# Lecture Notes in Artificial Intelligence    11987

Subseries of Lecture Notes in Computer Science

More information about this subseries at http://www.springer.com/series/1244

Purushothama B. R. · Veena Thenkanidiyoor ·
Rajendra Prasath · Odelu Vanga (Eds.)

# Mining Intelligence and Knowledge Exploration

7th International Conference, MIKE 2019
Goa, India, December 19–22, 2019
Proceedings

 Springer

*Editors*
Purushothama B. R. ⓘ
National Institute of Technology
Goa, India

Veena Thenkanidiyoor
National Institute of Technology
Goa, India

Rajendra Prasath ⓘ
Indian Institute of Information Technology
Sri City, India

Odelu Vanga
Indian Institute of Information Technology
Sri City, India

ISSN 0302-9743          ISSN 1611-3349   (electronic)
Lecture Notes in Artificial Intelligence
ISBN 978-3-030-66186-1          ISBN 978-3-030-66187-8   (eBook)
https://doi.org/10.1007/978-3-030-66187-8

LNCS Sublibrary: SL7 – Artificial Intelligence

This Springer imprint is published by the registered company Springer Nature Switzerland AG
The registered company address is: Gewerbestrasse 11, 6330 Cham, Switzerland

# Preface

This volume contains the papers presented at the 7th International Conference on Mining Intelligence and Knowledge Exploration (MIKE 2019), held during December 19–22, 2019, at the National Institute of Technology Goa, India (http://www.mike.org.in/2019/). MIKE 2019 received 83 qualified submissions from 17 countries and each qualified submission was reviewed by a minimum of two Program Committee members using the criteria of relevance, originality, technical quality, and presentation. A rigorous review process with the help of a distinguished Program Committee yeilded 31 submissions for presentation in the conference. Hence, the overall acceptance rate for this edition of MIKE is 37.35%.

MIKE is an initiative focusing on research and applications on various topics of human intelligence, mining, and knowledge discovery. Human intelligence has evolved steadily over several generations, and today human expertise is excelling in multiple domains and in knowledge-acquiring artifacts. The primary goal was to focus on the frontiers of human intelligence mining toward building a body of knowledge in this key domain. The focus was also to present state-of-the-art scientific results, to disseminate modern technologies, and to promote collaborative research in mining intelligence and knowledge exploration. At MIKE 2019, specific focus was placed on the "Learning to innovate using Internet of Things (IoT)."

MIKE 2019 identified 10 tracks topic wise, each led by 2–3 track coordinators to contribute and also handle submissions falling in their areas of interest. The involment from each of them, along with the supervision of the program chairs, ensured selection of quality papers for the conference. Each track coordinator took responsibility to fulfil the tasks assigned to him since we started circulating the first call for papers. This was reflected in every paper appearing in the proceedings with an impact in terms of the quality of the submissions.

The accepted papers were chosen on the basis of research excellence, which provides a body of literature for researchers involved in exploring, developing, and validating learning algorithms and knowledge-discovery techniques. Accepted papers were grouped into various subtopics, including evolutionary computation, knowledge exploration in IoT, artificial intelligence, machine learning, image processing, pattern recognition, speech processing, information retrieval, natural language processing, social network analysis, security, fuzzy rough sets, and other areas not included in the above list. Researchers presented their work and had an excellent opportunity to interact with eminent professors and scholars in their area of research. All participants have benefitted from discussions that facilitated the emergence of new ideas and approaches.

We were pleased to have the following notable scholars serving as advisory members for MIKE 2019: Prof. Ramon Lopaz de Mantaras, Artificial Intelligence

Research Institute, Spain; Prof. Mandar Mitra, Indian Statistical Institute, Kolkata, India; Prof. Agnar Aamodt, Prof. Pinar Ozturk, Prof. Bjorn Gamback, and Dr. Kazi Shah Nawaz Ripo, Norwegian University of Science and Technology, Norway; Prof. Sudeshna Sarkar and Prof. Niloy Ganguly, Indian Institute of Technology, Kharagpur, India; Prof. G. Kannabiran, Indian Institute of Information Technology, Sri City, India; Prof. Philip O'Reilly, University College, Ireland; Prof. Nirmalie Wiratunga, Robert Gordon University, UK; Prof. Paolo Rosso, Universitat Politècnica de València, Spain; Prof. Chaman L. Sabharwal, Missouri University of Science and Technology, USA; Prof. Tapio Saramaki, Tampere University of Technology, Finland; Prof. Vasudeva Verma, Indian Institute of Technology, Hyderabad, India; Prof. Grigori Sidorov, NLTP Laboratory CIC–IPN, Mexico; Prof. Genoveva Vargas-Solar, CNRS, France; Prof. Ildar Batyrshin, National Polytechnic Institute, Mexico; and Dr. Krishnaiyya Jallu, Bharat Heavy Electronics Limited, Thiruchirappalli, India.

We sincerely express our gratitude to Prof. Bayya Yegnanarayana, INSA Senior Scientist, International Institute of Information Technology, Hyderabad, India, and Prof. Chaman Lal Sabharwal, Missouri University of Science and Technology, USA, for their continued support to MIKE 2019. Their guidance, suggestions, and constant support have been invaluable in planning various activities of MIKE 2019.

Several eminent scholars, including Prof. Sankar Kumar Pal, Distinguished Scientist and Former Director, Indian Statistical Institute, Kolkata, India; Prof. Sung-Bae Cho, Yonsei University, South Korea; Prof. Alexander Gelbukh, Instituto Politecnico Nacional, Mexico; and Prof. N. Subba Reddy, Gyeongsang National University, South Korea, also extended their kind support in guiding us in organizing MIKE conference even better than the previous edition.

Prof. C. Chandra Sekhar, Indian Institute of Technology Madras, Chennai, India; Dr. Nikhil Rasiwasia, Amazon Bangalore, India; Prof. N. Subba Reddy, Gyeongsang National University, South Korea, delivered invited talks on Deep Learning Models based Approaches to Image and Video Captioning, Applied Machine Learning, and Extraction of Knowledge in Materials Science by Machine Learning respectively.

A large number of eminent professors, well-known scholars, industry leaders, and young researchers participated in making MIKE 2019 a great success. We recognize and appreciate the hard work put in by each individual author of the articles being published in these proceedings. We also express our sincere thanks to the National Institute of Technology, Goa, India, for hosting MIKE 2019.

We thank the Technical Program Committee members and all reviewers for their timely and thorough participation in the reviewing process. We thank Prof. (Dr.) Gopal Mugeraya, Director, National Institute of Technology Goa (NIT Goa), India, for his support in organizing MIKE 2019 in NIT Goa this year. We appreciate the time and effort put in by the members of the local organizing team at NIT Goa, India, and IIIT, Sri City, India. We are very grateful to all our sponsors for their generous support to MIKE 2019.

Finally, we acknowledge the support of EasyChair in the submission, review, and proceedings creation processes.

We are very pleased to express our sincere thanks to Springer staff members, especially Mr. Alfred Hofmann, Ms. Anna Kramer, and the editorial staff, for their support in publishing the proceedings of MIKE 2019.

December 2019

Purushothama B. R.
Veena Thenkanidiyoor
Rajendra Prasath
Odelu Vanga

# Organization

## Advisory Committee

| | |
|---|---|
| Adrian Groza | Technical University of Cluj-Napoca, Romania |
| Agnar Aamodt | Norwegian University of Science and Technology, Norway |
| Aidan Duane | Waterford Institute of Technology, Ireland |
| Alexander Gelbukh | Instituto Politécnico Nacional (IPN), Mexico |
| Amit A. Nanavati | IBM India Research Labs, New Delhi, India |
| Anil Vuppala | IIIT Hyderabad, India |
| Ashish Ghosh | Indian Statistical Institute, Kolkata, India |
| B. Yegnanarayana | IIIT Hyderabad, India |
| Bjorn Gamback | Norwegian University of Science and Technology, Norway |
| Chaman Lal Sabharwal | Missouri University of Science and Technology, USA |
| Debi Prosad Dogra | Indian Institute of Technology, Bhubaneswar, India |
| Genoveva Vargas-Solar | CNRS, France |
| Grigori Sidorov | NLTP Laboratory, CIC-IPN, Mexico |
| Hrishikesh Venkataraman | IIIT, Sri City, India |
| Ildar Batyrshin | Instituto Politécnico Nacional (IPN), Mexico |
| Kazi Shah Nawaz Ripon | Norwegian University of Science and Technology, Norway |
| Krishnaiyya Jallu | BHEL Hyderabad, India |
| Mandar Mitra | Indian Statistical Institute, Kolkata, India |
| Manish Shrivastava | IIIT Hyderabad, India |
| Maunendra S. Desarkar | Indian Institute of Technology, Hyderabad, India |
| N. Subba Reddy | Gyeongsang National University, South Korea |
| Niloy Ganguly | Indian Institute of Technology, Kharagpur, India |
| Nirmalie Wiratunga | Robert Gordon University, UK |
| P. V. Rajkumar | Texas Southern University, USA |
| Paolo Rosso | Universitat Politècnica de València, Spain |
| Philip O'Reilly | University College Cork, Ireland |
| Pinar Ozturk | Norwegian University of Science and Technology, Norway |
| Radu Grosu | Vienna University of Technology, Austria |
| Rajarshi Pal | IDRBT Hyderabad, India |
| Ramon Lopez de Mantaras | IIIA-CSIC, Spain |
| Saurav Karmakar | GreyKarma Technologies, India |
| Sudeshna Sarkar | Indian Institute of Technology Kharagpur, India |
| Sudip Misra | Indian Institute of Technology Kharagpur, India |
| Susmita Ghosh | Jadavpur University, Kolkata, India |

| | |
|---|---|
| T. Kathirvalavakumar | VHNSN College (Autonomous), India |
| Tanmoy Chakraborty | IIIT Delhi, India |
| Tapio Saramäki | Tampere University of Technology, Finland |
| V. Ravi | IDRBT Hyderabad, India |
| Vasile Rus | University of Memphis, USA |
| Vasudeva Verma | IIIT Hyderabad, India |
| Yannis Stylianou | University of Crete, Greece |

## Technical Program Committee

| | |
|---|---|
| Aakanksha Sharaff | National Institute of Technology, Raipur, India |
| Anca Hangan | Technical University of Cluj-Napoca, Romania |
| Anca Marginean | Technical University of Cluj-Napoca, Romania |
| Animesh Dutta | National Institute of Technology, Durgapur, India |
| Arun Kumar Yadav | National Institute of Technology, Hamirpur, India |
| Baisakhi Chakraborty | National Institute of Technology, Durgapur, India |
| Basant Subba | National Institute of Technology, Hamirpur, India |
| Birjodh Tiwana | LinkedIn Inc., USA |
| Bogdan Iancu | Technical University of Cluj-Napoca, Romania |
| Bunil Balabanataray | National Institute of Technology, Meghalaya, India |
| Camelia Chira | Babes-Bolyai University, Romania |
| Camelia Lemnaru | Technical University of Cluj-Napoca, Romania |
| Chaman Lal Sabharwal | Missouri University of Science and Technology, USA |
| Ciprian Oprisa | Technical University of Cluj-Napoca, Romania |
| Costin Badica | University of Craiova, Romania |
| Cristina Feier | University of Bremen, Germany |
| Debasis Ganguly | Dublin City University, Ireland |
| Deepak Gupta | National Institute of Technology, Arunachal Pradesh, India |
| Deepanwita Das | National Institute of Technology, Durgapur, India |
| Denis Trcek | University of Ljubljana, Slovenia |
| Dileep A. D. | Indian Institute of Technology, Mandi, India |
| Dinesh Tyagi | Malaviya National Institute of Technology Jaipur, India |
| Koushlendra Kumar Singh | National Institute of Technology, Jamshedpur, India |
| Surendiran B. | National Institute of Technology Puducherry, India |
| Veena T. | National Institute of Technology, Goa, India |
| Earnest Paul Ijjina | National Institute of Technology, Warangal, India |
| Florin Craciun | Babes-Bolyai University, Romania |
| Florin Leon | Technical University Gheorghe Asachi Iasi, Romania |
| Gheorghe Sebestyen | Technical University of Cluj-Napoca, Romania |
| Gloria Inés Alvarez | Pontificia Universidad Javeriana - Cali, Colombia |
| Goutam Sarker | National Institute of Technology, Durgapur, India |
| Goutham Reddy A. | Kyungpook National University, South Korea |
| Hans Moen | University of Turku, Finland |
| Himabindu K. | National Institute of Technology, Andhra Pradesh, India |

| Rupesh Kumar Dewang | Motilal Nehru National Institute of Technology Allahabad, India |
| Samir Borgohain | National Institute of Technology, Silchar, Assam, India |
| Santhana Vijayan Arumugam | National Institute of Technology Tiruchirappalli, India |
| Satyendra Singh Chouhan | Malaviya National Institute of Technology Jaipur, India |
| Sergio Alejandro Gomez | Universidad Nacional del Sur, Argentina |
| Sergiu Zaporojan | The Technical University of Moldova, Moldova |
| Shanmuganathan Raman | Indian Institute of Technology Gandhinagar, India |
| Somaraju Suvvari | National Institute of Technology Patna, India |
| Srilatha Chebrolu | National Institute of Technology, Andhra Pradesh, India |
| Sujit Das | National Institute of Technology, Warangal, India |
| Sung-Bae Cho | Yonsei University, South Korea |
| Tanmay Basu | Ramakrishna Mission Vivekananda Educational and Research Institute, India |
| Thoudam Doren Singh | National Institute of Technology, Silchar, Assam, India |
| Udai Pratap Rao | Sardar Vallabhbhai National Institute of Technology, India |
| Victoria Bobicev | The Technical University of Moldova, Moldova |
| Vivek Nallur | University College Dublin, Ireland |
| Vlad Muresan | Technical University of Cluj-Napoca, Romania |
| Zeyar Aung | Masdar Institute of Science and Technology, UAE |

## Additional Reviewers

Augasta, M. Gethsiyal
Christopher, Gladis
Dubey, Shiv Ram
Kathirvalavakumar, T.
Kumaran, T.
Mitra, Rangeet
Prasath, Rajendra
T., Kumaran
Thakur, Mainak
Vanga, Odelu

# Contents

# On the Differences Between Human Agents and Logic-Based Software Agents Discourse Understanding

Adrian Groza[✉] [iD]

Technical University of Cluj-Napoca, Cluj-Napoca, Romania
Adrian.Groza@cs.utcluj.ro
http://users.utcluj.ro/~agroza

**Abstract.** We are interested in the differences between how a human agent and a logic-based software agent interpret a text in natural language. When reading a narrative, the human agent has a single interpretation model. That is the preferred model among the models consistent with the available information. The model is gradually adjusted as the story proceeds. Differently, a logic-based software agent works with a finite set of many models, in the same time. Of most interest is that the number of these models is huge, even for simple narratives. We compare here the reduction strategies of humans and software agents to keep the discourse more intelligible and tractable. One the one hand, the human agent extensively uses common knowledge, contextual reasoning and closes the world as much as possible. On the other hand, the logical agent adds domain knowledge (such as ontologies) and applied reduction strategies (such as identifying isomorphisms). The differences are analyse with puzzles in First order logic, Description logic and Dynamic epistemic logic.

**Keywords:** Machine comprehension · Discourse understanding · Interpretation models · Logical agents · Logical puzzles

## 1 Interpretation Models in First Order Logic

Let the classic love story between Abelard and Heloise, with the text *Abelard and Heloise are in love*. The human agent interpretation is that there are two individuals Abelard ($a$) and Heloise ($h$) that love each other (see Fig. 1). Instead, for the logical agent, the number of these models is huge, even for such simple narratives. The variety of interpretation models depends on at least two factors: (i) the errors and ambiguities introduced during natural language processing (NLP) or (ii) the way in which the interpretation are built based on the resulted formalisation of the text.

First, assume during natural language processing, the statement is interpreted as *Abelard is in love and Heloise is in love*. The formalisation in First Order Logic is:

This research is part-funded by the ExNanoMat-21PFE grant.

© Springer Nature Switzerland AG 2020
B. R. Purushothama et al. (Eds.): MIKE 2019, LNAI 11987, pp. 1–10, 2020.
https://doi.org/10.1007/978-3-030-66187-8_1

**Fig. 1.** The unique interpretation model of the human agent.

$$A_1: \exists x, \; love(abelard, x)$$
$$A_2: \exists x, \; love(heloise, x)$$

This formalisation is explained by the fact that NLP is based on statistical analysis. Based on statistics, our sentence will follow the same pattern as: *Abelard and Heloise are in park* (that is $inPark(abelard) \land inPark(heloise)$ or *Abelard and Heloise are in happy* ($happy(abelard) \land happy(heloise)$)).

Second, we are interested how many models does a FOL-based model finder compute for axioms $A_1$ and $A_2$? To answer this question we played with the MACE4 [10]. First, we closed the domain to 4 individuals (see Listing 1.1). Figure 2 illustrates the output of MACE4: there are 278,528 models.

**Listing 1.1.** Finding models with domain closed to 4 individuals.

```
assign(max_models, -1).
assign(domain_size, 4).
formulas(assumptions).
    exists x love(abelard,x).
    exists x love(heloise,x).
end_of_list.
```

```
============================= STATISTICS ====================
For domain size 4.

Current CPU time: 0.00 seconds (total CPU time: 5.66 seconds)
Ground clauses: seen=2, kept=2.
Selections=278522, assignments=557049, propagations=18, curr
Rewrite_terms=23, rewrite_bools=20, indexes=18.
Rules_from_neg_clauses=0, cross_offs=0.

============================= end of statistics ============

User_CPU=5.66, System_CPU=10.18, Wall_clock=25.

Exiting with 278528 models.

------ process 4061 exit (all_models) ------

Process 4061 exit (all_models) Sun Jul 28 11:51:49 2019
```

**Fig. 2.** MACE4 finds 278,528 interpretation models (domain is closed to four individuals only).

As these variety of models of unexpected (recall that the domain was restricted to four individuals), we took a look at the generated models (see

Fig. 3). Here, $a$ stands for *abelard*, $h$ for *heloise*, while $c_1$ and $c_2$ are the Skolem constants generated for the existential quantifiers in $A_1$ and $A_2$. As the domain is closed to four individuals we work only with the set of integers $\{0, 1, 2, 3\}$. The first model (first row, left) is consistent with the human interpretation: *abelard* and *heloise* do love each other. Note also that all four individuals are distinct: $a \rightarrow 0$, $b \rightarrow 1$, $c_1 \rightarrow 2$, $c_2 \rightarrow 3$. In the second model (first row, center), abelard loves an individual $c_1$, while heloise loves a distinct individual $c_2$. In the third model (first row, right), both abelard and heloise love the same individual $c_1$. Moreover, no one sad that the *love* relation is not reflexive. One such model is the fourth one (second row, left), where both abelard and heloise love each other. The variety of the models is also increased by different possible love relations involving $c_1$ and $c_2$. For instance in the fourth model, $c_1$ loves heloise and $c_2$ loves $c_1$. Similarly, no one sad that someone can love only one person at the same time. Therefore, the fifth model (second row, center) is possible. Here, abelard loves both heloise and $c_1$. The largest influence is given by the fact that the logical agent can interpret that some individuals are not distinct. In the sixth model (second row, right) abelard and heloise are interpreted as the same individual ($a \rightarrow 0$, $h \rightarrow 0$) referred by two distinct names.

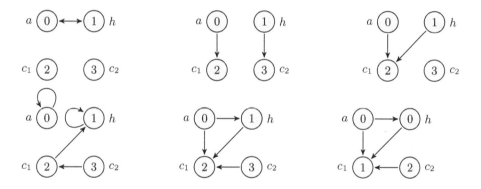

**Fig. 3.** Sample of interpretation models for the software agent.

The above analysis explains how the logical agent has indeed 278,528 interpretation models for the simple sentence *Abelard and Heloise are in love*. Moreover, all these models are equally plausible for the software agent. Given this gap (278,528 models vs. one model of the human agent), the natural question is *How the two agents would understand each other?* Our approach is to reduce the number of interpretation models for the software agent.

## 2  Reducing the Interpretation Models of the Logical Agent

To reduce the number of interpretation models, the knowledge base of the logical agent should be extended with several constraints.

First, the unique name assumption (UNA) can be added. In the MACE4 case, this is explicitly added with

$$A_3 : abelard \neq heloise$$

Models like the sixth one in Fig. 3 are removed. Note that we cannot apply this assumption on the Skolem constants that are generated during the FOl theory is processed. Under UNA, there are still 163,840 remaining models.

Second, we can assume that the love relation is not narcissistic. That is

$$A_4 : \forall x, \ \neg love(x, x)$$

With this constraint models like the fourth one in Fig. 3 are removed, leading to 5,120 remaining models.

Third, we add the somehow strong constraint that someone can love only one person at a time. That is

$$A_5 : love(x, y) \wedge love(x, z) \rightarrow y = z$$

Models like the fifth one in Fig. 3 are removed. The remaining models are 80. Unfortunately, love is not a symmetric relation. Hence, we cannot add the axiom $\forall x, y \ love(x, y) \leftrightarrow love(y, x)$.

Forth, we can exploit the fact that some of these models are isomorphic. After applying the MACE4's algorithm to remove isomorphic models [10], we keep 74 non-isomorphic models.

Fifth, recall that there are 2 Skolem constants after converting axioms $A_1$ and $A_2$. If we are not interested in the love relations of individuals represented by these constants, we can ignore them. This would result in 17 models obtained with the extended knowledge base from Fig. 2.

Some observations follow.

First, the order in which we apply the reductions is computationally relevant. For instance, it would be prohibitively to search for isomorphic models in the initial two steps, when there are 278,528 or 163,840 models. Mace4 reduces the initial 278,528 models to 186,976 non-isomorphic models in a User CPU time of ~2 h. Hence, the above strategy was to add domain knowledge to the initial narrative discourse, and then to search for the isomorphic structures.

Second, which domain knowledge to add is subject to interpretation. For instance, axiom $A_5$ might be too strong. There are various contexts, in which someone can love more than one individual in the same time. There are some contexts in which the human agent would have as the interpretation model, (the second model in Fig. 3). We argue that the decision what domain knowledge to activate should rely on some contextual reasoning step.

Third, the interpretation models vary as the story evolves. Let the following statement in the story:

*Abelard and Heloise are in love. They are getting married.*

This statement has the same pattern as:

*Abelard and Heloise are in park. They are playing chess.*

Assume the translation from natural language to FOL is the one in Listing 1.2. Note that we have already included here the domain knowledge to reduce the number of models: domain is closed to 4 individuals (line 2); UNA is applied on the named individuals (line 6); love is not narcissistic (line 7); love is a functional relation (line 8); the anaphora is correctly identified by the translator - that is the pronoun *they* is correctly replaced by Abelard and Heloise (lines 9 and 10); one person cannot married to him/herself (line 11); each person can be married with maximum one person at the same time (line 12). Given the above restrictions, MACE4 computes 5,242,880 models.

**Listing 1.2.** Increasing number of models as the story evolves. There are 5.242.880 models for the theory below.

```
1   assign ( max_models , −1).
2   assign ( domain_size , 4).
3   formulas ( assumptions ).
4      exists x love ( abelard ,x).
5      exists x love ( heloise ,x).
6      abelard != heloise .
7      all x −love (x,x).
8      love (x,y) & love (x,z) −> y = z.
9      exists married ( abelard ,x).
10     exists married ( heloise ,x).
11     all x −married (x,x).
12     married (x,y) & married (x,z) −> y = z.
13  end_of_list .
```

If one wants to assure to the logical agent the same view of the story as the human agent, the burden seems to be on the NLP to FOL translator. A theory that is closer to the human interpretation is the one in Listing 1.3. Here the main advantage is that existential quantifiers do not appear and thus the domain can be closed to 2 individuals only.

**Listing 1.3.** FOL theory closed for the human model.

```
1   assign ( max_models , −1).
2   assign ( domain_size , 2).
3   formulas ( assumptions ).
4      love ( abelard , heloise ).
5      love ( heloise , abelard ).
6      abelard != heloise .
7      all x −love (x,x).
8      love (x,y) & love (x,z) −> y = z.
9      married ( abelard , heloise ).
10     married ( heloise , abelard ).
11     all x −married (x,x).
12     married (x,y) & married (x,z) −> y = z.
13  end_of_list .
```

Here we focused on restricting interpretation models given a statistical-based translation from NLP to FOL. For some reasoning tasks the aim is indeed to have a single interpretation model of a narrative. One example is when specifying commands or tasks to a robot. Let the command: *Bring two espresso coffees to Abelard and Heloise.* In order to assure the correct interpretation, the agent should compute a single model for this command. We are interested next, in which situations when reducing models is not required.

## 3    When More Models Are Better?

For some reasoning tasks (e.g. solving lateral thinking puzzles [3]) keeping all possible models might be desirable. Let the following puzzle:

> *Two American Indians were sitting on a log - a big Indian and a little Indian. The little Indian was the son of the big Indian, but the big Indian was not the father of the little Indian. How do you explain this?*

Most of the people are able to quickly figure out the solution. However, the online forums indicate that there are human agent having difficulties to identify an interpretation model.

The logical agent does not have difficulties to compute the one interpretation model. Let the formalisation in Description Logic (DL) below. We picked DL as it is easier to import domain knowledge as ontologies are available on the Web. The family ontology is particularly useful here[1]. Relevant here is that the concept *Father* is disjoint to *Mother*. Also, in line 9, the relation *hasSon* is included in the more general relation *hasChild*. That is, if two individuals are related through the *hasSon* relation, the logical agent infers that they are also related through the *hasChild* relation. Additionally to this terminological box ((lines 1 to 9)), the information from puzzle is formalised in the assertional box in lines 10–13. Here, *littleIndian* and *bigIndian* are instances of the concept *AmericanIndian* (lines 10–11). The *bigIndian* has son the *littleIndian* (line 12), while *bigIndian* is not an instance of the *Father* concept. Given the above knowledge to reasoner in DL (such as Racer [6]), the system is able to infer that *bigIndian* is an instance of the *Mother* concept.

---

[1] We assume the reader is familiar with the Description Logic syntax. Otherwise, the reader is referred to [1].

$$1 \quad Indian \sqsubseteq Person$$
$$2 \quad Woman \sqsubseteq Person$$
$$3 \quad Man \sqsubseteq Person$$
$$4 \quad Parent \sqsubseteq \exists hasChild.Person$$
$$5 \quad Father \equiv Man \sqcap Parent$$
$$6 \quad Mather \equiv Woman \sqcap Parent$$
$$7 \quad Parent \sqsubseteq Father \sqcap Mother$$
$$8 \quad Father \sqsubseteq \neg Mather$$
$$9 \quad hasSon \sqsubseteq hasChild$$
$$10 \quad hasDaughter \sqsubseteq hasChild$$
$$11 \quad littleIndian : AmericanIndian$$
$$12 \quad bigIndian : AmericanIndian$$
$$13 \quad (bigIndian, littleIndian) : hasSon$$
$$14 \quad bigIndian : \neg Father$$

This is one example in which the human agent might not have an interpretation model, while the logical agent has one. A more difficult lateral thinking puzzle for the human agent is the following one:

*Two girls are born to the same mother, on the same day, in the same month and year and yet they're not twins. How can this be?*

The problem is that the human agent closes the world too much. What is relevant here to add to the family ontology are the axioms for the *Twin* or *Triplet* concept. Based on assertion that the girls are not Twin, the Racer reasoner deduces that they are triplets.

The problem here is that the human agent closed the world two much. The human agent fails to consider models in which a third individual exists. Differently, the software agent reasons here under the Open World Assumption.

Other examples in which the software agent is more aware of current world come from the epistemic puzzles. Let the following one:

There are 3 logicians at a table in a pub, The waitress asks them: "Does everyone want beer?" The first logician answers "I don't know". The second logician answers "I don't know". The third logician answer "Yes".

A logical agent, based on the possible worlds semantics of the Kripke structures [12] does not have problems to gradually reduce the interpretation models to the correct one.

Initially, there are 8 possible models, depending on which logician wants beer or not. Let $b_i$ true if logician $i$ wants beer, and false otherwise. Each world is characterised by three propositional variables: $b_1$, $b_2$ and $b_3$:

$$\{\langle 0,0,0 \rangle, \langle 0,0,1 \rangle, \langle 0,1,0 \rangle, \langle 0,1,1 \rangle, \langle 1,0,0 \rangle, \langle 1,0,1 \rangle, \langle 1,1,0 \rangle, \langle 1,1,1 \rangle\}$$

After the public answer of the first agent, all the models in which he does not want beer ($b_1 = 0$) are eliminated. That is because if he would not want beer the answer would have been "No". The words in which $b_1$ is false are eliminated for remaining four possible cases:

$$\{\langle 1,0,0\rangle, \langle 1,0,1\rangle, \langle 1,1,0\rangle, \langle 1,1,1\rangle\}$$

Similarly, after the second answer, all the agents will know that the second logician also wants beer. Otherwise, his answer would have been "No". Hence, the models with $b_2 = 0$ are eliminated:

$$\{\langle 1,1,0\rangle, \langle 1,1,1\rangle\}$$

Now the third agent can figure in which world there are. As he wants beer, the only possible model is $\{\langle 1,1,1\rangle\}$. This model is conveyed to waitress[2].

## 4   Discussion and Related Work

Both the human reader and the software agent aim to keep the story more intelligible and tractable. But they apply different reduction strategies. On one hand, humans understand stories by inferring the mental states (e.g. motivations, goals) of the characters, by applying parabolic projections of known stories into the target narrative [7], by extensively using commonsense reasoning [11] and fuzzy reasoning [9], or by closing the world as much as possible. On the other hand, logic-based software agents reduce the models by formalising discourse representation theories [8], by adding domain knowledge, or by identifying isomorphisms.

We also exemplified here how the number of interpretation models vary as the story evolves. Sentences introducing new objects and relations do increase the number of models. Sentences introducing constraints on the existing objects and relations contribute to the removal of some models. Adding domain knowledge also contributes to model removal. One research question is how to generate stories that end with a single interpretation model for the software agent. Another issue regards the amount of domain knowledge and commonsense knowledge that should be added, and which reduction strategy is better when the aim is to keep the number of models computationally feasible.

We focused here on the model explosion in logical frameworks and not on the translation from natural language into some logical formalism. Tools like Fred [4] aim to automatically translate natural language to description logic. Still, there are very limited. Given our sentence *Abelard and Heloise in love*, Fred translation[3] identifies *love* as an individual, not a relation: $in(abelard, love) \wedge in(heloise, love)$ (see Fig. 4). Note that Fred facilitate contextual reasoning by

---

[2] For one implementation of this puzzle, the interested reader is referred to SMCDEL symbolic model checker for Dynamic Epistemic Logic (https://github.com/jrclogic/SMCDEL) [2].

[3] http://wit.istc.cnr.it/stlab-tools/fred/demo/.

correctly identify the characters from DBpedia: Peter Abelard and the abbess Heloise. Another tool that aim to translate natural language to FOL is NLTK. NLTK has an interface with MACE4 and Prover9[4] to perform logical inference and model building of the translated FOL knowledge [5].

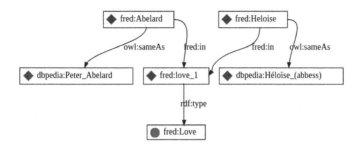

**Fig. 4.** Automatic translation from natural language into description logic.

We noticed that text models built with machine learning applied on big data, would benefit from some crash diet. In this line, we try to extract as much as we can from each statement, instead of statistically analysing the entire corpus. That is, the model of the story is built bottom-up and not top-down as machine learning does.

## 5    Conclusion

We compared the reduction strategies of humans and software agents to keep the discourse more intelligible and tractable. One the one hand, the human agent extensively uses common knowledge, contextual reasoning and closes the world as much as possible. On the other hand, the logical agent adds domain knowledge (such as ontologies) and applied reduction strategies (such as identifying isomorphisms).

For most of the reasoning tasks, the human agent keeps only one interpretation model. In this case, the aim to reduce the interpretation models of the software agent as much as possible in order to facilitate communication between human and software agent. In case of puzzles, some human agents fails to have an interpretation. Differently, the logical agent is able to compute a consistent model with the given knowledge, if such a model exists.

## References

1. Baader, F., Calvanese, D., McGuinness, D., Patel-Schneider, P., Nardi, D.: The Description Logic Handbook: Theory, Implementation and Applications. Cambridge University Press, Cambridge (2003)

---

[4] http://www.nltk.org/howto/inference.html.

2. van Benthem, J., van Eijck, J., Gattinger, M., Su, K.: Symbolic model checking for dynamic epistemic logic—S5 and beyond. J. Logic Comput. **28**(2), 367–402 (2017)
3. De Bono, E., Zimbalist, E.: Lateral thinking. Viking (2010)
4. Gangemi, A., Presutti, V., Recupero, D.R., Nuzzolese, A.G., Draicchio, F., Mongiovì, M.: Semantic web machine reading with FRED. Semant. Web **8**(6), 873–893 (2017)
5. Garrette, D., Klein, E.: An extensible toolkit for computational semantics. In: Proceedings of the Eighth International Conference on Computational Semantics, pp. 116–127. Association for Computational Linguistics (2009)
6. Haarslev, V., Hidde, K., Möller, R., Wessel, M.: The RacerPro knowledge representation and reasoning system. Semant. Web **3**(3), 267–277 (2012)
7. Herman, D.: Story Logic: Problems and Possibilities of Narrative. University of Nebraska Press, Lincoln (2004)
8. Kamp, H., Reyle, U.: From Discourse to Logic: Introduction to Model Theoretic Semantics of Natural Language, Formal Logic and Discourse Representation Theory, vol. 42. Springer, Dordrecht (2013)
9. Letia, I.A., Groza, A.: Modelling imprecise arguments in description logic. Adv. Electr. Comput. Eng. **9**(3), 94–99 (2009)
10. McCune, W.: Mace4 reference manual and guide. arXiv preprint cs/0310055 (2003)
11. Mueller, E.T.: Commonsense Reasoning: An Event Calculus Based Approach. Morgan Kaufmann, Burlington (2014)
12. Van Ditmarsch, H., van Der Hoek, W., Kooi, B.: Dynamic Epistemic Logic, vol. 337. Springer, Dordrecht (2007). https://doi.org/10.1007/978-1-4020-5839-4

# A Study on the Importance of Linguistic Suffixes in Maithili POS Tagger Development

Ankur Priyadarshi and Sujan Kumar Saha[⊠]

Computer Science and Engineering, Birla Institute of Technology, Mesra,
Ranchi, Jharkhand, India
priyadarshiankur81@gmail.com, sujan.kr.saha@gmail.com

**Abstract.** This paper presents our study on the effect of morphological inflections in the performance of a Maithili Part of Speech (POS) tagger. In the last few years, substantial effort is devoted to developing morphological analyzers and POS taggers in several Indian languages including Hindi, Bengali, Tamil, Telugu, Kannada, Punjabi and Marathi. But we did not find any open POS tagger or morphological analyzers in Maithili. However, Maithili is one of the official languages of India with around 50 million native speakers. So, we worked on developing a POS tagger in Maithili. For the development, we used a manually annotated in-house Maithili corpus containing 52,190 tokens. The tagset contains 27 tags. We first trained conditional random fields (CRF) classifier with various combination of word unigram, bigram, fixed-length suffix, and prefix features. There we observed that the fixed-length suffixes do not show the expected accuracy improvement. However, during the manual corpus annotation, we observed that suffixes played as a helpful clue. So, instead of using the fixed-length suffixes, we worked on identifying the morphological inflections in Mathili. When we used these morphological suffixes in the system, we found a noticeable performance improvement.

**Keywords:** Maithili NLP · Parts-of-speech · POS tagger · Morphological analyzer

## 1 Introduction

Automatic part of speech (POS) tagging is the method of assigning part of speech label or lexical class marker to each token based on its definition and context. In the grammatical background, a POS tag is defined as a signpost or label assigned to each word in a text corpus such as Noun, Pronoun, Adjective, Verb, and Adverb. It is an essential task as many language processing frameworks utilize POS tagger as a pre-processing step. POS tagging is often regarded as the primary task to perform computer processing of the language. Therefore, the development of POS tagger is a key research area, and automatic POS taggers have been developed for many languages. A substantial amount of effort has also

© Springer Nature Switzerland AG 2020
B. R. Purushothama et al. (Eds.): MIKE 2019, LNAI 11987, pp. 11–20, 2020.
https://doi.org/10.1007/978-3-030-66187-8_2

been devoted to POS tagger development in several Indian languages, including Hindi, Bengali, Telugu, Tamil, Kannada, and Punjabi. However, we did not find any open Maithili POS tagger and related resources. Therefore, we worked on the development of Maithili POS tagger.

Maithili is an Indo-Aryan language spoken mainly in the Bihar and Jharkhand states of India. It is also used outside India and is the second most predominant language of Nepal. There are around 50 million native speakers in Maithili. In 2003, Maithili was included in the Eighth Schedule of the Indian Constitution as a recognized regional language of India, which allows it to be used in education, government, and other official contexts[1]. In March 2018, Maithili acquired the second official language status in the Indian state of Jharkhand.

We used an in-house Maithili POS tagged corpus for the development. The corpus contains 52190 words that are manually annotated using 27 tags. We used the Conditional Random Fields (CRF) as the learning algorithm. Like in existing POS taggers in other Indian languages, initially, we considered the current and surrounding words, n-grams, suffix and prefix information in the feature set. We conducted several experiments with various combinations of these features to obtain the final feature set. The highest accuracy we achieved from these experiments is 81.51%. In these experiments, we also observed that the fixed-length suffixes and prefixes are not effective in improving the performance of the classifier. Rather, the accuracy degraded in certain cases. However, during the manual corpus annotation, we observed that suffixes played as a helpful clue. The fixed-length suffixes cause a large expansion of the feature set where many useless features were included. So, we worked on identifying the morphological inflections in Maithili words. Instead of using the fixed-length suffixes, we used the morphological suffixes. Then, we observed that the accuracy of the system is increased to 83.84%. This performance improvement demonstrates the necessity of the morphological analyzer in POS tagger development.

## 2   Related Work

Here we present an overview of the automatic part of speech tagging task with a particular focus to Indian languages.

As we found in the literature, POS tagging was initially explored in the sixties by [8]. In that initial phase, the tagging was done by manually prepared rules. A popular POS tagger of that phase is the TAGGIT system [7]. Several rule-based systems have been developed that aimed to improve accuracy and efficiency. Later, Machine Learning algorithms have been used in POS tagging task. In 2001 [9] proposed Conditional Random Fields (CRF) for POS tagging, and the CRF became one the mostly used algorithms for POS tagging task in the last decade.

Now, we will discuss some of the major part of speech taggers in Indian Languages. Hindi is the most widely used language in India, which is also the fourth

---

[1] https://en.wikipedia.org/wiki/Maithili_language.

most spoken language in the world. In the literature, we found [2] attempted the
first work on Indian language POS tagging. Later [12] worked on Hindi POS disambiguation. They used a morphological analyzer for the task. In 2006 [15] used
a Decision Tree for POS tagging in a limited resource scenario. They used stem-
mer, morphological analyzer and a verb group analyzer to handle the ambiguity
and unknown words. Another Hindi POS Tagger based on HMM was developed
by [14]. In this paper, the HMM approach was designed to advance the morphological richness of the languages without employing to complex and expensive
analysis. They used a tagged corpus of size 81751 tokens and achieved an accuracy of 93.12%. Several attempts have been made after that also. For example,
for Hindi POS tagging [6] developed a rule-based system, [10] developed another
rule-based system that achieved 85.45% accuracy.

Apart from Hindi, POS taggers have been developed in other major Indian
languages including Bengali, Telugu, Tamil. In 2007 [4] experimented with HMM,
Maximum Entropy and CRF for development of a Bengali POS tagger. The
created a training corpus consisted of 45,000 words and achieved an accuracy
of 88.61% with CRF. Use of morphological analyzer helped to improve the efficiency to 92.37. They also observed that in the POS tagging task, CRF performs
better than HMM and Maximum Entropy classifiers [3]. Another POS Tagger
in Bengali was developed by [5]. They utilized CRF using word suffix, named
entity information, length of the word, lexicon feature and symbols as features.
In Tamil, a hybrid POS tagger [1] has been developed in a combination of an
HMM-based tagger with a rule-based tagger. In 2011 [13] developed a Hidden
Markov Model-based system for Punjabi POS tagging. The system achieved an
accuracy of 90.11%.

Although we find POS tagger in several Indian languages, Maithili is not
explored. We did not find any open Maithili data or reporting on Maithili POS
tagger development. We were also unable to find any morphological analyzer or
root extractor in Maithili.

## 3    Maithili POS Tagger Development Using CRF

In this section, we discuss the CRF based Maithili POS tagger.

### 3.1    Training Data

For the development, we use a manually annotated corpus. The annotated
corpus contains a total of 2460 sentences. The sentences are collected from a
few web-resources including e-Maithili newspapers इसमाद [2], मैथिली जिन्दाबाद [3], and
मिथिला दैनिक [4] and e-Journals साहित् अकादेमी [5] (Sahitya Akademi - Central Institution for Literary Dialogue), and विदेह [6]. The tagset used during the corpus

---

[2] http://www.esamaad.com/.
[3] http://www.maithilijindabaad.com/.
[4] http://www.mithiladainik.in/.
[5] http://sahitya-akademi.gov.in/sahitya-akademi/index.jsp.
[6] http://www.videha.co.in/.

annotations consists of 27 tags which are illustrated in Table 1. Here we provide an example of manual annotation.

ई/PRO किताबसभ/NNS हमर/PRN अछि/VAUX ।/SYM

(ITRANS - ee kitAbasabha hamara achhi)

(English Translation - These books are mine.)

We use the Itrans[7] transliteration to denote the Devanagri or Maithili words.

**Table 1.** Part of speech tagset for Maithili [11]

| Sym | Description | Sym | Description | Sym | Description |
|-----|-------------|-----|-------------|-----|-------------|
| NN | Singular Common Noun | DEM | Demonstrative | CC | Conjunction |
| NNS | Plural Noun | MOD | Modals | CND | Conditional |
| NNP | Proper Noun | VM | Main Verb | IN | Interjection |
| NNL | Name Spatial and Temporal | VN | Dependent Verb | NEG | Negation |
| NTP | Name Title Person | VAUX | Auxiliary Verb | CD | Cardinal |
| PRN | Personal Pronoun | JJ | Adjective | OD | Ordinal |
| PRO | Pronoun | JJC | Quantifiers | FN | Foreign Word |
| PRF | Reflexive Pronoun | RB | Adverb | SYM | Symbol |
| PRQ | Question Words | PP | Preposition | PUNC | Punctuation |

The tagged corpus contains a total of 52,190 words. The corpus is split into two parts as training and test corpus. The training corpus subsists of 48,007 words and test corpus consists of 4183 words. The sentences in test corpus are chosen randomly from the whole corpus and are not included in the training data. In Table 2 we have provided the details of the annotated corpus.

**Table 2.** Statistics of the Maithili training and test corpus

| Corpus | Number of sentences | Number of words | Number of unique words | Ambiguous words (in%) |
|--------|---------------------|-----------------|------------------------|-----------------------|
| Train | 2298 | 48007 | 9231 | 1.6% |
| Test | 162 | 4183 | 1687 | 1.5% |
| Total | 2460 | 52190 | 9856 | 2.6% |

## 3.2  CRF Model Creation

Conditional Random Fields (CRFs) are the category of discriminative probabilistic graphical model associating the capability to compactly model multivariate

---

[7] https://www.aczoom.com/itrans/online/.

outputs **v** with the strength to leverage a large number of input features **x** for prediction. The classifier plays a vital role in labelling or parsing sequential data. CRFs outperform Hidden Markov Model (HMM) and Maximum Entropy models (ME) on a number of sequence labeling tasks as HMM achieve joint distribution $P(x, y)$ of the state and the observed sequence, although in the estimation issue, we need a conditional probability $P(Y|X)$ whereas in ME model it overcomes by avoiding label bias problem.

For the training of the CRF model, in addition to training and testing file, we need to define a suitable feature set. The training is based on LBFGS (Limited-Memory Broyden-Fletcher-Goldfarb-Shanno), a quasi-newton algorithm for the large-scale numerical optimization problem. Several experiments were carried out with a distinct set of features, inspected our results and then accustomed based on the error analysis. For the implementation we used CRF++-0.58[8]. We have used the default parameter settings of the tool except c = 1.5 and f = 3. Here, 'c' parameter trades the balance between over-fitting and under-fitting, and the 'f' parameter sets the cut-off threshold for the features. These values gave the best result in our experiments. More details of the parameters and possible values or range can be found in the Readme file of the tool.

Initially, we used the Unigram and Bi-gram features to train the model where the number of surrounding words varied in different test sets as 3, 5 and 7. Then we incorporated the suffix and prefix information in the feature set. These suffixes and prefixes we used in the feature set are just the fixed length set of characters, not the linguistic suffixes that cause inflection of the words. For example, when the target word is ' रखलाह ' the suffixes of length 3 and 4 are 'Оहिहिहीह' and 'लाह' respectively.

**Table 3.** Accuracy of the CRF based tagger using different feature sets

| Feature Id | Feature details | Accuracy (in %) |
|---|---|---|
| f1 | Unigram (window = 3) | 81.20 |
| f2 | Unigram (window = 5) | 80.70 |
| f3 | Unigram (window = 7) | 79.56 |
| f4 | Bi-grams | 78.86 |
| f5 | f1 + suffix length 2 | 80.22 |
| f6 | f1 + suffix length 3 | 81.39 |
| f7 | f1 + suffix length 4 | 80.16 |
| f8 | f1 + suffix length 5 | 79.67 |
| f9 | f1 + suffix length (2 + 3 + 4 + 5) | 81.51 |
| f10 | f1 + prefix | 80.04 |

---

[8] https://taku910.github.io/crfpp/.

### 3.3   Accuracy of CRF Based System

To show the efficiency of the CRF-based classifier, we first developed a baseline system. The baseline system assigns a label to the word as per their occurrence and labelling in the training data. The predominant tag-based baseline system achieves an accuracy of 71.63%.

To develop the CRF classifier, several experiments were carried out using various combinations of individual features to identify the feature set that produces the best accuracy. In Table 3, we summarized the features used in the CRF classifier and corresponding accuracy values. In the word features, we used several combinations of preceding and subsequent words. There we found a word window of length three, containing the current, previous and next words, worked better. This is primarily because of the insufficiency of training data. A large number of features cause over-fitting when applied to small training data. Bigram features also give lower accuracy than the uni-gram features. Again, the suffix length was varied as 2, 3, 4 and 5 characters and the system achieved better accuracy when the length is 3. The highest accuracy achieved in these experiments is 81.51%.

### 3.4   Discussions

During annotation of the Maithili corpus, we observed that suffixes play a major role in categorizing the words into the POS classes. However, in our experiments, we did not achieve expected performance improvement through the suffix features. We feel that the issue arose due to the fixed-length suffixes. Fixed length suffixes of a particular length fail to cover all valid suffixes and cause inclusion of a large number of unnecessary features to the classifier. For example, if we consider suffix length 3 for two different word like 'बुझबाक' and 'रखलनि', the extracted suffix for 'बुझबाक' is 'बाक' which is not informative whereas for 'रखलनि' it is 'नि' which provides a clue towards the word class. Similarly, for suffix length 4 the word 'करबाक' extracted suffix is 'रबाक', while for word 'प्रवक्ताक' the suffix is 'ताक' which does not provide any clue towards the class. The suffix length 5 results in loss of significance of a word and rarely provides the relevant suffix. There are frequent common verb words like 'देबाक', 'करबाक' and 'बनाकय' generates non-linguistic suffixes as 'ेबाक', 'रबाक' and 'नाकय'. Finally, we can observe from these examples that, there are no fixed length suffixes which can extract morphological features for every words.

Additionally, the fixed-length suffixes result in an expansion of the feature space by a large amount. As the training data is not sufficient, a large number of features cause over-fitting and performance degradation. The experimental results also prove it. When we used suffixes of length 2, 4 or 5 along with the unigram features, the accuracy degraded. Only in length 3 suffixes, we achieved some amount of accuracy improvement, that too only 0.19%. When all suffixes are used as a combined feature set, the improvement becomes 0.31%.

However, in the literature we found, information regarding the root word and its morphological inflections help a lot in the POS tagging task. During the corpus annotation, we also observed that the suffixes played a major role in deciding the word class. So, we hope instead of using fixed length suffixes, if we can identify the morphological suffixes, then we can improvise the accuracy. The set of rules defined for other Indian languages have distinctive features which can not be borrowed for Maithili. However, we do not have access to any open morphological analyzer in Maithili. So, we worked on identifying morphological suffixes in Maithili and used them in the system. That study is discussed in the following section.

## 4  Morphological Analysis for Improving Maithili POS Tagger

In order to identify the inflections of the words, we study the morphological structures in the Maithili language.

### 4.1  Inflections in Maithili Words

Dissimilar to English or other Western-European languages, where a character is considered as the basic orthographic unit, Maithili uses syllable. A syllable is commonly a vowel center, which is anticipated before by zero or more consonants and pursued by a discretionary diacritic imprint. In this section, we explain the different morphological impact of inflections in various Maithili word classes. Like in other north Indian languages such as Hindi and Bengali, the inflections in Maithili place as a suffix to the stem. The word-formation after inflection can be represented as follows.
word := stem + inflections
inflections := null — inflection
inflections := inflection + inflections

Example: लिखनाय [likhnAy] < लिख [likh] (Stem) + नाय [nAy] (Inflection).

There are few inflections which were observed during manual annotation.

1. There are words in singular form, which have suffix inflections 'क' [ka] such as:
देशक [deshka] < देश [desh] (Stem) + क [ka](Inflection),
नेताक [netAka] < नेता [netA] (Stem) + क [ka] (Inflection)
The inflections occurred as 'क' [ka] are categorised under singular form of noun.

2. In Hindi, to denote multiples, the multiple denoting words like 'सभी' are used as a separate word along with the noun. So, the translation of 'all kids' is 'सभी बच्चे' in Hindi. For Example:
किताबसभ [kitAbasabh] < किताब [kitAba] (Stem) + सभ [sabh] (Inflection),
लड़कासब [la.Dakasab] < लड़का [la.Daka] (Stem) + सब [sab] (Inflection).
However, in Maithili we observed that the plural denoting words like 'सभ/सब' are attached with the noun and represented as a single word.

3. There are few suffixes inflections such as 'र' [ra] and 'आ' [aa]. For Example:
हुनकर [hunkara] < हुनक [hunak] (Stem) + [ra] (Inflection),
ओकरा [okarA] < ओकर [okar] (Stem) + [aa] (Inflection)
The suffix inflections incurred above are generally found in Maithili Pronouns.

4. There were large number of inflections which consist of suffixes such as, 'लक'
[laka]', 'ब' [ba], and 'ह' [ha]. For Example:
पढ़लक [pa.Dhalaka] < पढ़ [pa.Dha] (Stem) + लक [laka] (Inflection),
देखबह [dekhabah] < देख [dekha] (Stem) + ब [ba] (second person future inflection) + ह [ha] (Inflection)
The above inflected suffixes are generally occurred in different Verb forms of
Maithili.

5. Similarly, inflections such as 'ल' [la] and 'नि' [ni] also affects Maithili words.
For Example:
देखलनि [dekhalani] < देख [dekha] (Stem) + ल [la] (Inflection) + नि [ni] (Honorific suffix)
This verb form often occurs when honorific words occur in Maithili.

6. Another important inflection in Maithili is 'न' [na]. For Example:
एहन [ehan] < एह [eh] (Stem) + न [na] (Inflection).
The following inflections commonly occurs in Demonstrative, Interrogative
and Quantifying Adjectives.

7. Similarly, in Maithili inflection like, 'क' [ka] is also majorly found. For Example:
कतेक [ktaik] < कते [ktai] (Stem) + क [ka] (Inflection),
जतेक [jatek] < जते [jate] (Stem) + क [ka] (Inflection)
Above inflections categorically lies under Adjectives too.

8. In Maithili, morphologically affected token based on emphasis is not commonly found. But, still there are few instances such as:
लड़कासबस [la.DakAsabsa] < लड़का [la.Daka] (Stem) सब [sab] (Inflection) + स
[sa] (Inflection representing emphasis).

A detailed linguistic analysis of the Maithili words might lead more type of
inflections and rules. However, a deeper analysis requires linguistic expertise. As
our primary objective here is to see the effect of morphological inflections on the
performance of POS tagger, we used these identified inflections in the system to
find the performance.

## 4.2   Accuracy with Morphological Suffixes

In Table 4, we have summarized the overall results obtained during the development of Maithili POS Tagger. The predominant tag-based CRF model without
any feature sets which achieved an accuracy of 71.63%. Later, we implemented
n-grams of various window sizes to obtain the best feature set which improved

the accuracy to 81.20%. Eventually, we incorporated affixes varying the length which improved the system performance minimally to 81.51%.

Table 4. Overall accuracy of the Maithili POS tagger

| Model description | Accuracy (in %) |
| --- | --- |
| Baseline: Predominant tag | 71.63 |
| CRF with Unigram (window = 3) | 81.20 |
| CRF With Unigram and Fixed length suffixes | 81.51 |
| CRF With Unigram and linguistic suffixes | 83.84 |

The linguistic study in Sect. 4 depicts the future development and improvement of Maithili POS tagger. The system performance can be improved by creating a separate indexed dictionary during manual annotation for inflected words, to avoid loss of information occurred during suffix based development. The constructed dictionary and existing n-grams features can improve system performance. When these features are used in the classifier, it achieves an accuracy of 83.84%. This performance improvement proves the superiority of morphological features over the fixed-length features in the POS tagging task.

## 5   Conclusion

This paper presented our effort on the development of a POS tagger in Maithili as well as a study on the effectiveness of linguistics suffixes in the POS tagging task. As in the literature, no previous work is there on Maithili POS tagger or morphological analyzer, we had to work on POS corpus labelling and finding inflections of the Maithili words. In these experiments, we have achieved an accuracy of 83.84% in the POS tagger. Also through experiments, we have shown the superiority of the linguistic suffixes over the fixed-length suffixes.

There is ample scope to extend the present work. The training data is not sufficient, so expanding the training data is one of the directions where one can work on in the future. Identifying a deeper set of inflection rules or developing a full-fledged morphological analyzer is another future direction. Finding solutions to handle morphological richness and ambiguity, exploring possibilities of applying other learning algorithms are the other possible directions to work on in future. As the POS tagging is the most fundamental NLP task, it opens the scope of developing other NLP systems including parser, semantic level processing, and machine translation.

**Funding.** This work was supported by Science and Engineering Research Board, India [Grant No: EEQ/2016/000241].

# References

1. Arulmozhi, P., Sobha, L.: A hybrid POS tagger for a relatively free word order language. In: Proceedings of the First National Symposium on Modeling and Shallow Parsing of Indian Languages, pp. 79–85 (2006)
2. Bharati, A., Chaitanya, V., Sangal, R., Ramakrishnamacharyulu, K.: Natural Language Processing: A Paninian Perspective. Prentice-Hall of India, New Delhi (1995)
3. Dandapat, S.: Part-of-speech tagging for Bengali. Department of Computer Science and Engineering, Indian Institute of Technology, Kharagpur (2009)
4. Dandapat, S., Sarkar, S., Basu, A.: Automatic part-of-speech tagging for Bengali: an approach for morphologically rich languages in a poor resource scenario. In: Proceedings of the 45th Annual Meeting of the ACL on Interactive Poster and Demonstration Sessions, pp. 221–224. Association for Computational Linguistics (2007)
5. Ekbal, A., Haque, R., Bandyopadhyay, S.: Bengali part of speech tagging using conditional random field. In: Proceedings of Seventh International Symposium on Natural Language Processing (SNLP 2007), pp. 131–136 (2007)
6. Garg, N., Goyal, V., Preet, S.: Rule based Hindi part of speech tagger. In: Proceedings of COLING 2012: Demonstration Papers, pp. 163–174 (2012)
7. Greene, B.B., Rubin, G.M.: Automatic grammatical tagging of English. Department of Linguistics, Brown University (1971)
8. Harris, Z.S.: String analysis of sentence structure, no. 1, Mouton (1962)
9. Lafferty, J., McCallum, A., Pereira, F.C.: Conditional random fields: probabilistic models for segmenting and labeling sequence data (2001)
10. Modi, D., Nain, N.: Part-of-speech tagging of Hindi corpus using rule-based method. In: Afzalpulkar, N., Srivastava, V., Singh, G., Bhatnagar, D. (eds.) Proceedings of the International Conference on Recent Cognizance in Wireless Communication & Image Processing, pp. 241–247. Springer, New Delhi (2016). https://doi.org/10.1007/978-81-322-2638-3_28
11. Priyadarshi, A., Saha, S.K.: Towards the first Maithili part of speech tagger: resource creation and system development. Comput. Speech Lang. **62**, 101054 (2019)
12. Ranjan, P., Basu, H.V.S.S.A.: Part of speech tagging and local word grouping techniques for natural language parsing in Hindi. In: Proceedings of the 1st International Conference on Natural Language Processing (ICON 2003). Citeseer (2003)
13. Sharma, S.K., Lehal, G.S.: Using hidden Markov model to improve the accuracy of Punjabi POS tagger. In: 2011 IEEE International Conference on Computer Science and Automation Engineering, vol. 2, pp. 697–701. IEEE (2011)
14. Shrivastava, M., Bhattacharyya, P.: Hindi POS tagger using Naive stemming: harnessing morphological information without extensive linguistic knowledge. In: International Conference on NLP (ICON 2008), Pune, India (2008)
15. Singh, S., Gupta, K., Shrivastava, M., Bhattacharyya, P.: Morphological richness offsets resource demand-experiences in constructing a POS tagger for Hindi. In: Proceedings of the COLING/ACL on Main Conference Poster Sessions, pp. 779–786. Association for Computational Linguistics (2006)

# Text Cohesion in CQA - Does It Impact Rating?

Lalit Mohan Sanagavarapu$^{(\boxtimes)}$, Jahfar Ali Pichen, Syed Mohd Ali Rizwi,
Y. Raghu Reddy, and Dipti Sharma

IIIT Hyderabad, Hyderabad, India
{lalit.mohan,jahfar.ali}@research.iiit.ac.in,
syedmohdali.rizwi@students.iiit.ac.in, {raghu.reddy,dipti}@iiit.ac.in

**Abstract.** Community Question and Answer (CQA) platforms are expected to provide relevant content that is not readily available through search engines. With an increase in the number of users and growth of internet, CQA platforms have transitioned from generic to domain specific systems. Expert rating, machine learning and statistical methods are being used for assessing the quality of answers. However, the research on importance of consistency as a quality parameter in the form of text cohesion in CQAs is limited. We extracted 109,113 CQAs from StackExchange related to Information Security of the last 8 years to evaluate text cohesion in answers. An empirical study conducted with 246 participants (Information Security Experts, Software Engineers and Computational Linguists) on the extracted answers stated that lack of text cohesion impacts the rating of answers in CQA. Software Engineers are seekers and viewers of answers, they responded to a survey that lack of text cohesion leads to difficulty in reading and remembering. Information Security Experts providing answers to CQA stated that they need text cohesion for understandability.

**Keywords:** Crowdsourcing · Question and Answers · Quality · Text cohesion

## 1 Introduction

With improved digital literacy, affordable computing devices and growing internet user base (4+ Billion users), crowdsourcing platforms are becoming part of mainstream work. The contributions in macro (logo design, task or procedure oriented questions, software development and others) tasks is growing along with micro (image tagging, language translation, survey, and others) tasks on crowdsourcing platforms. Amazon MTurk, StackExchange, Reddit, Google Maps and Wikipedia are among the popular crowdsourcing systems. Crowdsourcing 'Question and Answers' (Q&A) is commonly referred as Community Question and Answering (CQA); StackExchange and Quora are some the widely used CQA systems. While the motivation to contribute on crowdsourcing platforms can be

© Springer Nature Switzerland AG 2020
B. R. Purushothama et al. (Eds.): MIKE 2019, LNAI 11987, pp. 21–31, 2020.
https://doi.org/10.1007/978-3-030-66187-8_3

extrinsic or intrinsic, motivation to contribute on CQA systems is mostly intrinsic (internal satisfaction). With increasing contributions and varying motivation, the quality of answers are not consistent and considered to contain casual and misleading answers [5,15]. Machine learning, follow graphs, game theory, rating and other techniques have been the research focus for quality assessment [1]. Most of the research on CQA is to assess the quality of questions, estimate the number of answers to a question, assignment of multiple questions to a single responder, on question type (factoid, procedural and others) based response rate, clicks, syntactic and semantic factors [9,14]. The quality of answers is our focus area with increasing contributors and Machine2Machine communication.

Quality is a key attribute in software engineering as well; code, documents and other deliverables are assessed for quality. To improve the quality of deliverable, the importance of completeness, consistency and correctness in information capturing and reporting are emphasized and used as software engineering quality principles [3] and ISO/IEC 25010:2011. We hypothesize that *'answers that are complete, consistent and correct are expected to have better ratings and views on CQA platforms'*. Completeness means that the answer to the question contains all the available information or is self-contained. Consistency in an answer indicates that semantic or syntactic terms in the sentence(s) do not contradict with each other. Correctness relates to conformance of the answer to a question with reference to ground truth. The fuzziness/interplay among these quality principles has to be dealt before measuring them independently [23]. Correctness and completeness are with reference to world knowledge and ground truth whereas consistency is related to continuity of topic being discussed that helps better comprehension or interpret-ability. Building ground truth of world knowledge is difficult and never-ending effort [17].

In the current study, we limited our study to the role of consistency in answer text and its impact on ratings and views. Consistency is realised through the interpretability of text, which is composed of 'word interpretation', 'syntactic parsing', and 'semantic integration' [12] that leads to successful formation of a mental representation. Consistency reminds the major property of the text to facilitate formation of the right mental representation. Assessing consistency as text interpret-ability depends on textual and subject variables [16]. The subject variables (coherence) are about relevant knowledge and skill set that the reader brings to the text. Hence, the subject variables are confined to the knowledge of readers [13] within the discourse context of the text. The textual variables are linguistic signals (cohesive devices) that mark the relations between the sequence of text constituents. The textual continuity and the relations between the sequences of textual constituents cannot be determined by a finite number of explicit linguistic markers [6] and are computationally elusive task. It also depends on the cognitive ability of the reader to interpret and construct the continuity in the discourse context. In our study, we included various textual cohesion variables such as adding extraneous information, identification of anaphoric references, and supplying background information as identified by Crossley [7], McNamara [16] and Kintsch [4].

In the experiment, we validated the need of text cohesion on ratings and views of StackExchange[1] related to Information Security domain or topic specific answers. Though there were over 149 features [11] to feature cohesion, we experimented with *sentence linking, order, opposition, reason and purpose* features after dimensionality reduction on a sample of 343 responses. Based on the identified features, a survey was conducted to assess the importance of text cohesion in CQA with participation from 3 different groups - Computational Linguists, Software Engineers and Information Security Experts. The survey results on text cohesion were analyzed to understand the differences in responses across the three groups. In the remainder sections of the paper, we describe in (ii) Sect. 2, the approach to obtain StackExchange CQA and the process followed for obtaining survey responses; (iii) Sect. 3, results and analysis on the participants' responses to the survey; (iv) Sect. 4, conclusion and the potential future work.

## 2   Approach

We adopted an experimental approach with quantitative analysis on a sample to validate our hypothesis that *'answers that are consistent are expected to have better ratings and views on CQA platforms'*. The steps in our approach for measuring importance of cohesion in CQA are shown in Fig. 1. We limited cohesion assessment to a domain so that a focused group or subject matter experts can be identified for the study. We used StackExchange dataset as it provides an SQL interface to obtain domain specific Q&A [20]. Using StackExchange SQL interface, we extracted records containing questions, their related answers, question posted date, answer date and the score (user rating) given to the answer using *Question, Answer and Posts* tables into a *.csv* file. We selected 'Information Security' as a domain on StackExchange. Attention towards Information security[2] increased with increasing digital usage. As part of the approach, answers

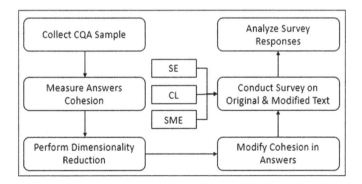

**Fig. 1.** Process diagram for measuring text cohesion

---

[1] https://security.stackexchange.com/.
[2] https://tinyurl.com/PWCSecurity.

rating/score, difference in answer date vis-a-vis question date, cascading/full answers, answer length, count of answers to a question are factored to identify a sample of answers for cohesion analysis. We extracted 109,113 ($N$) Question and Answers on 'Information Security' for a period of 8 years (StackExchange started in 2009 with very few records and our study happened in 2018, hence, our extract contains data from 2010-17). A stratified sampling is performed on the extracted CQA to identify a sample ($S$) answers that represents the population $N$ as mentioned in the following steps -

- The length of answers ranged from 38 to 27,596 characters. Approximately 80% of answers have 500 characters. Based on the character size filter, the sample size is reduced to 87,293 ($S'$) records.
- Interestingly, some questions were answered even after 6 years. However, >80% of the questions were answered within 15 min. With this filter, sample size is further reduced to 74,647 ($S"$) unique answers.
- There are answers that were negatively scored and some answers have been highly scored. As some questions had more than one answer, we selected answers that had the highest score amongst the available answers for a question. The median score or rating of answers is 12 of the initial extract ($N$) as well as the filtered sample ($S"$). After the filtering based on median score, the sample size reduced to 343 ($S$) answers, this sample was used for measuring text cohesion.

To measure cohesion features in text, CohMetrix of McNamara [16] and his co-author Kristopher Kyle's TAACO [8] are widely used tools. We used TAACO (149 features, $F$) as it has more features (CohMetrix has 106 features) and ease of set-up for identifying various cohesion features in StackExchange answers. To identify impactful, tractable and unrelated features, we performed dimensionality reduction on the cohesion feature values of $S$ answers. While there are many dimensionality reduction techniques [21], we use PCA and Pearson Correlation Analysis for feature identification. On performing PCA, we observed that we can represent all the $F$ features with 90% accuracy by using these 30 features as shown in Fig. 2. However, PCA gives only a tentative number of features to be used but doesn't give any specific information about the significant features as the values are combined and transformed to principal components. We performed Pearson correlation [19] analysis that examines the relationship between two sets of variables/features. A +1 is a case of perfect direct (increasing) linear relationship (correlation), −1 is a case of a perfect decreasing (inverse) linear relationship (anticorrelation), and some value in the open interval (−1, 1) in all other cases, indicating the degree of linear dependence between the variables. The correlation coefficients of $F$ features of $S$ is available in TextCohesion-Correlation Analysis spreadsheet on Google drive [18]. The features were correlated in the mean range of −0.297 to 0.658 ($\mu$). The coefficient score range ±0.3 is considered to contain weak relationship, we used this range to identify the features that are least or not correlated but have an impact on text cohesion. The six ($D$) text cohesion features *sentence linking*, *order*, *reason* and *purpose*, *opposition*, *temporal* and *quantpro* from TAACO were identified as least correlated features. The number

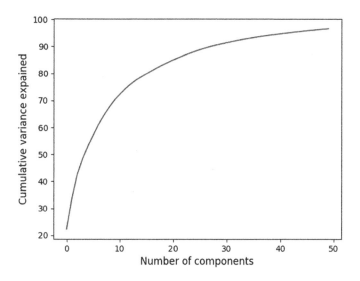

**Fig. 2.** Principal component analysis results

of significant features identified by correlation analysis to represent text cohesion were less as compared to principal components identified by PCA, hence, we used features identified by correlation analysis for further study.

We conducted a survey to identify the impact of these features on answer rating, i.e., on the quality of answer. We shortlisted 3 questions per year (answers without any grammatical errors) along with their answers from 343 sample $(S)$ records. The selected answers were modified on $D$ cohesion features. The modified answer text set was prepared by removing explicit cohesive markers, which makes the answer less accessible as compared to the original answer text. The key intent contained in the answer text was not removed in the iterative process of re-writing the answer text. Apart from removing the explicit connectives and other references, complex sentences were simplified in to multiple sentences with lesser explicit connectives across them. To restrict the role of implicit discourse signals, which activate default choice of continuity [2] between sentences, order of sentences from the original texts were changed. For every iteration of re-writing, the text was validated using TAACO to ensure a difference from the original answer text in terms of cohesion features. While modifying the text, grammar was maintained intact as the focus is evaluating cohesion of the text. The identified cohesion features *sentence linking, order, opposition* were mapped to the survey question on *reading* and *remembering* and cohesion feature *reason* and *purpose* was mapped to the survey question on *understanding*. We did not modify temporal and *quantpro* (quantitative pronouns such as *many*) features in answer as the focus was on *reading, remembering* and *understanding*. The 24 original and 24 modified answers (available as Cohesion Survey Questions on Google drive [18]) were shared with Information Security Experts, Computational Linguists and Software Engineers to rate on an ordinal scale (rating from 1–6 with value 6 being the highest and 1 being the lowest, we used an even number scale to reduce the chance of participants taking a middle path). Information Security Experts are considered to be contributors/responders in CQA. Software Engineers are considered to be viewers or seekers of responses in CQA. Computational Linguists are expected to be particular about features of text cohesion, are neither consumers or contributors of Information Security CQA. The first 3 questions in the survey capture the participant profile and the next 3 survey response ratings were on correctness, *reading*, *remembering* and *understanding* of the answer. Each participant was provided with 3 Stack-Exchange questions followed by its answer with a mix of original and modified answers. No participant was given the original and modified text of the same answer to avoid bias and to measure responses as independent samples.

- Q1: Name, Email ID and Educational Qualification of the participant were requested. The purpose of capturing this information was to bring seriousness to the survey and validity to the data for any future reference. The response to this question will not be used for analysis.
- Q2: How regularly do you use crowdsourcing platforms like StackExchange, Quora and MTurk, etc? This question validates the level of participation on CQA platforms. This question was expected to allude survey participants that authors were interested on CQA quality assessment. However, participants were not informed on the type (cohesion in the text) of quality assessment.
- Q3: What is your professional/personal familiarity in Information Security domain? The selected StackExchange sample CQA were related to information security, the domain familiarity provides an insight into participants response on correctness of the StackExchange answer.
- R1: Is the given answer responding to the question? As StackExchange is moderated and we selected answers that have median score 12, answers were expected to be near correct. This survey question was posed to eliminate non-serious survey participants and understand technical challenges of non-security domain participants.
- R2: What is the ease of reading and remembering the answer? The response to this survey question identify the ease of *reading* and *remembering*, i.e. related to *sentence linking*, *order*, *opposition* cohesion features. We combined the question on reading and remembering together as text is just not a combination of words but words that form a sentence for remembrance.
- R3: What is the difficulty level of the answer text? The response to this survey question identifies the *understandability*, ability to gather the intent of the text and relates to *reason* and *purpose* cohesion features.

## 3   Survey Results and Analysis

We used online and physical forms to interact with Group 1 - Subject Matter Experts referred as SMEs (Academicians, Chief Information Security Officers, Research Students with expertise in Information Security), Group 2 - CLs (Computational Linguists from academia) and Group 3 - SEs (industry professionals and research students in Software Engineering) over a period of 6 months

(April - September 2018) for the survey. A total of 246 participants provided 697 responses as shown in Table 1 with approximately 50% were SMEs, survey responses are available on Google drive [18]. We had minimum 5 responses to each of the original and modified sample answers from each of the groups. In response to $Q2$, 72% of the participants rated between 4–6 on their participation on crowdsourcing platforms, this confirmed that most of the participants are familiar with StackExchange or other CQA systems. For $Q3$ on familiarity to Information Security domain, Fig. 3 shows a near normal distribution suggesting that we have SMEs; all CLs and SEs that may not have security knowledge. We observed that participants grouped in SMEs have rated themselves at different levels on security expertise; 13% of the group have rated themselves low on domain expertise. As shown in Fig. 3, In response to the correctness of the response ($R1$), we observed that about 5% of the responses were rated answer as not correct (rated response between 1 and −3) and we considered these participants as casual and were removed from further analysis, these participants were present in all 3 groups (SE, CL and SME). These participants also gave same rating as $R1$ to $R2$ and $R3$. In response to $R2$, 83% of the responses rated modified text as relatively less readable and difficult to remember, shown in Table 2. Further analysis at individual question also showed that 70% of the participants had difficulty in *reading* and *remembering*. For $R3$, we analyzed the impact of

**Table 1.** Summary of survey participation

| Group | Count | Response |
|---|---|---|
| Linguists (CL) | 76 | 105 |
| Software Engineers (SE) | 36 | 111 |
| Security Experts (SME) | 134 | 427 |
| **Total** | **246** | **643** |

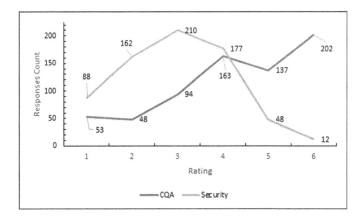

**Fig. 3.** Participants CQA and security familiarity

**Table 2.** Reading and remembering of text

| Rating | R2 | | R1 on answer correctness | | | | | |
|--------|------|-----|------|-----|------|-----|------|-----|
| | Orig | Mod | 4 | | 5 | | 6 | |
| | | | Orig | Mod | Orig | Mod | Orig | Mod |
| 1 | **23** | **29** | 6 | 4 | **7** | **10** | **8** | **11** |
| 2 | 87 | 59 | 20 | 12 | 35 | 23 | 22 | 7 |
| 3 | 81 | 67 | **29** | **35** | 28 | 14 | 8 | 4 |
| 4 | 91 | 62 | 25 | 16 | 29 | 16 | 15 | 9 |
| 5 | 43 | 42 | 16 | 14 | **9** | **12** | 7 | 3 |
| 6 | 13 | 5 | 4 | 2 | 2 | 1 | 5 | 1 |

*understandability* with original (*Orig*) and modified (*Mod*) answers. Approximately 75% of the participants rated original text higher on *understandability* than modified text (relatively less cohesive) as shown in Table 3, cells marked bold in the table deviate from the observed pattern. Only 68% of the participants had more than 3 rating and no response had a mean rating of $\geq 5$, this states that answers text need to be cohesive for improved understanding. The statistical mode value (variance of $\approx 1.29\%$) on the rating for all 3 groups is lower for modified answer text as compared to the original answer text. The participants gave a higher mean rating (4) for $R2$ as compared to $R3$ that had a mean of 3 for modified answers. However, rating by SE and SMEs had same mode value for original and modified text. This states that cohesion of text was relatively more important for understanding of the text as compared to reading and remembering. The Fig. 4 confirms that participants had varying difficulty in *reading*, *remembering* and *understanding* of text though the correctness of the answer text was maintained. We performed ANOVA analysis on the original and modified text in response to $R2$ and $R3$, data is shown in Table 4. The calculated $F_{Value}$ is greater than $F_{Critical}$ score for confidence level of 95%, this confirmed our hypothesis that text cohesion has an impact on rating.

The $F_{Critical}$ was greater than $F_{Value}$ for $R3$ for SME, however, the $P$ value was 0.17 and greater than $\alpha$ value. This observation reiterated that the text cohesion had an impact on rating for SMEs as well. Based on the ratings, we also observed that text cohesion is more significant for $R2$ (reading and remembering) to SEs and CLs and $R3$ (understanding) to SMEs. The margin of difference of rating between original and modified text is higher for $R3$ as compared to $R2$, similar observations [18] were obtained with one tail and two tail T Test (inferential statistics). Amongst the primary users (SME and SE) of the StackExchange, SMEs gave importance to *reason* and *purpose* to state that responses should be understandable. SEs stated their need of text cohesion is more for *reading* and *remembering* as compared to *understanding*, hence, lack of text cohesion impacts CQA rating. Similar to our experiment, the role of content and domain knowledge was conducted [10,22] on school children, it showed that background

**Table 3.** Understandability of original and modified text

| Rating | R3 | | R1 on answer correctness | | | | | |
| --- | --- | --- | --- | --- | --- | --- | --- | --- |
| | Orig | Mod | 4 | | 5 | | 6 | |
| | | | Orig | Mod | Orig | Mod | Orig | Mod |
| 1 | **9** | **12** | 2 | 2 | **2** | **5** | 2 | 2 |
| 2 | 53 | 25 | 16 | 4 | 10 | 5 | 8 | 3 |
| 3 | 73 | 57 | 26 | 20 | 25 | 10 | 3 | 3 |
| 4 | 96 | 67 | 37 | 27 | 26 | 23 | 17 | 4 |
| 5 | 75 | 49 | **15** | **16** | 36 | 16 | 17 | 5 |
| 6 | **35** | **51** | **3** | **13** | **12** | **16** | 18 | 18 |

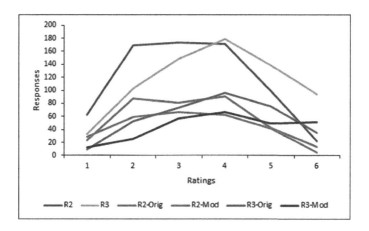

**Fig. 4.** Distribution of response ratings

**Table 4.** F scores of R2 and R3

| Group | R2 | | R3 | |
| --- | --- | --- | --- | --- |
| | F value | F critical | F value | F critical |
| SME | 0.87 | 0.78 | **1.04** | **1.29** |
| SE | 0.97 | 0.61 | 0.78 | 0.61 |
| CL | **0.66** | **0.68** | 0.91 | 0.67 |

knowledge played a vital role than the reader's decoding skills, and that text cohesion and genre depends on prior knowledge. Their results also revealed that cohesion cues without elaboration information do not facilitate comprehension, particularly for challenging texts. Another related study [7] described that elaboration and improved cohesion led to higher rating of coherence compared to original and elaborated versions.

## 4    Conclusion

The empirical study confirmed that cohesion improves *reading*, *remembering* and *understanding* of CQA text and impacts on quality or rating of CQA. Based on the ratings across groups, it is identified that importance of text cohesion is more significant for *understanding* as compared to *reading* and *remembering*. SMEs stated the need of cohesion for understanding whereas SEs stated the need for reading and remembering of the CQA text. Based on these analyses, a plugin for cohesion assessment of the text can be built, thereby, to validate the quality of web text on a page. Based on the ratings from SMEs on importance of cohesion for understandability, we state that validating text cohesion will enhance algorithms that are used for building/enhancing ontologies. The text cohesion may also improve credibility of a web page and assist in identifying fake content. Our experiment was limited to 643 responses obtained from 246 users on a sample 24 questions, extending the sample size or user base may provide more insights on text cohesion. Having traditional linguists as compared to computational linguists as survey participants would strengthen our observations on the need of text cohesion. The survey questions can be extended to open domain to validate if there are any different observations.

## References

1. Allahbakhsh, M., Benatallah, B., Ignjatovic, A., Motahari-Nezhad, H.R., Bertino, E., Dustdar, S.: Quality control in crowdsourcing systems: issues and directions. IEEE Internet Comput. **17**(2), 76–81 (2013)
2. Ariel, M.: Accessibility theory: an overview. Text Represent.: Linguist. Psycholinguist. Aspects **8**, 29–87 (2001)
3. Boehm, B.W., Brown, J.R., Lipow, M.: Quantitative evaluation of software quality. In: Proceedings of the 2nd International Conference on Software Engineering, pp. 592–605. IEEE Computer Society Press (1976)
4. Britton, B.K., Gülgöz, S.: Using Kintsch's computational model to improve instructional text: effects of repairing inference calls on recall and cognitive structures. J. Educ. Psychol. **83**(3), 329 (1991)
5. Burghardt, K., Alsina, E.F., Girvan, M., Rand, W., Lerman, K.: The myopia of crowds: cognitive load and collective evaluation of answers on stack exchange. PLoS ONE **12**(3), e0173610 (2017)
6. Charolles, M., Ehrlich, M.F.: Aspects of textual continuity linguistic approaches. In: Advances in Psychology, vol. 79, pp. 251–267. Elsevier (1991)
7. Crossley, S.A., McNamara, D.S.: Say more and be more coherent: how text elaboration and cohesion can increase writing quality. Institute of Educational Sciences (2016)
8. Crossley, S.A., Kyle, K., McNamara, D.S.: The tool for the automatic analysis of text cohesion (TAACO): automatic assessment of local, global, and text cohesion. Behav. Res. Methods **48**(4), 1227–1237 (2016)
9. Dahiya, Y., Talukdar, P.: Discovering response-eliciting factors in social question answering: a reddit inspired study. Director **24196**(3295), 13–61 (2016)

10. McNamara, D.S., Ozuru, Y., Floyd, R.G.: Comprehension challenges in the fourth grade: the roles of text cohesion, text genre, and readers' prior knowledge. Int. Electron. J. Element. Educ. **4**, 229–257 (2011)
11. Graesser, A.C., McNamara, D.S., Louwerse, M.M., Cai, Z.: Coh-Metrix: analysis of text on cohesion and language. Behav. Res. Methods Instrum. Comput. **36**(2), 193–202 (2004)
12. Halliday, M.A.K.: Explorations in the functions of language. Can. J. Linguist./Revue canadienne de linguistique **21**(2), 196–199 (1976)
13. Kintsch, W., Van Dijk, T.A.: Toward a model of text comprehension and production. Psychol. Rev. **85**(5), 363 (1978)
14. Li, B., Jin, T., Lyu, M.R., King, I., Mak, B.: Analyzing and predicting question quality in community question answering services. In: 21st International Conference on World Wide Web, pp. 775–782. ACM (2012)
15. Liu, J., Shen, H., Yu, L.: Question quality analysis and prediction in community question answering services with coupled mutual reinforcement. IEEE Trans. Serv. Comput. **10**(2), 286–301 (2017)
16. McNamara, D.S., Kintsch, W.: Learning from texts: effects of prior knowledge and text coherence. Discourse Process. **22**(3), 247–288 (1996)
17. Mitchell, T., et al.: Never-ending learning. Commun. ACM **61**(5), 103–115 (2018)
18. For Now A: CQA Text Cohesion Analysis (2019). https://tinyurl.com/CQACohesion/. (Accessed 20 Dec 2019)
19. Ratner, B.: The correlation coefficient: its values range between ±1, or do they? J. Target. Meas. Anal. Mark. **17**(2), 139–142 (2009)
20. Ravi, S., Pang, B., Rastogi, V., Kumar, R.: Great question! Question quality in community Q&A. In: Eighth International AAAI Conference on Weblogs and Social Media 2014, pp. 426–435 (2014)
21. Van Der Maaten, L., Postma, E., Van den Herik, J.: Dimensionality reduction: a comparative review. J. Mach. Learn. Res. **10**, 66–71 (2009)
22. Rupley, W.H., Willson, V.L.: Content, domain, and word knowledge: relationship to comprehension of narrative and expository text. Read. Writ. **8**, 419–432 (1996)
23. Zowghi, D., Gervasi, V.: The three Cs of requirements: consistency, completeness, and correctness. In: International Workshop on Requirements Engineering: Foundations for Software Quality, pp. 155–164. Essener Informatik Beitiage, Essen, Germany (2002)

# Person Name Segmentation with Deep Neural Networks

Tokala Yaswanth Sri Sai Santosh[1], Debarshi Kumar Sanyal[2(✉)],
and Partha Pratim Das[1]

[1] Department of Computer Science and Engineering,
Indian Institute of Technology Kharagpur, Kharagpur 721302, India
santoshtyss@gmail.com, ppd@cse.iitkgp.ac.in
[2] National Digital Library of India, Indian Institute of Technology Kharagpur,
Kharagpur 721302, India
debarshisanyal@gmail.com

**Abstract.** Person names often need to be represented in a consistent format in an application, for example, in <Last Name, Given Name, Suffix> format in library catalogs. Obtaining a normalized representation automatically from an input name requires precise labeling of its components. The process is difficult owing to numerous cultural conventions in writing personal names. In this paper, we propose deep learning-based techniques to achieve this using sequence-to-sequence learning. We design several architectures using a bidirectional long short-term memory (BiLSTM)-based recurrent neural network (RNN). We compare these methods with one based on the hidden Markov model. We perform experiments on a large collection of author names drawn from the National Digital Library of India. The best accuracy of 94% is achieved by the character-level BiLSTM with a conditional random field at the output layer. We also show visualizations of the vectors (representing person names) learned by a BiLSTM and how these vectors are clustered according to name structures. Our study shows that deep learning is a promising approach to automatic name segmentation.

**Keywords:** Name segmentation · Recurrent neural network · Long short-term memory · Hidden Markov model · Deep learning · Digital Library

## 1 Introduction

Many applications entail organizing personal names in a consistent format. For example, library catalogs generally mention the last name at the beginning followed by the given name. Many official forms ask users to segregate the different components of his/her name into separate text boxes. The open-source tool ReCiter that automatically generates investigator profiles using citation databases like PubMed and Scopus requires as input an investigator's name in a formatted manner with components like last name and given name identified [9].

© Springer Nature Switzerland AG 2020
B. R. Purushothama et al. (Eds.): MIKE 2019, LNAI 11987, pp. 32–41, 2020.
https://doi.org/10.1007/978-3-030-66187-8_4

Name segmentation is also useful in big data processing used by marketing companies, personal information management, automatic genealogy analysis, and name disambiguation. Given a personal name where it is unknown which component is the first name, which one is the last name, etc., it is difficult to achieve this segmentation *automatically*.

Given the cultural and ethnographic diversity in names and ways to write them, it is difficult to enumerate all rules to segment a name correctly into a given set of classes. So it is useful to explore machine learning techniques that can automatically learn the rules of name segmentation from labeled data. In this paper, we develop a framework for automatic name segmentation using deep learning. In particular, we model it as a sequence labeling problem where the input sequence consists of the different (unlabeled) components of the name, and the output sequence comprises the labels: last name (LN), suffix (SFX), and remaining name (RN), that are assigned to the components. For example, if the input name is Sharma Ramesh Chandra, the input sequence becomes <Sharma, Ramesh, Chandra> and the output sequence is <LN, RN, RN>. We choose only these three labels because the identification of the last name is most important in many applications, including that of library catalogs and bibliographic databases such as the National Digital Library of India (NDLI) hosted at https://www.ndl.gov.in. It is also important to identify the suffix as many bibliographic formats like APA (American Psychological Association), Chicago, and MLA (Modern Language Association) styles put them after the author's given name although one conventionally writes it after the last name (e.g., John Forbes Nash, Jr. is written as Nash, John Forbes, Jr. in a bibliography). We use a recurrent neural network (RNN) architecture with bidirectional long short-term memory (BiLSTM) cells to translate an input sequence to an output sequence. To the best of our knowledge, this application of BiLSTM is completely novel. We compare our proposed technique to a hidden Markov model (HMM)-based framework for parsing name components. Experiments performed on a dataset of author names from NDLI shows that a character-level bidirectional LSTM network with a conditional random field (CRF) layer at the output (the model is called BiLSTM-CRF in short) reaches an accuracy of 94% while an HMM produces 83.5% accuracy. Our code and dataset are available at https://github.com/dksanyal/Name-Parsing.

## 2   Related Work

The automatic segmentation of unstructured text into well-defined records is an important activity in data cleaning and normalization. The plethora of techniques to achieve it can be classified broadly into three categories: (1) rule-based, (2) statistical learning-based, and (3) hybrid of the preceding two categories. Statistical learning techniques either use generative models like HMM or discriminative models like CRFs [15]. The choice of the model often depends on the application with no clear winner among them [14]. HMM is used for address and name segmentation in [1], where the authors show that nested HMMs with a dictionary of semantic dependencies and an absolute discounting-based smoothing function can achieve higher accuracy than rule-based systems. References [2] and [7] employed HMMs to normalize Australian person names and person names in medical databases respectively. However, they did not find HMMs to perform better than the traditional rule-based methods. We have used HMM as the baseline in our experiments. Note that CRF can be used for record segmentation, but it requires manually identified features [3]. We do not focus on manual feature engineering. Moreover, the dataset of names we use is prepared in such a way that common features like capitalization and the positions of the name components are not useful for classification (because the names are lower-cased and the components within a name are shuffled). Hence, we do not use CRF as a baseline in our experiments.

Recently, deep learning has shown tremendous success in speech recognition, handwriting recognition, computer vision, and natural language translation [4]. RNNs are used for sequence processing. Unlike conventional feedforward neural networks, an RNN allows a layer to affect itself through a feedback mechanism and thus, can store infinite history [11]. A problem with RNNs is that the gradients propagating back through the layers over several time steps can become vanishingly small or explode to large values. LSTM networks (or simply, LSTMs) are a specific kind of RNNs that solve the above hidden and vanishing gradient problems of RNNs [8]. Both HMM and LSTM can be used to analyze sequential data. However, LSTMs can capture information from an arbitrarily long context window and hence, generally achieve higher performance [11]. A BiLSTM reads a sequence backwards and forwards. So it improves the performance of LSTM even further (see, for example, [17]). We use BiLSTM for our purpose. The problem addressed in this paper shares some characteristics with the *named entity recognition* (NER) problem where LSTMs have been used [16] successfully. However, name segmentation also has important differences from it: while NER aims at identifying text spans referring to an entity in text and leverages the considerable context around the entity mentions, our problem is focused on classifying name components where each component has a very limited context that simply comprises the other components in the same name.

## 3   Problem Formulation

The problem of name segmentation can be formally modeled as translating an input sequence $X = <x_1, x_2, \cdots, x_n>$ (comprising the components in the name) of length $n$ to a target sequence $Y = <y_1, y_2, \cdots, y_n>$ (comprising the labels) of the same length $n$. In practice, we seek $Y^*$ that maximizes the conditional probability $p(Y|X, \Lambda)$ where $\Lambda$ is the set of model parameters:

$$Y^* = \arg \max_{Y} p(Y|X, \Lambda) \tag{1}$$

$$p(Y|X, \Lambda) = p(y_1, \cdots, y_n | x_1, \cdots x_n, \Lambda) \tag{2}$$

Supervised machine learning models use a validation set to choose the best set of model parameters that optimize some performance measure on that set. The resultant model is evaluated on the test set. In our case, the performance measure is accuracy.

# 4 Proposed Approach

We describe the deep learning-based and HMM-based methods in the following subsections.

## 4.1 RNN-Based Segmenter

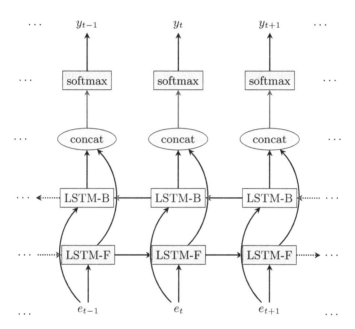

**Fig. 1.** Bidirectional RNN with LSTM cells (or simply, BiLSTM) to segment person names. The input symbols $e_i$ are embeddings. For word-level model, they are word embeddings; for character-level model, they are character embeddings. LSTM-F denotes an LSTM that reads the input sequence forwards while LSTM-B denotes an LSTM that reads the sequence backwards. An yellow oval denotes the concatenation of the hidden states from the forward and the backward LSTMs. The softmax layer generates a probability distribution over {LN, SFX, RN} in the word-level model and over {NONE, LN, SFX, RN} in the character-level model; the class with the highest probability is output as a label for the input symbol. In BiLSTM-CRF models, the softmax layer is replaced with a CRF layer. (Color figure online)

We have used the Keras deep learning library with Theano backend [10]. We designed an RNN that takes an input sequence containing a *representation* of a person name, passes it through a hidden layer, and outputs a sequence that labels each component of the name from the set {LN, SFX, RN}. Formally, given an input sequence $\Phi = [\phi_1, \phi_2, \cdots, \phi_n]$ where $\phi_i \in \mathbb{R}^d$ (in our case, the input sequence is a sequence of *embeddings* representing a name), at each time-step, a hidden state is produced, resulting in a hidden sequence $[h_1, h_2, \cdots, h_n]$ where $h_t$ is a function $f$ of the current input $\phi_t$ and previous hidden state $h_{t-1}$, that is, $h_t = f(\phi_t, h_{t-1})$. To avoid the vanishing gradient problem, we use LSTM cells when calculating the hidden state $h_t$; each LSTM cell contains an input gate, a forget gate, and an output gate [8]. At each time-step, an output is produced, resulting in an output sequence $[\psi_1, \psi_2, \cdots, \psi_n]$. It has been observed that in sequence processing tasks, contexts from both past and future are useful. So we design a bidirectional LSTM network that has two recurrent layers – one processing the input from left to right (forward) and another from right to left (backward) – and combine their hidden states at each timestamp as shown in Fig. 1. To avoid overfitting, we use dropout of 0.1. Let the output layer apply a function $g(.)$ on the BiLSTM outputs. We design two variants of the output layer: (1) $g(.)$ is the softmax function, (2) $g(.)$ is a CRF. While softmax predicts the output label for each token independently, CRF models the output labels as random variables forming a Markov Random Field conditioned upon the input sequence. By modeling the dependency among the output labels, a CRF usually predicts the labels more accurately than a model that treats each label independent of others. Thus, 2 models are designed: (1) BiLSTM with softmax, (2) BiLSTM-CRF. Each of the above architectures is again of three types based on the input: word level, character level, and word + character level.

**Word Level.** For the word level model, we restrict an input name to its first 9 components, zero-padding shorter ones. The word embeddings are trained with the model by backpropagation through time on the training mini-batches. Each word representation that flows out of the BiLSTM layer is a 1000-dimensional vector formed by concatenating two 500-dimensional vectors produced by the two LSTMs. The softmax or the CRF layer generates a probability distribution over {LN, SFX, RN}.

**Character Level.** In this model, a name is considered as a sequence of characters that are passed through the RNN that predicts labels for each character. Each character embedding is a 1000-dimensional vector and generated as the model is trained. The softmax or the CRF layer generates a probability distribution over {NONE, LN, SFX, RN}. One of the labels LN, SFX, RN should be output for the preceding name component whenever whitespace is encountered. For other characters, the output label should be NONE. An advantage of character-based models is their improved ability to handle out-of-vocabulary (OOV) words.

**Word + Character Level.** In this model, each name component is represented as a combination of a word embedding and a representation of the characters of the word. The character representation is generated with another BiLSTM. The BiLSTM layer in the segmenter runs over the concatenated representations. The final outputs are generated by a softmax or a CRF layer.

## 4.2  HMM-Based Segmenter

As an alternative to the deep learning model, we use an HMM to map name components to states. Here, $X$ denotes a sequence of observations and $Y$ a sequence of hidden states that produced $X$. An HMM $\lambda$ is a finite state machine in which state transitions are stochastic and states emit symbols stochastically, i.e., it is a bivariate stochastic process [13]. Formally, it is defined as a 4-tuple $\lambda = (S, V, \mathbf{A}, \mathbf{B})$:

1. a set of $n$ (=5) states $S = \{\texttt{START}, \texttt{LN}, \texttt{SFX}, \texttt{RN}, \texttt{END}\}$; the states are hidden in the sense that one can observe a sequence of emissions, but does not know the sequence of states the model went through to generate the emissions; the $\texttt{START}$ and $\texttt{END}$ states do not emit any symbols,
2. a vocabulary of $m$ observation symbols $V = \{w_1, w_2, \ldots, w_{m-1}, w_m\}$ where $w_1, \ldots w_{m-1}$ are the symbols seen during training and $w_m$ is a special symbol $\texttt{[UNK]}$ that represents symbols not seen during training,
3. an $n \times n$ *state transition matrix* $\mathbf{A} = [a_{ij}]$ where $a_{ij}$ denotes the probability of making a transition from state $i$ to state $j$, and
4. an $n \times m$ *emission probability matrix* $\mathbf{B} = [b_{jk}]$ where $b_{jk}$ is the probability of emitting symbol $w_k$ in state $j$.

The matrices $\mathbf{A}$ and $\mathbf{B}$ are learned from training data as follows.

$$a_{ij} = \frac{\text{Number of transitions from state } i \text{ to state } j}{\text{Total number of transitions out of state } i} \tag{3}$$

$$b_j(w_k) = \frac{\text{Number of times } w_k \text{ is emitted from state } j}{\text{Total number of symbol-emissions from state } j} \tag{4}$$

We use two smoothing techniques, *Laplace smoothing* and *absolute discounting* to assign an emission probability to $\texttt{[UNK]}$. In the former, we choose a pseudocount $\mu = 1$ and assume that each symbol in $V$ appears at least $\mu$ times so that $\texttt{[UNK]}$ does not get zero probability. In case of absolute discounting, we subtract a small quantity $\delta$ from the emission probability of each known symbol $w_k$ ($1 \leq k \leq m - 1$) emitted from state $j$ so that $w_k$ now gets an emission probability $b'_j(w_k) = b_j(w_k) - \delta$ in state $j$ where $b_j(w_k)$ is as calculated in Eq. 4. The total subtracted probability is divided equally among the symbols not seen in state $j$. Thus, if $T_j$ unique symbols are seen in state $j$ during training, the probability of an unseen symbol to be emitted from state $j$ is $\frac{T_j \delta}{m - T_j}$; we choose $\delta = \frac{1}{T_j + m}$ [1]. We use the Viterbi algorithm to find the most likely state sequence $Y^*$ that generated the input sequence $X$ [6]. This gives us the final output sequence made of $\{\texttt{LN}, \texttt{SFX}, \texttt{RN}\}$.

## 5  Experiments and Results

We trained the RNN models for 15 epochs in mini-batches of 1000 sequences. We have used the most 30K name components as the vocabulary for training the word-level RNN models and the HMM.

## 5.1   Dataset

There is no benchmark dataset for name segmentation. Therefore, we prepared a dataset for our study. Our corpus contains author names from IEEE publications indexed in NDLI. They are available in the form <LN+, SFX?, RN+>. Note that there are multi-part last names (for example, van Cutsem) in a complete name. We remove all separating commas and augment the dataset by circular right-shifting each name so that there are <RN+, LN+, SFX?> names, too. Otherwise, the segmenter will only learn to output <LN+, SFX?, RN+>. Finally, the training dataset holds 1.3 million author names while test set has 341588 names, that is, the corpus is divided in the ratio 80:20 to form the training and the test subsets, respectively. Figure 2 shows the distribution of the number of components in a name.

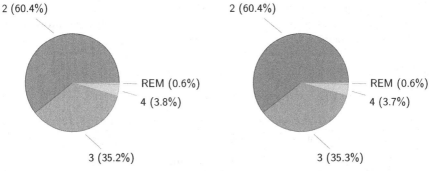

(a) Training corpus. REM comprises names of lengths 1,5,6,7,8,9.

(b) Test corpus. REM comprises names of lengths 1,5,6,7,8,9.

**Fig. 2.** Distribution of the number of components in an author name in the corpus. Each sector has a distinct color and is labeled with '$N$ ($p\%$)' or 'REM ($p\%$). In '$N$ ($p\%$)', $N$ is the number of components in a name and $p$ is the percentage of names with $N$ components in the given corpus. REM comprises names not covered by the other sectors. (Color figure online)

## 5.2   Results

We used the most 30K words as the vocabulary to train the word-level deep learning models and the HMM but no such bound naturally applies to the character-level models. The results for RNN are shown in Table 1. Clearly, the character-level BiLSTM with CRF (shown as **CharacterEmb-BiLSTM-CRF**) produces the highest accuracy of 94%. This is not unexpected as LSTMs can leverage the training data better than HMMs, and character embeddings can handle OOV better. We have observed that increasing the number of hidden layers in the BiLSTM does not change the accuracy appreciably but increases the training

**Table 1.** Performance of deep learning-based segmenters.

| Model | Vocabulary size (#words) | Accuracy (%) |
|---|---|---|
| WordEmb-BiLSTM-SoftMax | 30K | 90.05 |
| CharacterEmb-BiLSTM-SoftMax | X | 93.78 |
| (Word + Char)Emb-BiLSTM-SoftMax | 30K | 92.64 |
| WordEmb-BiLSTM-CRF | 30K | 91.85 |
| **CharacterEmb-BiLSTM-CRF** | **X** | **93.97** |
| (Word + Char)Emb-BiLSTM-CRF | 30K | 93.09 |

**Table 2.** Performance of HMM-based segmenter.

| Vocabulary size (#words) | Smoothing function | Accuracy (%) |
|---|---|---|
| 30K | Laplace | 83.5 |
| 30K | Absolute discounting | 81.98 |

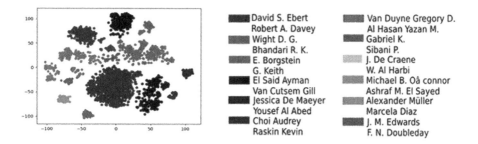

**Fig. 3.** Name embeddings. *Left:* We build the final embedding of a name by concatenating the hidden states of the name components (flowing through the red edges in Fig. 1) in the word-level BiLSTM. We collect embeddings for a large subset of names, cluster them with DBSCAN, and plot with t-SNE. *Right:* We show a few representative names appearing in some of the clusters. Observe the clusters learn distinct name structures like `<RN, RN, LN>` (e.g., `<David, S., Ebert>`) where the middle component is a single letter; `<LN, LN, RN, RN>` (e.g., `<Van, Duyne, Gregory, D.>`) where the leftmost `LN` is a particle and the rightmost `RN` is a single letter. (Color figure online)

time considerably. Table 2 shows the accuracy achieved by the HMM. Although training with Laplace smoothing gives the highest accuracy of 83.5%, the two HMM configurations display comparable performance.

## 5.3   Visualization of the Learned Representations

We wanted to understand what the RNN was learning. So given a name, we extracted the embeddings for the 9 components output to the CRF classifier in the word-level BiLSTM. We then concatenated them to form a 9000 dimensional vector. We did this for a large set of representative names drawn from the training set. Then we clustered the vectors with DBSCAN [5] (we have chosen it over alternatives like $k$-means as it does not require the number of clusters as input). Finally, we visualized the clusters by plotting them in 2-dimensional space with t-SNE [12]. The results are shown in Fig. 3. We observe that a cluster indeed corresponds to names of a distinct structure. We did not check this for the character BiLSTM as the concatenated vector will be too large.

## 6   Conclusion

We presented a novel deep learning-based name segmentation technique. With character BiLSTM, we achieve an accuracy of 94%, which vastly surpasses that of an HMM. Thus, an RNN provides an automatic method to parse person names for applications like library catalogs and bibliographies. Our results set a baseline for more complex name segmentation techniques that we intend to develop in the future. We would also explore if active learning can increase the accuracy further.

**Acknowledgements.** This work is supported by the *National Digital Library of India Project* sponsored by the Ministry of Human Resource Development, Government of India at IIT Kharagpur.

## References

1. Borkar, V., Deshmukh, K., Sarawagi, S.: Automatic segmentation of text into structured records. In: ACM SIGMOD Record, vol. 30, pp. 175–186. ACM (2001)
2. Churches, T., Christen, P., Lim, K., Zhu, J.X.: Preparation of name and address data for record linkage using hidden Markov models. BMC Med. Inform. Decis. Mak. **2**(1), 9 (2002)
3. Das, G.S., Li, X., Sun, A., Kardes, H., Wang, X.: Person-name parsing for linking user web profiles. In: Proceedings of the 18th International Workshop on Web and Databases, pp. 20–26. ACM (2015)
4. Deng, L.: A tutorial survey of architectures, algorithms, and applications for deep learning. APSIPA Trans. Signal Inf. Process. **3**, e2 (2014)
5. Ester, M., Kriegel, H.P., Sander, J., Xu, X., et al.: A density-based algorithm for discovering clusters in large spatial databases with noise. In: Proceedings of the SIGKDD Conference on Knowledge Discovery and Data Mining 1996, pp. 226–231 (1996)
6. Forney, G.D.: The Viterbi algorithm. Proc. IEEE **61**(3), 268–278 (1973)
7. Gonçalves, R.D.C.B., Freire, S.M.: Name segmentation using hidden Markov models and its application in record linkage. Cadernos de Saude Publica **30**(10), 2039–2048 (2014)
8. Hochreiter, S., Schmidhuber, J.: Long short-term memory. Neural Comput. **9**(8), 1735–1780 (1997)
9. Johnson, S.B., Bales, M.E., Dine, D., Bakken, S., Albert, P.J., Weng, C.: Automatic generation of investigator bibliographies for institutional research networking systems. J. Biomed. Inform. **51**, 8–14 (2014)

10. Keras-Team: Keras documentation (2018). https://keras.io/. Accessed 09 Mar 2019
11. Lipton, Z.C., Berkowitz, J., Elkan, C.: A critical review of recurrent neural networks for sequence learning. arXiv preprint arXiv:1506.00019 (2015)
12. van der Maaten, L., Hinton, G.: Visualizing data using t-SNE. J. Mach. Learn. Res. **9**(Nov), 2579–2605 (2008)
13. Rabiner, L.R.: A tutorial on hidden Markov models and selected applications in speech recognition. Proc. IEEE **77**(2), 257–286 (1989)
14. Sarawagi, S.: Information extraction. Found. Trends Databases **1**(3), 261–377 (2008)
15. Sutton, C., McCallum, A.: An introduction to conditional random fields. Found. Trends® Mach. Learn. **4**(4), 267–373 (2012)
16. Yadav, V., Bethard, S.: A survey on recent advances in named entity recognition from deep learning models. In: Proceedings of the 27th International Conference on Computational Linguistics, pp. 2145–2158 (2018)
17. Zeyer, A., Doetsch, P., Voigtlaender, P., Schlüter, R., Ney, H.: A comprehensive study of deep bidirectional LSTM RNNs for acoustic modeling in speech recognition. In: Proceedings of the IEEE International Conference on Acoustics, Speech and Signal Processing (ICASSP), pp. 2462–2466. IEEE (2017)

# Convex vs Convex-Concave Objective for Rare Label Classification

Nagesh Bhattu Sristy[1]([✉]), Satya Krishna Nunna[2,4], D. V. L. N. Somayajulu[3,4], and N. V. Narendra Kumar[2]

[1] NIT Andhra Pradesh, Tadepalligudem 534101, Andhra Pradesh, India
nageshbhattu@nitandhra.ac.in
[2] IDRBT, Castle Hills, Road No.1, Masab Tank, Hyderabad 500057, India
satya.krishna.nunna@gmail.com, nvnarendra@idrbt.ac.in
[3] IIITDM Kurnool, Jagannathagattu Hill, Kurnool 518007, Andhra Pradesh, India
somadvlns@gmail.com
[4] NIT-W, Warangal 506004, Telangana, India

**Abstract.** Machine learning algorithms based on semi-supervised strategies have drawn the attention of researchers due to their ability to work with limited labeled data making use of huge number of unlabeled samples. Graph based semi-supervised algorithms make an assumption of similarity of examples in lower dimensional manifold and use an objective that ensures similarity of labels as enforced by the similarity graph. Such methods typically make use of a L2 regularization term to avoid over-fitting. Regularization term further ensures convexity of the overall objective leading to efficient learning algorithms. Addressing the problem of low-supervision and high class imbalance, prior work has shown state-of-the-art results for anomaly detection and other important classification problems by using a convex-concave objective. The current work analyses such performance improvements of convex-concave objective thoroughly. Our study indicates that a KL-Divergence based loss function for semi-supervised learning has performed much better than the convex-concave objective based on L2-Loss. It is also seen that the one-versus-rest setting for multi-class classification using convex-concave objective is performing much weaker compared to the naturally multi-class KL-Divergence based multi-class classification setting.

**Keywords:** Semi-supervised learning · Multi-class classification · Convex-Concave

## 1 Introduction

Semi-supervised learning (SSL) is an important area of machine learning meant for addressing the scarcity of labeled training data. SSL believes in the observation that the unlabeled data (usually available abundantly) can also be used by the learning algorithm along with the limited labeled data. SSL for generative approaches such as naive Bayes is studied in [14] using expectation

© Springer Nature Switzerland AG 2020
B. R. Purushothama et al. (Eds.): MIKE 2019, LNAI 11987, pp. 42–51, 2020.
https://doi.org/10.1007/978-3-030-66187-8_5

maximization algorithm. Such performance improvement is not extended for discriminative approaches such as logistic regression, support vector machines and neural networks as these methods model the discriminator directly, making the unlabeled examples useless. Graph based algorithms address semi-supervised learning problem with discriminative approaches using a graph based objective. The graph based objective combines the labeled and unlabeled examples using their feature representations connected over a similarity graph (a graph whose edges encode similarity of nodes in the form of a weight). [6] and [28] are some of the earlier works which used such an approach for SSL. Several such works are connected through the same underlying principles, which can be expressed as a single objective connecting the loss computed from limited labeled data, a graph based label smoothing objective and an additional regularization term such as loss or weight decay.

The work in [15] an important improvisation over this framework when applied to problems which have class imbalance and very low degree of supervision. [15] observed that when general purpose SSL objective is applied to such problems (low degree of supervision and high class imbalance), the regularizer pulls the labeling for unlabeled examples towards the boundary of class separation, making the classifier useless for many examples. Instead they proposed an approach to modify the regularization term to be negative making the total objective to be difference of two convex functions rather than being convex. A variant of gradient projection is used to solve the constrained optimization objective. Here after we refer to their approach as NCLP (non-convex label propagation) through out the paper.

The work in [18] addresses multi-class SSL problem elegantly using a loss function based on KL-Divergence. The authors in [18] proposed an alternating minimization approach which is much more efficient than the naive approaches for SSL with KL-Divergence based loss function. Looking at the impressive results observed in [15] for various scenarios of class imbalance and anomaly detection, the current work addresses two research objectives.

– How does the NCLP approach perform compared to KL-Divergence based SSL
– How does the NCLP approach work for imbalanced-multi-class classification scenarios

## 2   Related work

There are many different classes of SSL algorithms, such as self-training [17], co-training [7], inductive-learning and transductive learning [21] are implemented to solve different learning problems such as clustering, regression and classification [10,30]. Graph-based semi-supervised learning (GSSL - a transductive learning algorithm), is a special case of SSL algorithms, in which both the train and test datasets are jointly represent in a single connected graph [1,2,12,13,22,23,26,30].

Most of the GSSL algorithms are categorized into two classes based on propagation of label information methods such as *label-propagation* - it uses the graph structure to pass label information from labeled data points to unlabeled data points and *measure propagation* - it minimizes the loss function defined based on the smoothness constraints derived from the graph.

The works [20,28] presented GSSL algorithms for classification problem by propagating label information from labeled data points to unlabeled data points using Markov random walk and k-Nearest-Neighbour (kNN).

The work in [6] presented a graph mincut based SSL algorithm for classification using graph partitioning by minimizing the number of similar data points with different labels (by minimizing the leave-one-out cross-validation error over the entire dataset). A Gaussian random field model for GSSL using the minimization of harmonic energy function is presented in [29]. The works [3,4,8], presented the Laplacian regularization to exploit the geometry of the marginal distribution in SSL algorithms. Many GSSL algorithms [5,9,12,29] use the squared-loss function in their objective functions to learn the model. Though, it is feasible for a Gaussian noise model, it is not feasible for classification problems. The one-vs-rest GSSL algorithms [6,12] are implemented using $n$ binary classifiers to solve multi-class classification problems. Though, the one-vs-rest classifiers performs as well as true multi-class classifiers [16], our results, presented in this work, on GSSL model suggest the true multi-class classifier performs superior to the one-vs-rest.

## 3   Approach

Let there be a dataset $X = X_L \cup X_U$ of labeled ($X_L$) and unlabeled ($X_U$) examples. $|L|$ and $|U|$ are number of labeled and unlabeled examples respectively. Let $(d_i, l_i)$ be i'th example ($1 <= i <= |L|$)in the labeled dataset $X_L$ where $d_i \in \mathbb{R}^k$ is k dimensional feature vector representation of the example and $l_i \in \mathcal{C}$ is the label drawn from the set of all labels $\mathcal{C}$. For binary classification tasks, the set of labels is $\{-1, 1\}$ representing the two classes. Let $\mathbb{L}_L$ be the vector of all labels of labeled examples. We further extend this vector as $\mathbb{L}$ by filling 0's as label for all unlabeled examples. Similarly $d_i$ is the i'th example ($1 <= i <= |U|$) of unlabeled dataset $X_U$ (occupying index $L + i$ in the complete dataset X).

Let us consider the similarity between any pair of examples $x_i$ and $x_j$ in the dataset $X$. The similarity is defined as $sim(x_i, x_j) = f(d_i, d_j)$ where f is suitable function of similarity. For Gaussian kernel based similarity:

$$f(d_i, d_j) = exp^{\frac{-||d_i - d_j||_2^2}{2*\sigma^2}} \tag{1}$$

Gaussian kernel uses a precision parameter $\sigma$ for scaling the L2-squared norm of the difference vector $d_i - d_j$. Consider an undirected graph where each of the examples $x_i \in X_L$ are nodes. The edges between any pair of nodes $x_i$ and $x_j$ has weight given by $sim(x_i, x_j)$. As number of nodes becomes huge, maintaining the similarity across every possible pair of nodes poses serious difficulties for the subsequent optimization. From a practical perspective, for every node we maintain the top-k similar node connections in similarity graph. Let G(V, E) be such k-nearest neighbor graph where $v_i \in V$ identifies the node corresponding to i'th example of the dataset $x_i$. $(v_i, v_j) \in E$, if $x_j$ is among k-nearest neighbors of $x_i$. Let $A$ be a matrix of weights of all the edges in the similarity graph.

$$A(i,j) = \begin{cases} sim(x_i, x_j) & \text{if } v_i \text{ and } v_j \text{ are neighbors in k-nn graph} \\ 0 & \text{otherwise} \end{cases} \quad (2)$$

Let $D$ be a diagonal matrix with diagonal entries as row-wise sum of all entries in the particular row. $D(i,i) = \sum_{j=1}^{|L|+|U|} A(i,j)$. Let $H$ be a matrix obtained by either (i) $H = D - A$ (ii) $H = D^{-\frac{1}{2}}(D - A)D^{-\frac{1}{2}}$ indicating unnormalized graph laplacian and noramlized graph laplacian respectively.

### 3.1  Graph Based Semi-supervised Learning for Binary Classification

Numerous graph based SSL algorithms can be put in a common framework of optimization depicted in (3). A first portion of such minimization optimization objective is due to the loss from limited labeled data. Binary classification tasks have the label $(l_i)$ to be in $\{-1, 1\}$. The term $\hat{l}_i$ indicates the label predicted by the model. Model used for this prediction is $\hat{l}_i = g(d_i; \theta)$. The number of parameters in $\theta$ will match that of number of features k for linear/log-linear models. Neural networks model it using multiple layers of linear models, increasing the parameters by many folds. Predictions for the whole set of examples are put in a vector $\hat{\mathbb{L}}$. Predictions for the labeled portion of the dataset is represented as the vector $\hat{\mathcal{L}}_L$. The second part is due to the graph based label smoothner. It ensures that any two neighbors in k-nn graph have their label agreement proportional to the similarity of the two nodes in the graph. The same can be expressed as $\hat{\mathcal{L}}^t H \hat{\mathcal{L}}$. The last term acts as a regularizer expressed as norm of parameter vector $\theta$. The objective in (3) uses L2-Square norm for regularizing the loss function. Accounting for all the three sub-parts, the objective in (3) is minimized with respect to the model parameters to find the optimal. $\mu >= 0$ is the weight of graph regularization term and $\lambda >= 0$ is the weight of regularization term in the objective.

$$\mathcal{O}_{SQ-CO} = \sum_{i=1}^{|L|} (l_i - \hat{l}_i)^2 + \mu \sum_{i=1}^{|L|+|U|} \sum_{j \in \mathcal{N}(v_i)} A(i,j) *$$
$$(\hat{l}_i - \hat{l}_j)^2 + \lambda * ||\theta||_2^2 \quad (3)$$

Alternatively the same objective can be written as

$$\mathcal{O}_{SQ-CO} = (\mathcal{L} - \hat{\mathcal{L}})^t B(\mathcal{L} - \hat{\mathcal{L}}) + \mu * \hat{\mathcal{L}}^t H \hat{\mathcal{L}} \quad (4)$$

where B is a diagonal matrix with

$$B(i,i) = \begin{cases} 1 & if 1 <= i <= |L| \\ \lambda & otherwise \end{cases} \quad (5)$$

The works in [29] and [25] implement the objective in Eq. (3) differently. Zhu et al. 2003 [29] uses random walk based laplacian to encode the graph regularizer and does not use any regularization term. Zhou et al. 2003 [25] uses normalized graph laplacian and uses a regularization term towards the ending. Pimplikar et al. [15] furthered these prior works using a convex-concave objective. The application of such a technique is shown to be useful when the number of labeled examples is few and class imbalance is high. The constrained optimization problem being minimized in [15] represented in Eq. (6). The difference between Eqs. (3) and (6) is the addition of constraints for enabling the convex-concave objective to be solved. The regularization term towards the end of the objective is negative making the entire objective to be difference of two convex functions (i.e. convex-concave).

$$\mathcal{O}_{SQ-CCO} = ||\mathcal{L}_L - \hat{\mathcal{L}}_L||_2^2 + \mu * \hat{\mathcal{L}}^t H \hat{\mathbb{L}} - \lambda * ||\hat{\mathcal{L}}||_2^2$$
$$s.t.\text{-}1 <= \hat{\mathcal{L}} <= 1 \tag{6}$$

Pimplikar et al. [15] followed a gradient projection approach to solve the constrained convex-concave optimization problem. Yuille et al. [24] shows methods for solving several convex concave optimization problems. [15, Pimplikar et al.] have replaced the quadratic regularization term ($||\hat{\mathcal{L}}||_2^2$) in Eq. (6) with a linear term ($\hat{\mathcal{L}}_{Old}^t \hat{\mathcal{L}}$). Such modification keeps the convexity of optimization objective intact. Another technical issue that such modification to the graph based SSL algorithm has to deal with is a case when the k-nn graph has multiple connected components and each component does not have examples of each representative class. In such cases, the labels of unlabeled examples are pulled towards classes which are present in the respective connected component making the graph based objective useless. Such problem is addressed by adding additional edges into the k-nn graph making it a single connected component. All these issues become more complicated when working with multi-class classification setting.

## 3.2  KL-Divergence Based SSL

The work in [18, Subramanya et al.] presents a KL-Divergence based formulation of SSL which is non-parametric. A similar model is also presented in [11] in the context of learning from labeled features, where the model is parametric. Let us consider a probability vector $a_i$ predicted label for the i'th example $x_i \in X$ (by the SSL model). Let $l_i$ be the one hot vector representation of the labels over the label space $\mathcal{C}$.

Similar to the earlier formulation in Eq. (3), the KL-Divergence based formulation for SSL depicted in Eq. (7), is also separated into three parts. The first portion corresponds to loss due to limited amount of labeled data. The loss function is based on KL-Divergence as opposed to L2-Square loss used in earlier formulation. The second part of the formulation uses graph based loss term making using of KL-Divergence for measuring the dissimilarity. This term finds the KL-Divergence ($KL(a_i, a_j)$) where $v_i$ and $v_j$ are neighbors in the original graph. The weight of such loss function is proportional to the weight of the edge in the graph. Unlike the earlier L2-Square loss, this term is asymmetric but preserves the convexity. The last part of the objective is summation of entropies of all the probability vectors $(E(a_i))$, which means when all the other terms are ineffective, the label vector $a_i$ should be driven towards uniform distribution.

$$\mathcal{O}_{KL-AM} = \sum_{i=1}^{L} KL(a_i, l_i) + \mu * \sum_{i=1}^{|L|+|U|} \sum_{j \in \mathcal{N}(v_i)} A(i,j)KL(a_i, a_j)$$
$$- \lambda * \sum_{i=1}^{|L|+|U|} E(a_i) \qquad (7)$$

We refer to the paper in [19] for proofs of convexity of the objective in Eq. (7) when $\mu, \lambda, A(i,j) >= 0$. The objective is optimized using an alternative minimization procedure whose complete details can be found in [19].

The approach in [15] was demonstrated for binary classification scenarios. We can also observe that such as approach [15] uses squared loss as opposed to KL-Divergence loss. Extending the performance gains of [15] for multi-class scenarios requires either one-vs-rest strategy or one-vs-one strategy. When the gains of NLCP formulation are extrapolated to multi-class scenarios, we can observe that squared loss is increasingly inappropriate. The important research question addressed in this work is to methodically compare between the two approaches for multi-class graph based semi-supervised learning algorithms when there is class imbalance.

## 4 Experiments

This section summarizes the performance of three different models on nine bench mark datasets. The details of these datasets are as follows.

### 4.1 Datasets

The nine bench mark datasets include *optical-digits, image-segment, iso-let, KDDcup99, waveform, wine-quality, magic-gamma, ionosphere* and *ILPD*. Except KDD cup'99 dataset[1], all other datasets are collected from the UCI repository[2]. These datasets are considered with different characteristics, such as class imbalance, degree of supervision, more number of classes and large size feature vectors. As shown in Table 1, the datasets size (i.e number of instances) varies from 351 to 492598, number of features varies from 10 to 10000 and number of classes varies from 2 to 30. The columns 6 to 11, summarize the number of labelled instances considered for our experimentation. As described in Sect. 3 we build a k-NN graph[3] for each dataset with fixed parameters *(5 nearest-neighbours, cosine similarity, radial basis kernel function)*.

---

[1] http://kdd.ics.uci.edu/databases/kddcup99/kddcup99.html.

[2] http://archive.ics.uci.edu/ml.

[3] The source code used to build k-NN graph is a sub module of the frame work available at: http://download.joachims.org/sgt_light/current/sgt_light.tar.gz.

**Table 1.** Datasets description. # **Instants**: Total number of instances, # **Features**: Number of feature attributes and one class attribute, #**classes**: Total number of class labels, **CI**: Class Imbalance, # **LP**: Number of labeled points,

| Degree Of Supervision ———> | | | | | 0.5% | 1% | 2% | 5% | 10% | 20% |
|---|---|---|---|---|---|---|---|---|---|---|
| Dataset Name | # Instances | # Features | #classes | CI | # LP | # LP | # LP | # LP | # LP | # LP |
| Optical digits | 5620 | 64+1 | 10 | 0.0 | 29 | 57 | 113 | 281 | 562 | 1124 |
| ImageSegment | 2310 | 19+1 | 7 | 0.15 | 12 | 24 | 47 | 116 | 231 | 462 |
| Isolet | 7797 | 617+1 | 26 | 0.0 | 39 | 78 | 156 | 390 | 780 | 1560 |
| KDDcup99 | 492598 | 41+1 | 2 | 0.95 | 2463 | 4926 | 9852 | 24630 | 49260 | 98520 |
| Waveform | 5000 | 21+1 | 3 | 0.52 | 25 | 50 | 100 | 250 | 500 | 1000 |
| WineQuality | 4898 | 11+1 | 7 | 0.44 | 25 | 49 | 98 | 245 | 490 | 980 |
| MagicGamma | 19020 | 10+1 | 2 | 0.71 | 96 | 191 | 381 | 951 | 1902 | 3804 |
| Ionosphere | 351 | 34+1 | 2 | 0.71 | 2 | 4 | 8 | 18 | 36 | 71 |
| ILPD | 583 | 10+1 | 2 | 0.74 | 3 | 6 | 12 | 30 | 59 | 117 |

## 4.2  Results

In our experimentation, we keep the class labels for randomly selected $l$ (computed based on the DoS value) number of instances and then mask the class labels for the remaining set of instances. While randomly selecting, we ensure that the class imbalance of labeled instances is similar to the class imbalance of the overall dataset. We experimented 20 times for each combination of the dataset and DoS value by selecting different instances as labeled examples in each time. Final average F-score of all these 20 outputs are presented in Table 2. These values show the average performance of each method for each combination.

In Table 2 we compare the performance of two base-line methods (one-vs-rest gssl-based classifiers LGC [25, 27] and NCLP [15]) with a multi-class classifier implemented using measure propagation [18] with $kl$-divergence similarity. The following insights are observed from our experimentation.

As shown in Table 2, the two models NCLP and MP outperforms the LGC method. Considering the NCLP and MP methods, MP performs better than NCLP in all cases except for two datasets, *optical-digits* and *image-segments*.

The datasets *KDD, waveform, wine-quality, magic-gamma, ionosphere* and *ILPD* are having high class imbalance (presented in Table 1) compared to the remaining datasets. The average F-score of MP method (for different DoS values) is approximately 16.49%, 25.66% and 8.52% superior to the NCLP on *KDD, waveform and wine-quality* datasets respectively. Similarly, on *magic-gamma, ionosphere* and *ILPD* datasets, MP method performs 11.65%, 6.44% and 30.06% superior to the NCLP method respectively. The MP method has consistent improvement in its performance, in terms of F-score, with increase in the DoS value. For high class imbalance and low DoS, MP method performs better than NCLP. As shown in Table 2, for 0.5% DoS, MP method performs 3.92%, 70.63%, 7.86%, 27.85%, 9.71% and 41.78% superior to the NCLP method on *KDD, waveform, wine-quality, magic-gamma, ionosphere* and *ILPD* datasets respectively.

As shown in Table 1, the datasets *optical-digits, image-segments* and *isolet* are having very low class imbalance. Similar to the high class imbalance datasets, the MP method performs better for all low class imbalance datasets (in terms of average F-score on different DoS values) except for *optical-digits* dataset. It performs 0.31%, 29.9% superior to the NCLP on *image-segment* and *isolet* datasets respectively. For low DoS (0.5%), in terms of F-score, MP method performs 18.25%, 28.55% superior to the NCLP on *image-segment* and *isolet* datasets respectively. Though, MP method shows less performance on *optical-digits* dataset, it reaches to the near performance of NCLP by adding just 1.5% labeled instances (shown with yellow color in Table 2).

With these results, we summarize our observations in concise way as follows:

- For high class imbalance and low DoS, the measure propagation with *kl*-divergence similarity (GSSL) method performs better than other GSSL methods. (The results are shown in red colour)
- For high class imbalance, low DoS and high volume of data, MP performs better than all other GSSL methods. (KDDcup99 dataset with DoS = 0.5%)
- For large size feature vector, more number of classes and low DoS, the MP method is superior than NCLP. (Isolet dataset with DoS = 0.5%)

**Table 2.** F1-score comparison of three models for different DoS levels on different bench mark datasets.

| Dataset | DoS: 0.5% | | | DoS: 1.0% | | | DoS: 2.0% | | |
|---|---|---|---|---|---|---|---|---|---|
| | LGC | NCLP | MP | LGC | NCLP | MP | LGC | NCLP | MP |
| Optdigits | 0.1639 | 0.9981 | 0.7579 | 0.1627 | 0.9982 | 0.8874 | 0.1618 | 0.998 | 0.9609 |
| Image-segment | 0.223 | 0.2196 | 0.4021 | 0.2215 | 0.5375 | 0.4923 | 0.223 | 0.6576 | 0.637 |
| Isolet | 0.0694 | 0.1223 | 0.4078 | 0.0707 | 0.0564 | 0.5387 | 0.0698 | 0.1358 | 0.6158 |
| KDDcup99 | 0.0414 | 0.5541 | 0.5933 | 0.0559 | 0.5245 | 0.6928 | 0.0582 | 0.6299 | 0.7672 |
| Waveform | 0.3968 | 0.0367 | 0.71 | 0.3942 | 0.1042 | 0.6961 | 0.3933 | 0.5176 | 0.7339 |
| Winequality | 0.0079 | 0.0692 | 0.1479 | 0.007 | 0.1111 | 0.1541 | 0.008 | 0.0583 | 0.1679 |
| Magicgamma | 0.4138 | 0.3424 | 0.6209 | 0.4133 | 0.4455 | 0.6225 | 0.4117 | 0.5356 | 0.6488 |
| Ionosphere | 0.4325 | 0.4307 | 0.527 8 | 0.4264 | 0.5639 | 0.6748 | 0.4327 | 0.5584 | 0.6217 |
| ILPD | 0.3613 | 0.1023 | 0.5201 | 0.3665 | 0.1546 | 0.4756 | 0.362 | 0.2678 | 0.475 |
| Dataset | DoS: 5.0% | | | DoS: 10.0% | | | DoS: 20.0% | | |
| | LGC | NCLP | MP | LGC | NCLP | MP | LGC | NCLP | MP |
| Optdigits | 0.1601 | 0.9981 | 0.9618 | 0.1588 | 0.9981 | 0.9772 | 0.1567 | **0.9982** | 0.983 |
| Image-segment | 0.2248 | 0.7887 | 0.7406 | 0.2294 | 0.8543 | 0.8286 | 0.2249 | **0.8891** | 0.8649 |
| Isolet | 0.0693 | 0.3997 | 0.7031 | 0.0693 | 0.5879 | 0.777 | 0.069 | 0.7396 | **0.7938** |
| KDDcup99 | 0.0451 | 0.6626 | 0.8463 | 0.0382 | 0.6974 | 0.9168 | 0.0475 | 0.7248 | **0.9664** |
| Waveform | 0.3922 | 0.7114 | 0.7285 | 0.3867 | 0.7523 | 0.7581 | 0.383 | 0.778 | **0.7799** |
| Winequality | 0.0075 | 0.0895 | 0.1841 | 0.0081 | 0.1089 | 0.1887 | 0.0075 | 0.0871 | **0.1928** |
| Magicgamma | 0.4129 | 0.6171 | 0.6756 | 0.4127 | 0.6515 | 0.6859 | 0.4096 | 0.6695 | **0.7071** |
| Ionosphere | 0.4314 | 0.667 | 0.6819 | 0.4206 | 0.713 | 0.7271 | 0.4266 | 0.7407 | **0.827** |
| ILPD | 0.3606 | 0.2345 | 0.5395 | 0.3553 | 0.2644 | 0.5991 | 0.3624 | 0.3148 | **0.5328** |

# 5 Conclusion

In this work we study the extension of a convex-concave formulation for SSL for problems with low degree of supervision and high class imbalance. We studied the performance comparision of L2-Loss earlier approach for convex-concave objective based SSL with that of KL-Divergence based SSL. We found that the performance of KL-Divergence based SSL is superior in 8 out of 9 datasets being worked out under varying degree of supervision. We also see a research challenge here as to whether such convex-concave formulations improve the performance of the classifiers in the general case.

# References

1. Belkin, M., Matveeva, I., Niyogi, P.: Regularization and semi-supervised learning on large graphs. In: Shawe-Taylor, J., Singer, Y. (eds.) COLT 2004. LNCS (LNAI), vol. 3120, pp. 624–638. Springer, Heidelberg (2004). https://doi.org/10.1007/978-3-540-27819-1_43
2. Belkin, M., Niyogi, P.: Semi-supervised learning on Riemannian manifolds. Mach. Learn. **56**(1–3), 209–239 (2004)
3. Belkin, M., Niyogi, P., Sindhwani, V.: Manifold regularization: a geometric framework for learning from labeled and unlabeled examples. J. Mach. Learn. Res. **7**(Nov), 2399–2434 (2006)
4. Belkin, M., Niyogi, P., Sindhwani, V.: On manifold regularization. In: AISTATS, p. 1 (2005)
5. Bengio, Y., Delalleau, O., Le Roux, N.: 11 Label Propagation and Quadratic Criterion, pp. 193–216. Semi-supervised Learning Edition. MIT Press, January 2006
6. Blum, A., Chawla, S.: Learning from labeled and unlabeled data using graph mincuts. In: Proceedings of the Eighteenth International Conference on Machine Learning, ICML 2001, pp. 19–26. Morgan Kaufmann Publishers Inc., San Francisco (2001). http://dl.acm.org/citation.cfm?id=645530.757779
7. Blum, A., Mitchell, T.: Combining labeled and unlabeled data with co-training. In: Proceedings of the Eleventh Annual Conference on Computational Learning Theory, pp. 92–100. ACM (1998)
8. Cai, D., He, X., Han, J., Huang, T.S.: Graph regularized nonnegative matrix factorization for data representation. IEEE Trans. Pattern Anal. Mach. Intell. **33**(8), 1548–1560 (2010)
9. Chapelle, O., Schölkopf, B., Zien, A.: Label propagation and quadratic criterion (2006)
10. Chapelle, O., Scholkopf, B., Zien, A.: Semi-supervised learning (Chapelle, o. et al., eds.; 2006) [book reviews]. IEEE Trans. Neural Netw. **20**(3), 542 (2009)
11. Druck, G., Mann, G., McCallum, A.: Learning from labeled features using generalized expectation criteria. In: Proceedings of the 31st Annual International ACM SIGIR Conference on Research and Development in Information Retrieval, SIGIR 2008, pp. 595–602. ACM, New York (2008). https://doi.org/10.1145/1390334.1390436
12. Joachims, T.: Transductive learning via spectral graph partitioning. In: Proceedings of the 20th International Conference on Machine Learning (ICML-2003), pp. 290–297 (2003)

13. Liu, W., He, J., Chang, S.F.: Large graph construction for scalable semi-supervised learning. In: Proceedings of the 27th International Conference on Machine Learning (ICML-2010), pp. 679–686 (2010)
14. Nigam, K., McCallum, A.K., Thrun, S., Mitchell, T.: Text classification from labeled and unlabeled documents using EM. Mach. Learn. **39**(2–3), 103–134 (2000). https://doi.org/10.1023/A:1007692713085
15. Pimplikar, R., Garg, D., Bharani, D., Parija, G.: Learning to propagate rare labels. In: Proceedings of the 23rd ACM International Conference on Information and Knowledge Management, CIKM 2014, pp. 201–210. ACM, New York (2014). https://doi.org/10.1145/2661829.2661982
16. Rifkin, R., Klautau, A.: In defense of one-vs-all classification. J. Mach. Learn. Res. **5**(Jan), 101–141 (2004)
17. Scudder, H.: Probability of error of some adaptive pattern-recognition machines. IEEE Trans. Inf. Theor. **11**(3), 363–371 (1965)
18. Subramanya, A., Bilmes, J.: Semi-supervised learning with measure propagation. J. Mach. Learn. Res. **12**, 3311–3370 (2011). https://dl.acm.org/citation.cfm?id=1953048.2078212
19. Subramanya, A., Bilmes, J.: Semi-supervised learning with measure propagation. J. Mach. Learn. Res. **12**(null), 3311–3370 (2011)
20. Szummer, M., Jaakkola, T.: Partially labeled classification with Markov random walks. In: Advances in Neural Information Processing Systems, pp. 945–952 (2002)
21. Vapnik, V.N.: An overview of statistical learning theory. IEEE Trans. Neural Netw. **10**(5), 988–999 (1999)
22. Wang, J., Jebara, T., Chang, S.F.: Graph transduction via alternating minimization. In: Proceedings of the 25th International Conference on Machine learning, pp. 1144–1151. ACM (2008)
23. Yang, Z., Cohen, W.W., Salakhutdinov, R.: Revisiting semi-supervised learning with graph embeddings. arXiv preprint arXiv:1603.08861 (2016)
24. Yuille, A.L., Rangarajan, A.: The concave-convex procedure. Neural Comput. **15**(4), 915–936 (2003). https://doi.org/10.1162/08997660360581958
25. Zhou, D., Bousquet, O., Lal, T.N., Weston, J., Schölkopf, B.: Learning with local and global consistency. In: Proceedings of the 16th International Conference on Neural Information Processing Systems, NIPS 2003, pp. 321–328. MIT Press, Cambridge (2003). http://dl.acm.org/citation.cfm?id=2981345.2981386
26. Zhou, D., Huang, J., Schölkopf, B.: Learning from labeled and unlabeled data on a directed graph. In: Proceedings of the 22nd International Conference on Machine learning, pp. 1036–1043. ACM (2005)
27. Zhou, D., Schölkopf, B.: A regularization framework for learning from graph data. In: ICML Workshop on Statistical Relational Learning and its Connections to Other Fields, vol. 15, pp. 67–68 (2004)
28. Zhu, X., Ghahramani, Z.: Learning from labeled and unlabeled data with label propagation. Technical Report (2002)
29. Zhu, X., Ghahramani, Z., Lafferty, J.: Semi-supervised learning using Gaussian fields and harmonic functions. In: Proceedings of the Twentieth International Conference on International Conference on Machine Learning, ICML 2003, pp. 912–919. AAAI Press (2003). http://dl.acm.org/citation.cfm?id=3041838.3041953
30. Zhu, X.J.: Semi-supervised learning literature survey. University of Wisconsin-Madison Department of Computer Sciences, Technical Report (2005)

# Skew Aware Partitioning Techniques for Multi-way Spatial Join

Prashanth Kadari[1], Avinash Potluri[2,3], Nagesh Bhattu Sristy[1(✉)],
R. B. V. Subramanyam[3], and N. V. Narendra Kumar[2]

[1] NIT Andhra Pradesh, Tadepalligudem 534101, Andhra Pradesh, India
`prashanthkadari99@gmail.com, nageshbhattu@nitandhra.ac.in`
[2] IDRBT, Castle Hills, Road No.1, Masab Tank, Hyderabad 500057, India
`potluri.avinash1@gmail.com, nvnarendra@idrbt.ac.in`
[3] NIT Warangal, Warangal 506004, Telangana, India
`rbvs66@gmail.com`

**Abstract.** With the massive increase in the usage of location-based services, there has been a huge increase in the availability of spatial data. Extracting hidden business value inherent in the spatial data like the migration of the customer base etc. has become mandate. With the recent advancement of open-source distributed computing techniques like Hadoop the computing power is made available at ease. SpatialHadoop, Hive, Impala are the popular tools used for querying spatial data. These tools generally use indexing methods to execute queries. Extensive work on optimizing joins has been done, but as the real-world spatial datasets contain huge skew, optimizing spatial joins is still a challenging problem. We investigate the problem of skew present in the spatial datasets by providing skew aware partitioning techniques for multi-way spatial joins. We solve the problem by distributing the data symmetrically across the cluster nodes. Our algorithms implemented in Hadoop mapreduce framework offers skew aware partitioning techniques by further reducing the communication cost. We implemented a binary split partitioning approach and strip partitioned technique for multi-way spatial join and compared with the baseline approaches sequential join and controlled replicate. We observed that our approaches are in line with the existing approaches for uniformly distributed datasets, whereas for the skewed datasets, our techniques outperformed the exiting techniques. Our experiments indicate that effective partitioning strategies, distribute the data evenly across the reducers, and have a better overall turn around time compared to the baseline methods.

**Keywords:** Big data · Multi-way spatial join · Skew

## 1 Introduction

The availability of high-performance computing devices and the rapid amelioration of technologies has enabled users to use various applications for their general concerns extensively. These applications gather some vital information from the

© Springer Nature Switzerland AG 2020
B. R. Purushothama et al. (Eds.): MIKE 2019, LNAI 11987, pp. 52–61, 2020.
https://doi.org/10.1007/978-3-030-66187-8_6

users like language, location, and age. With the technological shift towards the usage of location based services there is a huge swift in business, which lead the users and business owners to query spatial data for their timely analysis. Specifically, to understand the hidden business value in spatial data, it has become essential to process and analyze this massive amount of spatial data.

The GIS (geographic information system) [4] has become the greatest scientific invention and the source for the generation of spatial data. GIS is a system capable of storing, managing, studying, and visualizing spatial information. GIS is directly included in numerous applications of communications, protection, insurance, administration, logistics, and business. For instance, Uber uses customer location i.e., latitude and longitude extracted from the smartphone to provide service. The government of India uses spatial data of the railway passengers to find patterns of people migrating across the country. This has lead to the generation of massive amounts of spatial data. The spatial querying processing systems like spatialhadoop,[1] hive[2] and pig[3] are used to visualize and analyze spatial data. A complex spatial query can find a place that is neighboring to forest, hill station, and sea. To answer these queries, we need to join three huge datasets i.e., forests, hill stations, and seas.

Hadoop Map-Reduce is an open-source distributed computing programming framework for building high performance distributed clusters using commodity systems. Using the Hadoop Map-Reduce framework, we implemented various skew aware partitioning techniques to perform multi-way spatial join and provided a comparative analysis mentioning better strategies.

The contributions in this paper include:

1. We propose Skew aware partitioning strategies for multi-way spatial join in Map-Reduce.
2. We prove that tuning the partitioning schemes significantly improves the turn around time.
3. We compare and analyze the overall performance of the proposed and baseline techniques.

## 2   Spatial Join

The spatial join algorithms involving only two relations are addressed in the literature [3]. These provide the solutions by using the project-split-replicate technique.

**Project:** Project operation identifies the cell of the rectangle based on the starting point of the rectangle, and for each rectangle, a key:value pair is generated with cell number as key and rectangle as value. Let u be the rectangle, and it's cell be the $c_u$ then $(c_u, u)$ is a key value pair generated. Mathematically represented as, Project(u, C) $\rightarrow (c_u, u)$, where C is set of all the cells of a grid.

---

[1] spatialhadoop.cs.umn.edu.

[2] hive.apache.org.

[3] pig.apache.org.

**Split:** Split operation identifies all the cells of a rectangle having at least one point in common with partition cells in the grid. For each such cell generates a key:value pair with cell number as key and rectangle as value. Mathematical representation is given below. $\text{Split}(u, C) \rightarrow (c_i, u)$, $\forall$ (i) s.t. $u \cap c_i = \emptyset$.

**Replicate:** Replicate operation identifies the cells which are in the fourth quadrant with respect to the rectangle. Next, we understand how it can be evaluated on map-reduce platform and how the multi-way joins are performed. According to the grid structure mentioned above, the two-way spatial join can be computed by splitting the every input record and by sending them to their respective reducers and further by applying the appropriate algorithm at the reducers.

For example, consider the two sets A and B of spatial objects, such that $a \in A$ and $b \in B$. Due to its spatial property, one object may spread to more than one cell in the grid, so there is a chance of getting duplicates. There are two solutions to avoid this problem. One is to compute the output and scan the output to remove duplicates. As we are dealing with large amounts of input data, the amount of output generated is also huge, so this approach is expensive and leads to case time complexity. So the second alternative is by adopting a duplicate avoidance strategy that can eliminate the duplicates on the go. By using the duplicate avoidance mechanism, the output to be computed exactly in one reducer.

## 3   Multi-way Spatial Join Techniques

We illustrate a case of multi-way spatial join with a 3-way join involving four spatial object collections A, B, C, D, respectively. In this specific case Multi-way spatial join involves a search for tuples of the form $<a, b, c, d>$ where rectangles $a \in A, b \in B, c \in C$ and $d \in D$. Overlaps(a, b), Overlaps(b, c) and Overlaps(c, d) are all true simultaneously. The two naive methods used to perform spatial join are Sequential join and All-Replicate. The algorithms discussed below have better algorithmic design to perform spatial join.

### 3.1   Controlled-Replicate

To improve the performance of the sequential approach and All-Replicate approach, we perform the join using a better approach called Controlled-Replicate. In the All-Replicate technique [3] the spatial region is divided into rectangular partitions as discussed earlier. This is done in a single map-reduce phase. In the first map phase of All-Replicate all the rectangles are replicated to the fourth quadrant with respect to the starting point of the rectangle. The cell containing the starting point takes care of replicating the rectangle to its fourth quadrant. This causes huge overload to the reducers, which are in the upper right corner. In the reduce phase, we compute the output i.e., the overlaps. A duplicate avoidance strategy is used to avoid duplicates.

In this strategy, we reduce the number of replications to only forth quadrant cells. The controlled replicate strategy is done in a series of two map-reduce phases. The first map phase consists of a split operation. The rectangles are sent to all the reducers, which contain at least one point in common with the cell. In the first reduce phase, rectangles that lie completely inside the cell boundary are outputted if the overlap condition is satisfied. The rectangles, whose starting point is within the cell region and overlapping with the cell boundary, are marked for the processing in the next phase. Assume that a, b, c, d are rectanlges of sets A, B, C, D respectively. If b overlaps with c and cell boundary, further c overlaps with a rectangle d within the cell boundary then b, c and d are marked for replication. If c overlaps with cell boundary while having a overlapping ractangle b (though completely inside) and such b overlaps with a, mark all a, b and c for replication. If both b and c are not overlapping with cell boundary, nothing is marked for replication.

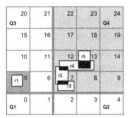

**Fig. 1.** Replication area

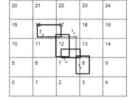

**Fig. 2.** Reducer selection

In the second map-reduce phase, the mapper replicates of the marked rectangles from the $1^{st}$ map-reduce phase to all the fourth quadrant cells with respect to the starting point of the corresponding rectangle. The reducer computes the remaining output.

For example, consider Fig. 1 as the rectangle $r_1$ in cell number 5 is not overlapping with any of the rectangles from other relations and does not have overlap with the cell boundary, so we need not compute it. The rectangles $r_2, r_3, r_4$, and $r_5$ are qualified as the output tuples, and no single cell is receiving all the rectangles information. So, for getting all the rectangle information at one place(cell) we replicated all to the cells which are in fourth quadrant with respect to each rectangle i.e the rectangles $r_2$ and $r_3$ are replicated to the cells 7–9, 12–14, 17–19 and 22 to 24, The rectangle r4 replicates to 12–14, 17–19 and 22 to 24. The rectangle $r_5$ is also replicated in the same way as $r_2, r_3, r_4$ i.e to the cells present in the $Q_4$ with respect to $r_5$ i.e 13, 14, 18, 19, 23 and 24. While replicating the rectangles to the fourth quadrant cells there is a possibility that more than one reducers compute the same tuple, to avoid this a duplicate avoidance strategy is used.

### 3.2   SLC

The Strip partitioning algorithm [1] follows a data-oriented partitioning strategy. In this strategy, the grid is divided into non-uniform partition cells. Strip partitioned multi-way spatial join is carried out in three map-reduce phases. Preliminarily we sort the input data in the ascending order based on the $Y_1$ coordinate to obtain the horizontal partitions. This can also be interchanged with $X_1$ coordinate to obtain vertical partitions based on the user's interest. A threshold parameter, which is a total number of records divided by the number of reducers, is defined for distributing the data evenly across the reducers. This can be termed as payload for each partitioning cell and are guaranteed to be consisting of tuples not exceeding the predefined threshold (payload) value $'t'$. This can be assumed to be a sliced cake.

Specifically, in the first map-reduce phase, we find the partition (cell) boundaries. The obtained partition boundaries are stored in the distributed cache to make it available to the next map reduce jobs. Distributed cache is a mechanism in hadoop map reduce framework, which makes the data available for all the mappers at a time before the start of the job. In the second map-reduce phase, we compute the partial output, which can be computed within the cell boundary, and we mark the set of rectangles that need to be processed in the next phase. The rectangles included in this set are the rectangles overlapping with the cell boundary. The boundary objects are addressed as follows. Let us consider a $\in$ A, b $\in$ B, c $\in$ C, and d $\in$ D be tuples from different relations. If the tuples b, C overlaps, and if b overlaps with cell boundary and there exits any overlapping d for c then we mark all the b, c, and d. Similarly, if c overlaps with cell boundary and there exits any overlapping a for b, then we mark all the a, b, and c. If b and c have no overlap with cell boundary, then we omit these rectangles. In the third map reduce phase, the mapper projects the *bandc* tuple received from the second reducer and replicates *aandd* to all the reducers. Finally, the reducer computes the actual join result. Consider the Fig. 3 and assume the threshold value to be $t = 1000$ and the total number of records to be $N = 7000$. We initially scan the input in sorted order, and whenever the number of records reaches the threshold, we make the first partition i.e., with 1 to 1000 input records. This process is continued for each input.

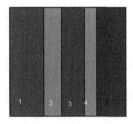

**Fig. 3.** SLC

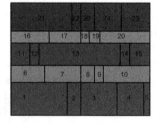

**Fig. 4.** BSP

**Algorithm 1.** MR-StripPartitionJoin(U,V,W,X)

1: **Map0** Input: $\langle \Phi; r \in$ any of the sets $U, V, W, X \rangle$, Payload p. emit $\langle (c; r) \rangle$

2: **Reduce0** Input: $\langle c; L_c = \{r | r \in U \cup V \cup W \cup X\} \rangle$ sort($L_c$, d);

3: U = Spatial Universe($L_c$);

4: **while** R is not empty **do**

5:     s = cutStrip(U , $L_c$, b);

6:     **for** $r_i$ in R **do**

7:         **if** not $r_i$ intersects with s **then** break;

8:     emit $(c_s; r)$

9:     **if** s contains $r_i$ **then** remove $r_i$ from R;

10:   emit $\langle (\Phi; s) \rangle$

11: **Map1** Input: $\langle c; r \in$ any of the sets $U, V, W, X \rangle$ emit $\langle (c; r) \rangle$

12: **Reduce1** Input: $\langle c; L_c = \{r | r \in U \cup V \cup W \cup X \wedge Overlap(r, c)\} \rangle$

13: Partition $L_c$ into $U_c = \{r | r \in U\}$ , $V_c = \{r | r \in V\}, W_c = \{r | r \in W\}$ and $X_c = \{r | r \in X\}$

14: **for** $(v, w) : v \in V_c \wedge w \in W_c \wedge Overlaps(v, w)$ **do**

15:     **if** $!CrossesCellBoundary(v) \wedge !CrossesCellBoundary(w)$ **then**

16:         **for** $u \in U_c \wedge Overlaps(u, v)$ **do**

17:             **for** $s \in X_c \wedge Overlaps(w, x)$ **do**

18:             emit($\langle \Phi; (u, v, w, x) \rangle$)        ▷ Generate part of the output

19:     **else**

20:         **for** $u \in U_c \wedge Overlaps(u, v)$ **do**

21:             Mark(u,(h(v),*))

22:         **for** $x \in X_c \wedge Overlaps(w, x)$ **do**

23:             Mark(x,(*,h(w)))

24:         Mark(v,(h(v),h(w)))

25:         Mark(w,(h(v),h(w)))

26: **for** $u \in U_c$ **do**

27:     **if** $Marked(u)$ **then** emit($\langle \Phi; (u, \mathcal{C}_{V_u}) \rangle$)

28: **for** $v \in V_c$ **do**

29:     **if** $Marked(V)$ **then** emit($\langle \Phi; (v, \mathcal{C}_{W_v}) \rangle$)

30: **for** $w \in W_c$ **do**

31:     **if** $Marked(w)$ **then** emit($\langle \Phi; (w, \mathcal{C}_{V_w}) \rangle$)

32: **for** $x \in X_c$ **do**

33:     **if** $Marked(x)$ **then** emit($\langle \Phi; (x, \mathcal{C}_{W_x}) \rangle$)

34: **Map2**

35: **if** Input is of type $(u, \mathcal{C}_{V_u})$ **then**

36:     **for** $c \in \mathcal{C}_{V_u}$ **do** emit $\langle (c); u \rangle$

37: **else if** Input is of type $(v, \mathcal{C}_{W_v})$ **then**

38:     **for** $c \in \mathcal{C}_{W_v}$ **do** emit $\langle (c); v \rangle$

39: **else if** Input is of type $(w, \mathcal{C}_{V_w})$ **then**

40:     **for** $c \in \mathcal{C}_{V_w}$ **do** emit $\langle (c); w \rangle$

41: **else**        ▷ Input is of type $(x, \mathcal{C}_{W_x})$

42:     **for** $c \in \mathcal{C}_{W_x}$ **do** emit $\langle (c); x \rangle$

43: **Reduce 2 Input:** $\langle c; L_c = \{r | r \in U \cup V \cup W \cup X\} \rangle$

44: Partition $L_c$ into $U_c = \{r | r \in U\}$ , $V_c = \{r | r \in V\}$

45: $W_c = \{r | r \in W\}$ and $X_c = \{r | r \in X\}$

46: **for** $(u, v, w, x) : u \in U_c \wedge v \in V_c \wedge w \in W_c \wedge x \in X_c$

47: $\wedge Overlaps(u, v) \wedge Overlaps(v, w) \wedge Overlaps(w, x)$ **do**

48:     **if** c can compute the output tuple $(u, v, w, x)$ **then**    ▷ Duplicate Avoidance

49:         emit $\langle \Phi; (u, v, w, x) \rangle$

### 3.3   BSP-Binary Split Partition Method

The Binary Split Partition [1] is a data-oriented partition strategy and is a variant of SLC [1]. The traditional grid partitioning strategies like the uniform grid does not evenly distribute the data among the cluster nodes. We follow a bidirectional partition strategy to distribute the data (Fig. 4). In the Binary Split Partition method, initially, the grid is partitioned in the horizontal direction based on a Y-payload, and in the next iteration, each such partition is partitioned in the vertical direction based on X-payload.

The BSP based join is computed in three map-reduce phases. We call the first mapreduce phase as the zeroth phase, as it does not compute the actual join. Here we compute the partition-(cell) boundaries. In the first map-reduce phase, the partial output is computed based on the set of tuples satisfying the overlap condition and lying completely inside the boundary. The rectangles which overlap with the cell boundary are also marked and sent to the next phase. In the second mapreduce phase, we replicate the boundary objects to all the fourth quadrant cells w.r.t the starting point of the rectangle and compute the remaining tuples based on the overlapping condition which is the final output.

## 4   Results and Discussion

Our experimentation consists of the comparison of mainly three algorithms, namely Controlled replicate, SLC, and BSP. The critical observation is that when the size of the dataset is increasing, SLC is working better than C-Rep and BSP, with SLC, BSP, and C-Rep in order of performance high to low. Furthermore, when skew in the dataset is increasing, BSP is working better than C-Rep and SLC, with BSP, SLC, and C-Rep in order of performance high to low. The performance of all the algorithms is shown below.

We have experimented with all our algorithms on a 17 node hadoop-Yarn cluster, which includes one master node and 16 slave nodes. Each machine in the cluster is 8 core CPU Intel i5 7th generation system with 16 GB of memory and 500 GB of disk space. All the experiments were imposed on both synthetic and real-world [2] datasets. Gowalla is a real-time location-based networking website, where users can share their spatial location by checking-in. The fields in the Gowalla dataset are user, check-in time, latitude, longitude, location id. Other real world dataset, is taken from OpenStreetMap[4] considering the spatial features of water and icesheet.

Our experiments are evaluated on both synthetic and real world datasets. An R script is used to generate the synthetic datasets. The parameters used for generating synthetic datasets are (a) Number of records ($n_I$), (b) Relation index (c) Rectangle coordinates ($X_1,Y_1$) and ($X_2,Y_2$). (c) The maximum length and breadth of rectangles ($[l_{min}, l_{max}]$, $[b_{min}, b_{max}]$) is defined by the overlap parameter. In the Tables 4 and 5 the turn around time and in Tables 1, 2 and 3

---

[4] https://osmdata.openstreetmap.de/info/.

the turn around time and the boundary objects i.e rectangles replicated are shown for all the methods.

The results in Table 1 describes the experimental results for uniform distribution. We varied the size of the dataset from 1 million to 5 million by keeping the overlap fixed to 100. SLC and BSP show better performance compared to CREP. It is observed that as the size of the dataset increases, there is a huge difference in the turn around time. In SLC, the grid partitioning is done only based on y coordinate. So the boundary objects overlapping with the boundary are more compared to BSP and CREP, which follow bidirectional partitioning.

**Table 1.** Turn-around time and boundary objects for normal distribution

| Dataset size | CREP | SLC | BSP | CREP (obj) | SLC (obj) | BSP (obj) |
|---|---|---|---|---|---|---|
| 1M 100 | 3 m 0 s | 2 m 13 s | 2 m 8 s | 0.25 L | 3.4 L | 0.7 L |
| 2M 100 | 10 m 2 s | 4 m 44 s | 4 m 3 s | 0.64 L | 11.5 L | 1.6 L |
| 3M 100 | 26 m 41 s | 9 m 27 s | 10 m 57 s | 1.06 L | 23.4 L | 2.7 L |
| 4M 100 | 1 h 9 m 15 s | 24 m 16 s | 19 m 04 s | 1.51 L | 39.0 L | 3.8 L |
| 5M 100 | >3 h | 3 6m 8 s | 1h 8 m 9 s | – | 58.6 L | 5.0 L |

Table 2 is a real-world data set with a huge skew. We varied the overlapping factor by keeping the size of the dataset fixed. It is observed that the performance of BSP based partitioning technique is magnifying as the overlap factor is increasing. The skew inherent in the real world dataset is handled efficiently by the BSP as it follows both non-uniform and bidirectional partitioning strategy.

**Table 2.** Turn-around time and boundary objects for real world gowalla

| Dataset size | CREP | SLC | BSP | CREP (obj) | SLC (obj) | BSP (obj) |
|---|---|---|---|---|---|---|
| 1M 15 | 43 m 5 s | 25 m 33 s | 43 m 22 s | 0.01 L | 0.8 L | 0.05 L |
| 1M 25 | 55 m 32 s | 51 m 30 s | 39 m 25 s | 0.02 L | 1.0 L | 0.08 L |
| 1M 35 | 1 h 49 m 46 s | 1h 7 m 52 s | 49 m 58 s | 0.03 L | 1.3 L | 0.12 L |
| 1M 40 | 3 h 32 m 22 s | 2h 1 m 45 s | 1 h 15 m 12 s | 0.04 L | 1.4 L | 0.15 L |

Table 3 differs from the early discussed results. Normal distribution and real-world datasets consist of similar characteristics. In the uniform distribution, the load on each reducer is almost the same. As there is an additional sorting cost involved in the proposed methods, they are either in-line or behind the CREP.

**Table 3.** Turn-around time and boundary objects for uniform distribution

| Dataset size | CREP | SLC | BSP | CREP (obj) | SLC (obj) | BSP (obj) |
|---|---|---|---|---|---|---|
| 4M 100 | 1 m 44 s | 2 m 43 s | 3 m 2 s | 0.4 L | 0.9 | 0.4 L |
| 8M 100 | 3 m 48 s | 5 m 17 s | 4 m 59 s | 1.3 L | 3.5 | 1.0 L |
| 12M 100 | 9 m 1 s | 10 m 46 s | 9 m 26 s | 2.5 L | 7.5 | 1.8 L |
| 16M 100 | 15 m 58 s | 14 m 13 s | 17 m 49 s | 3.8 L | 12.5 | 2.6 L |
| 20M 100 | 20 m 19 s | 57 m 1 s | 25 m 43 s | 5.2 L | 18.4 | 3.5 L |

Table 4 considers OSM-Ice dataset. Sizes of rectangles are varied considering the overlap factor from 100 to 500 with fixed 3 Million objects. In table 5 the number of tuples are varied from 2M to 8M, with fixed overlap factor of 100.

**Table 4.** Turn-around time for OSM Ice dataset

| Dataset size | CREP | SLC | BSP |
|---|---|---|---|
| 3M 100 | 5 m 54 s | 3 m 28 s | 3 m 11 s |
| 3M 200 | 22 m 34 s | 9 m 48 s | 10 m 8 s |
| 3M 300 | 1 h 3 m 54 s | 15 m 13 s | 11 m 44 s |
| 3M 400 | 2 h 12 m 11 s | 25 m 1 s | 28 m 39 s |
| 3M 500 | >3 h | 57 m 3 s | 1 h 10 m 58 s |

**Table 5.** Turn-around time for OSM Water dataset

| Dataset Size | CREP | SLC | BSP |
|---|---|---|---|
| 2M 100 | 2 m 20 s | 2 m 11 s | 6 m 9 s |
| 4M 100 | 4 m 37 s | 3 m 36 s | 23 m 4 s |
| 8M 100 | 13 m 34 s | 7 m 37 s | 1 h 24 m 50 s |

## 5    Conclusion and Future Work

The performance of multi-way spatial join methods over uniform and non-uniform grid is analyzed. From the experimental results, it is observed that the boundary objects are more in SLC, but the replication cost is less, whereas the replication cost is more in BSP, but the boundary objects are less. The proposed methods are in line and take marginally higher time compared to the baseline technique for uniform datasets since an additional sorting cost is involved. For skewed datasets, our approaches are better, and the difference in the turn around time increases with the increase in the size of datasets and overlap factor.

# References

1. Aji, A., Hoang, V., Wang, F.: Effective spatial data partitioning for scalable query processing (2015)
2. Cho, E., Myers, S.A., Leskovec, J.: Friendship and mobility: user movement in location-based social networks. In: Proceedings of the 17th ACM SIGKDD International Conference on Knowledge Discovery and Data Mining, pp. 1082–1090. ACM (2011)
3. Gupta, H., Chawda, B., Negi, S., Faruquie, T.A., Subramaniam, L.V., Mohania, M.: Processing multi-way spatial joins on map-reduce. In: Proceedings of the 16th International Conference on Extending Database Technology, pp. 113–124. ACM (2013)
4. Madurika, H., Hemakumara, G.: Gis based analysis for suitability location finding in the residential development areas of greater matara region. Int. J. Sci. Technol. Res **4**, 96–105 (2015)

# The Relationship Between Sentiments of Social Media and Economic Indicators

Pin-Hsuan Huang[1], Ping-Yu Hsu[1], Ming-Shien Cheng[2]([✉]), Chen-Wan Huang[1], and Ni Xu[1]

[1] Department of Business Administration, National Central University, No. 300, Jhongda Rd., Jhongli City, Taoyuan County 32001, Taiwan (R.O.C.)
984401019@cc.ncu.edu.tw
[2] Department of Industrial Engineering and Management, Ming Chi University of Technology, No. 84, Gongzhuan Rd., Taishan Dist., New Taipei City 24301, Taiwan (R.O.C.)
mscheng@mail.mcut.edu.tw

**Abstract.** Gross National Happiness (GNH) has been a popular issue since King of Bhutan, King Jigme Singye Wangchuck declared in 1972, 'Gross National Happiness is more important than Gross Domestic Product.' Since then, GNH is discussed by multiple researchers. Their researches are to determine its accuracy and the representative. Many Countries have announced taking this indicator to be one of the national performance review indexes. In year 2013, Taiwan has considered GNH as one of the performance review indexes. Among 2013 to 2018, Taiwan's Happiness scores have been rising. Taiwan is now the happiest country in Asia. Nonetheless, there's no research shows that it can actually represent Taiwanese happiness emotion. In order to testify this issue, we took 3600 articles from one of Taiwan most used social media-Gossiping board of PPT, to identify Taiwanese emotion among 2015 to 2017. We used Sentiment Analysis to calculate the monthly sentiment score of the media. In the end, we found that Taiwanese Sentiment scores among social media are rising as well as GNH scores. We used regression analysis to find out which one of GDP growth rate, GNI growth rate, are having significantly positive correlation with social media's sentiment scores. We can then use our conclusion to determine that social media's sentiment score can probably be one of the leading indicators of Economic indexes.

**Keywords:** Sentiment analysis · Gross national happiness · Economic indicator · Social media

## 1 Introduction

In 1972 the king of Bhutan, Jigme Singye Wangchuck, proposed and quantified the concept of 'Gross National Happiness, GNH' as the citizen economic index of the Buddhist Bhutan and shared the study with the rest of the world. Since then the gross national happiness index or the happiness index has become a benchmark for national development commensurate with that of gross national product. The core of GNH is to have a quality higher GNP in terms of measuring a country's quality. When people's

© Springer Nature Switzerland AG 2020
B. R. Purushothama et al. (Eds.): MIKE 2019, LNAI 11987, pp. 62–71, 2020.
https://doi.org/10.1007/978-3-030-66187-8_7

material and spiritual development occur at the same time, enhancing and supplementing each other, it will be salubrious to human social development (Alkire and Ura 2012). The definition of happiness is very subjective. The current most widely used is that by Andrew and Whitney (1976). They think that the feeling of happiness is a result of the degree of satisfaction of the people in regard to their life as a whole, in which it includes exterior evaluation standard personal subjective feelings. Now nine important indices make up the GNH index. As Fig. 1 illustrated, from the combination of the nine indices, a comprehensive happiness index is composed of traditional economic index, people's subjective feelings, and state of health, etc. As time goes on, many countries including Britain, Japan, Canada, and the European Union countries, have announced that they are starting the survey of national happiness index and life satisfaction rate. According to the World Happiness Report published by the United Nations (UN) and the happiness index report by the Taiwan government, it appears that Taiwan happiness index since 2013 has an upward trend annually.

**Fig. 1.** The 9 indices of GNH

However, the researches on happiness index and its component indices, in the past were mostly measuring the difference between the index and other indices (Blanchflower and Oswald 2005) and the degree of change upon which national activity and policy has brought (Nam and Lee 2014). No one has actually explored if the calculated results of the above happiness index matches the public opinions of the citizens. Do the feelings expressed by the people of Taiwan conform to the happiness index reported by the UN and the Taiwanese government in an upward trend? Therefore, this research will compare, through observing the public opinions of Taiwan's local forum, the feelings expressed by the people, and the happiness index reported by the institution and then observe the consistency and relationship of the trend.

This paper organized as follow: (1) Introduction: Research background, motivation and purpose. (2) Related work: Review of scholars researches on the relevant indices of the happiness and sentiment analysis. (3) Research methodology: Content of research process in this study. (4) Statistical analysis: Experimental results and the discussion of the test results. (5) Conclusion and future research: Contribution of the study, and possible future research direction is discussed.

## 2   Related Work

### 2.1   The Relevant Indices of the Happiness Index

GNH has been used frequently for related national policy research is because the happiness index is that the people do not focus only on the traditional economic index as the only one standard of a national strength. Therefore, many scholars have explored the relationship and paradox between happiness index and traditional index as a standard for measuring a nation's strength (Blanchflower and Oswald 2005; Leigh and Wolfers 2006; Dolan et al. 2016) researched on the changes in the people's happiness index of a nation that sponsors the Olympic Games to deduce indirectly the relationship between sports events and happiness index. The question of that happiness index as a new index can have a positive influence on national policy is also the research target of many researchers. (Prycker 2010). In the most recent researches, researchers have found in social media like Facebook and Twitter that the happier individuals will use more positive words; conversely, the words the article publisher used can be used to decide whether or not the writer is happy about his life (Kramer 2010; Wang and Kosinski 2012; Quercia et al. 2012). In this research, we will decipher the user's emotion by the characteristics of the words that appeared in the articles and derive a general life satisfaction rate.

There are many ways to calculate the happiness index (Alkire and Ura 2012; Bate et al. 2009), but this research will exclude the subjective feeling of the people and use the following formula as a base to dissect the component indices of the happiness index: Therefore, the factors included in the happiness index: gross national income, unemployment rate and inflation rate will be discussed in this section

$$\text{Gross National Happiness Index} = \text{The increase in income} / \text{Gini coefficient} *$$
$$\text{unemployment rate} * \text{inflation rate}$$

### 2.2   Sentiment Analysis

Sentiment Analysis Related Research has two aspects, first is constructing a sentiment analysis, which will establish the accuracy rate of sentiment analysis. Second is the recognition and identification of sentiment including the method of identifying sentiment.

There are two methods often used in identifying sentiment, one is Lexicon-Based method, the other is Machine Learning approaches. Lexicon-Based uses dictionary that has sentiment tags/labels. By comparing the strength of the words in the dictionary and that in the article or sentence, and discerning the frequency and strength of the sentiment words used to decipher the sentiment propensity of the article or sentence. Machine learning approach is using already polarity-categorized dictions as training material, and it classifies the characteristics of the diction. Discern and learn the sentiment polarity of the words, sentence, and article based on the rules of the characteristics. The common machine learning approach are Support Vector Machine (SVM), K-Nearest Neighbor (KNN), and Naïve Bayes Classifier (NB).

The research deployed sentiment analysis to calculate a sentiment numerical value/score of social media users on the internet, and use these scores to execute analysis with the happiness index and relevant indices. The research further explores that whether the directional trend of Taiwan public opinion is the same with that of these indices.

## 3   Research Methodology

The research structure is illustrated in Fig. 2. After collecting articles from the tabloid edition of the Internet for him PTT, we performed text segmentation to find sentiment actions; and use the national Taiwan University Sentiment Dictionary to tag the directions with sentiment values after text segmentation treatment. The research calculated monthly sentiment scores using a month as a basis on the articles. Next, the research deployed linear regression on sentimental scores and relevant indices of happiness index to derive the final research results and to decipher the relationship between the two.

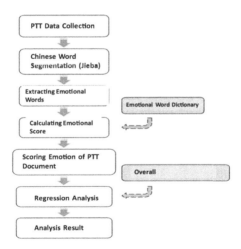

**Fig. 2.**  Research process

### 3.1   Research Method

Calculation of sentiment scores is based on the sentiment dictions captured from internet articles. After text segmentation, calculation of cinema score is based on the already segmented directions. Because the research adopted lexicon-based method, the next step was to execute the construction and deployment of sentiment analysis dictionary. The research used the National Taiwan University Sentiment Dictionary, NTUSD as the basis for positive or negative sentiment scores. The research will cross-examine the captured cinnamon words with the words in the National Taiwan University Sentiment Dictionary. The research assigned a +1 point for positive sentiment words, and assigned to negative words with −1 point for calculation, and in combining other factors considered below to arrive a final sentiment score. Positive sentiment word is denoted in the formula as W1, and negative word as W2.

Besides the sentiment strength of the diction itself, the research also takes into consideration the degree adverb and non-affirmative diction in front of the sentiment words. If these two types of diction's appear in front of the sentiment word, the strength of the cinema word will change. According to the dissertation of Zhang et al. (2009), Chinese degree adverbs are classified into different weight level based on the strength of its meaning. Sentiment words will be classified into D0, D1, D2, and D3. and assign a weight of 1, 1.5, 2 and 3 points respectively. Non-affirmative words has a weight of −1 because non-affirmative words will reverse the character a positive or negative word represents, thus through means of adding weight to change it's positive or the negative meaning. Table 1 below is the table of part of the classified degree words and non-affirmative words used in the research.

**Table 1.** Classified degree words and non-affirmative words table

| | Classification | Weight | Dictionary |
|---|---|---|---|
| Degree Adverb | Weak Degree (D1) | 1.5 | 一直、一點、又、也、不斷、比較、如此、多麼、有些、有點、何其、那麼、依舊、到底、始終、居然、果然、的確、相當、挺、根本、真的、略、竟然、終於、這麼、都、都比、都能、幾乎、實在… |
| | Medium Degree (D2) | 2 | 蠻、3倍、一倍、大、大力、大大、大半、大幅、大量、不錯、太、太大、太多、尤其、太過、亦甚、多、好、好一、好多、多次、好幾、有夠、老是、更、更是、明顯、非常、很、很久… |
| | Strong Degree (D3) | 3 | 愈來愈、十分、天大、世界、完全、到不、到爆、非常、很大、重大、最、最大、最、最好、超、超級、極大、極度、嚴重… |
| Negative Words | Negative | −1 | 不、不一定、不了、不力、不久、不切實際、不及、不少、不止、不比、不只、不可、不可不、不可以、不可能、不用… |

Putting together the above factors will derive the following formula. Add all the articles through the formula above to get a total to calculate the final monthly sentiment score for the ensuing analysis.

$$S = \sum D_n * N * W_n;$$

$D_n$: weight of degree adverbs, N: weight of non-affirmative; $W_n$: weight of positive or negative meaning.

## 3.2  Data Collection

The data the research has used are mainly one, the articles in the tabloid edition of internet forum PTT between 2014 and 2017 and two, the happiness index-related indices in Taiwan during that period of time. The tabloid addition has the largest volume of all. Whenever there is a major event occurring in Taiwan, be it protest demonstrations, elections, even international sports events, the tabloid edition will have tens of thousands of people logging in for discussions. On the night of November 25, 2018 election, the Taipei mayoral election was at a stalemate, there was a record of 106, 728 people online at the same time. So the research regards articles in that addition can best represent the opinions and sentiments of the Taiwanese people.

The research, using one month as its benchmark, randomly selects 100 articles every month. After collating and extracting the sentiment words by text segmentation, cross examining with the positive negative sentiment words in the sentiment dictionary to arrive at a sentiment score. The score will be standardized after calculation in order to reach accuracy. The research has collected articles from the tabloid edition from January 2014 to December 2017 for a total of 36 months and 3600 articles.

The source of that collected general statistical indices is from the general statistics database of the Republic of China, of which the gross national income (GNI) and gross domestic product (GDP) had only quarterly information, only data from January 2015 to December 2017 for a total of 3 years and 12 sets of data were used.

## 3.3  Calculation of Emotion Scores

After calculating the monthly sentiment scores, due to the more negative sentiments in the tabloid articles, we standardized the data in order to derive relative numbers so to know the real direction of the sentiment. There are a total of 3600 articles that led to the final 36 monthly sentiment scores.

We performed linear regression on standardized sentiment scores individually and separately with the gross domestic product (GDP), gross national income (GNI), unemployment rate, and inflation rate in order to find the relationship between the two factors. Of the indices in the above, GDP and GNI are quarterly indices, one index per three months. So when performing linear regression on these two indices, the monthly sentiment scores were calculated to get an average score of every three months to represent a quarterly score in order to be used in performing linear regression. Table 2 below lists the statistical data volume the research has used:

**Table 2.** Data volume

| Data type | PTT gossip board emotional score | GNH | GDP | GNI | Unemployed rate | Inflation rate |
|-----------|-----------------------------------|-----|-----|-----|-----------------|----------------|
| Volume | 36 | 3 | 12 | 12 | 36 | 26 |

## 4   Research Results

### 4.1   The Relationship Between Happiness Index and Forum Sentiment

First, we observe the trend of the monthly Taiwan forum sentiment score calculated before. Figure 3 shows the monthly sentiment score from the tabloid articles on PTT forum from 2015 to 2017: By observing Fig. 3, we find in the graph four low points, May and June 2015, December 2016, and February 2017 where there are four apparent low sentiment points. Further exploration finds that these low points all occurred when there were major issues that happened in Taiwan.

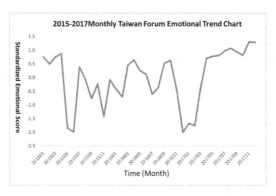

**Fig. 3.** 2015–2017 monthly Taiwan forum trend chart

In order to understand the happiness index published by the United Nations can truly reflect the emotions of Taiwanese people, the research took an average value of the monthly sentiment scores and combined with the happiness index in the trend chart to observe the direction of the trend. Illustrated in Fig. 4: we find that the happiness index trend and that of Taiwan forum between 2015 and 2017 are both in an upward trend; however, the degree of increase are not the same. In 2016, the sentiment score did not have the same degree of increase as that of the United Nations happiness index. If by only looking at that data of these three years, we can still see that direction of the Taiwanese people public opinion and the happiness index are both in an upward trend.

### 4.2   The Relationship Between GDP Annual Rate of Increase and the Forum Sentiment

The linear regression result on the quarterly rate of increase in GDP between 2015 and 2017 with the sentiment data in the tabloid edition of the Taiwan PPT that is illustrated in Table 3: From the table we find that the result of linear regression analysis on annual rate of increase of GDP with forum sentiments scores is substantial (P-value < 0.05) and the relationship between the two is highly positive (0.73). The coefficient of determination of 0.54 also represents that the annual rate of increase in GDP can explain the sentiment score changes in the tabloid edition of PTT. From the above result, we know that the

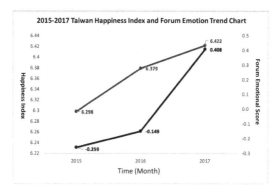

**Fig. 4.** 2015–2017 Taiwan happiness index and forum emotion trend chart

annual rate of increase of gross Domestic product (GDP) will affect the direction of the public opinion of the Taiwanese people. There is a positive relationship between forum sentiment and the annual rate of increase of GDP represents that the Taiwanese people value economic development very much. The size of economic growth will also affect the sense of happiness in the Taiwanese people on life. In a stable economic growth, people will more likely express positive emotions. Such a result complies with the researchers conducted by previous scholars.

**Table 3.** Regression analysis result of GDP growth rate and emotional score of PTT gossip board

| Annual GDP Growth Rate and Emotional Score of PTT Gossip Board Regression Analysis Results | | | | |
|---|---|---|---|---|
| Model | B | S.E | T | P |
| Explanatory Variable | 20.393 | 5.990 | 3.405 | 0.007* |
| Constant | -0.931 | 0.207 | -4.502 | 0.001 |

*P-value < 0.05 / $\alpha = 0.05$ / R=0.733 / $R^2$=0.537   Independent: Emotional Score of PTT Gossip Board
Dependent: Annual GDP Growth Rate

### 4.3   The Relationship Between GNI Annual Rate of Increase and the Forum Sentiment

The linear regression result on the quarterly rate of increase in GDP between 2015 and 2017 with the sentiment data in the tabloid edition of the Taiwan PPT that is illustrated in Table 4. From the table we find that the relationship between the annual rate of increase of GNI and forum sentiment scores is substantially positive (P-Value < 0.05, R = 0.642), meaning that as the annual rate of increase of GNI increases, the sentiments the Taiwanese people expressed in their articles in the tabloid section are more positive; conversely, as GNI decreases, the sentiments the Taiwanese people expressed in their articles in the tabloid section are more negative. Even though there is no absolute explaining power between the two ($R^2 = 0.412$), but there is certainly a positive relationship between the two. The result shows that the Taiwanese people have a feeling for the increase rate of income. Higher income will lead to more positive result in the Taiwanese people. However, the quarterly index of the annual rate of increase in the income of the Taiwanese people has been all positive indicating that the economic standard in Taiwan has been actually in a steady climb.

**Table 4.** Regression analysis result of GNI growth rate and emotional score of PTT gossip board

| Annual GNI Growth Rate and Emotional Score of PTT Gossip Board Regression Analysis Results | | | | |
|---|---|---|---|---|
| Model | B | S.E | T | P |
| Explanatory Variable | 17.699 | 6.689 | 2.646 | 0.024* |
| Constant | -0.798 | 0.215 | -3.722 | 0.004 |

*P-value < 0.05 / $\alpha = 0.05$ / R=0.642 / $R^2$=0.4: **Independent: Emotional Score of PTT Gossip Board**
**Dependent: Annual GNI Growth Rate**

## 5  Conclusion and Future Research

Since the happiness index proposed by the king of Bhutan, related researches have been conducted by many people. Many scholars have wanted to understand through researches the importance of this index and the influence that it brings because happiness is an important issue to many people. The research also tried to combine this index with people's opinions to verify the representation power of the happiness index.

According to the result of the last section, we can find that the people's sentiment represented in the Taiwan forum articles between 2015 and 2017 has the same upward trend as that of the happiness index. Moreover, in happiness index related economic indices, we find that unemployment rate and inflation rate do not have substantial relationship with sentiment due to their small degree of fluctuations. The annual rate of increase of GDP and GNI both have noticeable positive relationship with the sentiment of the people extracted from the Taiwan forum. The result illustrates that the GDP used by all Nations to evaluate and compare the economic growth is actually able to reflect people's sense of happiness.

The research result finds that the annual rate of increase of GDP has a high positive relationship with the sentiment reflected in the forum. We can deduce that as the sentiment in the forum increases, the annual rate of increase in GDP will also increase. Through prior investigations and sentiment analysis, we can investigate the rate of increase in forum sentiment in this quarter or this year. We can then predict the growth rate of GDP of this quarter or this year. However, the research was limited by the insufficient collection of data and inability to collect all the indices that can be part of the happiness index and be used to calculate not only the happiness index but also through cross-examination of these indices, seek out the most relevant index that will cause fluctuations of the people's sentiment for a more accurate research result. The future researchers can conduct further analysis and investigations with more related and broader information.

# References

Alkire, S., Ura, K., Zangmo, T., Wangdi, K.: A short guide to gross national happiness index. Centre for Bhutan Studies, Thimphu (2012)

Andrews, F.M., Withey, S.B.: Social Indicators of Well-Being (1976). https://doi.org/10.1007/978-1-4684-2253-5

Bates, W.: Gross national happiness. Asian Pac. Econ. Lit. **23**(2), 1–16 (2009). https://doi.org/10.1111/j.1467-8411.2009.01235.x

Blanchflower, D., Oswald, A.: Happiness and the human development index: the paradox of Australia (2005). https://doi.org/10.3386/w11416

Dolan, P., et al.: The host with the most? The effects of the olympic games on happiness. SSRN Electron. J. (2016). https://doi.org/10.2139/ssrn.2818834

Kramer, A.D.: An unobtrusive behavioral model of "gross national happiness". In: Proceedings of the 28th International Conference on Human Factors in Computing Systems - CHI 2010 (2010). https://doi.org/10.1145/1753326.1753369

Leigh, A., Wolfers, J.: Happiness and the human development index: Australia is not a paradox. Aust. Econ. Rev. **39**(2), 176–184 (2006). https://doi.org/10.1111/j.1467-8462.2006.00408.x

Nam, M., Lee, M.: Factors influencing subjective happiness index of health behavior, self esteem and major satisfaction by nursing students. J. Digit. Convergence **12**(10), 363–374 (2014). https://doi.org/10.14400/jdc.2014.12.10.363

Prycker, V.D.: Happiness on the political agenda? PROS and CONS. J. Happiness Stud. **11**(5), 585–603 (2010). https://doi.org/10.1007/s10902-010-9205-y

Quercia, D., Ellis, J., Capra, L., Crowcroft, J.: Tracking "gross community happiness" from tweets. In: Proceedings of the ACM 2012 Conference on Computer Supported Cooperative Work - CSCW 2012 (2012). https://doi.org/10.1145/2145204.2145347

Wang, N., Kosinski, M., Stillwell, D.J., Rust, J.: Can well-being be measured using Facebook status updates? Validation of Facebook's gross national happiness index. Soc. Indic. Res. **115**(1), 483–491 (2012). https://doi.org/10.1007/s11205-012-9996-9

Stefano, B., Andrea, E., Fabrizio, S.: SENTIWORDNET 3.0: an enhanced lexical resource for sentiment analysis and opinion mining (2010)

National Taiwan University Sentiment Dictionary (NTUSD). http://academiasinicanlplab.github.io/

World Happiness Report (n.d.). https://worldhappiness.report/

Republic of China Statistics Network - General Database. https://statdb.dgbas.gov.tw/pxweb/Dialog/statfile9L.asp

Taiwan PPT gossip board. https://disp.cc/b/Gossiping

Oxford Poverty & Human Development Initiative (OPHI) (n.d.). https://ophi.org.uk/policy/national-policy/gross-national-happiness-index/

# Entity and Verb Semantic Role Labelling for Tamil Biomedicine

J. Betina Antony[1](✉) [iD], N. R. Rejin Paul[2], and G. S. Mahalakshmi[3]

[1] Department of Computer Science and Engineering, Panimalar Institute of Technology, Poonamallee, Chennai, Tamil Nadu, India
betinaantony@gmail.com
[2] Department of Computer Science and Engineering, RMK College of Engineering and Technology, Puduvoyal, Thiruvallur, Tamil Nadu, India
rejinpaulcse@rmkcet.ac.in
[3] Department of Computer Science and Engineering, CEG, Anna University, Chennai, Tamil Nadu, India
gsmaha@annauniv.edu

**Abstract.** The primary task of Semantic Role Labelling (SRL) is to indicate exactly what semantic relations hold among a predicate and its associated participants. This type of role labelling yields a first level semantic representation of the text in question. Since the field of computation in Tamil Biomedicine is rather unexplored, SRL is introduced to label the named entities with specific roles in the given domain. In contrast to many state-of-the-art SRL systems, we devise a new approach to define roles to predicate terms along with its constituent terms. In order to achieve this, a MEM based classifier model is built using the features obtained from parsed input sentences. The parsing is done on a syntactic level and a dependency parse tree is built. The classifier model is further strengthened by verb frame training, as their probability give an extra edge to determine verb roles. The MEM model is compared with linear classifiers such as SVM and Linear Regression classifier and is found to perform better than the others.

**Keywords:** Semantic Role Labelling · Maximum entropy · Predicate labelling · Tamil biomedicine

## 1 Introduction

The most common application in NLP is identifying named entities and finding its significance in a context. This involves the determination of the semantic relations of the entities and their roles in the event they are associated with [1]. The roles usually involve answering a number of "wh" questions such as "who" did "what" to "whom", "why" and "how". Most IE systems are based on domain specific frame or slot template filling. These set of slots are required in understanding NLP tasks for new applications in a domain.

Semantic Role Labelling (SRL) [2] is a task of analyzing the predicates (mostly verbs) of a given sentence, and fill all the constituent entities in the sentence with domain-specific semantic roles. Like any NLP task, developments in SRL are built from manually

© Springer Nature Switzerland AG 2020
B. R. Purushothama et al. (Eds.): MIKE 2019, LNAI 11987, pp. 72–83, 2020.
https://doi.org/10.1007/978-3-030-66187-8_8

created semantic rules and knowledge bases for supporting text interpretation. A number of manually annotated corpora have been developed with semantic roles paving way for the development of statistical models for SRL thereby leading to its application on NLP tasks involving semantic interpretation. Some of them are NomBank [3], FrameNet [4] and PropBank [5].

The two main tasks in SRL given a sentence and a designated verb are identifying the constituent arguments around the verb predicate (argument identification) and labeling them with semantic roles (argument classification) [6]. The first step involves identifying (mostly filtering) the potential predicate and drawing boundaries for the surrounding argument candidates. These arguments may be continuous or in segments. The second step is the learning phase, where identified candidates are assigned roles by a trained classifier model.

Semantic roles are the underlying relation that a constituent has with the main verb in a clause. There is no definite set of roles that applies to every context. They may be highly domain specific and elaborate (such as *protein_ase* as in gene corpus) or totally generic and confined (such as *agents and theme*). Some of the commonly identified roles that substantially applies to all domains are

1. Agent (A0) – This role denotes an entity who is the doer of an action. They form the protagonist of the context as they are the reason an action took place.
2. Patient (A1) – This role denotes the beneficiary of the action. This role is given a number of names such as object, beneficiary, recipient etc. They are whom the action is being done to. In some cases, there might not be a beneficiary to an activity.
3. Co-agent (A3) – They are actors usually assisting the agent for the action to take place. The significance of these co-agents highly depend on the domain of interest. For example, co-agents have higher priority in medical literature than in a newswire domain.
4. Theme (AM) – This includes a broad set of elements that denote the manner in which an action is done. The role is quite generic that does not have a borderline rule to include set of constituent entities.
5. Action (AC) – The role action is nothing but the predicate (mostly verb) around which all the other roles exits. This is the actual work that is being done by the *Agent* on the *Patient* with the help of the *Co-agents* under the *Theme*. The role Action ranges between two extremes. In some cases, they are just labelled '*predicate*', while in others a specific verb is labelled *action* with arguments that are applicable to that particular verb. An example of these roles on a sentence from Tamil Siddha medical text is discussed below.

---

Eg.[அகத்திக்கீரையைப்]_A0  [பிழிந்து]_AC  [அதன்சாற்றில்]_A3  [இருதுளிமூக்கில்]_AM [விட்டால்]_AC [காய்ச்சல்]_A1 [நீங்கும்]_AC.
*Transliteration: [AkaththikkIraiyaip]_A0 [pizinthu]_AC [athan sARRil]_A3 [iru thuLi mUkkil] ]_AM [vittAl]_AC [kAyccal]_A1 [nIngum]_AC.*
Translation: If the leaves of Agati grandiflora are squeezed and two drops of its juice is administered in the nose, fever will be cured.

Note that the above sentence has three action roles பிழிந்து(*pizinthu*) (squeeze), விட்டால்(*vittAl*) (administer) and நீங்கும்(*nIngum*) (cure). Also as mentioned in the earlier chapters, Tamil follows Subject-Object-Verb format while forming phrases, clauses or sentences. In this paper, a MEM model for identifying semantic roles of candidate terms in the field of Tamil Siddha medical texts is built. These roles are pertaining to both entities and predicates. For the predicate roles, a verb frame based training is carried out.

## 2 Related Works

The concept of semantic roles was introduced in 2002. A system based on statistical classifier was trained with sentences with hand-annotated semantic roles [7]. The concept of syntactic trees from which various lexical and syntactic features such as phrase type, grammatical structure and position can be obtained was introduced here. Another SRL system with dependency trees formulated the labelling process as the linear classification of dependency relations [8]. An unsupervised method of labelling with bootstrapping algorithm used verb, slot, and noun class information as the basis for the iterative probability model [9].

In 2005, number of SRL methods was developed as part of the CoNLL-2005 shared task. Some of them are a joint model that captures dependencies among arguments of a predicate using log-linear model in discriminative re-ranking framework [10], a model with different syntactic view and SVM classifier to eliminate errors due to parsing [11], a Tree CRF model over the structure of each sentence's syntactic tree [12]. Some of the recent trends in SRL include dependency based neural model [13] using a stat bidirectional LSTM encoder. The model has been enhanced using Recurrent neural frame work [14] or linguistic integrated self-attention model [15], both recording their share of advantages, accuracies and also limitations.

SRL for biomedical documents was introduced by the system BIOSMILE [16] that uses a maximum entropy (ME) machine-learning model to extract biomedical relations with automatically generated template features. A semantic role labeller for Tamil documents had a verb frame based and MEM based training module and an ensemble evaluator module to identify roles from input system [17]. The system is optimized by EM classifier.

The main idea for this research came from [18], where a manually tagged clinical text was used in a question answering system. The model used domain adaptation algorithm and gave an accuracy level of 81%. The corpus used here is from PropBank. The three levels of adaptation learning are pruning incorrect data, transfer semi supervised learned information and finally augmenting features into higher dimension. Once the data is labelled, the model provided direct information for questions raised. Our system is a slight adaptation of this technique but it provides all information instead of query based.

## 3 SRL for Tamil Biomedical Texts

Tamil biomedical text consists of a selective pattern of statements and hence the roles of neighboring candidate elements to the verb terms follow specific patterns. In this system, the semantic roles are identified and labelled based on the features obtained from POS tags and syntactic tree structure. The overall SRL process is shown in Fig. 1. This system is a simplified version derived from [17] 's SRL system.

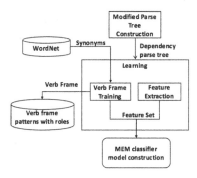

**Fig. 1.** Overall SRL system for tamil biomedicine

### 3.1 Domain-Specific Verb Semantic Roles

The main contribution of our SRL system is its ability to label verb phrases in addition to the standard roles identified. The verb phrases are usually tagged as a single role 'VBR-PHR' and their part in building the sentence is usually ignored. But in the case of Tamil Biomedicine, the verb phrases carry clues that can be used to differentiate the type of arguments involved. These labels of arguments and verb clue are employed in identifying sentences and labelling them accordingly for gathering information from Siddha texts. Thus a verb phrase (splitting node) in the context of Tamil Biomedicine can take up five different roles based on the surrounding noun phrase role pattern. The five roles are as follows.

#### 3.1.1 Procedural Verbs (VBR-PRO)

The verbs that denote a procedure to prepare a particular medicine is labelled 'PRO'. Siddha system of medicine is all about creating a medicine at home with easily or naturally available ingredients by meticulously following a set of instructions. Hence it is but natural that the text includes various verbs denoting execution and they dominate the verb set. The most common procedure verbs include கலந்து*(kalanthu)* (mix), சேர்த்து*(cErththu)* (add), அரைத்து*(araiththu)* (grind) etc.

#### 3.1.2 Do Verb (VBR-DO)

These verbs denote the procedure to follow in order for the medicine to work. There is only a narrow line of difference between 'DO' verbs and 'PRO' verbs. While PRO verbs deal with the procedure in preparing the medicine, DO verbs portray the directions in which the medicine is administered. The reason for giving separate role for these verbs is hence to differentiate the roles between Agent (A0) - Co-Agent (A3) and Agent

(A0) – Patient (A1). Some commonly used verbs include குடித்து(*kutiththu*) (drink), உண்டு(*uNtu*) (eat), தேய்த்து(*thEyththu*) (apply) etc.

### 3.1.3   Solution Verb (VBR-SOL)

Since the domain deals with disease-cure kind of statements predominantly, most sentences have a predicate that holds the meaning of cure to a particular ailment. These cure cues are nothing but 'SOL' verbs. They hold the information of what happens to the Patient (A1) word. In our context, the patient usually denotes an ailment.

### 3.1.4   Information Verb (VBR-INFO)

The dataset used includes information details about a disease or the various native ingredients used. These are expressed using 'INFO' verbs that shares the significance of an ingredient or a disease in the context. Some common informational verbs are இருக்கும்(*irukkum*) (present), கொண்டது(*koNtathu*) (has), பயன்படுகிறது(*payanpatukiRathu*) (used) etc.

### 3.1.5   None of the Above (VBR-NONE)

There are yet many verbs that do not belong to any of these four categories. They are labelled 'NONE' since their role is unpredictable, and if predicted can be inaccurate in the given context. These roles though large in number have minimum frequency of occurrence.

### 3.2   Feature Engineering and Verb Frame Extraction

In any NLP task, devising the perfect set of features plays a crucial role in obtaining superlative results. This is similar in SRL where features are devised carefully to encode candidate arguments and its associated predicate. Given a verb and a candidate argument (a syntactic phrase) that needs to be assigned semantic labels, three broad categories of features are usually gathered. They are candidate argument features, verb predicate features and relational features between candidates and predicate. The set of features considered for training the model to identify roles of constituent terms surrounding the predicate are listed in Table 1.

The ability of a verb to choose its subcategories and complements and the computations associated with it is called verb subcategorization frame or simply verb frame [19]. Verb frame contains information about verb and the pattern of semantic roles that can come with them. In our verb frame extraction, we estimate the probability of a particular verb cluster by analyzing the corpus and determine its probability using a regression based classifier. All possible verb frames for a given verb class is analyzed and a probability is assigned based on their position, count and slots filled. The various steps involved in verb frame extraction are discussed below (Fig. 2).

**Table 1.** Features for SRL Learning

| Feature | Definition |
| --- | --- |
| POS of term | Parts-of-speech tag of the constituent word |
| Headword POS | Parts-of-speech of the first word in the given phrase |
| Sentence position | Position of the term in the sentence |
| Phrase position | Position of the term in the phrase under consideration in sentence |
| No of words in phrase | Total number of words in a given phrase |
| No of noun phrases | Total number of noun phrases |
| Predicate distance | Distance of the constituent word from the predicate verb |
| Predicate POS | Parts-of-speech of the predicate verb |
| Category of parent | Category of the parent phrase of the given phrase |
| Category of previous term | Category of the previous term from the constituent term |

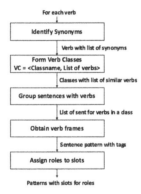

**Fig. 2.** Verb frame extraction

Verb Frame identification and extraction involves the following steps.

**Step 1:** For each verb, its corresponding synonyms are identified from the WordNet.
**Step 2:** The verb classes are formed by combining terms with similar meaning. This is to imply that any term 'a' in a class will satisfy a verb frame of every other term in the same class.
**Step 3:** All the sentences containing a verb are obtained from the corpus and are grouped together for each class.
**Step 4:** For these classes, the possible verb frames are obtained. Here verb frames are sentences with the verb and different combination of category of words.
**Step 5:** Finally, roles are assigned to the slots before and after each verb based on the pattern and verb label

The value of verb label is obtained from a listing file prepared prior to this operation based on their frequency, position and sense and undergoes a cross-fold validation using a multinomial logistic regression classifier with maximum-likelihood. A sample output of the above steps is shown in Fig. 3. **Note:** Verb frame extraction is an extended step of verb frame training. Verb frame training involves calculating the possible label for a verb in a given phrase based on certain features such as their position, frequency, POS, and surrounding words using a simple likelihood regression model. Whereas, verb frame extraction determines the semantic roles for both the verbs and the surrounding candidate arguments based on the patterns and verb labels.

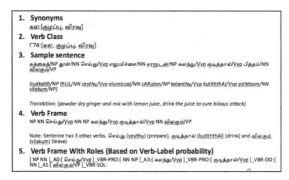

**Fig. 3.** Verb frame extraction for verb '**கலந்து**'(kalanthu) (mix)

### 3.3 Maximum Entropy Based Training Model

Maximum Entropy (ME) based training model is a widely used discriminative probability model for the task of SRL. The reason behind the popularity of this model is its ability to adapt to increasing rate of randomness. Thus in the course of the learning curve, the model tries to build a probability function that maximizes its entropy for a non-uniform distribution of data [20].

ME based SRL gained recognition in the CONLL - 2005 shared task [21] where majority of the teams deployed ME classifier model for learning process. After thorough analysis, we inferred that a multinomial logistic regression classifier is a preferred choice for its robust structure, accuracy in determining the labels and ease of computation for stochastic set of data. So we deploy a Maximum Entropy classifier to classify the labels of constituent terms and verb frames. We follow a semi supervised approach where the model learns as it builds from new data.

## 4  Experiments and Results

Our SRL is done in three stages. The first stage is to construct the dependency tree using the POS tags for the give sentences. Next is the learning step where a role classifier model is learnt based on the feature set and verb frame scores obtained from the parsed sentence. Finally, a classifier model is constructed to label the roles for the constituent terms and predicate term in the sentence.

## 4.1 Dataset

We use a small corpus with 1180 documents of instruction for training. The sentences in the document are tokenized and are POS tagged. The training data is neither ingredient oriented not disease related. However, the test dataset had set of documents taken from ingredient based instruction documents and disease oriented documents separately to determine if the content of dataset had impact on the performance of the SRL classifier.

## 4.2 Dependency Parse Tree

The first task in SRL is to parse the sentences into parse trees. Before the learning process, the sentences are converted to a dependency tree (parse tree) [22]. Our tree is a modification of the original dependency tree that used arc standard principles of dependency grammar. In our dependency tree, the nodes represent terms along with their POS tags in a sentence (similar to phrase structure trees). The modification here is that the height of the tree grows only if a verb phrase is encountered. Here a single world can also be called verb phrase due to the agglutination property of Tamil words. Thus the terms between a predicate term and its parent predicate form a chunk of constituent phrases for role labelling. This denotes that a verb phrase can act as a median between two different roles (parent and child node) and also determine the number and type of roles in the given phrase (sibling nodes). The dependency tree for the sample sentence in Sect. 1 is shown in Fig. 4.

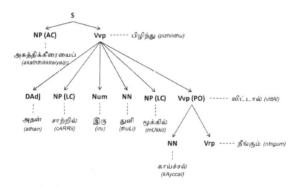

**Fig. 4.** Dependency tree for the example sentence

Note that the height of the tree is equal to the number of predicates in the given sentence. Also parsing is done by assembling the siblings of each predicate into constituent phrase for analysis. Thus the above example sentence is divided into three phrases. They are [அகத்திக்கீரையைப்_NP பிழிந்து_Vvp], [அதன்_Dadj சாற்றில்_NP இரு_Num துளி_NN மூக்கில்_NP விட்டால்_Vvp]and [காய்ச்சல்_NN நீங்கும்_Vrp].

## 4.3 Experimental Setup

Once the parse trees are constructed, the phrases undergo two separate learning process, the former for labelling constituent terms surrounding the predicate and the latter for labelling the predicate themselves. The separate features of the two learning are combined together to form a single classifier model using MEM classifier.

### 4.3.1   Feature Based Learning for Constituent Terms

For a set of 1268 instances with the above mentioned features, the ME classifier for 4 labels (Agent, Patient, Co-Agent and Predicate Verb) gave an f-score of 81%. Of all the roles, the score for co-agents is considerably low as a solid line of separation for determining them in a sentence is not present. The results might improve if semantic properties are considered in addition to the syntax grammar. Also the f-score for verb phrases is high as they are generic and straightforward when considering POS tags.

The evaluation results for the argument labelling is shown in Table 2. The recall of VBR-PHR is 100% as all the verbs in the given set of instances are identified. Also, all the verbs fall into a single role, hence assigning of role is straight forward hence the f-score is as high as 97%. There is however a drop in the recall (37.5%) and f-score (46.2%) of role co-agent (A3) as opposed to the other two constituent roles Agent (A0) (f-score 82%) and Patient (A1) (f-score 75.7%). The reason for this vast difference is the lack of a distinct feature to separate the roles. For example, in some cases, based on the predicate distance and no of words in the phrase, a candidate term occurring in the middle position is tagged as patient (A1) or a disease instead of co-agent (A3) or helping ingredient. This is due to the lack of semantic features that can determine the purpose of a word in a context. Also the uncertainty in determining the primary ingredient adds to the difficulty of determining which ingredient falls into the role agent or co-agent.

**Table 2.** Evaluation results for determining role of constituent terms using ME classifier

| Semantic role | Precision | Recall | F-score |
|---|---|---|---|
| Agent (A0) | 0.781 | 0.862 | 0.820 |
| Patient (A1) | 0.778 | 0.737 | 0.757 |
| Co-Agent (A3) | 0.600 | 0.375 | 0.462 |
| Predicate verb (VBR-PHR) | 0.955 | 1.000 | 0.977 |
| Total | 0.809 | 0.818 | 0.810 |

### 4.3.2   Verb-Frame Based Learning for Predicate Terms

In case of Verb-Frames, their main purpose is to determine the type of verbs associated with terms in a phrase. Thus a verb frame carries, in addition to the constituent term features, some cues to determine the type of sentence/phrase and ultimately enhances or strengthens the roles of constituent terms. For this purpose, each verb phrase is given a probability value boosted by MaxEnt method based on their position, verb sense, frequency in context and verb category. The verb phrases gave an overall f-score of 71.9% when cross-validated using a MaxEnt classifier. The solution to improve this measure is still open for discussion as the type of verb feature to boost the performance of a verb frame without hard coding is still brain wrecking.

## 4.4  Combined Results and Discussion

On analyzing individually, the ME models for constituent terms and predicate verbs, we were able to visualize the impact of each feature in determining the semantic role for a given term. Thus a single ME model is built using the above analyzed features to label all the terms in a given sentence. The training corpus contained total of 1180 documents from which a random 3300 sentences were obtained. From them a feature set containing 19,767 instances were extracted. Each instance was provided with values for 11 attributes and the label and the classification system is expected to classify the terms into 9 labels. The overall f-score was found to be about 80.2%. The details of the classifier output are shown in Table 3.

**Table 3.** Evaluation results for SRL using ME classifier

| Class | Precision | Recall | F-score |
|---|---|---|---|
| A0 | 0.836 | 0.818 | 0.827 |
| A1 | 0.779 | 0.698 | 0.736 |
| A3 | 0.674 | 0.738 | 0.705 |
| VBR-INFO | 0.800 | 1.000 | 0.889 |
| VBR-SOL | 0.907 | 0.961 | 0.933 |
| VBR-DO | 0.894 | 0.917 | 0.909 |
| VBR-PRO | 1.000 | 0.909 | 0.952 |
| VBR-NONE | 0.875 | 0.977 | 0.923 |
| NONE | 0.674 | 0.732 | 0.794 |
| Total | 0.839 | 0.768 | 0.802 |

The evaluation scores for the different roles infer that the verb based roles show better precision than the other roles. This denotes the significance of verb frame based learning that can categorize the different verb semantic roles accurately. The f-scores of the non-verb roles are A0 (0.827), A1 (0.736) and A3 (0.705). Among the non-verb roles, the role of co-agent (A3) is still lagging behind as their discrete semantic features are not considered. The recall of the role patient (A1) or diseases (0.698) also has a slight set back. This is mainly due to the fact that position of the word is taken as prominent feature. Hence when an ingredient is placed in the same position as a disease, their role is still assigned as patient (A1) and not agent (A0). The miscellaneous role NONE has no defining scope to it. Hence the accuracy of it is rather trivial. One way to avoid it and thereby boosting the accuracy of the entire system is to define all the roles explicitly.

The MaxEnt model when compare with other linear classification models gave slightly better results. A comparison of MaxEnt classifier with Linear Regression (LR) model and SVM model is shown in Fig. 5. The reason for selecting these two models is that both LR [10] and SVM model [11] gave better results compared to the others in CoNLL 2005.

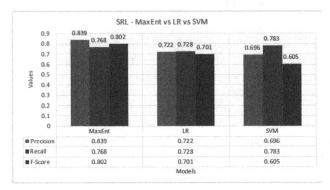

**Fig. 5.** Comparison between MaxEnt vs LR vs SVM for SRL in Tamil Biomedicine. Here X-axis denotes various classification models and Y-axis denotes their values between 0–1

The slight overhead of MEM (0.802) over LR (0.701) may be attributed to the effect of iterative re-ranking. On comparing ME with SVM (0.605), the probability framework has an upper hand over linear planar function. Also since the data points do not have a visible separation margin, the choice of maximum likelihood on logistic regression is found to be the better technique. But when calculating recall (number of correctly tagged roles over total number of roles present), SVM is found to give 2% better result than MEM. This may be due to high sensitivity of MEM on outliers when compared to the SVM model. Hence due to rapid change in the cost function on encountering a non-predictable word, the number of tagged words in the MEM model drops considerably thereby bringing down the recall value.

## 5    Conclusion

The SRL model built was a rudimentary model with limited yet essential features. The model can be strengthened in many levels. For instance, many other semantic roles related to manner, purpose, time etc. can be identified for constituent term that may help in improving the efficiency of the content tagging process. Also, the SRL constituent roles and predicate roles can be strengthened by using certain semantic features in addition to the syntactic features. And finally, the system can be experimented with many other machine learning models to find the optimal solution.

## References

1. Màrquez, L., Carreras, X., Litkowski, K.C., Stevenson, S.: Semantic role labeling: an introduction to the special issue. Comput. Linguist. **34**(2), 145–159 (2008)

2. Carreras, X., Màrquez, L.: Introduction to the CoNLL-2005 shared task: semantic role labeling. In: Proceedings of the CoNLL-2005 Shared Task. Ann Arbor, MI USA (2005)
3. Meyers, A., Reeves, R., Macleod, C., Szekely, R., Zielinska, V., Young, B.: The NomBank project: an interim report. In: Proceedings of the HLTNAACL 2004 Workshop: Frontiers in Corpus Annotation, Boston (2004)
4. Fillmore, C., Ruppenhofer, J., Baker, C.: FrameNet and representing the link between semantic and syntactic relations. In: Huang, C.-R., Lenders, W.L.: Computational Linguistics and Beyond, pp. 19–59 (2004)
5. Palmer, M., Gildea, D., Kingsbury, P.: The Proposition Bank: An Annotated Corpus of Semantic Roles, Computational Linguistics, vol. 31, pp. 71–106. MIT Press, Cambridge (2005)
6. Xue, N., Palmer, M.: Calibrating features for semantic role labeling. In: Proceedings of EMNLP-2004, Barcelona, Spain (2004)
7. Gildea, D., Jurafsky, D.: Automatic labeling of semantic roles. Comput. Linguist. 28(3), 245–288 (2002)
8. Hacioglu, K.: Semantic role labeling using dependency trees. In: Proceedings of the 20th International Conference on Computational Linguistics, vol. 1273 (2004)
9. Swier, R.S., Stevenson, S.: Unsupervised semantic role labelling. In: Proceedings of the 2004 Conference on Empirical Methods in Natural Language Processing, vol. 95, no. 102 (2004)
10. Haghighi, A., Toutanova, K., Manning, C.D.: A joint model for semantic role labeling. In: Proceedings of the Ninth Conference on Computational Natural Language Learning, pp. 173–176 (2005)
11. Pradhan, S., Ward, W., Hacioglu, K., Martin, J.H., Jurafsky, D.: Semantic role labeling using different syntactic views. In: Proceedings of the 43rd Annual Meeting on Association for Computational Linguistics, pp. 581–588 (2005)
12. Cohn, T., Blunsom, P.: Semantic role labelling with tree conditional random fields. In: Proceedings of the Ninth Conference on Computational Natural Language Learning, pp. 169–172 (2005)
13. Marcheggiani, D., Frolov, A., Titov, I.: A simple and accurate syntax-agnostic neural model for dependency-based semantic role labeling, arXiv preprint. arXiv:1701.02593 (2017)
14. Do, Q.N.T., Bethard, S., Moens, M.F.: Improving implicit semantic role labeling by predicting semantic frame arguments. arXiv preprint. arXiv:1704.02709 (2017)
15. Strubell, E., Verga, P., Andor, D., Weiss, D., McCallum, A.: Linguistically-informed self-attention for semantic role labeling. arXiv preprint. arXiv:1804.08199 (2018)
16. Tsai, R.T.H., et al.: BIOSMILE: a semantic role labeling system for biomedical verbs using a maximum-entropy model with automatically generated template features. BMC Bioinf. 8(1), 325 (2007). https://doi.org/10.1186/1471-2105-8-325
17. Pandian, S.L., Geetha, T.V.: Semantic role labeling for Tamil documents. Int. J. Recent Trends Eng. 1(1), 483 (2009)
18. Zhang, Y., Tang, B., Jiang, M., Wang, J., Xu, H.: Domain adaptation for semantic role labeling of clinical text. J. Am. Med. Inform. Assoc. 22(5), 967–979 (2015)
19. Schulte im Walde, S.: The induction of verb frames and verb classes from corpora. In: Corpus Linguistics, An International Handbook. Mouton de Gruyter, Berlin (2009)
20. Nigam, K., Lafferty, J., McCallum, A.: Using maximum entropy for text classification. In: IJCAI-99 Workshop on Machine Learning for Information Filtering, vol. 1, pp. 61–67 (1999)
21. Carreras, X., Màrquez, L.: Introduction to the CoNLL-2005 shared task: semantic role labeling. In: Proceedings of the CoNLL-2005 Shared Task, Ann Arbor, MI USA (2005)
22. Nivre, J.: Dependency grammar and dependency parsing, MSI report 5133.1959, pp. 1–32 (2005)

# Exploring Chinese Dynamic Sentiment/Emotion Analysis with Text Mining—Taiwanese Popular Movie Reviews Comment as a Case

Hao-Hsun Li[2], Ming-Shien Cheng[2]([✉]), Ping-Yu Hsu[1], Yen Huei Ko[1], and Zhi Chao Luo[1]

[1] Department of Business Administration, National Central University, No. 300, Jhongda Rd., Jhongli City, Taoyuan County 32001, Taiwan (R.O.C.)
{PingYuHsu984401019,YenHueiKo984401019,
ZhiChaoLuo984401019}@cc.ncu.edu.tw
[2] Department of Industrial Engineering and Management, Ming Chi University of Technology, No. 84, Gongzhuan Rd., Taishan Dist. New Taipei City 24301, Taiwan (R.O.C.)
{Hao-HsunLimscheng,MingShienChengmscheng}@mail.mcut.edu.tw

**Abstract.** With the rapid development of technology, viewers' opinions are no longer passed on by word-of-mouth in the real world but expressed on the Internet. In the six categories of life, food, clothing, housing, travel, education, and entertainment, every part is inseparable from comments. The most common entertainment in the six majors is watching movie. When people are interested in a movie, they might collect information online firstly so they might spend a lot of time reading online reviews and ratings. In order to have a general understanding of the movie, they will check different reviews and ratings on different online platforms. Thus, it is very meaningful to sort out helpful reviews from a large number of reviews and comments from other people. In this paper, we apply text exploration technology to the comments of movie and the analysis will allow the viewers to clearly identify the information they need. This study collects movie reviews from the online platform (YAHOO film) for text exploration and analysis. Many comments don't align with the ratings, so the primary goal of research is to verify whether the netizens' comments are consistent with the ratings, then discuss the connection between movie date and the emotional words. The viewers can refer to these overall analysis and emotional time dynamics in the future when they want to check feedbacks from other people. The result shows that the time dynamic analysis has significant differences in emotional words in the third week so it would be better to the viewers referring to the third-week rating as a quick check before watching movies.

**Keywords:** Sentiment/emotion analysis · Movie reviews · Text mining · Time dynamic analysis

## 1 Introduction

The daily life activities, food, clothing, housing, transportation, education, and entertainment, not all can escape from comments. Of the six activities listed above, entertainment

© Springer Nature Switzerland AG 2020
B. R. Purushothama et al. (Eds.): MIKE 2019, LNAI 11987, pp. 84–93, 2020.
https://doi.org/10.1007/978-3-030-66187-8_9

has no age limit from children to the seniors. Going to the movies is the most common in the entertainment activity of the six. Before going to the movies, people will go on line and collect information. Since there is no refund or test viewing of the movie, people pay even more attention to the reviews. There is much information, repetitive and subjective alike. In addition, the contents in the review platform are dispersed and the recommending platforms all use a five-star format on the products. All has made the users must spend very much time on reading the review and comparison of each writer. However, the user cannot differentiate and identify the authenticity of the review and comment. In order for users to have a comprehensive knowledge of the movies, doing research on movie reviews by filtering out those comments that are conducive so that the users may have a better reference for choice in the future is quite meaningful. In the dissertation, we deploy the text mining technology analysis so the users can differentiate unequivocally the needed information.

Currently of the many forms of entertainment, the rise in the popularity of movies renders with it movie reviews in which the use of sentimental wording is easier to identify if the review is toward a positive or negative direction. The research focuses on finding useful information among the multitude of movie reviews to understand the trend and fluctuation of sentimental diction.

There are more reviews on hit movies so the research bases on the top 10 selling movies as research material. In consideration of the authenticity of the reviews on each movie, the research adopts linear regression on both the sentiment and star strength and the intensity of sentimental dictions for two benefits. First is to explore the consistency of the number of stars with that of the review content where five stars and strong sentimental diction indicate that the review is authentic and where five stars and weak sentimental diction indicate a negative authenticity. Second is that the pre-text mining stage can be considered as noise which is mainly due to data mistake or outlier.

After the dealing with the pre-text mining stage, for the need to understand the trend of sentiment diction of each movie and fluctuations, time dynamic analysis is used to do research on the top 10 selling movies. Due to the differences in ticket sales, grouping was used to solve this problem. Then for the need to know the trend and fluctuations, we chose four weeks as the unit for the movie's in-theater time instead of one month or one day as the dividing standard. Next, we explored the changes in the sentimental dictions during the four weeks.

This paper organized as follow: (1) Introduction: Research background, motivation and purpose. (2) Related work: Review of scholars researches on the sentiment and emotion analysis. (3) Research methodology: Content of research process in this study. (4) Research result: Experimental results and the discussion of the statistic analysis. (5) Conclusion and future research: Contribution of the study, and possible future research direction is discussed.

## 2   Related Work

### 2.1   Sentiment and Emotion Analysis

The objective of sentiment analysis is to find the viewpoint and attitude of the commentator. The attitude may be the personal judgment or evaluation of the commentator, or it may be his emotional state at the time (the sentimental state of the writer when he wrote his words), or the commentator's exchange of feelings (the sentiment which the commentator wanted the reader to experience). One of the basic steps of sentiment analysis is to classify that part of a known text in the article. The classification is for deciding whether the viewpoint expressed by the text is positive, negative, or neutral in sentiment. An even more accurate emotional analysis will seek out even more complex sentiment states. Sentimental dictions are words that convey superficial characteristics or emotions. It includes meaning and sentiment concurrently.

Sentimental dictions are words that convey superficial characteristics or emotions. It includes meaning and sentiment concurrently. Related researches on sentiment analysis include "Construction of Dictionary of Sentiment Analysis", "Sentimental Identification and Classification" and "Sentimental Identification Method".

1. "Construction of Dictionary of Sentiment Analysis" currently is mainly collecting large quantity of vocabulary into the databank and then relies on human labor to tag sentiment words and polarity, which is very time consuming, and the tags are limited. Now "Dictionary Method" (NTUSD 2018) and "Machine Learning Method" have been developed (Yang et al. 2007).
2. There are two main "Sentimental Identification" methods. The first one is "Machine Learning Method", which trains by using already classified words and draws out special characteristics, then automatically deciphers and learns the new word based on the special characteristics. Second is the "Dictionary Method" using already tagged sentimental dictionary of emotion to integrate with the words by comparing the new unknown word with the words in the dictionary that is close to the new word to decide on the sentiment of the unknown word.
3. "Sentimental Identification and Classification" includes Subjectivity Analysis, Polarity Classification, and recognition of the strength of the polarity, all of which are basic research in sentiment analysis (Chang 2012).

## 3   Research Methodology

Text mining requires collecting series of information. The object of the research is the movie reviews, and through a set of regimented procedures to sort out unknown and unstructured information in order to find useful data so that analysis can be performed.

The process of the research is: data collection, pre-treatment, authentication of review content, dynamic analysis of sentiment/emotion categories, and observation of the sentiment category after analysis, statistical verification and analysis of the final result. The process is explained in more details in the following. The research process is illustrated in Fig. 1:

### 3.1   Data Collection

In terms of data collection, the object of the research is the movie reviews. Under the heading of movies, the movie topics for the research are further divided. However, there is an enormous quantity of data on the internet, and many on-line platforms can provide

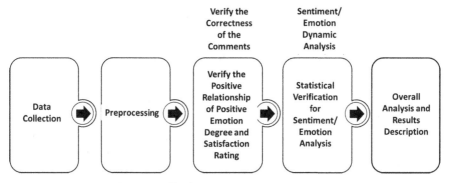

**Fig. 1.** Research process

movie review contents. For this reason, the research must select the platform that is appropriate for the topics of the research. In terms of area, as many Taiwan review platforms were selected as possible so that the review data can conform to Chinese language culture and the limitation of Taiwan ticket sales. Open platforms in Taiwan are the sources of the data. The research simply uses one year worth of reviews on top selling movies in Taiwan as research material, the quantity of which is sufficient enough. Discussions on hot movies are very high, reaching the highest especially during the showing period. Extracting useful data in the midst of big data is exactly the objective of text mining.

## 3.2 Pre-processing

The real data is very erratic; and the data colleting tools do not perform accurate checking resulting unusable data from the collected pool of data. Eighty percent of the time in data mining is spent on pre-processing that includes data cleaning, format transforming, and linking of the tables.

The research used review content, time of the review, and satisfaction rating selections as the setting for acquiring data content. Then quick read-through by human labor to select and delete advertisements saves the hassles of integrating data, excluding noise, and recording time for each type of data.

## 3.3 Verification of Authenticity of the Review Content

In order to understand if the content of the commentator conforms to the rating, there have been times where the content and the number of stars given do not match so that verification of the authenticity of the review is necessary. The research analyzed the relationship between the satisfaction rating (in number of starts) and sentiment strength, and presents it as data and charts to explore if a positive relationship exists between the two.

If the result from the above denotes a causal relationship, it means that the consumer who wrote the review has been giving his/her true emotion when giving the review and rating. In addition, that the credibility of this research and later research is high in that the review contents are realistic and the quality of the data is high.

### 3.4 Sentiment and Emotion Time Dynamic Analysis

In terms of emotion time dynamic analysis, there are big differences of ticket sales so the research groups the movies. The 10 movies in 2017 are sorted based on ticket sales dollar amount and presented in a slope graph as the basis for grouping.

Realizing that no matter how long a movie has been decommissioned from the movie theater, as long as there is a source for a movie, there will be a never-ending stream of reviews. The time and labor for processing and analyzing will be enormous. The basic thinking of the research is, just like the goal of data mining, to extract highly valuable data among the massive amount of data. We chose the time between beginning and ending of showing of a movie as the limit for the quantity of data for analysis because during such time the discussions about a movie will hit the highest peak, which we will use as the index of the research. We also divide the time with one day, one week, and one month as a unit to observe the changes in the sentiment words. We later aborted the one-day unit due to the lack of enough data. We chose one week as the unit and passed on the one-month unit because the beginning and ending time duration for a movie is usually one month so that time dynamic analysis will not apply.

In terms of the sentiment words, the research adopts the traditional Chinese dictionary of LIWC (Linguistic Inquiry and Word Count) as the research tool. LIWC tabulates the appearing frequency of a word by category in the article, for example, the relative percentages of usages of sentiment words, feeling words, and causal words. The research focused on the weekly discrepancy of emotion words and chose six categories from the Chinese LIWC dictionary to analyze the differences: Affect, Positive emotion (Posemo), Negative emotion (Negemo), Anxiety, Anger, Sad.

## 4    Research Results

We used the online application software import.io as the tool to collect data. In the pre-processing step, for the Chinese word segmentation, the CKIP Chinese word segmentation system of Academia Sinica was used. For verifying the authenticity of the review content, the traditional Chinese version of the sentiment dictionary vocabulary was used. LIWC was used in the time dynamic analysis to calculate the frequency of occurrence of the word class used in the article. Finally, the SPSS statistical software verified the data collected.

### 4.1 Data Collection

The data used in this research came from the Movie edition of YAHOO. We used import.io software to collate articles in PTT by using, as the basis, the top selling movies of 2017 that were announced at the end of each year, Fig. 2 shows the top 10 Taipei movie ticket sales in 2017 - billboard boxoffice- PTT Corp., no date). The articles related to all the top 10 movies that appeared in the chart were downloaded from YAHOO Movie. The numbers of articles for the top 10 selling movies in 2017 are 3150.

## 4.2  Pre-processing

First, the Chinese text segmentation system of Academia Sinica was used for text segmentation and classification. The space between words is how the LIWC detect the border of a word; however, there is no space in Chinese writing so that before importing the articles into LIWC for analysis, text segmentation must be performed. Every segment after being treated by the system may have different export format, the user must export the file as a txt file. Only the segmented texts with spaces were preserved and other extra marks were deleted.

The text segmentation was deployed on the top 10 selling movies of 2017. The segmentation only selected sentiment dictions as statistics to be compiled because the objective of the research is to explore the relationship between the view on a movie and the sentiment dictions used in the article.

## 4.3  Verification of the Authenticity of the Review Content

Deciding on the authenticity is a complex job. Before proceeding with the rest of the research, verification of the authenticity of each of the articles is the first job in order. After completing text segmentation, the research used the National Taiwan University's sentiment dictionary, in which the strength of each sentiment word is provided. The strength of the sentiment word can make each word have a positive or negative polarity and each word to be digitized. Analysis can then be performed conveniently. The bigger the number value the stronger the sentiment, the smaller means the opposite. After calculating the result of sentiment strength and satisfaction rating, the research deployed linear regression in which the smallest square root function is used on one or multiple independent variables and dependent variables to construct a regression analysis model to verify if the number of stars is related to the sentiment words. The results are as illustrated in Fig. 2–3.

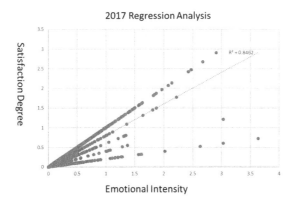

**Fig. 2.** Regression analysis of emotional intensity with satisfaction degree for 2017 top ten movie

From the above figures, there is a certain relationship between sentiment strength and the number of stars, meaning the credibility of the review in the ensuing research is

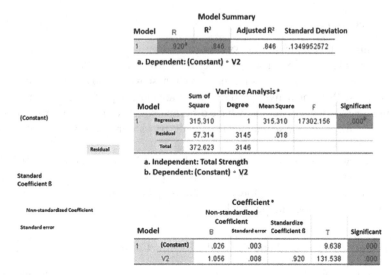

**Fig. 3.** Statistic summary of regression analysis of emotional intensity with satisfaction degree

high where the review was not written by a hired gun or out of malicious attack or spite. The quality of the data is very high.

### 4.4 Sentiment and Emotional Time Dynamic Analysis

After the regression analysis, the first target is to use LIWC to analyze the various categories of the sentiment dictions in the reviews on the top 10 selling movies of 2017. After classification analysis, ticket sales are grouped and analyzed. Since there are differences in ticket sales, so they are divided into 3 groups, the result of which is shown in Fig. 4.

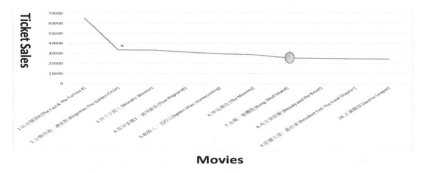

**Fig. 4.** 2017 grouped analysis of movie ticket sales

After the preparations, the research explored to see if discrepancy existed in the reviews between the showing time of movie in theater and the time after the movie being decommissioned; such times were partitioned and time-differentiated with one week as the partitioning standard. Some movies have longer showing time in theater so the one-month standard is defined as 4 weeks. Certain types of words are sorted out. Words of emotional journey, positive sentiment, negative sentiment, anxiety, anger, and sadness are the categories for the research. The research selected the above six categories and deployed time dynamic analysis to derive the result shown in Fig. 5.

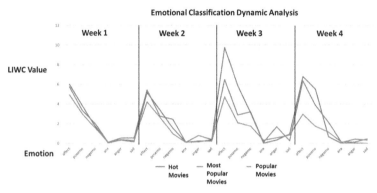

**Fig. 5.** Emotion classification analysis dynamic analysis

**Verification Statistics (Week 3)**

|  | affect | negemo | posemo | anx | anger |
|---|---|---|---|---|---|
| N | 214 | 214 | 214 | 214 | 214 |
| 中位数 | 4.155000000 | .0000000000 | 1.330000000 | .0000000000 | .0000000000 |
| 卡方缸定 | 17.574$^a$ | 27.029$^c$ | 21.858$^d$ | 8.763$^s$ | 20.107$^t$ |
| 自由度 | 9 | 9 | 9 | 9 | 9 |
| 渐近 顯著性 | .040 | .001 | .009 | .459 | .017 |

**Verification Statistics (Week 3)**

|  | sad |
|---|---|
| N | 214 |
| 中位数 | .0000000000 |
| 卡方缸定 | 6.567$^s$ |
| 自由度 | 9 |
| 渐近 顯著性 | .682 |

**Fig. 6.** Statistic summary of emotion dynamic analysis in week 3

From the result of the analysis, ticket sales are the hottest in week 3. The Posemo and Negemo emotions were both less than 0.05 in significance, which is the more obvious discrepancy. For the result, please refer to Fig. 6.

From the result of the time dynamic analysis, besides the emotional journey, which can be demonstrated as positive, or negative, the third week after the movie went on in the theater had apparent criticism and positive and negative reviews, proving that a great relationship exists between the time of a movie showing in theater and the commentator being able to write down accurately his/her words of sentiment. It is even more noticeable in the higher ticket sales category. The result is shown in Fig. 7.

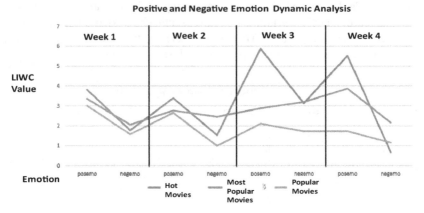

**Fig. 7.** Positive and negative emotion dynamic analysis

## 5   Conclusion and Future Research

With the rise of movie entertainment, the influence power of movie reviews cannot be overlooked. In a sea of movie review contents, to find the reviews that have value is the objective of this research so that the consumers can make quick judgment and selection and save time in the future.

Before exploring the relationship between movie reviews and ticket sales, we need to verify the authenticity of the movie review because false data will lead to false results. After the verification procedure, the trend of the ticket sales in terms of timing is next to be explored. There exists discrepancy in ticket sales, so the research deployed 'grouping' to form a slope chart and divided into 3 groups. In terms of timing, the time of a movie going on showing in movie theater and being decommissioned is the partitioning standard, which has one week as a unit out of 4 weeks in which sentiment and emotion time dynamic analysis is conducted. Comprehensive analysis on the prominent weeks is performed to understand what are the reasons and factors all audience focused on and which of the reasons and factors will contribute to future research. The research also found that there is a noticeable difference in sentiment fluctuation in the reviews during the third week. When applied to reading the review content, much time can be reduced and as a result, decisions can be derived by reading the star rating of the third week.

Many deficiencies were discovered after the end of the research. We have provided 2 points below in terms of limitations and recommendations:

1. In terms of collecting movie information and data, we hope to expand the research to larger markets such as China and the United States instead of being limited to Taiwan.

2. If the sentiment words in a review were found to be more persuasive to the consumers when making a choice, these words can be used for commercial purposes in commercials so that it is more likely to induce the consumers and to enhance their spending.

## References

Chang, Y.-R.: Using emotional analysis to evaluate library user satisfaction evaluation. Master's thesis, Library and Information Science, National Chung Hsing University (2012)

Import.io - Wikipedia (2019). https://en.wikipedia.org/wiki/Import.io

National Taiwan University Sentiment Dictionary (NTUSD) (2018). http://academiasinicanlplab.github.io/

Taiwan 2017 Annual Box Office TOP100 - Kanban Boxoffice - Batch kicking industrial workshop (2018). https://www.ptt.cc/bbs/boxoffice/M.1516302922.A.D68.html

Yahoo Movies (2018). https://movies.yahoo.com.tw/

Yang, C., Lin, K.H., Chen, H.: Emotion classification using web blog corpora. In: IEEE/WIC/ACM International Conference on Web Intelligence (WI07) (2007). https://doi.org/10.1109/wi.2007.51

# Detection of Misbehaviors in Clone Identities on Online Social Networks

Rishabh Kaushal[1,2(✉)], Chetna Sharma[2], and Ponnurangam Kumaraguru[1]

[1] Precog Research Group, Indraprastha Institute of Information Technology,
Delhi, India
{rishabhk,pk}@iiitd.ac.in
[2] Indira Gandhi Delhi Technical University for Women, Delhi, India
chetna712@gmail.com

**Abstract.** The account registration steps in Online Social Networks (OSNs) are simple to facilitate users to join the OSN sites. Alongside, Personally Identifiable Information (PII) of users is readily available online. Therefore, it becomes trivial for a malicious user (*attacker*) to create a spoofed identity of a real user (*victim*), which we refer to as *clone identity*. While a victim can be an ordinary or a famous person, we focus our attention on clone identities of famous persons (*celebrity clones*). These clone identities ride on the credibility and popularity of celebrities to gain engagement and impact. In this work, we analyze celebrity clone identities and extract an exhaustive set of 40 features based on posting behavior, friend network and profile attributes. Accordingly, we characterize their behavior as *benign* and *malicious*. On detailed inspection, we find benign behaviors are either to promote the celebrity which they have cloned or seek attention, thereby helping in the popularity of celebrity. However, on the contrary, we also find malicious behaviors (*misbehaviors*) wherein clone celebrities indulge in spreading indecent content, issuing advisories and opinions on contentious topics. We evaluate our approach on a real social network (Twitter) by constructing a machine learning based model to automatically classify behaviors of clone identities, and achieve accuracies of 86%, 95%, 74%, 92% & 63% for five clone behaviors corresponding to promotion, indecency, attention-seeking, advisory and opinionated.

**Keywords:** Online social networks · User clone identities · Behavioral detection

## 1 Introduction

Online Social Networks (OSNs) offer people in the real world to create accounts to avail plethora of social services being offered in the virtual world. While in the real world, it is readily feasible to verify the identity of an individual, it is quite tricky in OSNs [15]. The process of account creation is offered in quick and easy steps to encourage the adoption of OSNs platforms. This helps users create their accounts (also referred to as identities) with much ease. While it

© Springer Nature Switzerland AG 2020
B. R. Purushothama et al. (Eds.): MIKE 2019, LNAI 11987, pp. 94–103, 2020.
https://doi.org/10.1007/978-3-030-66187-8_10

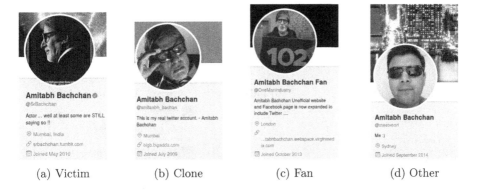

(a) Victim            (b) Clone            (c) Fan            (d) Other

**Fig. 1.** Illustration of Victim, Clone, Fan and Other Identities in Twitter.

helps genuine users create identities easily, on the flip side, it also enables a malicious user to create identity *similar* to a genuine user (victim), which we refer to as *clone identity*[1] [2]. The public availability of Personally Identifiable Information (PII) of users, like, profile picture, bio details and name, makes the task of a malicious user even more trivial [18]. We note that clone identities are different from *fake* identities (or *sybils*) in which an attacker creates a random profile without impersonating any individual.

In this work, we focus our attention on the clone identities of celebrities. The motivations for a malicious user to create clone identities are many-fold as exhibited by their behaviors. For instance, Fig. 1 depicts victim (well known Indian film celebrity Amitabh Bachchan on Twitter, Fig. 1a) along with his clone identity (Fig. 1b), which has been in existence for a long time (since 2009 in this case). Fan identity (in case of celebrity) also exists as shown in Fig. 1c along with an identity (Fig. 1d), which has the same name but is neither clone nor fan. Clone identities indulge in several behaviors as depicted in Fig. 2 such as promotion (Fig. 2a), indecency (Fig. 2b), attention-seeking (Fig. 2c), advisory (Fig. 2d) and opinionating (Fig. 2e). In the case of *celebrity cloning* [6], the apparent motivation is to ride on the popularity and reputation of known celebrities to influence users on OSN platforms. While behaviors associated with promotion and attention-seeking are *benign*, on the other hand, the behavior of spreading indecency is undoubtedly *malicious*. Also, the behaviors that involve sending advisories and opinions, particularly on contentious issues, that misrepresent celebrities, would be considered as *malicious* behaviors. Besides celebrities, clone identities are being created for ordinary individuals as well, in order to create *real-looking* profiles. These profiles are subsequently used to launch social engineering attacks like fake-following [3,8], fake-likes [17], spear-phishing [16]. In this work, we do not consider clones of ordinary people since their reach and impact is mostly limited to the victim alone.

---

[1] It is also referred as impersonation attack or identity clone attack.

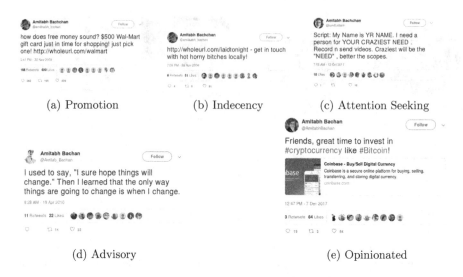

(a) Promotion      (b) Indecency      (c) Attention Seeking

(d) Advisory               (e) Opinionated

**Fig. 2.** Behavioral characteristics exhibited by clone identities.

Our proposed solution of behavior characterization of clone identities consists of the following steps. In the first step, we find suspected clone identities of the victim. These suspected identities are marked as *clone* identities, *fan*[2] identities (in case of celebrities), and *none*. In the second step, behavioral characterization of each of the clone identity is performed into predefined categories based on their behavior, as shown in Fig. 2. Five categories are considered namely promotion, indecency, attention-seeking, advisory, and opinionated. Our *behavioral characterization model*, pre-trained on 692 clones gives accuracies of 86%, 95%, 74%, 92% & 63%, respectively.

## 2 Related Work

Clone identities are a particular case of fake identities in which the victim's PII are leveraged by an attacker to create real-looking identities. Detection of fake identities, referred to as Sybil attacks are well studied. SybilGuard from Yu et al. [21] examines the impact of multiple fake identities (Sybil nodes) on honest nodes. Viswanath et al. [19] summarize the design of Sybil defense space from the perspective of detecting Sybils and tolerating (quantifying) their impact. Cao et al. [7] introduce a notion of ranking nodes (*SybilRank*) regarding their likelihood of being fake. While these works leverage network-based information in their solution approaches, Wang et al. [20] explore the possibility of a crowd-sourced solution for the detection of Sybils. Gupta et al. [11] leverage the machine learning approach for the detection of fake accounts on Facebook.

---

[2] Fan identities are created by supporters of celebrities with benign intentions of popularizing the celebrity. They may also be created by celebrities themselves, however, we don't delve into these issues, since our key focus is on behavior of clone identities.

In the context of clone detection, proposed solutions have exploited the fact that the attacker creates clone identities with attributes similar to that of the victim. Bilge et al. [5] demonstrate an identity theft attack on existing users of a given OSN and improve the trustworthiness of these identities by sending a friend request to friends of cloned victims. In another attack, they create cloned identities of victims across other OSNs where victims did not have their presence. Jin et al. [13] exploit attribute similarity and common friends as critical indicators to find clone identities. Kharaji et al. [14] also explore the similarity of attributes and strength of relationships as essential features to detect clone identities. However, both [13] and [14] could not validate their proposed approach on real OSN platform due to unavailability of verified and their clone identities. He et al. [12] propose a scheme to protect users from identity theft attacks. Gogo et al. [10] propose a technique for the collection of impersonation attacks. Their findings suggest that these attacks are targeting even ordinary individuals to create pseudo-real fake identities to evade detection.

# 3   Data Collection and Ground Truth

Among the various OSN platforms, we choose Twitter to evaluate our approach for many reasons. *First*, it is a popular short message service; users read and forward the tweets instantaneously. *Second*, it provides simple steps for account creation and has among the best support for developers, so creating a clone [9] is trivial. *Third*, Twitter follows a verification process for celebrities and grant a blue colored verify badge[3] indicating verified account. For selecting celebrities,

**Table 1.** Distribution of Suspected Clone Identities into Three Categories namely Clones, Fans and None

| Victim account | Clones | Fans | None | Total |
|---|---|---|---|---|
| Narendra Modi | 84 | 38 | 41 | 163 |
| Shah Rukh Khan | 56 | 11 | 41 | 108 |
| Amitabh Bachchan | 86 | 8 | 78 | 172 |
| Salman Khan | 23 | 7 | 42 | 72 |
| Akshay Kumar | 17 | 6 | 176 | 199 |
| Sachin Tendulkar | 107 | 10 | 70 | 187 |
| Virat Kohli | 79 | 30 | 20 | 129 |
| Deepika Padukone | 129 | 15 | 74 | 218 |
| Hrithik Roshan | 94 | 9 | 86 | 189 |
| Aamir Khan | 20 | 0 | 157 | 177 |
| Total | 695 | 134 | 785 | 1,614 |

---

[3] Verified Accounts on Twitter: https://help.twitter.com/en/managing-your-account/about-twitter-verified-accounts.

we use TwitterCounter[4], a web-based service to get 10,977 top influential (most followed) Twitter users spread across 227 countries. Due to computational constraints, we select the ten most influential users[5] from India. For each of them, we perform user search on Twitter using Search API[6] using various combinations of the name of user (first name only, first letter of first name + last name, both first name + last name and first name + first letter of last name). As a result, we obtain 1,614 suspected clone identities. We manually inspected each of these identities to find out whether they are indeed cloned identities or fan accounts (created to publicize or support their celebrities) or none of these. Out of 1,614 suspected clone identities, 695 were found to be clones, 134 fan identities, and the remaining 785 were neither clones nor fans, which forms ground truth for clone detection. Table 1 explains the breakup of these suspected clone identities. Further, we prepare ground truth for the behavior characterization

**Table 2.** Distribution of Five Behavioral Categories (C1:Promotion, C2:Indecency, C3:Advisory, C4:Opinionating, C5:Attention) among Clones and Fans

| Victim account | C1 | C2 | C3 | C4 | C5 |
|---|---|---|---|---|---|
| Narendra Modi | 8 | 9 | 7 | 61 | 27 |
| Shah Rukh Khan | 7 | 1 | 11 | 20 | 16 |
| Amitabh Bachchan | 14 | 3 | 12 | 28 | 29 |
| Salman Khan | 7 | 1 | 2 | 9 | 8 |
| Akshay Kumar | 5 | 0 | 1 | 12 | 5 |
| Sachin Tendulkar | 26 | 5 | 4 | 47 | 26 |
| Virat Kohli | 18 | 4 | 5 | 33 | 33 |
| Deepika Padukone | 27 | 12 | 10 | 52 | 42 |
| Hrithik Roshan | 19 | 7 | 9 | 30 | 28 |
| Aamir Khan | 6 | 0 | 1 | 6 | 6 |
| Total | 137 | 42 | 62 | 298 | 220 |

of clones and fans. Out of 829 of these identities (695 clones and 134 fans), we found that 22 of them got suspended, and 115 of them did not post even a single tweet. So, ignoring these, we focused our attention on the remaining 692 identities by manually inspecting all the tweets posted by them and engagement received. Based on the kind of content being posted, we narrowed down their behavior into *five behavioral categories* namely promotion, indecent, advisory,

---

[4] https://twittercounter.com/pages/100/.

[5] Narendra Modi, Shah Rukh Khan, Amitabh Bachchan, Salman Khan, Akshay Kumar, Sachin Tendulkar, Virat Kohli, Deepika Padukone, Hrithik Roshan and Aamir Khan.

[6] Twitter Search API: https://developer.twitter.com/en/docs/tweets/search/api-reference/get-search-tweets.html.

opinions, and attention seeking. The distribution of identities belonging to these categories are 137, 42, 62, 298, and 220, respectively as mentioned in Table 2. We observed that all these numbers add up to 759 which means that some of these identities exhibited more than one behavior.

## 4 Proposed Approach

Once we have detected clones, as explained in data collection, the next step is to characterize their behavior. There are *five* behavioral categories that we focus upon namely promotion, indecent, opinionated, advisory, and attention-seeking. During our behavioral characterization study of clones, as depicted in Fig. 3, we found that clones exhibit lessor activity weekly in terms of tweets posted (Fig. 3a) and tweets retweeted (Fig. 3b) as compared to victims who are influential users on Twitter.

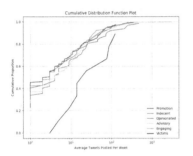
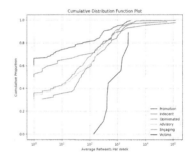

(a) Average Tweets Posted Per Week            (b) Avg. Retweets Received Per Week

**Fig. 3.** Behavioral characteristics exhibited by clone identities.

Table 3 describes the details of 40 features employed for behavioral characterization. We compute each of the features marked with '*' weekly, and we consider minimum, maximum, average, and standard deviation for each of them as features. We divide features into three categories namely content, network and profile, depending upon the type of attribute used as the source for feature computation.

– **Content Based Features**: The kind of content posted by clones provides a good indication of the type of behavior exhibited. The presence of URLs could lead users to inappropriate sites or promotional content. For instance, promotional keywords [4] would indicate promotion (or advertisement) class. Currency symbols could attract users towards some promotion. The presence of question marks and engaging words (like *who*, *what*, *when*, and *where*) could be used to invite attention or engagement. Swear words [1] would indicate the

**Table 3.** Features for behavioral characterization

| Features type | List of features |
|---|---|
| Content based Features (21) | URLs, Promotional Keywords, Mentions, Currency Symbols, Question Marks, Engaging Words, Swear Words, Quotes, Advisory Keywords, Days Since Last Tweet, Time* Between Two Tweets, Tweet* Length, Exclamation, Colon-Semicolon |
| Network based Features (14) | Tweets* per week, Retweet* Count & Favorite* Count, Followers, Following |
| Profile based Features (5) | Bio Analysis - URLs, Length, Victim Tag, Fan or Clone, Mention, Handle Mention |

presence of indecency. Special characters like quotes and advisory keywords (like *should*, *said*, and *quote*) could indicate self-help or advisory. Besides these, we use generic features like hashtags, tweet length, time between two tweets, days since the last tweet, presence of exclamation symbol and colon-semicolon.

– **Network Based Features**: Behavior of clone identities with their ego network can be studied by measuring the engagement. Therefore features like retweet count, favorite count, tweets per week, number of followers, and number of following are computed here in network-based features.
– **Profile Based Features**: Twitter has very few profile attributes among which *user bio* is worth investigating. We compute the number of occurrences of URLs, victim name (or tag) along with the length of bio in user bio field as features. Also, to capture the nature of profile as described by the user, we look into the occurrence of some common words. A clone may use words like *real account* or *official account*, whereas a fan page bio may have *unofficial page*, *parody account*, or *fan association* mentioned.

## 5   Evaluation and Results

We explain our evaluation methodology and corresponding results in this section. Recall from Table 2 that 692 clones (and fan) identities were analyzed to categorize them into one (or more) of the behavioral types. In particular, 137 were found to be involved in the promotion, 42 in spreading indecency, 64 in advisory, 298 in opinionating, and 220 in attention-seeking. We use this as ground truth and answer the following research questions (RQs).

– RQ1: Which is the best classifier for behavior characterization of clones?
– RQ2: Does detection accuracy improve with more training?

**Identifying Best Classifier.** To identify the best classifier, we compute 40 features on the 692 identities and ran over 12 off-the-shelf classifiers namely Random Forest, Decision Tree, Logistic Regression, KNeighbors, ExtraTreesClassifier, Logistic Regression, Ridge Classifier, ExtraTree Classifier, Neural Network - MLPClassifier, LinearSVC and Naive Bayes Classifier (Bernoulli and Gaussian). In our experimental set-up, we consider the multi-class (five classes) problem as five different binary classification problems in which the goal is to detect the presence or absence of a specific behavior in a given clone identity. It turns out that there is no single classifier, which performs best for all behavior types. Random forest works the best (94%) for detecting indecency, Naive-Bayes detects promotion with 86% accuracy, Logistic Regression gives 74% accuracy for attention-seeking behavior, RidgeClassifier gives 92% accuracy for advisory behavior whereas ExtraTreesClassifier gives 63% accuracy for opinionated content spreading.

**Table 4.** Accuracy scores with different training-testing split

| Train-test | Promotion | Indecency | Attention seeking | Advisory | Opinionated |
|---|---|---|---|---|---|
| 80-20 | **0.86** | **0.94** | **0.92** | **0.63** | **0.74** |
| 70-30 | 0.73 | 0.94 | 0.90 | 0.56 | 0.68 |
| 60-40 | 0.82 | 0.91 | 0.90 | 0.54 | 0.61 |
| 50-50 | 0.80 | 0.92 | 0.90 | 0.54 | 0.65 |

**Training-Testing Split.** In this evaluation, we study the effect of train-test split on classifier performance. As evident from Table 4, the classification accuracy is improved in all behavioral types as we increase the train-test ratio from 50-50 to 80-20, which suggests that as training size would size, the accuracies will improve. Also, we observe that the accuracy of the advisory class is low due to less number of clones spreading advisory behavior (Table 2). On the contrary, the accuracy of the indecent class is high, even though the number of indecent instances is less. We attribute it to the fact that swear words in indecency are limited and highly discriminative.

# 6    Limitations and Future Work

There are a few limitations to this work. We carefully select Twitter as the social network platform because it provides a mechanism of *verified accounts* in which a blue tick appears in user profile. This helped us in correctly identifying the real account from the cloned identities. It will be difficult to obtain ground truth in social networks that do not have any in-built mechanism for verification. Owing to computation limitations, we restrict ourselves to suspected 1,614 clones of the top ten celebrities on Twitter only from India. Therefore, we have a limited and biased dataset. Nevertheless, it is a good first step. In the future, it would be nice to extend the work on celebrities in other countries as well to understand the influence of cultural factors on the clone behaviors. We conveniently selected celebrities as victims because ground truth for them is readily available, and they have more clones than ordinary persons. Lastly, while the accuracies of behavioral prediction of promotion (86%), indecent (95%) and advisory (92%) are quite decent, at the same time, the accuracies for categories like attention (74%) and opinions (63%) are way too less to be of practical use. More data needs to be collected to improve accuracies for predicting these behaviors. Moving forward, this work can also be extended to build an application that alerts celebrities whenever any clone indulges in any misbehavior. We understand that every celebrity would have a public relations team, who can benefit from such an application.

## 7    Conclusion

In this work, we present our solution approach for the behavioral characterization of clones. We *recast* the problem as a binary classification problem and conventional classifiers are applied and empirically evaluated. We extract an exhaustive set of features from network, content, and profile of celebrity clone identities. Best classifiers achieve accuracies of 86%, 95%, 74%, 92% and 63% for five clone behaviors namely promotion, indecency, attention seeking, advisory, and opinionated, respectively.

## References

1. List of 723 bad words to blacklist & how to use facebook's moderation tool. Front Gate Media (May 2014). https://www.frontgatemedia.com/a-list-of-723-bad-words-to-blacklist-and-how-to-use-facebooks-moderation-tool/, [Online; posted 12 May 2014]
2. What is facebook cloning and how can i protect myself from it? Hoax Slayer (July 2017). https://www.hoax-slayer.net/what-is-facebook-cloning-and-how-can-i-protect-myself-from-it/, [Online; posted 25 July 2017]
3. Aggarwal, A., Kumar, S., Bhargava, K., Kumaraguru, P.: The follower count fallacy: detecting twitter users with manipulated follower count (2018)
4. Author, C.: Magic marketing words you should be using. Vertical Response (September 2017). https://www.verticalresponse.com/blog/the-30-magic-marketing-words/, [Online; posted 19 September 2017]
5. Bilge, L., Strufe, T., Balzarotti, D., Kirda, E.: All your contacts are belong to us: automated identity theft attacks on social networks. In: Proceedings of the 18th international conference on World wide web, pp. 551–560. ACM (2009)
6. Buxton, M.: The social scam: for a-listers, imposters still loom large. Refinery29 (May 2018). https://www.refinery29.com/2018/05/195519/celebrity-impersonation-accounts-fake-instagram-twitter, [Online; posted 2 May 2018]
7. Cao, Q., Sirivianos, M., Yang, X., Pregueiro, T.: Aiding the detection of fake accounts in large scale social online services. In: Proceedings of the 9th USENIX Conference on Networked Systems Design and Implementation. pp. 15–15. USENIX Association (2012)

8. Cresci, S., Di Pietro, R., Petrocchi, M., Spognardi, A., Tesconi, M.: Fame for sale: efficient detection of fake twitter followers. Decis. Support Syst. **80**, 56–71 (2015)
9. Glover, R.: Building a twitter clone. The Meteor Chef (August 2017). https:// themeteorchef.com/tutorials/building-a-twitter-clone, [Online; posted 31 August 2017]
10. Goga, O., Venkatadri, G., Gummadi, K.P.: The doppelgänger bot attack: exploring identity impersonation in online social networks. In: Proceedings of the 2015 Internet Measurement Conference, pp. 141–153. ACM (2015)
11. Gupta, A., Kaushal, R.: Towards detecting fake user accounts in facebook. In: Asia Security and Privacy (ISEASP), ISEA 2017, pp. 1–6. IEEE (2017)
12. He, B.Z., Chen, C.M., Su, Y.P., Sun, H.M.: A defence scheme against identity theft attack based on multiple social networks. Expert Syst. Appl. **41**(5), 2345–2352 (2014)
13. Jin, L., Takabi, H., Joshi, J.B.: Towards active detection of identity clone attacks on online social networks. In: Proceedings of the first ACM Conference on Data and Application Security and Privacy, pp. 27–38. ACM (2011)
14. Kharaji, M.Y., Rizi, F.S., Khayyambashi, M.R.: A new approach for finding cloned profiles in online social networks. arXiv preprint arXiv:1406.7377 (2014)
15. Lips, A.: Everyone wants to get verified on social media, but it's not usually an easy process. Social Media Week (March 2018). https://socialmediaweek.org/ blog/2018/03/can-i-get-verified-verification-guidelines-for-social-media/, [Online; posted 16 March 2018]
16. Parmar, B.: Protecting against spear-phishing. Comput. Fraud Secur. **2012**(1), 8–11 (2012)
17. Sen, I., Aggarwal, A., Mian, S., Singh, S., Kumaraguru, P., Datta, A.: Worth its weight in likes: towards detecting fake likes on instagram. In: Proceedings of the 10th ACM Conference on Web Science, pp. 205–209. ACM (2018)
18. Slotkin, J.: Twitter 'bots' steal tweeters' identities. Market Place (May 2013). https://www.marketplace.org/2013/05/27/tech/twitter-bots-steal-tweeters-identities, [Online; posted 27 May 2013]
19. Viswanath, B., et al.: Exploring the design space of social network-based sybil defenses. In: 2012 Fourth International Conference on Communication Systems and Networks (COMSNETS), pp. 1–8. IEEE (2012)
20. Wang, G., et al.: Social turing tests: crowdsourcing sybil detection. arXiv preprint arXiv:1205.3856 (2012)
21. Yu, H., Kaminsky, M., Gibbons, P.B., Flaxman, A.: Sybilguard: defending against sybil attacks via social networks. In: ACM SIGCOMM Computer Communication Review, vol. 36, pp. 267–278. ACM (2006)

# Contextual Predictability of Texts for Texts Processing and Understanding

Olga Krutchenko, Ekaterina Pronoza$^{(\boxtimes)}$, Elena Yagunova, Viktor Timokhov, and Alexander Ivanets

St. Petersburg State University, St. Petersburg, Russian Federation
krutchenko.olga@gmail.com, katpronoza@gmail.com,
iagounova.elena@gmail.com, viktor-timohov@mail.ru,
sookol98@yandex.ru

**Abstract.** This paper is the first part of contextual predictability model investigation for Russian, it is focused on linguistic and psychology interpretation of models, features, metrics and sets of features. The aim of this paper is to identify the dependence of the implementation of contextual predictability procedures on the genre characteristics of the text (or text collection): scientific vs. fictional. We construct a model predicting text elements and designate its features for texts of different genres and domains. We analyze various methods for studying contextual predictability, carry out a computational experiment against scientific and fictional texts, and verify its results by the experiment with informants (cloze-tests) and word embeddings (word2vec CBOW model). As a result, text processing model is built. It is evaluated based on the selected contextual predictability features and experiments with informants.

**Keywords:** Contextual predictability · Language model · Dice · Surprisal · Conditional probability · Informational entropy · Cloze test · Fiction texts · Scientific corpora

## 1 Introduction

Information redundancy is an inherent feature of any text, especially from the point of view of information theory. And it is precisely because of this property that a person successfully perceives and understands both oral and written text. Redundancy is an inherent property of any language and is therefore inherent in all texts, without exception, but to varying degrees, depending on the functional style of the text [1].

The concept of contextual predictability is closely connected to the process of predicting words based on their context. The effect of contextual predictability is essentially the opposite of information redundancy, demonstrating that not all the words are equivalent for perception and understanding of a text.

In this paper, an analysis of various computational methods of contextual predictability is carried out, and the most adequate metrics are selected for further verification during constructing a language model. The research involves computational analysis based on

© Springer Nature Switzerland AG 2020
B. R. Purushothama et al. (Eds.): MIKE 2019, LNAI 11987, pp. 104–119, 2020.
https://doi.org/10.1007/978-3-030-66187-8_11

the corpora of scientific and fictional texts and experiment with informants and word embeddings.

Our aim is to identify the dependence of the implementation of contextual predictability procedures on the genre and style characteristics of the text.

Contextual predictability involves consideration of many aspects, since this topic is interdisciplinary. One of them is the psychological aspect. There are many different studies about the dependence of contextual predictability and the speed of reading of a person, their eye movement when reading [2], etc.

On the other hand, contextual predictability is directly connected with the fields of linguistics, psychology, perception and analysis of the text. Such research methods as cloze-tests, tests aimed at restoring missing elements of the text, allow to assess the degree of informants knowledge of the language, readability of the text (solving the problem of the comprehensibility of texts) [4], as well as analyze issues which may arise while teaching/studying this language [4–8].

But the issue of contextual predictability in computational linguistics, when solving problems associated with automatic text processing, is particularly relevant [9]. For example, contextual predictability is highly relevant for the recognition and correction of typos in the text when solving various problems associated with further text processing. Using the principles of contextual predictability, if it is impossible to recognize a word, we can assume that there is a typo in it, and then to restore the correct word with the help of the context.

Contextual predictability can also help in extracting keywords and collocations from text [10]. Since a collocation phrase has signs of a holistic semantic and syntactic unit; contextual predictability indicators values are usually high for collocations. Keywords, on the contrary, are the main source of new and significant information in the text, therefore, their contextual predictability is expected to be small, especially when they occur in the text for the first time.

Contextual predictability is also relevant for the task of predicting the words missing from text, by their context: the higher contextual predictability of text is, the easier it is to predict the missing words (and it is proved in the experiments with both the informants and automatic word prediction model).

Thus, the relevance and practical significance of the research of contextual predictability is very high for a variety of areas related to automatic text processing.

## 2 Related Work

### 2.1 General Approaches to Analyzing Contextual Predictability

From the point of view of computational linguistics, the predictability of words in the context has been little studied. However, there has been an increasing amount of research on this topic recently.

The main approaches in the contextual predictability research are the analysis of statistical data based on corpus of texts and the conduct of cloze-tests with informants. To conduct a comprehensive study, it is necessary to use a combination of the two approaches and compare the results at each of the stages. At the initial stage of the analysis of the data, two main questions arise: how to evaluate contextual predictability based on statistical data and on the basis of what corpora to conduct research.

Contextual predictability of the word in the text can be assessed in various ways. First of all, there are statistical measures of association, mainly used to identify collocations. These are measures such as MI, t-score, Dice [10, 14, 15] and others. They may be useful for both separate texts and the corpora [16]. Another possible approach to contextual predictability involves calculating informational entropy and conditional probability. These measures will be considered in Sect. 2.3 in detail.

### 2.2  Contextual Predictability Analysis via Cloze-Test

Cloze-test can be considered the oldest form of analyzing contextual predictability. Cloze-test was proposed by V. Taylor [6] to determine the readability of the text (an indicator of how difficult the text is for reading and perception). Its method is as follows: a prose passage of 100 to 400 words is selected, in which each n-th word is skipped. An informant is asked to recover the missing words. The success of this text is directly dependent on the time it takes for the informant to understand the entire text and restore the connection between the events. This, in turn, is determined by the informant's knowledge of the vocabulary of a given language, the extent to which he/she has developed a language guess and how adequately he/she understands the text of each specific situation [6].

This test can be used to control the process of learning a foreign language, since it allows one to accurately and objectively establish the degree of the formation of reading skills and level of vocabulary knowledge when reading.

Cloze texts have also other possible applications. Using this type of test, one can evaluate language model of a particular language. For example, in [4] it is shown that detailed information about the performance of the language model can be obtained through cloze-tests with informants.

The method of cloze-tests is also used to assess the understanding of speech by ear. Moreover, this approach is important not only for the purpose of control in teaching a foreign language, but also to study the mechanisms of perception of sounding speech, which has its own distinctive features: ellipsis, unclear pronouncing of unstressed syllables, objective interference of a communication channel, etc. This issue is considered in detail in [11] and [12].

### 2.3  Statistical Models for Contextual Predictability

If we consider studies that propose objective criteria for determining the complexity of an arbitrary language and ranking various languages by complexity, the paper by McWarter [17] can be considered the first work in this direction. In his work, he criticizes the prevailing opinion about the equal complexity of all languages and proves that some modern languages are simpler than the "old" ones. Later, the ideas of McWarter were developed in the works of other researchers, such as Wouter Küsters [18], Esten Dahl [19], Peter Tradgil [20], and others.

The development of contextual predictability models in computer science and related disciplines is more relevant to the our research. Such models often rely on hidden Markov processes. Hidden Markov models allow us to consider the text as a set of processes of transition from one state to another. In this case, if we analyze the text of a sufficiently large volume, we can use n-gram frequencies to obtain the transition probabilities. For example, after analyzing Liyus Carroll's fairy tale "Alice's Adventures in Wonderland", we found out that the state "l" (the letter "l") occurs 100 times in the text. The next state is likely to be the state "i", since the word "Alice" is a fairly frequent word in the text selected for the initial analysis [13].

In general, statistical models like Hidden Markov models and Conditional Random Fields are often used in natural language processing for such tasks as language modelling, document classification, clustering and information extraction [21].

It should be noted that work related to the study of informational redundancy in text, was also carried out in Russia in the 1960 s (see, for example, the studies of N. N. Leontyeva, R. G. Piotrovsky, T. N. Nikitina, M. I. Otkupshchikova, specifically devoted to this topic [22]). This issue is considered in detail by P.G. Piotrovsky ([23] and [24]).

At the first stage of the current research, Hidden Markov models were considered and preliminary results were obtained. However, these results had no strict and formalized linguistic interpretation. Thus we organized our research as follows: firstly, we focus on the statistical metrics of contextual predictability and their interpretation (see this paper); secondly, we compare results of the statistical metrics with other models like Hidden Markov models.

Further in this section we describe several statistical metrics we used in this research. *Informational entropy* is calculated as follows:

$$H(x) = -log_2 P(x), \tag{1}$$

where $P(x)$ denotes the probability of occurrence of the word $x$ in text. This is a term from informational theory, and it is a measure of uncertainty of the appearance of a symbol of the primary alphabet.

*Conditional probability* is the probability of one event, provided that another event has already occurred [25]. Conditional probability for contextual predictability of the word is calculated as follows:

$$P(x|context) = \frac{f(x, context)}{f(context)}, \tag{2}$$

where $f(x, context)$ is the frequency of joint occurrence of the word x after the specified context, and $f(context))$ is the frequency of meeting of the context.

*Mutual information (MI)* is also a notion from information theory referring to the strength of the connection and allows one to assess the independence of the appearance of two words in the text. In this paper we use pMI which is calculated by the formula:

$$pMI(x_1 x_2) = log_2 \frac{f(x_1 x_2) \times N}{f(x_1) \times f(x_2)}, \tag{3}$$

where $x_2$ is the word under study, $x_1$ is the preceding word, $f(x_1 x_2)$ is the frequency of the occurrence of the two words together, $f(x_1)$ and $f(x_2)$ are the word frequencies of $x_1$ and $x_2$ respectively and $N$ is corpus size (in the number of words) [10, 14]. MI tends to assign greater importance to combinations of rare words, including words with misprints and foreign words. Therefore, it is necessary to consider a threshold for word frequency values in the corpus [10, 16].

*T-score* is an association measure which refers to the asymptotic criteria for hypothesis testing. It is calculated by the formula:

$$t - score(x_1, x_2) = \frac{f(x_1 x_2) - \frac{f(x_1) \times f(x_2)}{N}}{\sqrt{f(x_1 x_2)}}, \tag{4}$$

where $x_2$ is the word under study, $x_1$ is the preceding word, $f(x_1 x_2)$ is the frequency of occurrence of the two words together, $f(x_1)$ and $f(x_2)$ are the word frequencies of $x_1$ and $x_2$ respectively and $N$ is corpus size (in the number of words) [10, 14].

*The Dice coefficient*, like MI, refers to the point estimate of a measure of connection. It is calculated by the formula:

$$Dice(x_1, x_2) = \frac{2 * f(x_1 x_2)}{f(x_1) + f(x_2)}, \tag{5}$$

where $x_2$ is the word under study, $x_1$ is the preceding word, $f(x_1 x_2)$ is the frequency of occurrence of the two words together, $f(x_1)$ and $f(x_2)$ are the word frequencies of $x_1$ and $x_2$ respectively. There is also a logarithmic variant of Dice, logDice, which is often used in text processing tasks):

$$log Dice(x_1, x_2) = log_2 \frac{2 * f(x_1 x_2)}{f(x_1) + f(x_2)}. \tag{6}$$

This measure (both Dice and logDice) does not depend on the size of the corpus (unlike MI and t-score); it takes into account only the frequency of joint occurrence and independent frequencies. However, like MI, this measure gives an overestimation of low-frequency phrases [14, 15], although this overestimate is much less critical for the Dice measure than for the MI measure. To study contextual predictability, the following algorithm can be interesting for estimating n-word combinations using the Dice measure: for all pairs of words in a body (or text), the Dice coefficient is considered, then the elements are arranged into chunks, or linked text segments, according to a particular principle (so-called cosegment procedure [15, 26]).

The term chunk term was introduced as a cognitive term in [3] to designate a fragment (in other words, a piece) of text from several words that are commonly used together in a fixed expression. An example of such phrases: "in my opinion", "Do you know what I mean?" and others. The selection of these phrases (chunks) was made as part of the study of mastering a foreign language [30].

The union of words in chunks occurs on the basis of a previously discussed feature of the connectivity of the two elements of the text (words).

There are two options when linked text segments extraction is concerned. The first option is as follows: pairs of words are united into one text element based on the value of the coefficients of this pair of words and the closest context. A word is not attached to the previous one, if the value of the Dice coefficient for this pair is lower than the threshold, or if it is lower than the arithmetic average of the same coefficient for the left and right pair. A condition is imposed that related chains cannot consist of more than 7 words [15]. This algorithm was introduced and described in detail by V. Daudaravicius (for example, [26]).

The second option is as follows: for each phrase a group is formed by successively merging it with context phrases. For each group, the Dice coefficient is calculated by taking into account five phrases from the left context and two phrases from the right context (such sizes of the context window is selected as this is approximately how a human perceives context).

In a computational experiment, the Dice coefficient for each bigram has to be calculated.

In this research, a condition based on the arithmetic average of two values of the Dice coefficient to the right and left of the studied words was selected as a feature for combining the two words.

The first word analyzed is always a chunk. To add each subsequent word to the chunk, the following condition must be met:

$$Dice(word2, \; word3) \; > \; \frac{Dict(word1, word2) \; + \; Dice(word3, \; word4)}{2}. \tag{7}$$

A word does not join the previous one if the value of the Dice coefficient for this pair is below the threshold, i.e. than the arithmetic mean of the same coefficient for the left and right pair. An additional limit is imposed on the length of the chunks: the number of elements (words) is not more than 7 [15, 26].

The *surprisal* metric is a measure of the content of information associated with an event in a probabilistic space. The smaller the probability of an event, the greater is the surprisal coefficient associated with the information that this event will occur [27].

This measure, proposed by H. Levvi in 2001 [28], has become standard for the tasks related to the assessment of contextual predictability. It is calculated by the formula:

$$I(x, \; context) = log_2 \frac{1}{P(x \vee context)} \tag{8}$$

where $P(x \vee context)$ is the conditional probability of the occurrence of the word $x$ in a given context.

The *salience* metric for assessing the compatibility of words is much less common than MI and t-score metrics. However, it can be considered a normalized variant of the Dice metric. The salience coefficient is calculated using the formula:

$$salience(x_1, x_2) = 14 + log_2 \frac{2 \times f(x_1 x_2)}{f(x_1) + f(x_2)}, \tag{9}$$

where $x_2$ is the word under study, $x_1$ is the preceding word, $f(x_1 x_2)$ is the frequency of occurrence of the two words together, $f(x_1)$ and $f(x_2)$ are the word frequencies of $x_1$ and $x_2$ respectively [14].

## 3   Data

As mentioned earlier, redundancy is an essential feature of natural language and natural language text in particular, which is necessary for perception and understanding by a human. Redundancy is inherent in all texts, without exception, but it is not a constant value and depends on many parameters, one of which is the functional style of the text [1, 12].

The total amount of information contained in the text is called the information richness of the text. Information richness is an absolute indicator of the quality of the text (as opposed to informativeness, which depends on the degree of novelty of the topic for the reader, and therefore is a relative indicator of quality). According to the degree of information richness, the five main functional styles can be arranged as follows in ascending order: colloquial, fictional, publicistic, scientific, official business [1, 29].

According to the defined classification, conversational and artistic styles have the greatest redundancy, while the scientific and official business styles tend to increase the information richness, i.e. to reduce redundancy.

Therefore, for the study of contextual predictability, we selected two functional styles for comparison: the scientific and the fictional ones, which are expected to be the opposites in terms of the redundancy of the texts (and the value of contextual predictability for scientific texts is expected to be much higher compared to the fictional ones due to greater information richness).

We prepared two datasets of scientific text, each of which belongs to one subject area and is homogeneous in genre and theme.

For the corpus of fictional texts, we selected texts that differed in the following parameters: text volume in terms of words number, genre and the "recognition" of the work of art.

The corpus of fictional texts consists of 6 texts. By the number of words, texts range from 9 500 to 363 500 words. The total number of words in the corpus is 782 300.

As for the scientific texts, 2 subcorpora were formed: scientific articles on corpus linguistics (15 093 articles) and cognitive psychology (22 703 articles). The total number of words in the corpus is 37 796.

As the amount of scientific articles is quite small, it makes sense to carry out an analysis directly on the whole corpus, while fictional texts can be considered separately. The results of the analysis of the corpus of scientific texts and individual fictional texts can be comparable due to the common theme of scientific articles, belonging to one subject area, the presence of similar keywords (corpus of scientific articles similar in these characteristics can be perceived as a single text).

The formed corpus of texts serves as the basis for our research and for obtaining preliminary results.

For the experiment with missing words prediction we prepared a third-party fictional corpus of 337 texts and a scientific corpus of 1095 texts. Preprocessing stage included tokenization and lemmatization (using Mystem morphological parser). Continuous Bag-of-Words (CBOW) models were trained on the lemmatized corpora with the following parameters: size = 300, window = 4, min_count = 5 for scientific corpus and size = 500, window = 2, min_count = 5 for fictional corpus.

## 4   Text Model Construction

All the considered metrics for detecting contextual predictability can be classified as follows: probabilistic estimates (entropy characteristic, conditional probability, surprisal), pointwise (MI, Dice, salience) and asymptotic (t-score) estimates of communication measures. Some of them are very similar to each other, differing only by normalization. For the practical part of the research, the following measures are of interest:

– Conditional probability and entropy characteristic, since they are the main probability metrics.
– Surprisal, because this metric is a standard for assessing contextual predictability.
– Dice coefficient, which will be used to implement the algorithm of combining collocation into linked text segments.

The selected metrics are quite diverse, and as a result are interesting for comparing their performance. And also all of them have their own characteristics, advantages and disadvantages. In this regard, they are most interesting for further testing on the corpus of texts and individual texts in the course of building a model and analyzing its work. Comparison of various methods allows us to visually identify their differences and work efficiency and analyze the results separately for each of the metrics.

The selected metrics were combined and represented as a graph. This model is a graph (see Fig. 1) where the nodes refer to the words (on the lemma level), and the edges correspond to the connections between the words and their contexts. The edges are annotated with all possible metrics and their values, and the nodes are annotated with morphological information (i.e., lemma, grammemes, etc.).

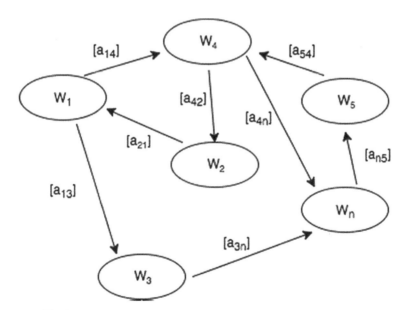

**Fig. 1.** Graph model for context predictability metrics representation.

To build such a model, the textual data is sequentially processed in several stages, such as:

– preprocessing, which includes tokenization and lemmatization;
– creating a frequency dictionary of tokens;
– extracting bigrams from the text and creating their frequency dictionary;
– calculating necessary attributes and metrics for each of the bigrams;
– generating the graph text model.

As part of the computational experiment, we also extracted linked text segments form the texts using Dice coefficient as described in Sect. 2.3.

## 5   Results Discussion

As a result of the computational experiment, text models (consisting of context predictability metrics values) for each corpus were obtained. For further analysis and comparison of the results, it is necessary to take into account the volume and lexical variety of the texts in question (see Table 1).

**Table 1.** Volume and lexical variety of the texts.

| Text (corpus) | Volume (tokens number) | Percentage of unique wordforms, % | Percentage of unique lemmas, % |
|---|---|---|---|
| Scientific corpus 1 (cognitive psychology) | 13434 | 30.4 | 23.3 |
| Scientific corpus 2 (computational linguistics) | 13434 | 39.6 | 25.6 |
| "Catching minnows in Georgia" by V. Astafev | 9624 | 50.2 | 36.6 |
| "The problem of a werewolf…" by V. Pelevin | 10472 | 38.0 | 25.3 |
| "Station on the Horizon" by E.M. Remark | 49568 | 28.3 | 16.0 |
| "Ivanhoe" by W. Scott | 148466 | 19.7 | 8.3 |
| "Singing in the thorns" by C. McCullough | 200852 | 17.3 | 7.8 |
| "The Count of Monte Cristo" by A. Dumas | 363554 | 12.1 | 4.7 |

To analyze the results obtained for each text, we calculated the arithmetic mean value for each of the studied metrics. Such mean values are shown in Table 2.

**Table 2.** Mean values of context predictability metrics.

| Text (corpus) | Conditional probability | Entropy | MI | Dice | Surprisal |
|---|---|---|---|---|---|
| Scientific corpus 1 (cognitive psychology) | 0.45 | 11.4 | 23 | 0.27 | 2.35 |
| Scientific corpus 2 (computational linguistics) | 0.39 | 11.2 | 22.6 | 0.29 | 2.43 |
| "Catching minnows in Georgia" by V. Astafev | 0.53 | 10.7 | 21.7 | 0.32 | 2.26 |
| "The problem of a werewolf..." by V. Pelevin | 0.42 | 10.3 | 21.2 | 0.22 | 2.68 |
| "Station on the Horizon" by E.M. Remark | 0.35 | 11.8 | 23.6 | 0.14 | 3.64 |
| "Ivanhoe" by W. Scott | 0.27 | 12.4 | 25.2 | 0.09 | 4.38 |
| "Singing in the thorns" by C. McCullough | 0.25 | 12.5 | 25.3 | 0.09 | 4.72 |
| "The Count of Monte Cristo" by A. Dumas | 0.2 | 12.5 | 25.8 | 0.06 | 5.3 |

At this stage of the research, it can be concluded that the values of the selected metrics depend not only on the contextual predictability of the text, but also on the volume of the given text. This suggests that we need to increase the corpus for further research. In spite of this, on the basis of the results obtained, it can already be concluded that the hypothesis of the expected higher values of contextual predictability features for the body of scientific texts in comparison with the fictional ones is confirmed.

It should be notes that the constructed text models can be used to solve practical natural language processing tasks, for example, those related to the removal of ambiguity and the correction of typos (see Table 3).

**Table 3.** Example of typos correction.

| Context | Word | Entropy | Dice | Surprisal | Lemma |
|---|---|---|---|---|---|
| сегодня /today/ | вечером /evening/ | 12 | 0.079 | 4.2 | вечер /evening/ |
| сегодня /today/ | вчером /evening/ | **18** | 0.026 | 6.2 | Unknown |

To recognize typos, one needs to identify such pairs of words where the two words differ in one letter, and lemma for one of the words is not known (in practice, it means that lemma cannot be found by a morphological parser). In this case, one can to compare the entropy values for these words. If the entropy value of one of the words is higher than the total entropy of the text, then there can be a typo in this word and it is necessary to check the values of other features with the same context for these words (if there is a context).

Another case of applying the results of the research in practice is the disambiguation task. Since morphological analysis is carried out automatically, it is imperfect, and errors are possible. To verify its results, it is necessary to compare the values of some contextual predictability features for the same words with different contexts. First of all, it is necessary to pay attention to the values of the surprisal metric, which is significantly higher than the average value in the text for rare bigrams (and this is the case when a disambiguation error takes place) – see Table 4.

**Table 4.** Disambiguation example.

| Context | Word | Entropy | Dice | Surprisal | Lemma |
|---------|------|---------|------|-----------|-------|
| моя /my/ | вина /guilt/ | 16 | 0.026 | **6.0** | вино /wine/ |
| глоток /sip of/ | вина /wine/ | 13 | 0.045 | **1.6** | вино /wine/ |

As a result of the experiments with chunks extraction, a list of linked text segments was obtained, with their lengths ranging from 1 to 7 elements.

Comparing the results obtained for fictional and scientific functional styles, the following tendencies are found out:

- The average length of chunks in fiction texts is 5 elements, while in scientific ones it is 3 elements.
- In scientific style, each sentence is almost completely divided into chunks, while in fictional style only 1–2 integrated blocks are more common in long sentences.
- Chunks in scientific style texts are cliche phrases, introductory constructions and turns. In fictional style chunks are constituted by steady combinations and collocations.

To evaluate the performance of the constructed contextual predictability model, we conducted cloze-tests with informants.

We selected 4 fragments of texts (2 fragments of fictional style, 2 – of scientific style), belonging to various works. Each of the fragments ranges from 100 to 120 words in volume. In each fragment, 10 words are missing, which are proposed to be restored by the informants.

The choice of the omitted words was made on the basis of the surprisal (which is a standard for such procedure) and entropy metrics. In each text fragment, words with high (8–11), medium (4–8), and low (0–3) meanings of the surprisal metric were selected to be missing. It is assumed that a higher surprisal value means that the given word is worse recovered from the context. The results of the experiment with surprisal metric are also compared with those with the entropy metric.

The cloze-test in our research consists of two parts - the main and the additional. The first one contains the content part (fragments of texts with missing words), the second one includes questions for informants that need to be answered after passing the test (regarding their age category, sex and whether they recognized the books from which the fragments were taken). The informants were offered instructions for passing the test and a test form, they were no time restrictions.

In our experiment, 10 informants participated.

Some of the excluded words, together with the informants' results, are presented in Table 5 and 6 for the text fragments selected for the cloze-test, and an example of such text fragment (with omitted words) is provided as follows:

**Table 5.** Cloze-test results for fictional texts (a fragment).

| Original word | Answer 1 | Answer 2 | ... | Amount of correct answers | Percent of correct answers, % | Amount of correct part of speech tags | Percent of correct part of speech tags, % |
|---|---|---|---|---|---|---|---|
| увидела /saw/ | увидела /saw/ | увидела /saw/ | | 10 | 100 | 10 | 100 |
| сиянье /glow/ | облако /cloud/ | солнце /sun/ | | 1 | 10 | 10 | 100 |
| солнце /sun/ | солнце /sun/ | светило /luminary/ | | 9 | 90 | 10 | 100 |
| бортом /board/ | бортом /board/ | ней /her/ | | 4 | 40 | 10 | 100 |
| собой /self/ | собой /self/ | бриллианты /brilliants/ | | 5 | 50 | 6 | 60 |
| водой /water/ | землей /earth/ | небом /sky/ | | 4 | 40 | 10 | 100 |

*"She walked on the deck and 1) _____ new, unfamiliar Australia. In the transparent, colorless 2) _____ was slowly spreading, rose above the pearl rose 3) _____, and already in the east, on the edge of the ocean there rose 4) _____, the newborn scarlet light turned into a white day...".*

In Table 5, results of the experiment on fictional texts are presented, and Table 6 contains the results obtained for the scientific corpora.

According to the results of the informants' answers, the main assumption of the experiment was confirmed: the words with low surprisal value are restored by the informants correctly or using synonyms in 85–100% of cases.

We also selected a group of words (10% of the total number of the missing words), which are unequivocally restored by informants, but have a high surprisal value (from 8 to 11). Initially it was assumed that this group of words would be less recoverable. However, entropy values of these words slightly exceed the average entropy of the text (they make 13–14, with the average entropy of the text equal to 11).

**Table 6.** Cloze-test results for scientific texts (a fragment).

| Original word | Answer 1 | Answer 2 | ... | Amount of correct answers | Percent of correct answers, % | Amount of correct part of speech tags | Percent of correct part of speech tags, % |
|---|---|---|---|---|---|---|---|
| иначе /else/ | иначе /else/ | иначе /else/ | | 8 | 80 | 8 | 80 |
| многообразие /variety/ | обширность /vastness/ | разнообразие /diversity/ | | 2 | 20 | 10 | 100 |
| несмотря /despite/ | несмотря /despite/ | взгляды /views/ | | 7 | 70 | 8 | 80 |
| правило /rule/ | правило /rule/ | чувство /sense/ | | 3 | 30 | 8 | 80 |
| рассматривают /consider/ | считают /think/ | определяют /define/ | | 1 | 10 | 10 | 100 |
| сталкиваются /encounter/ | работают /work/ | исследуют /investigate/ | | 5 | 50 | 10 | 100 |
| опыт /experience/ | опыт /experience/ | опыт /experience/ | | 9 | 90 | 10 | 100 |

This result can be explained by the fact that for the calculation of the surprisal measure one previous word was used as the context, and the informant, filling in the blanks, was guided by the context of greater length. The fact that the context is used more widely is confirmed by the fact that the words of this group are included in the selected chunks formed on the basis of the Dice metric with the broader context (five words from the left side and two words from the right side).

For example, in the sentence "She went on deck and saw a new, unfamiliar Australia" the word "saw" was omitted. According to the results of the experiment, 100% of the informants correctly restored the word form in this case. The value of the surprisal metric for the missing word is 10.7. However, despite the high value of the surprisal metrics, when allocating chunks based on the Dice metric, the "went and saw" chain was selected. This example in particular and the whole group of these words in general confirm the need to use a broader context in the study of contextual predictability, which is closer to human perception of information.

It should also be noted that the words of this group (easily restored and with high surprisal value) in the fragments of fictional texts are more than twice as many as compared with the scientific ones.

In scientific texts, words that are cliches are almost unmistakably (in 95% of cases) restored (e.g., "in other words", "despite", "first, ..., second, ..." and others. But despite the low surprisal value (and therefore supposedly the best recoverability from the context), the terms and scientific vocabulary in fragments of scientific texts in 75% of cases are not restored by informants.

In general, the results confirm the effectiveness of the contextual predictability text model built during the computational experiment. However, some characteristics of human perception were not taken into account in the experiment (e.g., analysis of a wider context, certain knowledge and experience of a particular informant).

Our second experiment was similar to cloze test but the language model had to fill in the missing words instead of the informants. We trained two CBOW models (using word2vec tool) on fictional and scientific third-party corpora and automatically predicted missing words from their context. Results of this experiment for the two text collections are shown in Table 7.

**Table 7.** Missing word prediction task results.

| Text collection | Percent of correct* answers, % | Percent of correct part of speech tags, % |
|---|---|---|
| Fictional | 30 | 20 |
| Scientific | 0 | 10 |

Since cloze-test is a hard task for a language model, its answer is considered correct when the true missing word or its synonym is present in top-10 most probable words returned by the model. Results of the missing words prediction task are much worse than that of the informants, which is not surprising. At the same time, the three correct answers given by the language model refer to the situations when a word is actually a part of the collocation (e.g., "your" in "your excellency", "say" in "better say"), while other words, not predicted by the language model correctly, are less dependent on their context.

## 6 Conclusion

In this paper, we consider various metrics for calculating contextual predictability and construct language model using these metrics. Our data includes scientific and fictional texts, and we experiment with informants (cloze tests) and word embeddings language models (missing words prediction task).

Results of the experiments prove that the implementation of contextual predictability procedures depends on the genre and style characteristics of the text. Words with higher context predictability values of various metrics are easier restored by both human informants and language models than those with lower context predictability values.

**Acknowledgements.** The authors acknowledge the RSF for the research grant 18-18-00114.

## References

1. Yagunova, E.V.: Fundamentals of theoretical, computational and experimental linguistics, or Reflections on the place of the linguist in computational linguistics. In: Bolshakova, E.I.,

Klyshinsky, E.S., Lande, D.V., Noskov, A.A., Peskova, O.V., Yagunova, E.V.-M.: Automatic Processing of Texts in Natural Language and Computational Linguistics: Studies. Allowance. MIEM (2011). (in Russian)

2. Biemann, C., Remus, S., Hofmann, M.J.: Predicting word 'predictability' in cloze completion, electroencephalographic and eye movement data. Natural language processing and cognitive science. In: Bernadette, S., Wiesław, L., Rodolfo, D. (eds.) Libreria Editrice Cafoscarina, Venezia, pp. 83–95 (2015)

3. Miller, G.A.: The magical number seven, plus or minus two: some limits on our capacity for processing information. Psychol. Rev. **63**(2), 81–97 (1956)

4. Owens, M., O'Boyle, P., Mcmahon, J., Ming J., Smith F.: A comparison of human and statistical language model performance using missing-word tests. Lang. Speech **40**(4), 377–389 (1997)

5. Robinson, R.D.: The cloze procedure: a new tool for adult education. Adult Educ. Quart. **23**, 97–98 (1973)

6. Taylor, W.L.: Cloze procedure: a new tool for measuring readability. J. Quart. **30**, 415–433 (1953)

7. Oller Jr., J.W., Yii, G.K., Greenberg, L.A., Hurtado R.: The learning effect from textual coherence measured with cloze. In: Oller Jr., J.W., Jonz, J. (Eds.) Cloze and coherence, Cranbury, NJ, pp. 247–268 (1994)

8. Nusbaum, H.C., et al.: Why cloze procedure? In: Oller Jr., J.W., Jonz, J. (eds.) Cloze and Coherence, Cranbury, NJ, pp. 1–20 (1994)

9. Yagunova, E.V.: Study of the contextual predictability of text units using corpus resources. In: Proceedings of the International Conference "Corpus Linguistics – 2008". SPSU, SPb, pp. 396–403 (2008). (in Russian)

10. Yagunova, E.V., Pivovarova, L.M.: The nature of collocations in the Russian language. The experience of automatic extraction and classification on the material of news texts. In: Proceedings of STI, Series 2, no. 6 (2010). (in Russian)

11. Yagunova, E.V.: Variability of perception strategies of sounding text (experimental research based on Russian-language texts of various functional styles). SPSU – Perm (2008). (in Russian)

12. Yagunova E.V.: Investigation of the redundancy of Russian sounding text. In: Voeikov, M.D. (ed.): Redundancy in the Grammatical Structure of the Language. SPb, Science, p. 462 (2010). (in Russian)

13. Markov Models for Text Analysis. Purdue University, Department of Statistics (2009). http://www.stat.purdue.edu/~mdw/CSOI/MarkovLab.html. Accessed 15 Apr 2016

14. Khokhlova, M.V.: The study of lexical-semantic compatibility in Russian with the help of statistical methods (based on corpus text), St. Petersburg (2010). (in Russian)

15. Yagunova, E.V., Pivovarova, L.M.: Study of the structure of news text as a sequence of connected segments. In: Izd-vo Rsuh, M.: Computational Linguistics and Intellectual Technologies: Based on the Materials of the Annual International Conference "Dialogue", Bekasovo, 25–29 May 2011, vol. 10, no. 17 (2011). (in Russian)

16. Yagunova, E.V.: Study of the contextual predictability of text units using corpus resources. In: Proceedings of the International Conference "Corpus Linguistics – 2008". SPb, SPSU, pp. 396–403 (2008). (in Russian)

17. McWhorter, J.: The world's simplest grammars are creole grammars. Linguist. Typol. **5**(2–3), 125–166 (2001)

18. Kusters, W.: Linguistic complexity: the influence of social change on verbal inflection, Utrecht (2003)

19. Dahl, Ö.: The growth and maintenance of linguistic complexity, Amsterdam (2004)

20. Trudgill, P.: Sociolinguistic typology: social determinants of linguistic complexity, Oxford (2011)

21. Sun, Y., Deng, H., Han, J.: Probabilistic models for text mining. In: Aggarwal, C., Zhai, C. (eds.) Mining Text Data, pp. 259–295. Springer, Boston (2012). https://doi.org/10.1007/978-1-4614-3223-4_8
22. Berdichevsky, A.: Language complexity (language complexity). Questions of linguistics, no. 5 (2012). (in Russian)
23. Piotrovsky, R.G.: Linguistic Automaton (in research and continuous learning), SPb (1999). (in Russian)
24. Piotrovsky R.G.: Informational measurements of language (1968). (in Russian)
25. MacKay, D.: Information Theory, Inference, and Learning Algorithms. Cambridge University Press, Cambridge (2003)
26. Daudaravicius, V.: Automatic identification of lexical units. In: Computational Linguistics and Intelligent text processing CICling (2009)
27. Decision Trees: Entropy, Information Gain, Gain Ratio. Marina Santini. http://www.slideshare.net/marinasantini1/lecture-4-decision-trees-2-entropy-information-gain-gain-ratio-55241087?related=1. 18 May 2016
28. Myslín, M., Roger L.: Codeswitching and predictability of meaning in discourse. Language **91**(4), 871–905 (2015)
29. Babaylova, A.E.: Text as a product, means and object of communication in teaching a non-native language. Saratov University (1987). (in Russian)
30. Miller J.A.: The magic number is seven plus or minus two. In: Gippenreiter, Y.B., Romanov, V.Y. (eds.) On Some Limits of Our Ability to Process Information, CheRo, Moscow, pp. 564–582 (1998). (in Russian)

# Haralick Features from Wavelet Domain in Recognizing Fingerprints Using Neural Network

K. S. Jeyalakshmi[1] and T. Kathirvalavakumar[2(✉)]

[1] Department of Computer Science, N.M.S.S.Vellaichamy Nadar College,
Madurai 625019, India
jeyal2007@gmail.com
[2] Research Centre in Computer Science, V.H.N. Senthikumara Nadar College,
Virudhunagar 626001, India
kathirvalavakumar@yahoo.com

**Abstract.** Towards digitalization in the world, fingerprints are captured for personal identification and most of the recognitions of these captured fingerprints are having wide range of preprocessing tasks such as segmentation for extracting region of interest, enhancement for better visualization of minutiae features, orientation field estimation for fingerprint classification and minutiae matching. It is not worthy if recognition spends more time in prepocessing tasks while handling voluminous fingerprint database. Hence this work aims to recognize fingerprint without preprocessing tasks but with better accuracy and less time. In this method, wavelet co-occurrence features are extracted from approximation image of fingerprint image obtained from wavelet decomposition process and is recognized using feedforward neural network. The proposed method uses four wavelet co-occurrence features namely contrast, correlation, energy and homogeneity for recognition. The experimental results of FVC 2000, 2002 and 2004 databases show that better accuracy with less time is achieved.

**Keywords:** Fingerprint recognition · Wavelet decomposition · Wavelet co-occurrence matrix · Neural network

## 1 Introduction

In this digital era, fingerprint the one of the biometrics is widely accepted for personal identification because of their uniqueness nature, ease of use and affordability. Fingerprint recognition is an automated process of confirming the identity of individual person based on matching. In any Automatic Fingerprint Identification System (AFIS) there are voluminous data in the fingerprint database but it needs a speedy recognition process. In the literatures more number of fingerprint recognition systems are proposed by many authors. Each fingerprint recognition system is competing the other by its accuracy, speed, novelty, methodology, memory, and complexity.

© Springer Nature Switzerland AG 2020
B. R. Purushothama et al. (Eds.): MIKE 2019, LNAI 11987, pp. 120–130, 2020.
https://doi.org/10.1007/978-3-030-66187-8_12

JuchengYang et al. have proposed fingerprint matching algorithm with the preprocessing tasks namely removal of background and noise, by image enhancement through Discrete Wavelet Transform, and reference point detection. They have constructed seven invariant moment features for learning vector quantization neural network [1]. WangYuan et al. have proposed fingerprint recognition by minutiae matching algorithm with image enhancement as preprocessing [2]. Montesanto et al. have presented a fingerprint recognition system by applying fuzzy operator on the extracted minutiae. They have used filtering process as preprocessing task to remove fingerprint distortion [3]. Abrishambaf et al. have proposed a fully cellular neural network based fingerprint recognition system with contrast stretc.hing, Gabor filtering and binarization as preprocessing and ridge line thinning for extracting feature points as postprocessing [4]. Jucheng et al. have presented a fingerprint matching system with preprocessing and with the classifiers extreme learning machine (ELM) and regularized ELM [5]. Kumar et al. have presented a fingerprint matching system using feedforward neural network. Local directional patterns are used·in training the network. They have used normalization and segmentation as preprocessing tasks in the system [6]. Bahaa-Eldin et al. have proposed fingerprint matching algorithm with feature vector distance matching and they have performed thinning as postprocessing task [7]. Luo et al. have proposed [8] fingerprint verification system using the modified version of minutiae matching algorithm of A.K.Jain et al. [9]. Qader et al. [10] have used Zernike moment invariant as shape descriptor in their fingerprint recognition. Liu et al. have proposed a fingerprint recognition system using pore matching by adopting coarse-to-fine strategy where a tangent distance and sparse representation based pores matching are used in coarse level and a weighted RANdom SAmple Consensus(RANSAC) algorithm is used in fine level [11]. Win et al. have proposed a method for recognizing low quality fingerprint image using textural features [12]. They have used orientation image estimation and Gabor filtering as preprocessing. Pornpanomchai et al. have proposed a fingerprint recognition system using Euclidean distance with the average access time of 19.68 s and they have followed sharpness adjustment process and core point detection in the preprocessing [13]. In general, time consumption in the preprocessing task slow down the fingerprint recognition process while handling voluminous fingerprint database. Hence, efficient recognition without preprocessing is a need of the day.

Gray Level Co-occurrence Matrix (GLCM) features extracted in spatial domain are frequently used in the field of image texture analysis [14]. Ribaric et al. have proposed novel palmprint recognition using local Haralick features [15]. Jafarpour et al. have proposed brain MRI classification using GLCM after extracting features by principle components analysis and reduction by linear discriminant analysis [16]. Wahid et al. have proposed an efficient low cost medical image reconstruction system with Daubechies wavelet and minimizing the approximation error by algebraic integer quantization [17].

In the proposed method, fingerprint image is transformed into wavelet domain with Daubechies wavelet. Wavelet co-occurrences features like contrast, correlation, energy, and homogeneity are calculated from the wavelet co-occurrence matrices and fingerprints are recognized using feedforward neural network with Levenberg-Marquardt training algorithm. This paper is organized as follows: Sect. 2 elaborates feature extraction. The feedforward neural network is briefly explained in Sect. 3. Section 4 presents the training algorithm of the proposed method and Sect. 5 discusses experimental results.

## 2    Feature Extraction

### 2.1    Wavelet Transform

Wavelet transforms are good for extracting textural information [18]. Fingerprint image is decomposed into three higher frequency coefficients (Details components LH,HL and HH) and lower frequency coefficients (Approximation component LL), in each level. High frequency coefficients are ignored as they are noise signals. Generally, wavelet transform is used in signal processing for compression, de-noising and feature extraction [19]. Different mother wavelets are used for wavelet transformation [20]. One among them is Daubechies wavelet which yield better results in signal processing [21]. This is most frequently used for mother wavelet as Daubechies' orthonormal basis has compact support interval. In the proposed method, single level decomposition is applied on the fingerprint image using Daubechies wavelet (db1). The obtained approximation image is used for further processing.

### 2.2    GLCM

One dimensional histogram is the simplest statistic measure but it is not a good texture measure [22]. Two-dimensional histogram introduced by Abutaleb et al. [23] consumes more time. GLCM overcomes the computational cost problem occur in two-dimensional histogram and also it overcomes the weakness of one dimensional histogram in the texture analysis. In spatial domain, statistical measures are computed for the conditional joint probabilities matrix called gray level co-occurrence matrix to generate second order texture features named Haralick features. In general, these statistics identify some characteristics of the structural texture of the input image by means of the arrangement of probabilities within a GLCM indexed on (i, j). The spatial window of interest for computing GLCM has two parameters: inter-pixel distance (d) and orientation ($\theta$) [24]. The spatial window of interest is shown in Fig. 1. The GLCM features are mostly used in texture based image analysis applications [14–16,25].

### 2.3    Wavelet Co-occurrence Features

GLCM becomes wavelet co-occurrence matrix in wavelet domain. Wavelet co-occurrence matrices are computed at a distance d = 1 and orientation ($\theta$) 0°, 45°, 90° and 135° for the approximation image obtained through wavelet transform. The computed wavelet co-occurrence matrices are the second order statistical

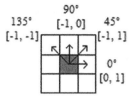

**Fig. 1.** Spatial window of interest

representation of the input fingerprint image. Among 16 features four wavelet co-occurrence features namely contrast, correlation, energy and homogeneity are selected for recognition and these can be estimated from the wavelets co-occurrence matrix (W) as follows:

$$Contrast = \sum_{i,j} |i - j|^2 . W_{i,j} \tag{1}$$

$$Correlation = \sum_{i,j} \frac{(i - \mu i)(j - \mu j) W_{i,j}}{\sigma_i \sigma_j} \tag{2}$$

$$Energy = \sum_{i,j} W_{i,j}^2 \tag{3}$$

$$Homogeneity = \sum_{i,j} \frac{W_{i,j}}{1 + |i - j|} \tag{4}$$

where mean $(\mu)$ and variance$(\sigma)$ are first order statistics.

## 3    Feedforward Neural Network

Feedforward neural network (FNN) is a fully interconnected supervised neural network. In this network, neurons in input layer are interconnected with adjacent hidden layer and neurons in hidden layer are interconnected with neurons in output layer with weights. The architecture of FNN is shown in Fig. 2. Levenberg-Marquardt algorithm is used to train the FNN. The Levenberg-Marquardt algorithm is a numerical optimization algorithm that combines the advantages of both the gradient descent method and the Gauss-Newton method [26].

## 4    Training Algorithm

1. For each fingerprint image, do the following steps.
   (a) **Wavelet transform** - Decompose the input fingerprint image one level with Daubechies wavelet (db1).

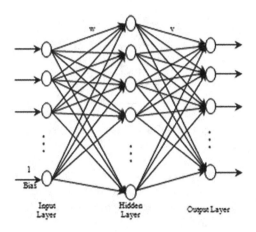

**Fig. 2.** FNN architecture

(b) **Feature extraction**

    i For the approximation image, calculate four wavelet co-occurrence matrices for four directions by varying parameters of spatial window of interest as $[0, 1]$, $[-1, 1]$, $[-1, 0]$ and $[-1, -1]$.

    ii From each wavelet co-occurrence matrix, extract four wavelet co-occurrence features named contrast, correlation, energy and homogeneity using Eqs. (1), (2), (3) and (4) respectively resulting 16 wavelet co-occurrence features.

    iii Generate pattern of size $1 \times 17$ by arranging first 4 contrast features, followed by 4 correlation features, 4 energy features, 4 homogeneity features and with the bias value 1.

2. **FNN Training** - Train the network for generated features using Levenberg-Marquardt algorithm.

3. Test the test patterns on the trained FNN.

## 5    Results and Discussion

The experiment is carried out on the public fingerprint databases namely set B of FVC 2000 [30], FVC 2002 [31], and FVC 2004 [32] to show the competency of the proposed method in terms of speed and accuracy. Every database contains 4 sub databases. Each sub database has 80 fingerprint images of 8 different impressions of 10 persons which lead to totally 960 fingerprint images. Among 80 patterns of each sub database 66 training and 14 testing patterns are selected randomly. The sensor type, image size, number of images and resolution of each database are depicted in Table 1. The proposed method is implemented using MATLAB 2013a on Intel(R) Xeon(R) CPU E5-16070 @ 3.00 GHz.

The input fingerprint image is transformed into wavelet domain with Daubechies wavelet (db1). Four wavelet co-occurrence matrices are obtained

**Table 1.** Characteristics of Fingerprint databases

| Database | Sensor type | Image size | No. of images | Resolution |
|---|---|---|---|---|
| FVC 2000 DB1_B | Low-cost Optical Sensor | $300 \times 300$ | 80 | 500 dpi |
| FVC 2000 DB2_B | Low-cost Capacitive Sensor | $256 \times 364$ | 80 | 500 dpi |
| FVC 2000 DB3_B | Optical Sensor | $448 \times 478$ | 80 | 500 dpi |
| FVC 2000 DB4_B | Synthetic Generator | $240 \times 320$ | 80 | About 500 dpi |
| FVC 2002 DB1_B | Optical | $388 \times 374$ | 80 | 500 dpi |
| FVC 2002 DB2_B | Optical | $296 \times 560$ | 80 | 569 dpi |
| FVC 2002 DB3_B | Capacitive Sensor | $300 \times 300$ | 80 | 500 dpi |
| FVC 2002 DB4_B | Synthetic | $288 \times 374$ | 80 | 500 dpi |
| FVC 2004 DB1_B | Optical Sensor | $640 \times 480$ | 80 | 500 dpi |
| FVC 2004 DB2_B | Optical Sensor | $328 \times 364$ | 80 | 500 dpi |
| FVC 2004 DB3_B | Thermal Sweeping Sensor | $300 \times 480$ | 80 | 500 dpi |
| FVC 2004 DB4_B | Synthetic | $288 \times 384$ | 80 | About 500 dpi |

**Table 2.** Neurons in different layers, training epoch, training time and accuracy

| Database | InpN | HN | OutN | Epoch | Time (s) | Accuracy(%) |
|---|---|---|---|---|---|---|
| FVC 2000 DB1_B | 17 | 15 | 10 | 50 | 11.379 | 97.9 |
| FVC 2000 DB2_B | 17 | 20 | 10 | 129 | 16.083 | 97.4 |
| FVC 2000 DB3_B | 17 | 15 | 10 | 14 | 0.58 | 100 |
| FVC 2000 DB4_B | 17 | 15 | 10 | 71 | 2.913 | 96.1 |
| FVC 2002 DB1_B | 17 | 15 | 10 | 28 | 1.139 | 97.5 |
| FVC 2002 DB2_B | 17 | 15 | 10 | 18 | 0.749 | 98.8 |
| FVC 2002 DB3_B | 17 | 15 | 10 | 6 | 0.453 | 100 |
| FVC 2002 DB4_B | 17 | 15 | 10 | 33 | 3.545 | 98.8 |
| FVC 2004 DB1_B | 17 | 15 | 10 | 29 | 1.248 | 92.5 |
| FVC 2004 DB2_B | 17 | 15 | 10 | 200 | 18.564 | 92.7 |
| FVC 2004 DB3_B | 17 | 15 | 10 | 3 | 0.25 | 100 |
| FVC 2004 DB4_B | 17 | 17 | 10 | 25 | 1.037 | 96.3 |

for four different orientations $0°$, $45°$, $90°$ and $135°$ corresponding to the spatial window of interest $[0, 1]$, $[-1, 1]$, $[-1, 0]$ and $[-1, -1]$ of the approximation image obtained through wavelet transform. The required wavelet co-occurrence features contrast, correlation, energy, and homogeneity are calculated from each wavelets co-occurrence matrix which generate the feature vector of size $1 \times 17$ including a bias value 1. Generating a single feature vector consumes $0.0386$ s.

FNN is configured with 17 neurons in input layer, 15 neurons in hidden layer and 10 neurons in the output layer for all sub databases except FVC 2000 DB2_B and FVC 2004 DB4_B. 20 hidden neurons are considered for FVC 2000 DB2_B and 17 neurons for FVC 2004 DB4_B. The number of hidden neurons

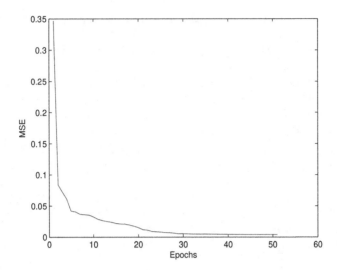

**Fig. 3.** Learning curve

**Table 3.** Comparison of performance with the method [8]

| Database | Method [8] | Proposed method |
|----------|-----------|-----------------|
| FVC 2000 | 91.8% | 97.8% |
| FVC 2002 | 91.5% | 98.75% |
| FVC 2004 | 91% | 95.4% |

**Table 4.** Comparison of performance with the method [11] and [7]

| Database | Method [11] | Method [7] | Proposed method |
|----------|------------|-----------|-----------------|
| FVC 2000 | 92% | 98% | 97.8% |

**Table 5.** Comparison of performance with the method [10]

| Database | Method [10] | Proposed method |
|----------|------------|-----------------|
| FVC 2002 | 92.89% | 98.75% |

is selected by trial and error. The network training is terminated when mean squared error reaches 0.00001. The network architecture, average epoch, training period and recognition accuracy of each sub database are shown in Table 2. The learning curve depicted in Fig. 3 exhibits that the convergence is guaranteed during training. Recognition accuracy of the proposed method is compared with [7,8,11] and [10] and are shown in Table 3, Table 4 and Table 5. A receiver operating characteristic (ROC) curve is a plot of FMR against (1 - FNMR) and is shown Fig. 4.

**Table 6.** Comparison of processing time

|  | Processing time in seconds | | |
|---|---|---|---|
|  | Method [28] | Method [29] | **Proposed method** |
| Orientation field estimation | 0.51 | - | - |
| Segmentation | 2.25 | - | - |
| Smoothing | 3.9 | - | - |
| Thinning | 2.45 | - | - |
| Feature extraction | 0.33 | 0.858 | **0.0386** |
| Matching | 0.148 | 5.83 | - |
| Neural network training & testing | - | - | **1.4715** |
| Verification | - | - | **0.022201** |
| **Total time** | 9.588 | 6.688 | **1.532301** |

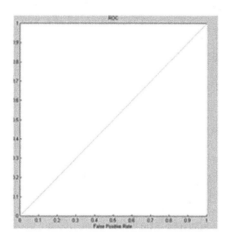

**Fig. 4.** Receiver operating characteristic

The performance of a supervised learning algorithm can be visualized using confusion matrix by means of the number of false positives, false negatives, true positives, and true negatives [27] and is a square matrix with 'n' number of actual classes and 'n' number of output classes. The confusion matrix shown in Fig. 5 is the performance of the proposed algorithm applied on FVC 2000 DB3_B database. The proposed method takes only 0.0386s for feature extraction than the methods [28] and [29] and is shown in Table 6.

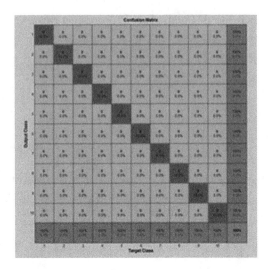

**Fig. 5.** Confusion matrix of FVC 2000 DB3_B

## 6    Conclusion

Fingerprint is recognized using only four different wavelet co-occurrence features namely contrast, correlation, energy and homogeneity. These features are extracted from four different wavelet co-occurrence matrices. Neural network is used to recognize the fingerprint with four different wavelet co-occurrence features. The experimental results show that the proposed method recognizes the fingerprint with good accuracy even without preprocessing but with minimum wavelet co-occurrence features. The main aim of the proposed method is fast effective fingerprint recognition without using preprocessing and is achieved in this work.

## References

1. Yang, J., Shin, J., Min, B., Park, J., Park, D.: Fingerprint matching using invariant moment fingercode and learning vector quantization neural network. In: 2006 International Conference on Computational Intelligence and Security, vol. 1, pp. 735–738. IEEE (November 2006)
2. Yuan, W., Lixiu, Y., Fuqiang, Z.: A real time fingerprint recognition system based on novel fingerprint matching strategy. In: 2007 8th International Conference on Electronic Measurement and Instruments, pp. 1–81. IEEE (August 2007)
3. Montesanto, A., Baldassarri, P., Vallesi, G., Tascini, G.: Fingerprints recognition using minutiae extraction: a fuzzy approach. In: 14th International Conference on Image Analysis and Processing (ICIAP 2007), pp. 229–234. IEEE (September 2007)
4. Abrishambaf, R., Demirel, H., Kale, I.: Establishing the finite word-length parameters for a CNN based fingerprint recognition system. In: Proceedings of the 5th International Symposium on Electrical and Computer Systems (EECS 2008) (2008)

5. Yang, J., Xie, S., Yoon, S., Park, D., Fang, Z., Yang, S.: Fingerprint matching based on extreme learning machine. Neural Comput. Appl. **22**(3–4), 435–445 (2013)
6. Kumar, R., Chandra, P., Hanmandlu, M.: Local directional pattern (LDP) based fingerprint matching using SLFNN. In: 2013 IEEE Second International Conference on Image Information Processing (ICIIP-2013), pp. 493–498. IEEE (December 2013)
7. Bahaa-Eldin, A.M.: A medium resolution fingerprint matching system. Ain Shams Eng. J. **4**(3), 393–408 (2013)
8. Luo, X., Tian, J., Wu, Y.: A minutiae matching algorithm in fingerprint verification. In: Proceedings 15th International Conference on Pattern Recognition, ICPR-2000, vol. 4, pp. 833–836. IEEE (2000)
9. Jain, A.K., Hong, L.: BR On-line fingerprint verification. IEEE Trans. Pattern Anal. Mach. Intell. **19**(4), 302–314 (1997)
10. Qader, H.A., Ramli, A.R., Al-Haddad, S.A.R.: Fingerprint recognition using zernike moments. Int. Arab J. Inf. Technol. **4**(4), 372–376 (2007)
11. Liu, F., Zhao, Q., Zhang, D.: A novel hierarchical fingerprint matching approach. Pattern Recogn. **44**(8), 1604–1613 (2011)
12. Win, Z.M., Sein, M.M.: Texture feature based fingerprint recognition for low quality images. In: 2011 International Symposium on Micro-NanoMechatronics and Human Science, pp. 333–338. IEEE (November 2011)
13. Pornpanomchai, C., Phaisitkulwiwat, A.: Fingerprint recognition by euclidean distance. In: 2010 Second International Conference on Computer and Network Technology, pp. 437–441. IEEE (April 2010)
14. Hazra, D.: Texture recognition with combined GLCM, wavelet and rotated wavelet features. Int. J. Comput. Electr. Eng. **3**(1), 146 (2011)
15. Ribaric, S., Lopar, M.: Palmprint recognition based on local Haralick features. In: 2012 16th IEEE Mediterranean Electrotechnical Conference, pp. 657–660. IEEE (March 2012)
16. Jafarpour, S., Sedghi, Z., Amirani, M.C.: A robust brain MRI classification with GLCM features. Int. J. Comput. Appl. **37**(12), 1–5 (2012)
17. Wahid, K.: Low complexity implementation of daubechies wavelets for medical imaging applications. In: Discrete Wavelet Transforms-Algorithms and Applications IntechOpen (2011)
18. Niwas, S.I., Palanisamy, P., Sujathan, K., Bengtsson, E.: Analysis of nuclei textures of fine needle aspirated cytology images for breast cancer diagnosis using Complex Daubechies wavelets. Sig. Proc. **93**(10), 2828–2837 (2013)
19. Chan, K.P., Fu, A.W.C.: Efficient time series matching by wavelets. In: Proceedings 15th International Conference on Data Engineering (Cat. No. 99CB36337), pp. 126–133. IEEE (March 1999)
20. Daubechies, I.: Ten lectures on wavelets, vol. 61. Siam (1992)
21. Rafiee, J., Rafiee, M.A., Prause, N., Schoen, M.P.: Wavelet basis functions in biomedical signal processing. Expert Syst. Appl. **38**(5), 6190–6201 (2011)
22. Mirzapour, F., Ghassemian, H.: Using GLCM and Gabor filters for classification of PAN images. In: 2013 21st Iranian Conference on Electrical Engineering (ICEE), pp. 1–6. IEEE (May 2013)
23. Abutaleb, A.S.: Automatic thresholding of gray-level pictures using two-dimensional entropy. Comput. Vision, Graphics Image Proc. **47**(1), 22–32 (1989)
24. Haralick, R.M.: Statistical and structural approaches to texture. Proc. IEEE **67**(5), 786–804 (1979)

25. Zaim, A., Sawalha, A., Quweider, M., Iglesias, J., Tang, R.: A new method for iris recognition using gray-level coccurence matrix. In: 2006 IEEE International Conference on Electro/Information Technology, pp. 350–353. IEEE (May 2006)
26. Marquardt, D.W.: An algorithm for least-squares estimation of nonlinear parameters. J. Soc. Ind. Appl. Math. **11**(2), 431–441 (1963)
27. Sarkar, S., Mukherjee, K., Jin, X., Singh, D.S., Ray, A.: Optimization of symbolic feature extraction for pattern classification. Sig. Proc. **92**(3), 625–635 (2012)
28. Maio, D., Maltoni, D.: Direct gray-scale minutiae detection in fingerprints. IEEE Trans. Pattern Anal. Mach. Intell. **19**(1), 27–40 (1997)
29. Awad, A.I., Baba, K.: Evaluation of a fingerprint identification algorithm with SIFT features. In: 2012 IIAI International Conference on Advanced Applied Informatics, pp. 129–132. IEEE (September 2012)
30. FVC2000 Set B Databases. http://bias.csr.unibo.it/fvc2000/download.asp
31. FVC2002 Set B Databases. http://bias.csr.unibo.it/fvc2002/download.asp
32. FVC2004 Set B Databases. http://bias.csr.unibo.it/fvc2004/download.asp

# Circular Local Directional Pattern for Texture Analysis

Abuobayda M. M. Shabat and Jules R. Tapamo(✉)📷

University of KwaZulu-Natal, Durban 4041, South Africa
abshabat@gmail.com, tapamoj@ukzn.ac.za

**Abstract.** This paper presents a novel texture feature extraction method, Circular Local Directional Pattern (CILDP), that is inspired by Local Binary pattern (LBP) and Local Directional Pattern (LDP). This method relies on circular shape to compute the directional edge responses based on Kirsch Masks using different radiuses. The performance of the proposed method is evaluated using five classifiers on textures from the Kylberg dataset. Results achieved establish that the proposed method consistently outperforms LBP and LDP when different radiuses are considered.

**Keywords:** Texture analysis · Local binary patterns · Local Directional Pattern · Classification · Kirsch Masks · Circular Local Directional Pattern

## 1 Introduction

Texture analysis is an important technique employed in many image analysis and computer vision applications. Some examples are object classification, face identification, pattern analysis, image segmentation. Although, widely used in computer vision and the many efforts to define it in universal terms, texture lacks a precise definition. One of the most accepted definition is that it is a function of the spatial variation in pixel intensities [1]. Many features methods have been proposed in the literature, such as grey-level co-occurrence matrix (GLCM) [2], local binary pattern [3], scale-invariant feature transform (SIFT) [4], speeded up robust features (SURF) [5], local directional pattern (LDP) [6], directional local binary pattern (DLBP) [7] and so much more. Some of these methods have been applied to surface characterization and texture analysis applications [8–10]. Among all the features methods, local binary pattern is one of the most recent and popular. It has been employed in several applications, including facial recognition [11], texture analysis [9] and remote sensing [12]. Instigated by the power and the simplicity of LBP, many researchers have proposed different improvements of LBP, such as dominant local binary pattern (DLBP) [13], complete local binary pattern (CLBP) [14] and center-symmetric local binary pattern (CSLBP) [15].

Researchers in recent years have started focusing on directional information instead of intensity information. The reason for that is because the directional

© Springer Nature Switzerland AG 2020
B. R. Purushothama et al. (Eds.): MIKE 2019, LNAI 11987, pp. 131–142, 2020.
https://doi.org/10.1007/978-3-030-66187-8_13

encoded is more stable than the pixel intensity [16]. Jabid *et al.* [6] presented a low-level feature, Local Directional Pattern, which uses the edge responses of eight different directions about each pixel. Luo *et al.* [16] presented the local line directional pattern (LLDP) using the line direction response instead of the gradient response. Shabat and Tapamo [7] presented the directional local binary pattern (DLBP) method using the center pixel as a threshold for the eight directional response values of the neighborhood.

Inspired by LBP and LDP, in this paper we propose a new LDP-structure descriptor, the Circular Local Directional Pattern.

## 2   Features Methods for Texture Analysis

The most important process in texture analysis is features extraction. Local Binary Pattern (LBP), Local Directional Pattern (LDP) and the proposed Circular Local Directional Pattern (CILDP) are presented below.

### 2.1   Local Binary Pattern

Local Binary Pattern changes the value of each pixel in the image. This modification is based on the relationship of each pixel in its 8-neighborhood. For each pixel $p$, LBP operator makes its gray value $g(p)$ a threshold, and for each neighbor $(n_i(p))$ (for $i = 0, 1, \ldots, 7$), if its gray value is greater than $g(p)$ then set gray value corresponding binary LBP bit code to 1 binary bit, otherwise, set it to 0. At the end convert the binary code obtain into decimal. An example is shown in Fig. 1. When LBP codes are produced for all pixels of an image, an histogram of these codes is generated and can be used as texture feature.

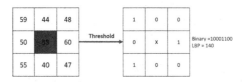

**Fig. 1.** LBP example

### 2.2   Local Directional Pattern

The LDP operator calculates an eight-bit binary code by comparing the different directional edge response values in the 8-neighborhood of each pixel. Given a pixel (x,y) in an image $I$, the 8-directional edge response vector, $(m_0, \cdots, m_7)$, is computed as shown in Eq. 1, by applying Kirsch masks in eight different rotations $M_0, \ldots, M_7$ shown in Fig. 2.

$$m_n = \sum_{l=-1}^{1} \sum_{k=-1}^{1} I(x+l, y+k) \times M_i(l,k) \qquad n = 0, 1, \ldots, 7 \qquad (1)$$

$$\begin{bmatrix} -3 & -3 & 5 \\ -3 & 0 & 5 \\ -3 & -3 & 5 \end{bmatrix} \quad \begin{bmatrix} -3 & 5 & 5 \\ -3 & 0 & 5 \\ -3 & -3 & -3 \end{bmatrix} \quad \begin{bmatrix} 5 & 5 & 5 \\ -3 & 0 & -3 \\ -3 & -3 & -3 \end{bmatrix} \quad \begin{bmatrix} 5 & 5 & -3 \\ 5 & 0 & -3 \\ -3 & -3 & -3 \end{bmatrix}$$

East $M_0$    North East $M_1$    North $M_2$    North West $M_3$

$$\begin{bmatrix} 5 & -3 & -3 \\ 5 & 0 & -3 \\ 5 & -3 & -3 \end{bmatrix} \quad \begin{bmatrix} -3 & -3 & -3 \\ 5 & 0 & -3 \\ 5 & 5 & -3 \end{bmatrix} \quad \begin{bmatrix} -3 & -3 & -3 \\ -3 & 0 & -3 \\ 5 & 5 & 5 \end{bmatrix} \quad \begin{bmatrix} -3 & -3 & -3 \\ -3 & 0 & 5 \\ -3 & 5 & 5 \end{bmatrix}$$

West $M_4$    South West $M_5$    South $M_6$    South East $M_7$

**Fig. 2.** Kirsch masks

Positions of the $k$ most significant edge responses are chosen to generate the binary LDP code. Hence, a 8-bit binary code is generated by setting to 1 the positions corresponding to the top $k^{th}$ edge responses (in absolute values), and the remaining $(8 - k)$ positions are set to 0. The LDP code of the given point is derived using the following formula

$$LDP_{x,y}(m_0, m_1, \ldots, m_7) = \sum_{n=0}^{7} s(m_n - m_k) \times 2^n \qquad (2)$$

where $m_k$ is the most prominent directions and $s(x)$ is define as

$$s(x) = \begin{cases} 1 & \text{if } x \geq 0 \\ 0 & \text{otherwise} \end{cases}$$

An example is shown in Fig. 3.

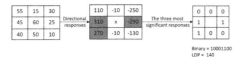

**Fig. 3.** Example of LDP code calculation

## 2.3    Circular Local Directional Pattern

In contrast to the regular LDP, which uses eight pixels in $(3 \times 3)$ window, CILDP uses the circle shape to allocate a set of points using different radius (1, 2, 3) as shown in Fig. 4. This leads to better analysis, specially with textures with different scales. However, it is limited to eight pixels because the Kirsch mask applies to eight values only.

Consider an image $I$ and let $p_c$ be an arbitrary pixel at the position $(x_c, y_c)$. Moreover, let $p_n$ denote the gray value of a sampling point in an evenly spaced circular neighborhood of 8 points and radius $R$ around $p_c$, as shown in Fig. 4. The circular neighborhood made of the 8 points $(x_0, y_0), (x_1, y_1), \ldots, (x_7, y_7)$ that are located using Eqs. 3 and 4, and the gray values $p_0, p_1, \ldots, p_7$ are found using Eq. 5

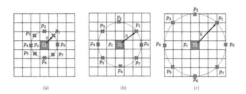

(a)                    (b)                    (c)

**Fig. 4.** The circular a.(8,1) b.(8,2) c.(8,3) neighborhoods. Bilinear interpolation is used to compute all the points that don't fall in the image matrix.

$$x_n = x_c + R cos(2\pi n/8) \tag{3}$$

$$y_n = y_c + R sin(2\pi n/8) \tag{4}$$

$$p_n = \begin{cases} I(x_n, y_n) & \text{if } (x_n, y_n) \text{ is in the image grid} \\ g_n & \text{otherwise} \end{cases} \quad n = 0, \ldots, 7 \tag{5}$$

where $g_n$ is computed using Eq. 16.

Given a point $p_c = (2, 2)$ and a radius $R = 2$. Table 1 shows the coordinates $(x_n, y_n)_{n=0,1,\ldots,7}$ of the 8 points in the circular neighborhood of the point $p_c$.

Bilinear interpolation is employed to compute the gray value $g_n$ (See Eq. 5) of each point that does not correspond to a pixel of the image grid. As shown in Table 1, points $(x_1, y_1), (x_3, y_3), (x_5, y_5)$ and $(x_7, y_7)$ don't correspond with any point in the image grid. If $(x, y)$ is such a point in an image $I$ as shown in Fig. 5, a bilinear interpolation method uses Eqs. 6–16 to compute the gray value $g_n$ of $(x, y)$.

$$ny_1 = \lfloor y \rfloor \tag{6}$$

$$ny_2 = \lceil y \rceil \tag{7}$$

**Table 1.** Computation of points on the circular neighborhood of radius $R = 2$

| $p_n$ | $x_n$ | $y_n$ |
|-------|-------|-------|
| $p_0$ | 4 | 2 |
| $p_1$ | 3.14 | 0.585 |
| $p_2$ | 2 | 0 |
| $p_3$ | 0.585 | 0.585 |
| $p_4$ | 0 | 2 |
| $p_5$ | 0.585 | 3.41 |
| $p_6$ | 2 | 4 |
| $p_7$ | 3.41 | 3.41 |

$$nx_1 = \lfloor x \rfloor \tag{8}$$

$$nx_2 = \lceil x \rceil \tag{9}$$

$$G_{11} = I(nx_1, ny_1) \tag{10}$$

$$G_{12} = I(nx_1, ny_2) \tag{11}$$

$$G_{21} = I(nx_2, ny_1) \tag{12}$$

$$G_{22} = I(nx_2, ny_2) \tag{13}$$

$$p_{x1} = \frac{nx_2 - x}{nx_2 - nx_1} G_{11} + \frac{x - nx_1}{nx_2 - nx_1} G_{21} \tag{14}$$

$$p_{x2} = \frac{nx_2 - x}{nx_2 - nx_1} G_{12} + \frac{x - nx_1}{nx_2 - x_1} G_{22} \tag{15}$$

$$g_n = \frac{ny_2 - y}{ny_2 - ny_1} p_{x1} + \frac{y - ny_1}{ny_2 - ny_1} p_{x2} \tag{16}$$

For each point $(x, y)$, after all the grey levels $p_0, p_1, \ldots, p_7$ of the 8 pixels in the circular neighborhood have been found, the eight directional edge responses vector $(m_0, m_1, \ldots, m_7)$ is computed with Eq. 17 by applying Kirsch masks $M_0, M_1, \ldots, M_7$.

$$
\begin{aligned}
m_n = {}& p_3 \times M_n(x - 1, y - 1) + p_2 \times M_n(x, y - 1) \\
& + p_1 \times M_n(x - 1, y + 1) + p_4 \times M_n(x - 1, y) \\
& + p_5 \times M_n(x - 1, y + 1) + p_6 \times M_n(x + 1, y) \\
& + p_7 \times M_n(x + 1, y + 1) + p_0 \times M_n(x, y + 1) \quad n = 0, 1, \ldots, 7
\end{aligned}
\tag{17}
$$

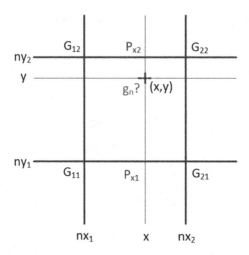

**Fig. 5.** Presentation of a computed point $(x, y)$ (see Eqs. 3 and 5) of a circular 8-neighborhood that is not in the image grid, but is surrounded by 4 points $(nx_1, ny_1), (nx_1, ny_2), (nx_2, ny_1)$, and $(nx_2, ny_2)$ of the image grid. The gray values $G_{11}, G_{12}, G_{21}$ and $G_{22}$ of these four points are used to compute the gray value $g_n$ of $(x, y)$.

In order to generate the CILDP code, the $k$ (here $k$ is chosen to be 3) most significant responses, of Kirsch masks application are identified. The decimal value, $CILDP_{x,y}$, of the CILDP binary code of the pixel $(x, y)$ is defined as

$$CILDP_{x,y}(m_0, m_1, \ldots, m_7) = \sum_{n=0}^{7} s(m_n - m_k) \times 2^n \qquad (18)$$

After transforming an input image $I$ of size $M \times N$ to an CILDP coded image, we can then extract a CILDP histogram of ${}^8C_3 = 56$ bins using the following formula

$$H_i = \sum_{x=0}^{M-1} \sum_{y=0}^{N-1} p(CILDP_{x,y}, C_i) \qquad (19)$$

where $C_i$ is the $i^{th}$ CILDP pattern value, $i = 1, \ldots, {}^8C_3$ and $p$ is defined as

$$p(x, a) = \begin{cases} 1 & \text{if } x = a \\ 0 & \text{otherwise} \end{cases}$$

For an image, $I$, and the number of significant responses considered equal to k $k$, the CILDP feature vector, $ldb_{k,I}$, is extracted from it is defined as

$$cildp_{k,I} = (H_1, H_2, \ldots, H_{8C_k}) \qquad (20)$$

Given an image $I$, Algorithm 1 summarises the extraction of CILDP features.

---

**Algorithm 1:** EXTRACTION OF CILDP FEATURES VECTOR FROM AN IMAGE

---

**Input:** Original image **I**
Number of significant bits **k**
Radius of the circular neighborhood **R**
**Output:** $H$ // CILDP Histogram feature vector of the image **I**
1 **convert** $I$ into gray level
2 **for** *all* $(x_c, y_c) \in$ **I do**
3 $\quad$ **compute** $(x_n, y_n)_{n=0,1,...,7}$ using Eqs. 3–4
4 $\quad$ **compute** $(p_n)_{n=0,1,...,7}$ using Eq. 5
5 $\quad$ **compute** $(m_n)_{n=0,1,...,7}$ using Eq. 17
6 $\quad$ **compute** $CILDP_{x_c,y_c}$ using Eq. 18
7 **for** $i \leftarrow 1$ *to* $8C_k$ **do**
8 $\quad$ **compute** $H_i$ using Eq. 19
9 $H \leftarrow (H_1, H_2, \ldots, H_{8C_k})$
10 **return** $H$

---

# 3 Experimental Results and Discussion

In this section, a description for the classification performance applied to Kylbreg Dataset using the proposed method CILDP, LDP and LBP are presented. The proposed methods are implemented using python framework, scikit-learn library and opencv.

## 3.1 Image Dataset

To evaluate the proposed method Kylberg image dataset is used. The Kylberg dataset consists of 4480 texture surfaces of 28 categories, with 160 samples per category as shown in Fig. 6. The images are homogeneous in terms of illumination and scale. The standard size of each sample is 576 pixels and it is available in different rotations $\theta \in [0, \frac{1}{6}\pi, \frac{2}{6}\pi, \ldots, \frac{11}{6}\pi]$.

## 3.2 Classification Evaluation

The effectiveness of these methods were evaluated using different classification measures, learning curve, accuracy, precision, recall, F-score and Cohen's kappa[18].

The learning curve is a very useful algorithm that evaluates the sanity of an algorithm. It plots the relation between the training set size and the performance. In a basic manner it shows the starting point where the classifiers begins to learn. Accuracy is the number of samples classified correctly, for example if the classifier accuracy is 50% it means that the classifier manage to classify correctly 50% of the dataset

$$Accuracy = \frac{\# \text{ of samples correctly classified}}{\# \text{ of samples}} \tag{21}$$

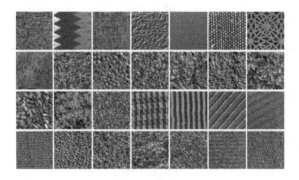

**Fig. 6.** Example of one sample of each category in the 28 classes in the Kylberg dataset

Precision is the ratio of a number of positive predictions to all the number of positive classes value predicted.

$$precision = \frac{TP}{TP + FP} \tag{22}$$

Sensitivity is the ratio of a number of positive predictions to all number of positive classes in test data.

$$recall = \frac{TP}{TP + FN} \tag{23}$$

Where $TP$ is the number of samples correctly classified as positive, $FP$ is the number of samples incorrectly classified as positive and $FN$ is the number of samples incorrectly classified as negative.

$F - score$ conveys the balance between the precision and the recall.

$$F - score = 2\frac{precision * recall}{precision + recall} \tag{24}$$

Cohen's kappa is a very good measure that can handle very well both multi-class and imbalanced class problem. It calculates the agreement between categorical data. If the value is less than or equal 0 it indicates that the classifier is useless. The following formula can be used to compute Cohen's kappa:

$$\kappa = \frac{Pr(a) - Pr(e)}{1 - Pr(e)} \tag{25}$$

where $Pr(a)$ and $Pr(e)$ are actual observed agreement and chance agreement respectively. Table 2 shows the interpretation of Kappa value.

Table 2. The interpretation of Kappa

| Interpretation | Conditions on $\kappa$ |
| --- | --- |
| Poor agreement | $\kappa \leq 0.20$ |
| Fair agreement | $0.20 < \kappa \leq 0.40$ |
| Moderate agreement | $0.40 < \kappa \leq 0.60$ |
| Good agreement | $0.60 < \kappa \leq 0.80$ |
| Very good agreement | $0.80 < \kappa \leq 1.00$ |

The dataset is split into two datasets 80% as a training set and 20% test set using 10-fold cross validations. Each classifier is trained using different parameters as shown in Table 3.

Table 3. Classifiers parameters

| Classifiers | Parameters |
| --- | --- |
| SVM | Polynomial linear kernel |
| | Configuration parameter $c = 0.025$ |
| k-NN | $k = 5$ |
| DT | Entropy |
| | The minimum number of split is 10 |
| RF | The number of the trees is 10 |
| | The maximum depth of the tree is 5 |
| Perceptron | The number of passes over the training data $= 100$ |
| | Constant eta $= 0.1$ |

### 3.3   Results Discussion

The performance of the proposed CILDP, LBP and LDP are tested in texture classification problem using Kylberg dataset [17]. In this paper, five classifiers have been applied, namely K-Nearest Neighbours, Support Vector Machine, Decision Tree, Random Forest and Perceptron. Table 4 shows the performance rates of CILDP, LDP and LBP using five different classifiers on Kylberg dataset. Overall, it can be seen that the CILDP in various distances performs equally or better compared to other methods. Figure 7 shows the learning curve for the proposed method CILDP compared to LDP using SVM as a classifier. Learning curve describes the relationship between the performance and the experience, where the performance is measured by the accuracy and the experience is the size of the training dataset or the number of iterations (cross validation) used to enhance the parameter of a classifier. In each graph there are two lines, the average square error on training set and the average square error on cross validation set. It is noticed that the performance rises when the training samples are between 250 to 750. Above 1500 the classifier starts gaining less knowledge and doesn't improve much. CILDP method in different distances did very well compared to LDP.

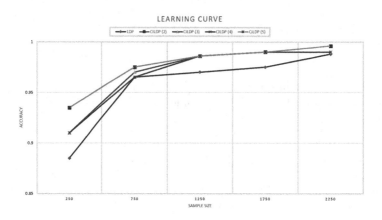

**Fig. 7.** The learning curve of LDP and CILDP

CILDP has the highest performance at 99% using SVM. CILDP has an improved performance ranging from 1% to 24% in all the classifiers as shown in Table 4. For example, CILDP performance using Perceptron classifier was 87%, while LDP performance was 74% and LBP 63%. This shows a performance improvement of 11% and 24%, respectively, compared to LDP and LBP. Table 4 illustrates that the proposed method CILDP either matches or outperforms LDP and LBP.

Table 5 shows the performance of SVM in which 80% is used as training dataset and the remaining 20% is used as test dataset.

In Table 5 different classifications evaluation are used to measure the comparative performances of CILDP and LDP. A proportion of 80% the dataset was uses as training dataset and the remainder as a test dataset. CILDP at distance 5 had the best Cohen kappa value with 96%, which is interpreted as very good agreement. All the results indicate the superiority of CILDP compared with LDP.

**Table 4.** The performance accuracy of CILDP, LDP and LBP applied on Kylberg dataset using five classifiers

| Classifiers | LBP | LDP | Circular LDP (Distance 2) | Circular LDP (Distance 3) | Circular LDP (Distance 4) | Circular LDP (Distance 5) |
|---|---|---|---|---|---|---|
| k-NN | **93** | 91 | 90 | **93** | 91 | **93** |
| SVM | 98 | 98 | 98 | **99** | 98 | 98 |
| DT | 87 | 89 | **91** | 89 | **91** | **91** |
| RF | 70 | 64 | 72 | 75 | **77** | 75 |
| Perceptron | 63 | 74 | 71 | **87** | 86 | 84 |

**Table 5.** Using different evaluation measures to evaluate CILDP and LDP

| Feature | Accuracy | Cohen Kappa | F1_score | Precision | Recall |
|---|---|---|---|---|---|
| LDP | 0.92 | 0.9 | 0.9 | 0.89 | 0.91 |
| CILDP 2 | 0.95 | 0.94 | 0.95 | **0.96** | 0.95 |
| CILDP 3 | 0.93 | 0.92 | 0.93 | 0.925 | 0.93 |
| CILDP 4 | 0.94 | 0.93 | 0.94 | 0.94 | 0.935 |
| CILDP 5 | **0.95** | **0.96** | **0.95** | 0.95 | **0.95** |

## 4    Conclusion

In this paper, we proposed a new texture feature method called CILDP. The method is based on using circle shape to compute the directional edge responses vector with different radiuses. To evaluate the performance of the proposed method, a comparative experiment between CILDP, LDP, and LBP has been carried out using five different classifiers to classify 28 categories of texture from the Kylberg dataset. The results establish the effect of variation of radiuses on the performance of CILDP; it is also shown that CILDP outperforms LDP and LBP. It will be interesting to investigate the performance of CILDP using different datasets and parameters.

## References

1. Pietikäinen, M., Hadid, A., Zhao, G., Ahonen, T.: Local binary patterns for still images. In: Computer Vision Using Local Binary Patterns. Computational Imaging and Vision, vol. 40. Springer, London. https://doi.org/10.1007/978-0-85729-748-8_2
2. Haralick, R.M., Shanmugam, K.: Textural features for image classification. IEEE Trans. Syst. Man Cybern. **SMC-3**(6), 610–621 (1973)
3. He, D.C., Wang, L.: Texture unit, texture spectrum, and texture analysis. IEEE Trans. Geosci. Remote Sens. **28**(4), 509–512 (1990)
4. Lowe, D.G.: Distinctive image features from scale-invariant keypoints. Int. J. Comput. Vis. **60**(2), 91–110 (2004)

5. Bay, H., Ess, A., Tuytelaars, T., Van Gool, L.: Speeded-up robust features (SURF). Comput. Vis. Image Underst. **110**(3), 346–359 (2008)
6. Jabid, T., Kabir, M.H., Chae, O.: Local directional pattern (LDP) for face recognition. In: Proceedings of Consumer Electronics Conference (ICCE), Digest of Technical Papers International, pp. 329–330 (2010)
7. Shabat, A.M., Tapamo, J.-R.: Directional local binary pattern for texture analysis. In: Campilho, A., Karray, F. (eds.) ICIAR 2016. LNCS, vol. 9730, pp. 226–233. Springer, Cham (2016). https://doi.org/10.1007/978-3-319-41501-7_26
8. Soh, L.K., Tsatsoulis, C.: Texture analysis of SAR sea ice imagery using gray level co-occurrence matrices. IEEE Trans. Geosci. Remote Sens. **37**(2), 780–795 (1999)
9. Mäenpää, T., Pietikäinen, M.: Texture analysis with local binary patterns. Handb. Pattern Recogn. Comput. Vis. **3**, 197–216 (2005)
10. Shabat, A.M., Tapamo, J.R.: A comparative study of local directional pattern for texture classification. In: World Symposium on Computer Applications & Research (WSCAR), pp. 1–7 (2014)
11. Ahonen, T., Hadid, A., Pietikäinen, M.: Face recognition with local binary patterns. In: Pajdla, T., Matas, J. (eds.) ECCV 2004. LNCS, vol. 3021, pp. 469–481. Springer, Heidelberg (2004). https://doi.org/10.1007/978-3-540-24670-1_36
12. Ojala, T., Pietikäinen, M., Maenpaa, T.: Multiresolution gray-scale and rotation invariant texture classification with local binary patterns. IEEE Trans. Pattern Anal. Mach. Intell. **24**(7), 971–987 (2002)
13. Liao, S., Law, M.W., Chung, A.C.: Dominant local binary patterns for texture classification. IEEE Trans. Image Process. **18**(5), 1107–1118 (2009)
14. Guo, Z., Zhang, L., Zhang, D.: A completed modeling of local binary pattern operator for texture classification. IEEE Trans. Image Process. **19**(6), 1657–1663 (2010)
15. Heikkilä, M., Pietikäinen, M., Schmid, C.: Description of interest regions with center-symmetric local binary patterns. In: ICVGIP, vol. 6, pp. 58–69 (2006)
16. Luo, Y.T., et al.: Local line directional pattern for palmprint recognition. Pattern Recogn. **50**, 26–44 (2016)
17. Kylberg, G.: Kylberg Texture Dataset v. 1.0. Centre for Image Analysis. Swedish University of Agricultural Sciences and Uppsala University (2011)
18. McHugh, M.L.: Interrater reliability: the kappa statistic. Biochem. Med. **22**(3), 276–282 (2012)

# A Deep Learning Approach for Automatic Segmentation of Dental Images

Vincent Majanga and Serestina Viriri[✉]

School of Mathematics, Statistics and Computer Science,
University of KwaZulu-Natal, Durban, South Africa
viriris@ukzn.ac.za

**Abstract.** Dental images segmentation helps to find important regions of a dental X-ray image: tooth isolation. A challenge presents itself in how to detect dental images for correct matching/classification. Edge-based methods have a significant potential role in image segmentation field. These edge based methods use edges to detect objects, boundaries, and other relevant information in an image. This research proposes a deep learning approach to include edge-based features. Firstly, the proposed technique employs data augmentation to address the limited number of dental images, and improvement of accuracy in the evaluation process. Secondly, the edge-based features are extracted using canny edge detection method. Lastly, the neural network features of the (Keras model), from the Keras tool package will be used for converging iterations of the segmentation process, and further classification. The proposed deep learning technique which combines image augmentation, and edge-based features, achieved a higher accuracy of 89% for both precision, and recall values.

**Keywords:** Deep learning · Dental segmentation · Another bitewing images

## 1 Introduction

Image segmentation is a critical process in computer vision. It plays an important role in image processing and its applications such as medical diagnosis. It involves dividing a visual input into segments or subgroups, of regions with respect to the appropriate locations, so as to simplify image analysis. Image segmentation still places a challenge due to many factors such as, feature extraction from images, contextual information, object granularity, and contour smoothness. This paper proposes a deep learning method to address this challenges. Dental cavities or tooth decay, is one of the most prevalent chronic diseases worldwide [1]. It forms through a complex interaction over time between acid-producing bacteria and fermentable carbohydrate, and other host factors, including saliva and teeth. The disease develops in both the crowns and roots of teeth. It can arise in early childhood as tooth decay that affects infants' and toddlers' primary teeth.

B. R. Purushothama et al. (Eds.): MIKE 2019, LNAI 11987, pp. 143–152, 2020.
https://doi.org/10.1007/978-3-030-66187-8_14

The risk for dental cavities includes environmental, physical, biological, behavioural, and lifestyle-related factors such as cariogenic bacteria, inadequate saliva flow, insufficient fluoride exposure, poor oral hygiene, poverty, inappropriate methods of feeding infants. The methods of cavity diagnosis and intervention are changing with time. Dentists have been using visual, tactical, and radiographic information to detect relatively advanced changes in the dental hard tissues [2]. The clinical management of dental cavities has been directed at the treatment of the consequences of the disease process by placing restorations and not at curing the disease. With emerging technology, dentists will be able to detect dental cavities at an earlier stage. These changes will permit dentists to adopt more conservative management strategies directed at the prevention, and cure of dental cavities. Artificial intelligence (AI), through deep learning is now used for real life problems, and applied across all sectors of society. The use of deep learning methods in dentistry, is advancing quite fast, beyond text to image based practices.

Diagnosis of dental caries through machine learning and deep learning methods has improved treatment levels. Automatic dental caries detection system is practical, and concentrates on certain parts such as edge segmentation, detection and dental caries classification. Each of the previous parts depend on certain criteria, for instance edge segmentation needs to be grouped in pixels such as intensity value range, texture or gradient information. This needs a lot of analytical knowledge of images and experience. But most of these medical institutions still use manual methods to detect dental caries and its time consuming. With the availability of emerging innovative efficient techniques, there is room of improving existing techniques of dental caries detection.

## 2   Related Work

Segmentation and classification algorithms have been developed by several scholars, for high accuracy evaluation of dental images. For instance algorithms, active contours [4], level set method [5] were used for teeth segmentation. Fourier descriptors [6] were extracted as features. Finally, Bayesian techniques, Support Vector Machines and linear models for classification purposes [7]. Most of the said algorithms perform manual image enhancement before segmentation. This leads to a huge workload, which impacts negatively to the performance of image recognition.

Deep learning has improved this drawbacks tremendously, with the introduction of an image enhancement process, which is faster and automated. Forensics experts in law enforcement have used forensic odontology, for postmortem identification. The problem of developing an automated system, for postmortem identification, using dental records (dental radiographs), has tried to be addressed. The automated dental identification system (ADIS) is used by security agencies in the United States, to locate missing persons using databases/datasets of dental X-rays, of human remains of missing persons. The search and identification process currently is carried out manually, thus time-consuming.

Therefore, a novel architecture for ADIS was proposed, which explains the functionality of various components, describing the techniques used to realize them [8].

Majority of deep learning algorithms often do image enhancement before the segmentation process, and feature extraction, and image features usually are extracted manually. This gives a large workload, and thus depreciation of evaluation performance. Extracted features are dependant significantly on the image enhancement and the recognition process. A research by [9], discovered that X-ray films, obtained from dead peoples' teeth, is usually compared with records in a dental images database. This is done so that the identity can still be determined effectively. Humans naturally have 32 teeth and if all are screened for comparison, the system will encounter a large computational burden leading to reduction in accuracy. Thus the segmenting of teeth from X-ray films, and performing the numbering of each tooth. This enables only testing of teeth that can be compared with those having the same numbers in the database, thus the computational efficiency and accuracy improved.

In [10], proposed a dental classification and numbering system to segment, classify, and number teeth in dental bitewing radiographs. An image enhancement method that combines homomorphic filtering, homogeneity-based contrast stretching, and adaptive morphological transformation. This is to improve both the contrast and illumination evenness of the dental images. In [11], trained a large, deep convolutional neural network so as to classify the 1.3 million high-resolution images in the LSVRC-2010 ImageNet training set, into the 1000 different classes. On the test data, they achieved top-1 and top-5 error rates of 39.7% and 18.9%, which is considerably better than the previous state-of-the-art results.

Performance of the neural network based on the number of images presented to it was impressive. In [12], there was an introduction of a layer to remove the fixed-size constraint of the neural network. Specifically, addition of a spatial pyramid pooling (SPP) layer on top of the last convolutional layer in their network. The SPP layer is to pool the features and thereafter generates fixed-length outputs, which are then fed into the fully-connected layers (or other classifiers). This is to enable information aggregation to be done at a deeper stage of the network, to avoid warping or cropping at the beginning. In [13], there is an introduction of a Region Proposal Network (RPN), that consists of full-image convolutional features, and a network detection feature. A Region Proposal Network(RPN) is a fully-convolutional network, that predicts simultaneously regions of objects and their scores. They are trained together to generate high-quality regions, which are used by the Fast R-CNN for object detection.

## 3    Methods and Techniques

The proposed framework proposes the segmentation process be undertaken in the steps below.

## 3.1  Data Augmentation

Given the less number of images available for the research, it is impossible to derive intelligent decisions through deep learning techniques. Deep learning networks need a large amount of training data to achieve good evaluation performance. Image augmentation is prescribed, which artificially creates training images through different ways of processing, or combination of multiple processing ways, such as random rotation, shifts, shear and flips. Data augmentation was initially popularized by [14] in order to make simulation more feasible and simple. Neural networks need data augmented so as to attain satisfactory performance.

Several data augmentation techniques include horizontally flipping images, random crops, and color jittering. Basically, just image shifts via the width shift, range and height shift, range arguments. Image flips through the horizontal and vertical flip arguments. Also image rotations, brightness, and zoom arguments. The Data Augmentation process [15] is described through the below steps. Flips: horizontal and vertical flip for each image I in the training set. Even though only horizontal flips are used in natural images, its believed that vertical flips capture a unique property of medical images, namely, invariance to vertical reflection.

Vertical flips capture a unique property of medical images, namely, invariance to vertical reflection. Conventionally, for natural images, only horizontal flips of the original images are used, since vertical flips often do not reflect natural images (i.e. an upside-down cat would not generally make a model more discriminative during training).

Scaling: Scale each I in either the x or y direction; specifically, we apply an affine transformation.

Powers: Take each I to a power. To calculate the power, p, we use the following equation, $p = n \cdot r + 1$, where n is a random float taken from a Gaussian distribution with mean $\theta$ and variance 1 while r is a number less than 1. Then, to generated the augmented image, Ia, we have,

Rotations: The following affine transformation,

$$A = (\cos\theta \sin\theta - \sin\theta \cos\theta) \tag{1}$$

where $\theta$ is between 10 and 175°, is applied.

## 3.2  Pre-processing

After dataset preparation, an edge segmentation method is introduced, which is a combination of Gaussian filter for image enhancement, to remove noise, and Canny edge detector for edge detection. Figure 1 shows the original image before pre-processing, noise removal through the Gaussian Blur, and canny edge detector for edge segmentation.

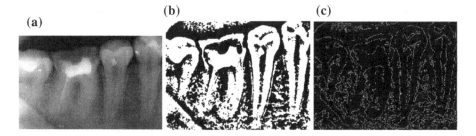

**Fig. 1.** a. Original image b. Gaussian Blur c. Canny edge detection

### 3.3  Classification

An object detection tool package based on (Keras model architecture) in the keras tool package, for multiple categories is selected for the neural network model.

The neural network model defined by Keras, is used as a network with one input layer, two hidden layers, and one output layer. A set of 8361 images is used to train and 2787 images for testing the neural network. A total of 3 classes are used for this exercise. The Scikit-learns' precision recall Fscore technique is selected as the metric for evaluation.

The precision is the ratio:

$$t_p/(t_p + f_p) \qquad (2)$$

where $t_p$ is the number of true positives and $f_p$ the number of false positives. The precision is intuitively the ability of the classifier not to label as positive a sample that is negative. The recall is the ratio:

$$t_p/(t_p + f_n) \qquad (3)$$

where $t_p$ is the number of true positives and $f_n$ the number of false negatives. The recall is intuitively the ability of the classifier to find all the positive samples.

The F-beta score can be interpreted as a weighted harmonic mean of the precision and recall, where an F-beta score reaches its best value at 1 and worst score at 0.

The F-beta score weights recall more than precision by a factor of beta. Beta = 1.0 means recall and precision are equally important.

The support is the number of occurrences of each class in $y_t rue$. If $pos_l abel$ is None and in binary classification, this function returns the average precision, recall and F-measure if average is one of 'micro', 'macro', 'weighted' or 'samples'

## 4   Experimental Results and Discussion

This method of [4], was used to extract the teeth contour of images. Image database has two types of dental radiographs, those obtained when a person is alive, and those after his death. Images were randomly selected and the tooth contour extraction algorithm was executed on these images and the results were manually categorized. A comparison was done for the same images but by the snake method. The active contours without edges tends to gather efficiently the boundary of segmentation of teeth as shown by the below images (Fig. 2):

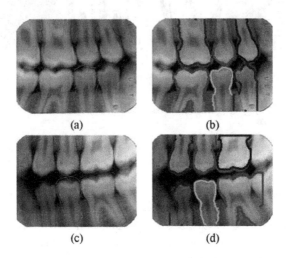

(a)    (b)

(c)    (d)

**Fig. 2.** (a) and (c) Snake method, (b) and (d) Active contour without edges.

In [9], the evaluation of performance of a CNN on a test dataset was compared to that of 3 expert dentists. Human annotation rules were, drawing minimum sized bounded boxes of each tooth on images and using the FDI numbering system. The experts were to learn how to do annotations from some ground truth annotations in the images of the training dataset. The annotations by the experts were matched with the ground truth data to calculate results for precision, recall and IOU.

This results had a higher accuracy for the more experienced expert dentists compared to the others. After the human exercise of evaluation, the previous fast neural network was trained with the same train and validation datasets. Basically this method compared results got from the human experts, against those of the automatic system, which in this case is the R-CNN. The introduction of post-processing to the neural network helped in increasing the performance of the automatic system.

The results were close to those of the dentists. The analysis of mismatch annotations by both human experts and automatic system, implied mistakes were similar especially in less complex cases. The difference though is critical for the dentists to overcome due to the insufficient time for them to go through and review reports. Thus this automatic system is a significant help if well developed further so as to assist in the diagnostic work of dentists.

In this research [14], the experiment was training a VGG-16 net (neural network) on 8 augmented sets. Each experiment the learning rate is set to 1e−3,

L2 regularization is set to 1e−7, and the dropout parameter p is 0.5. The VGG-16 net is then trained over its corresponding augmented training set for 2500 iterations. The network is trained for approximately 1.5 epochs, since the classification accuracy generally overfits around this point.

Visualization of the augmentation effect on the training set, presents the mean images result before augmentation, and after augmentation. This helps to explore relationship existing between the mean image results from an augmented training set, training and validation results of the VGG-16 net trained on that augmented set. Basically, does augmentation of original set affects training and validation accuracies (Fig. 3).

| Augmentation type | MI | Training acc | Validation acc |
|---|---|---|---|
| Noise | 2.27 | 0.625 | 0.660 |
| Gaussian Filter | 2.60 | 0.870 | 0.881 |
| Jitter | 2.59 | 0.832 | 0.813 |
| Scale | 2.67 | 0.887 | 0.874 |
| Powers | 2.33 | 0.661 | 0.737 |
| Rotate | 2.20 | 0.884 | 0.880 |
| Shear | 2.06 | 0.891 | 0.879 |
| Flips | 2.70 | 0.830 | 0.842 |

**Fig. 3.** Mutual Information between Mean images + Average accuracy.

Therefore, a higher mutual information of the images correlates to a higher classification accuracy (Fig. 4).

Dental image segmentation helps to find regions of interest namely, the gap valley and to isolate individual teeth. This is a challenge caused by noise and intensity variations. The use of gray and binary intensity integral curves have been used before. In the [16], proposed a novel method of finding a region of interest for the gap valley and tooth isolation using binary edge intensity integral curves. It uses the region growing approach, then canny edge detector. This automatically finds the ROI for both gap valley and tooth isolation. This is shown by Fig. 5 clearly identifying the tooth isolation and gap valley from binary integrated edge intensity curves.

This method was applied on 30 dental X-ray images and various values of thresholding selected experimentally. 83% was achieved with the images using this method. It clearly differentiates tooth isolation of teeth, and segmentation of both upper and lower jaws is done clearly. For a dental image with a large gap valley, this method gives a region of interest which passes through a larger portion of the gap valley.

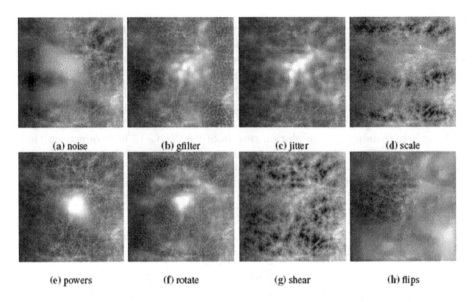

(a) noise          (b) gfilter          (c) jitter          (d) scale

(e) powers          (f) rotate          (g) shear          (h) flips

**Fig. 4.** Images after augmentation process.

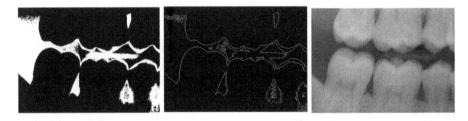

**Fig. 5.** Identified tooth isolation and gap valley from binary integrated edge intensity curves image

| Methods | Accuracy |
|---|---|
| Faster R-CNN [13] | 73.2% |
| SPP for object detection [12] | 31.8% |
| Imagenet classification with DNN [11] | 78.1% |
| Novel algorithm [16] | 83% |
| **Proposed method** | **89.0%** |

From the proposed method, Fig. 6 below shows graphs of training and validation process, for 50 iterations and 75 iterations respectively.

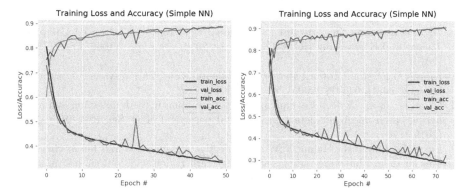

**Fig. 6.** Proposed method graph after 50 epochs and 75 epochs/iterations respectively.

# 5   Conclusion

From the various results of various quoted methods, it is clear that there is need of more images for training the neural network. Thus, the aspect of introducing data augmentation is important where the dataset is lacking. From the method proposed, and the iterations/epochs done in training the dataset, over-fitting was realised. This progressively reduced through data augmentation, and the increase of iterations/epochs. There is room for improvement as seen by the graphs presented by Fig. 6. The results can be improved further, by combining this method with other deep learning techniques. The challenges experienced are the inadequacy of dental images for training and testing purposes, and also ground truths for the dental images.

# References

1. Selwitz, R.H., Ismail, A.I., Pitts, N.B.: Dental caries. The Lancet **369**(9555), 51–59 (2007)
2. Zero, D.T.: Dental caries process. Dent. Clin. North Am. **43**(4), 635–664 (1999)
3. Litjens, G., et al.: A survey on deep learning in medical image analysis. Med. Image Anal. **42**, 60–88 (2017)
4. Shah, S., Abaza, A., Ross, A., Ammar, H.: Automatic tooth segmentation using active contour without edges. In: 2006 Biometrics Symposium: Special Session on Research at the Biometric Consortium Conference, September 2006, pp. 1–6. IEEE (2006)
5. Rad, A.E., Rahim, M.S.M., Norouzi, A.: Digital dental X-ray image segmentation and feature extraction. TELKOMNIKA Indones. J. Electr. Eng. **11**(6), 3109–3114 (2013)
6. Tangel, M.L., et al.: Dental classification for periapical radiograph based on multiple fuzzy attribute. In: 2013 Joint IFSA World Congress and NAFIPS Annual Meeting (IFSA/NAFIPS), June 2013, pp. 304–309. IEEE (2013)

7. Aeini, F., Mahmoudi, F.: Classification and numbering of posterior teeth in bitewing dental images. In: 2010 3rd International Conference on Advanced Computer Theory and Engineering (ICACTE), August 2010, vol. 6, pp. V6-66–V6-72. IEEE (2010)
8. Fahmy, G.F., et al.: Toward an automated dental identification system. J. Electron. Imaging **14**(4), 043018 (2005)
9. Chen, H., et al.: A deep learning approach to automatic teeth detection and numbering based on object detection in dental periapical films. Sci. Rep. **9**(1), 3840 (2019)
10. Lin, P.L., Lai, Y.H., Huang, P.W.: An effective classification and numbering system for dental bitewing radiographs using teeth region and contour information. Pattern Recogn. **43**(4), 1380–1392 (2010)
11. Krizhevsky, A., Sutskever, I., Hinton, G.E.: ImageNet classification with deep convolutional neural networks. In: Advances in Neural Information Processing Systems, pp. 1097–1105 (2012)
12. He, K., Zhang, X., Ren, S., Sun, J.: Spatial pyramid pooling in deep convolutional networks for visual recognition. IEEE Trans. Pattern Anal. Mach. Intell. **37**(9), 1904–1916 (2015)
13. Ren, S., He, K., Girshick, R., Sun, J.: Faster R-CNN: towards real-time object detection with region proposal networks. In: Advances in Neural Information Processing Systems, pp. 91–99 (2015)
14. Hussain, Z., Gimenez, F., Yi, D., Rubin, D.: Differential data augmentation techniques for medical imaging classification tasks. In: 2017 AMIA Annual Symposium Proceedings, vol. 2017, p. 979. American Medical Informatics Association (2017)
15. Van der Walt, S., et al.: Scikit-image: image processing in Python. PeerJ. **2**, e453 (2014)
16. Modi, C.K., Desai, N.P.: A simple and novel algorithm for automatic selection of ROI for dental radiograph segmentation. In: 2011 24th Canadian Conference on Electrical and Computer Engineering (CCECE), May 2011, pp. 000504–000507. IEEE (2011)

# Quality Assessment of Fingerprint Images Using Local Texture Descriptors

Ram Prakash Sharma$^{(\boxtimes)}$ and Somnath Dey

Indian Institute of Technology Indore, Simrol, India
{phd1501201003,somnathd}@iiti.ac.in

**Abstract.** Analyzing the fingerprint quality is of paramount importance as it affects recognition performance. The low-quality fingerprint images degrade the recognition performance as they produce spurious minutiae points. Therefore, estimation of fingerprint quality is essential to avoid performance degradation. Local texture descriptors utilizing micro-textural features for analyzing texture patterns are attaining popularity due to their flexibility and excellent performance. The proposed work aims at evaluating the competency of two well known texture descriptors, namely, Weber Local Descriptor (WLD) and Binarized Statistical Image Features (BSIFs) for fingerprint quality assessment. Computation of WLD features is inspired from the Weber's law which considers human visual perception of texture patterns while BSIFs are computed by automatically learning a predefined set of filters from a set of natural images instead of using manual filters. The features extracted using WLD and BSIFs are utilized individually to assess dry, wet, and good texture quality of fingerprint blocks. The fingerprint blocks of different qualities are classified into suitable quality classes using Support Vector Machine (SVM) classifier. Thereafter, block texture quality assessment method is used iteratively for fingerprint texture quality assessment. The experimental evaluations performed on publicly available low-quality FVC 2004 fingerprint data-sets show that proposed method outperforms other state-of-the-art methods of fingerprint quality assessment.

**Keywords:** Biometrics · Local texture descriptor · Fingerprint quality · Support Vector Machine

## 1 Introduction

Analyzing the biometric sample quality has attained considerable interest of many researchers due to their wide applicability in real-world applications. The recognition performance of biometric systems is heavily dependent on the quality of input data. Therefore, it is necessary to evaluate biometric sample quality indicating its ability to function as a biometric. From all the biometric modalities, fingerprint based recognition is the most widely used due to its performance, higher distinctiveness, and ease of use. To insure the higher performance of fingerprint recognition systems, it is essential to analyze the input fingerprint

© Springer Nature Switzerland AG 2020
B. R. Purushothama et al. (Eds.): MIKE 2019, LNAI 11987, pp. 153–164, 2020.
https://doi.org/10.1007/978-3-030-66187-8_15

quality. A poor quality fingerprint image can exhibit spurious features (minutiae) which degrades the recognition performance. In the quality assessment of fingerprint images, the ridge quality of the fingerprint images is analyzed. Therefore, analyzing the ridge quality can help to provide active quality feedback for rejecting poor quality fingerprint samples. Various factors such as wetness, dryness, dirt on the sensor, less or more pressure, etc. influence the fingerprint quality. Most of these factors (dryness, wetness, normal) can be identified at the time of fingerprint acquisition through proper ridge quality analysis. Based on the quality analysis, a quality feedback may be provided to the users which can help in acquiring a better quality fingerprint image. This supervised acquisition of fingerprint images will decrease the number of enrollment attempts, improved recognition performance, and better user experience.

In a recent work, Tertychnyi et al. [18] proposed the applicability of deep learning to recognize low-quality fingerprint images. These low-quality images are caused due to wetness, dryness, presence of dots, physical damage, and blurriness. The have utilized the VGG16 deep learning network for identification of low-quality (dry, blurred, wet, etc.) fingerprint images. They have also compared results of deep learning approach with SVM and Random Forest (RF) classifier based approaches. However, the comparative results exhibits that deep learning model outperform SVM and RF classifier. A quality based approach proposed by Sharma et al. [16] extracts some ridge-valley distribution based features (moisture, ridge-valley area uniformity, and ridge line count, etc.) to assess fingerprint quality. The Decision Tree (DT) classifier is used to detect different quality blocks (dry, good, normal dry, wet, and normal wet) using the extracted features. Awasthi et al. [1] have utilized consistency and orientation based features, ridge based features, pixel intensity, and directional contrast to identify the impairment (wet, dry, etc.) in fingerprint images. This impairment information is further utilized to provide quality scores to fingerprint images. A fingerprint quality clustering approach is proposed by Munir et al. [13] using hierarchical k-means clustering. They have classified images into normal, dry, and wet quality classes using a set of statistical and frequency features (mean, smoothness, uniformity, energy concentration, etc.). Their study on quality based fingerprint matching shows the improvement in performance of minutiae-based matcher. Lim et al. [11] have proposed a well-known fingerprint block quality classification approach. They have used a set of quality feature namely, sinusoidal local ridge/valley uniformity, directional strength, ridge/valley pattern, and core occurrences features for classification of fingerprint blocks in good or bad class. The classification results are obtained using Self-Organizing Map (SOM), Naive bayes classifier, and Radial Basis Function Neural Network (RBFNN) classifiers. In a recent approach, Sharma et al. [17] have proposed utilization of Local Phase Quantization (LPQ) descriptor for fingerprint quality assessment. Their work reports that the local descriptors are well suited for texture quality assessment of fingerprint images. Some other works evaluating the fingerprint quality can be found in [2,14,19]. Most of the existing works require computation of multiple quality-related features to assess fingerprint texture quality.

Therefore, the objective of this work is to propose a simple and robust fingerprint texture quality assessment method. In this work, the potential of Weber Local Descriptor (WLD) [4] and Binarized Statistical Image Features (BSIFs) [10] for fingerprint perceptual quality assessment is investigated. The WLD descriptor is based on the well known Weber's law [9]. WLD computes orientation and differential excitation feature for each foreground pixel of the image. The joint histograms of these two components construct discriminative features set. The BSIFs features have been used effectively for face recognition, texture classification [10], and fingerprint liveness detection [6]. Inspired from these successful applications of BSIFs, the potential of BSIFs is also explored for fingerprint texture quality assessment. In this work, dry, wet, and good perceptual quality of the fingerprint images are considered. The efficacy of the proposed method is tested on the low-quality fingerprint FVC 2004 data-sets. The FVC 2004 data-sets fingerprint images are partitioned into $32 \times 32$ sized blocks. These blocks are assigned wet, good, and dry quality by human experts having knowledge of fingerprint based recognition systems. Thereafter, the extracted features using WLD and BSIFs are fed individually to Support Vector Machine (SVM) classifier to train a quality classification model. This obtained classification models assign quality label to each foreground block of a fingerprint image. The fingerprint image is assigned an overall quality label based on the maximum foreground region of a particular quality class. The major highlights of the contributions made in this work are presented below.

- A simple and effective single feature based approach is proposed to assess the perceptual quality of fingerprint images.
- The potential of WLD and BSIFs are evaluated to assess fingerprint texture quality.
- Experimental evaluations exhibits suitability of WLD and BSIFs for fingerprint texture quality assessment.
- The experimental results exhibit that proposed approach outperform other recent fingerprint quality assessment methods.

## 2   Proposed Method

Quality assessment plays an important role to improve or control the input fingerprint in the system. Therefore, a simple and fast fingerprint quality assessment method is proposed which operates in two phases, namely, (i) block texture quality assessment, and (ii) fingerprint texture quality assessment. Schematic diagram of proposed method is illustrated in Fig. 1. In the initial phase, the proposed method extracts features from WLD and BSIFs to train a classification model which predicts wet, good, or dry quality of fingerprint blocks. The classification model of phase 1 is further utilized iteratively in second phase for fingerprint quality assessment. The intrinsic properties of wet, good, and dry quality classes are given below.

- **Wet** blocks are too dark and have mixed-up ridge-valley structure which is very difficult to separate. These fingerprint images are captured when the

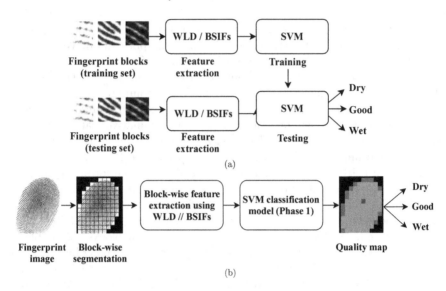

(a)

(b)

**Fig. 1.** Schematic diagram of proposed texture quality assessment method

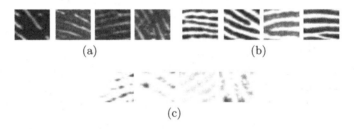

**Fig. 2.** Sample blocks of (a) Wet (b) Good, and (c) Dry quality

fingertip is having huge amount of sweat on it due to which valleys also makes contact with the scanner surface. The extra sweat on the fingertip needs to be wiped out to obtain a better quality of fingerprint. Figure 2(a) shows some samples of wet quality blocks.

- **Good** quality blocks have clearly separated ridge-valley structure. These fingerprint images need to be retained without any re-acquisition procedure. Figure 2(b) shows some sample of good quality blocks.
- **Dry** blocks are caused due to the dryness of the skin or low pressure on scanner surface which results in fainted ridge-valley structure as shown in Fig. 2(c). The possible solution to capture a better quality image is to moisten the fingerprint by rubbing it against the forehead, nose, or any other area of sweat pores.

In this work, we have focused on well-known texture descriptors which are widely utilized in different texture classification tasks and shown promising results. For fingerprint texture assessment, we have investigated use of WLD and BSIFs. Brief description of feature computation using WLD and BSIFs is provided in the following section.

## 2.1   Weber Local Descriptors

In [4,5], a simple and robust descriptor called Weber local descriptor is proposed. WLD is a combination of two components which are (i) differential excitation and (ii) orientation. The differential excitation component represents the ratio of a pixel's relative intensity differences from its neighbors and the intensity of that pixel. The human perception of the pattern can be stimulated by the differential excitation which indicates the salient variations within an image. The orientation component of WLD is obtained using gradient orientation [4]. The complete WLD histogram is constructed with the concatenation of these two components. The computation of these two components is done using Eq. 1 and Eq. 2.

$$F_2(x) = \xi(x) = \frac{\overline{I}_{3\times3} - I(x)}{I(x)} \tag{1}$$

$$F_1(x) = \theta(x) = angle(\triangledown I(x)) \tag{2}$$

Here $\overline{I}_{3\times3}$ represents the average of image $I$ over $3 \times 3$ pixel window which is centered on pixel $x$. The orientation angle is uniformly quantized in the range $[-\pi, \pi]$ with $N_1$ output levels. On the other hand, differential excitation is quantized non-uniformly using arctan non-linearity followed by a uniform $N_2$ level quantizer in $[-\pi/2, \pi/2]$ range. Finally, outputs of these two components are concatenated into a single integer with values in $[0, N_1 N_2 - 1]$ range using Eq. 3.

$$C(x) = WLD(x) = C_1(x)N_2 + C_2(x) \tag{3}$$

The final histogram with 960 values comprises $N_2 = 120$ bins for the differential excitation and $N_1 = 8$ bins for the orientation.

## 2.2   Binarized Statistical Image Features:

The BSIFs features have been used effectively for texture classification [10], face recognition [10], and fingerprint liveness detection [6]. The computation of BSIFs is stimulated by Local Binary Pattern (LBP) and LPQ descriptors. BSIF utilizes a set of natural images to learn a predefined set of filters instead of using manual filters as used in LBP and LPQ. Proposed approach consists of applied learning, instead of manual tuning for efficient quality representation of fingerprint images. This enables efficient encoding of information using simple element-wise quantization.

Histogram of BSIF code values is computed to obtain the texture properties of a fingerprint block. The response of a linear filter at zero threshold is binarized to obtain the value of each element in the BSIF binary code. The number of filters learnt from the training set of natural image patches determines the desired length of the bit string which will maximize the statistical independence of the filter responses [8]. The description of the filters computation can be found in [10]. The BSIFs computation is done as follows: For a given $l \times l$ pixel image patch $X$ and a linear filter $W_i$ of the same size, the filter response $s_i$ is obtained by Eq. 4.

$$s_i = \sum_{u,v} W_i(u, v)X(u, v) = w_i^T x \tag{4}$$

Here vector $w$ and $x$ contain the pixels of $W_i$ and $X$. The filters $W_i$ are learnt using Independent Component Analysis (ICA) by maximizing the statistical independence of $s_i$. The binary feature $b_i$ is computed using Eq. 5.

$$b_i = \begin{cases} 1, & \text{if } s_i > 0. \\ 0, & \text{otherwise.} \end{cases} \tag{5}$$

In the experiments, 13 natural images are used to learn a set of filters. These set of filters are learnt using 50,000 image patches of 13 natural images. Filter learning is performed by three-stage processing which are (a) subtraction of mean intensity of each patch, (b) dimension reduction and whitening via Principal Component Analysis (PCA), and (c) estimation of independent components. There are two parameters in the BSIF descriptor namely, the length $n$ of the bit string and filter size $l$. Further details regarding the implementation of BSIF can be found in [6,10].

### 2.3   Support Vector Machine

The assessment of fingerprint quality is done using SVM classification model [15] with Radial Basis Function (RBF) kernel. It requires two parameters [7], namely, penalty $(C)$ and kernel $(\gamma)$ parameters. The task of penalty parameter $C$ is to control the rate of misclassification error for training examples and kernel parameter $\gamma$ controls non-linear classification problems. The optimal values of these two parameters for the best classification results are obtained using grid search algorithm [3].

## 3   Experimental Results

The efficacy of the proposed method is tested on DB1, DB2, and DB4 data-set of FVC 2004 database [12]. These data-sets contain 800 fingerprint images of 100 individuals (8 sample per individual). The fingerprint images of these data-sets are captured with varying conditions of fingertip to obtain different texture pattern in fingerprint images (wet, normal, and dry). The quality sensitive acquisition of fingerprint images in these data-sets is suitable for fingerprint quality assessment. Some samples of wet, good, and dry fingerprint images are shown in Fig. 3.

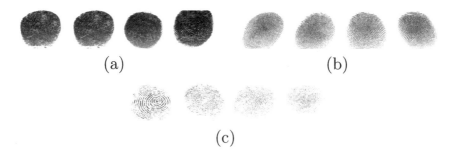

**Fig. 3.** Fingerprint images of (a) Wet (b) Good, and (c) Dry qualities

**Table 1.** Block quality classification results of the proposed method using SVM classifier

|  |  | Wet | Good | Dry | Total |
|---|---|---|---|---|---|
| Subjective quality | **WLD** |  |  |  |  |
|  | Wet | **193** | 6 | 1 | 200 |
|  | Good | 13 | **182** | 5 | 200 |
|  | Dry | 0 | 0 | **200** | 200 |
|  | Total | 206 | 188 | 206 | 600 |
|  | **Accuracy** | 96.50% | 91.00% | 100% | **95.83%** |
|  | **BSIF** |  |  |  |  |
|  | Wet | **192** | 8 | 0 | 200 |
|  | Good | 11 | **189** | 0 | 200 |
|  | Dry | 0 | 0 | **200** | 200 |
|  | Total | 203 | 197 | 200 | 600 |
|  | **Accuracy** | 96.00% | 94.50% | 100% | **96.83%** |

## 3.1   Block Texture Quality Assessment

Fingerprint images of FVC 2004 database (DB1, DB2, and DB4 data-sets) are partitioned into $32 \times 32$ size blocks. A quality labeled data-set of 3000 blocks (1000 for each quality class) is constituted by the human experts. The texture features extracted using WLD and BSIFs are obtained for all the blocks. In our experiments, the optimal penalty and kernel parameter are $C = 1.5$ and $\gamma = 0.0625$ for WLD, $C = 2$ and $\gamma = 0.0625$ for BSIFs which are providing the highest classification accuracy using grid search algorithm [3]. Results are obtained using the 5-fold cross-validation.

Table 1 presents the results of block quality classification. For the WLD, it shows that out of 200 wet blocks 193 are predicted correctly. Similarly, 182 and 200 are the number of blocks predicted correctly in good and dry quality class, respectively. The overall classification accuracy achieved using WLD is 95.83%. The similar experiments using BSIFs results in overall accuracy of 96.83%.

The obtained results are compared with some of the well-known quality assessment method for fingerprint images. To make our results comparable with all other methods, a single bad quality class is formed which contains both the dry and wet quality class. This results in only two quality classes (good and bad) of the fingerprint images. The comparative results given in Table 2 shows that the WLD and BSIFs performs better as compared with other methods in terms of overall classification accuracy. These results show that BSIFs performs better with 96.83% accuracy as compared with WLD which achieves 95.83% accuracy.

**Table 2.** Comparison of the proposed block texture quality assessment with other existing methods

| Methods | Classifier | Quality | | Overall accuracy |
|---------|-----------|---------|------|-----------------|
| | | Bad | Good | |
| Subjective quality | Manual | 400 | 200 | 600 |
| Sharma et al. [16] | DT | 379 (94.75%) | **191 (95.50%)** | 570 (95.00%) |
| Lim et al. [11] | Naive Bayes | 375 (93.75%) | 181 (90.50%) | 556 (92.66%) |
| Lim et al. [11] | SOM | 359 (89.75%) | 175 (87.50%) | 534 (89.00%) |
| Lim et al. [11] | RBFNN | 378 (94.50%) | 186 (93.00%) | 564 (94.00%) |
| Sharma et al. [17] | LPQ-SVM | **398 (99.50%)** | 173 (86.50%) | 571 (95.16%) |
| Proposed method | WLD-SVM | 393 (98.25%) | 182 (91.00%) | 575 (95.83%) |
| | BSIF-SVM | 392 (98.00%) | 189 (94.50%) | **581 (96.83%)** |

### 3.2  Fingerprint Texture Quality Assessment

Three human experts have classified the fingerprint images of DB1, DB2, and DB4 data-sets into wet, dry, and good quality to test performance of this phase of the proposed method. We have not selected the DB3 data-set of FVC 2004 database for quality assessment as most of the fingerprint images are darker as they were captured using thermal sweeper sensor. Due to this, it was very difficult to separate fingerprint images of different quality. The foreground blocks are identified and assigned an appropriate quality class using the classification model built in phase 1. The maximum number of blocks in either of the dry, wet, or good quality classes decides overall quality of the fingerprint image (Fig. 4).

The evaluation results of fingerprint texture quality assessment method are compared with subjective quality, Munir et al. [13], Awasthi et al. [1], Terty et al. [18], Sharma et al. [17] methods. The classification model of Terty et al. [18] method is used to classify texture of fingerprint images in wet, good, and dry classes. The normal quality class defined by Munir et al. [13] method is same as good quality class. The comparative results for DB1 data-set is given in Table 3. These results show that BSIFs based method attains the best classification accuracy of 93.87% as compared with 91.25%, 92.25%, 90.62%, 92.87%, and 92.62%, accuracy achieved by Munir et al. [13], Awasthi et al. [1], Terty et al. [18], Sharma et al. [17], and WLD based methods. It clearly shows that

**Table 3.** Comparative study on DB1 data-set for texture quality classification method

|  |  | Quality class | | | |
| --- | --- | --- | --- | --- | --- |
|  |  | Wet | Good | Dry | Overall |
| Subjective quality |  | 172 | 441 | 187 | 800 |
| Munir et al. [13] |  | 168 (97.67%) | 393 (89.11%) | 169 (90.37%) | 730 (91.25%) |
| Awasthi et al. [1] |  | 159 (92.44%) | **405 (91.83%)** | 174 (93.04%) | 738 (92.25%) |
| Terty et al. [18] |  | 163 (94.76%) | 387 (87.75%) | 175 (93.58%) | 725 (90.62%) |
| Sharma et al. [17] | LPQ | 168 (97.67%) | 393 (89.11%) | **182 (97.32%)** | 743 (92.87%) |
| Proposed method | WLD | 165 (95.93%) | 399 (90.47%) | 177 (94.65%) | 741 (92.62%) |
|  | BSIF | **169 (98.25%)** | 401 (90.92%) | 181 (96.79%) | **751 (93.87%)** |

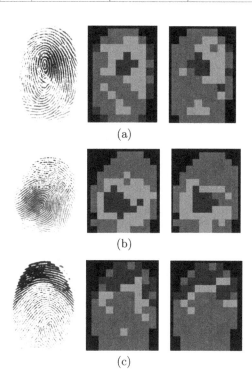

(a)

(b)

(c)

**Fig. 4.** Fingerprint images and their corresponding quality maps. The columns from left to right correspond to original image, WLD Maps, and BSIF Maps

the BSIFs performs better than other methods. The comparative results for the DB2 and DB4 data-sets are also reported in Table 4 and Table 5, respectively. The best classification accuracy of 95.12% and 95.62% for DB2 and DB4 data-sets is also achieved using the BSIFs based quality assessment method. These results assert that the BSIFs local descriptor is the best for fingerprint texture quality assessment.

**Table 4.** Comparative study on DB2 data-set for texture quality classification method

| | | Quality class | | | |
|---|---|---|---|---|---|
| | | Wet | Good | Dry | Overall |
| Subjective quality | | 77 | 491 | 232 | 800 |
| Munir et al. [13] | | 61 (79.22%) | 447 (91.10%) | 205 (88.36%) | 713 (89.12%) |
| Awasthi et al. [1] | | 68 (88.31%) | 453 (92.26%) | 213 (91.81%) | 734 (91.75%) |
| Terty et al. [18] | | 65 (84.41%) | 449 (91.44%) | 215 (92.62%) | 729 (91.12%) |
| Sharma et al. [17] | LPQ | 71 (92.20%) | 452 (92.05%) | 221 (95.25%) | 744 (93.00%) |
| Proposed method | WLD | 71 (92.20%) | 451 (91.85%) | 218 (93.96%) | 740 (92.50%) |
| | BSIF | **75 (97.40%)** | **459 (93.48%)** | **227 (97.84%)** | **761 (95.12%)** |

**Table 5.** Comparative study on DB4 data-set for texture quality classification method

| | | Quality class | | | |
|---|---|---|---|---|---|
| | | Wet | Good | Dry | Overall |
| Subjective quality | | 38 | 564 | 198 | 800 |
| Munir et al. [13] | | 33 (86.84%) | 511 (90.60%) | 172 (86.86%) | 716(89.50%) |
| Awasthi et al. [1] | | **36 (94.73%)** | 523 (92.73%) | 181 (91.41%) | 740 (92.50%) |
| Terty et al. [18] | | 35 (92.10%) | 518 (91.84%) | 179 (90.40%) | 732 (91.50%) |
| Sharma et al. [17] | LPQ | 33 (86.84%) | 529 (93.79%) | 189 (95.45%) | 751 (93.87%) |
| Proposed method | WLD | **36 (94.73%)** | 522 (92.55%) | 187 (94.44%) | 745 (93.12%) |
| | BSIF | 34 (89.47%) | **539 (95.56%)** | **192 (96.96%)** | **765 (95.62%)** |

# 4   Conclusion

This paper proposes an effective fingerprint texture quality assessment approach using WLD and BSIFs. The first phase of our proposed method classifies the blocks of fingerprint images into wet, good, and dry quality classes using SVM classifier. In the second phase, $32 \times 32$ blocks are extracted from the segmented fingerprint images and fed to the block quality classification model of first phase. The quality of a fingerprint is decided by the label of the quality class that contains the largest number of blocks. We evaluated the performance of our proposed method on FVC 2004 data-sets and the comparative analysis show that the proposed method is better than the current state-of-the-art fingerprint quality assessment methods. The achieved results show that the proposed approach can be effective to control fingerprint quality in the fingerprint recognition systems. The future research works can be directed towards analyzing other quality impairment such as blurring, scars, etc. in the fingerprint images.

**Acknowledgment.** This research work has been carried out with the financial support provided from Science and Engineering Research Board (SERB), DST (ECR/2017/000027), Govt. of India.

# References

1. Awasthi, A., Venkataramani, K., Nandini, A.: Image quality quantification for fingerprints using quality-impairment assessment. In: IEEE Workshop on Applications of Computer Vision (WACV), pp. 296–302 (2013)

2. Bharadwaj, S., Vatsa, M., Singh, R.: Biometric quality: a review of fingerprint, iris, and face. EURASIP J. Image Video Process. **2014**(1), 1–28 (2014). https://doi.org/10.1186/1687-5281-2014-34

3. Chang, C.C., Lin, C.J.: LIBSVM: a library for support vector machines. ACM Trans. Intell. Sys. Technol. **2**(3), 27:1–27:27 (2011). Software available at http://www.csie.ntu.edu.tw/cjlin/libsvm

4. Chen, J., et al.: WLD: a robust local image descriptor. IEEE Trans. Pattern Anal. Mach. Intell. **32**(9), 1705–1720 (2010)

5. Chen, J., Shan, S., Zhao, G., Chen, X., Gao, W., Pietikainen, M.: A robust descriptor based on Webers law. In: 2008 IEEE Conference on Computer Vision and Pattern Recognition, pp. 1–7 (2008)

6. Ghiani, L., Hadid, A., Marcialis, G.L., Roli, F.: Fingerprint liveness detection using local texture features. IET Biom. **6**(3), 224–231 (2017)

7. Hsu, C.W., Chang, C.C., Lin, C.J.: A practical guide to support vector classification. Department of Computer Science, National Taiwan University, Technical report (2010)

8. Hyvärinen, A., Oja, E.: Independent component analysis: algorithms and applications. Neural Netw. **13**(4), 411–430 (2000)

9. Jain, A.K.: Fundamentals of Digital Image Processing. Prentice-Hall Inc., Upper Saddle River (1989)

10. Kannala, J., Rahtu, E.: BSIF: binarized statistical image features. In: Proceedings of the 21st International Conference on Pattern Recognition, ICPR 2012, pp. 1363–1366 (2012)

11. Lim, E., Toh, K.A., Suganthan, P.N., Jiang, X., Yau, W.Y.: Fingerprint image quality analysis. International Conference on Image Processing (ICIP), vol. 2, pp. 1241–1244 (2004)

12. Maio, D., Maltoni, D., Cappelli, R., Wayman, J.L., Jain, A.K.: FVC2004: third fingerprint verification competition. In: Zhang, D., Jain, A.K. (eds.) Biometric Authentication, pp. 1–7 (2004)

13. Munir, M.U., Javed, M.Y., Khan, S.A.: A hierarchical k-means clustering based fingerprint quality classification. Neurocomputing **85**, 62–67 (2012)

14. Olsen, M.A., Smida, V., Busch, C.: Finger image quality assessment features: definitions and evaluation. IET Biom. **5**(2), 47–64 (2016)

15. Scholkopf, B., Williamson, R., Smola, A., Shawe-Taylor, J., Platt, J.: Support vector method for novelty detection. In: Proceedings of the 12th International Conference on Neural Information Processing Systems, pp. 582–588 (1999)

16. Sharma, R.P., Dey, S.: Fingerprint image quality assessment and scoring. In: Ghosh, A., Pal, R., Prasath, R. (eds.) MIKE 2017. LNCS (LNAI), vol. 10682, pp. 156–167. Springer, Cham (2017). https://doi.org/10.1007/978-3-319-71928-3_16

17. Sharma, R.P., Dey, S.: Quality analysis of fingerprint images using local phase quantization. In: Vento, M., Percannella, G. (eds.) CAIP 2019. LNCS, vol. 11678, pp. 648–658. Springer, Cham (2019). https://doi.org/10.1007/978-3-030-29888-3_53

18. Tertychnyi, P., Ozcinar, C., Anbarjafari, G.: Low-quality fingerprint classification using deep neural network. IET Biom. **7**(6), 550–556 (2018)
19. Yao, Z., Bars, J.M.L., Charrier, C., Rosenberger, C.: Literature review of fingerprint quality assessment and its evaluation. IET Biom. **5**(3), 243–251 (2016)

# Skeletal Age Estimation from Hand Radiographs Using Transfer Learning

Divyan Hirasen, Verosha Pillay, Serestina Viriri$^{(\boxtimes)}$, and Mandlenkosi Gwetu

School of Mathematics, Statistics and Computer Science,
University of KwaZulu-Natal, Durban, South Africa
{viriris,gwetum}@ukzn.ac.za

**Abstract.** This paper presents experimental results obtained from using weakly tuned deep learning models for skeletal age estimation from hand radiographs. By leveraging transfer learning, deep learning models were initialised with the ImageNet dataset weights and then tuned for 5 epochs on the target RSNA Bone Age dataset. Thereafter, the deep learned models were used to estimate skeletal ages and obtained a MAE of 9.96 months. With the exploration of weighted model ensemble the MAE reduced to 9.32 months. In the final ensemble, the best results achieved took into consideration predictions from one of the poor performing models. This improvement indicates that weakly tuned deep learned models still have a good prediction accuracy. Moreover, poor performing models such as the InceptionResNetV2 which achieved a MAE of 16.75 months was still needed in the ensemble for best results. This indicates that even poor performing models can still extract useful information which can be taken advantage of in ensemble situations such as weighted ensemble.

**Keywords:** Age estimation · Hand radiographs · Transfer learning · Convolutional neural network

## 1 Introduction

The method for assessing the bone age using left hand wrist radiographs is widely accepted due to its minimum radiation exposure, simplicity and choice of ossification centres for evaluation of maturity [5]. Any discrepancy between the chronological and assessed skeletal age of an individual can indicate abnormalities in the skeletal development [6]. Bone age assessment (BAA) methods usually start with taking a single X-ray image of the left hand, from the wrist to fingertips, as shown in Fig. 2 [3]. Bones in the X-ray image are compared with radiographs in a standardized atlas of bone development. The BAA considers three vital factors: The presence of primary and secondary centres of ossification, the development of both centres and lastly, the timing of the union of primary and secondary centres [4]. These bone age atlases are based on large numbers of radiographs collected from male and female individuals generally of the same ethnic group [3].

© Springer Nature Switzerland AG 2020
B. R. Purushothama et al. (Eds.): MIKE 2019, LNAI 11987, pp. 165–176, 2020.
https://doi.org/10.1007/978-3-030-66187-8_16

BAA had been an ideal target for automated image evaluation since the quantity of radiographs in hospitals is increasing and with standardised reports containing clear information on gender and age labels. This combination is an appealing target for machine learning, as it sidesteps many labour-intensive pre-processing steps such as using Natural Language Processing (NLP) to process radiology reports and extract information to be used as labels. In the domain of medical imaging, convolutional neural networks (CNN) have been successfully applied on a rage of problems such as diabetic retinopathy screening [7], breast cancer histology image analysis [8] and bone disease prediction [10], to name a few. Furthermore, transfer learning-based approaches demonstrated performance improvements over custom deep learning methods since the lack of freely available hand radiographs to train models was compensated using transfer learning. The general implementation of a deep learning model is to be trained until a desirable accuracy rate is obtained while avoiding overfitting. This approach can potentially take up a large amount of time and ,with the lack of openly available medical images for this problem, overfitting can become an issue. This is also due to some age groups have extremely minimal observations within a dataset. With ensemble approaches, weak deep learning models can be combined to produce a model which can provide desirable accuracy rates with the benefit of only being trained with a minimum number of iterations or epoch.

This paper provides initial results obtained when deep learning models initialised on the ImageNet dataset weights and fine-tuned with only 5 epochs of training on a target RSNA Bone Age dataset of hand radiographs. Moreover, an ensemble of these deep learning models are explored with performance improvements noted.

## 2   Transfer Learning

The goal of Transfer Learning is to adapt a classifier trained in a source domain $D_S$ with learning task $T_T$ with adequate samples to work effectively in a new target domain $D_T$ which has its own learning task $T_S$ and where the samples contain different distributions. In some cases, $D_S$ and $D_T$ may be similar in which case transfer learning models can be used while retaining the original layer weights. While in cases of $D_S$ and $D_T$ being different, fine-tuning of the respective model's hyperparameters can be done using $D_T$

Creating labelled data is time consuming and expensive, so actively leveraging existing datasets is key. Traditional machine learning models learn patterns from a source training dataset and apply this knowledge to generalise from an unseen target dataset. With the use of transfer learning, models can continue the generalisation process of patterns already learnt from datasets with large amounts of training data. Transfer learning and generalisation are highly similar on a conceptual level as individuals can solve new tasks in an ad-hoc manner by using experiences from other situations. The primary distinction is that transfer learning transfers knowledge across tasks, instead of generalising within a specific task. Deep learning, especially in the case of supervised learning, requires large amounts of labelled data to perform effectively. Transfer learning is a viable approach to reducing the required size of training datasets for new target tasks, making it more applicable to real life scenarios where large amounts of labelled data is not easily available.

A domain can be represented mathematically as $D = (xP(X))$, where

- $X$ is a feature space
- $P(X)$ is the edge probability distribution
- $X = \{x_1, x_2, ..., x_n\} \epsilon X$

A task can be represented mathematically as $T = \{y, g(x)\}$, where

- $y$ is the label space
- $g(x)$ is the prediction function, or conditional probability function $P(y|x)$

## 3    Ensemble Learning

Ensemble learning is a machine learning paradigm where multiple models, often called weak learners, are trained to solve the same problem and combined to get better results. The main hypothesis is that when weak models are correctly combined more accurate and robust models can be achieved.

There are three major kinds of meta-algorithms that aim at combining weak learners:

- Bagging, that often considers homogeneous weak learners, learns them independently from each other in parallel and combines them following some kind of deterministic averaging process
- Boosting, that often considers homogeneous weak learners and learns them sequentially in an adaptive way and combines them following a deterministic strategy
- Stacking, that often considers heterogeneous weak learners, learns them in parallel and combines them by training a meta-model to output a prediction based on the different weak model's predictions

Bagging will mainly focus at getting an ensemble model with less variance than its components whereas boosting and stacking will mainly try to produce strong models less biased than their components (even if variance can also be reduced). Bagging is the primary approach explored in this work with a final step of averaging and weighted averaging applied for ensemble.

### 3.1    Averaging

Similar to the max voting technique, multiple predictions are made for each data point in averaging. In this method, the average of predictions from all the models acquired from bagging are used to make the final prediction. Averaging can be used for making predictions in regression problems or while calculating probabilities for classification problems.

## 3.2  Weighted Average

Weighted average is an extension of the averaging method. All models are assigned different weights defining the importance of each model for prediction. This importance is obtained through evaluation of each bagging model on a test dataset. These weights allow more accurate models to have a stronger influence on the final prediction of the model.

# 4  Methodology

The main aim is to create deep learning models which are fined tuned to boot-strap segments of the training dataset. Thereafter use the bootstrap models to produce a final classification. Thereafter, combining the classification of different bootstrap model predictions using averaging and weighted averaging.

Initially, the entire dataset is pre-processed to remove noise, such as text on radiographs, and to extract the hand radiograph from the background. This is done by using a combination of thresholding and edge detection techniques. Thereafter, the dataset it split into training and testing. The training set is further split into 5 bootstraps. A deep learning model is then trained on each of the 5 bootstraps, and the model is holistically evaluated on the average of the 5-bootstrap model's classification on the test set. This is known as the plain model evaluation. Along with plain model evaluation, averaging and weighted evaluation is carried out. This is through the use of different deep learning models and ensembling the result during the test set classification. This methodology can be seen in Fig. 1.

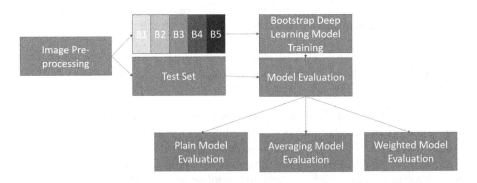

**Fig. 1.** The proposed framework for skeletal age estimation using hand radiographs

## 4.1  Dataset

Precise skeletal age estimation requires a dataset which is both large and of high quality. Moreover, the dataset needs to be representative for each skeletal age which could be assessed. Most of the time datasets could be unevenly distributed,

**Table 1.** The RSNA skeletal bone age dataset contains 6 833 male observations and 5 778 female observations ranging from 1 to 228 months of age

| Dataset | Size | Accessibility |
| --- | --- | --- |
| RSNA challenge dataset (Male) | 6 833 | Public |
| RSNA challenge dataset (Female) | 5 778 | Public |
| Total | 12 611 | Public |

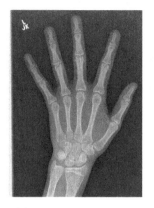  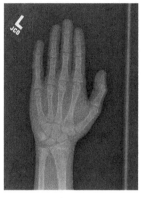  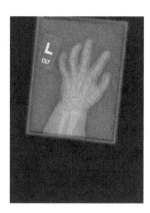

  (a) Female 180 Months      (b) Male 120 Months      (c) Female 36 Months

**Fig. 2.** Hand radiograph samples from the RSNA bone age dataset

either in terms of gender or by age categories. These cases of uneven distribution can be solved by the implementation of data augmentation techniques to evenly distribute the dataset and increase its size. The RSNA dataset had skeletal hand radiographs of males and females in the range from 1 to 228 months. Table 1 provides gender information about the RSNA dataset.

## 4.2 Evaluation Protocols

Evaluation protocols determine the test and performance measures. Successful strategies are generally representative of the dataset population and independent of the specific training data being used [1]. Therefore, skeletal estimation techniques need to be validated using data which is unseen to the model in the attempt to reduce overfitting and improve the generalisation performance of the model, thus making it representative of a population. A popular strategy for classification is cross-validation. This strategy entails splitting the dataset into subsets of training and validation, which are used to train and validate the model respectively. The training and validation sets have consecutive turns to 'cross-over' for every learning iteration of the model. This allows the model to be evaluated then increase its performance preferably through each learning iteration.

In each validation iteration, the absolute error (AE) for an age estimate is given by Eq. 1:

$$AE = |a_k - \bar{a}_k| \tag{1}$$

where $a_k$ is a of ground truth age and $\bar{a}_k$ is the respective estimate age. After all validation iterations are completed, the mean absolute error (MAE) can be defined as the average of all absolute errors. This is given by:

$$MAE = \frac{\sum_{k=1}^{n} |a_k - \bar{a}_k|}{n} \tag{2}$$

where $n$ is the total number of instances ground truth and estimate age pairs. This performance metric is commonly used, but in terms of age estimation it is advantageous to gather the MAE within age groups rather than through the entire dataset. The MAE can be modified to fit this requirement. Suppose the dataset is split into $j$ age groups, such that $D_s = a_1, a_2, ..., a_j$. Then the MAE for an age group is given by:

$$MAE_i = \frac{\sum_{k=1}^{n} |a_k - \bar{a}_k|}{n} \tag{3}$$

where $n$ is all the images in age group $i$. The overall MAE can be found as a sum of the MAE is each age group. Such that:

$$MAE_{total} = \frac{\sum_{k=1}^{j} MAE_k}{j} \tag{4}$$

In statistics, mean absolute error (MAE) is a measure of difference between two continuous variables. It measures the average magnitude of the errors in a set of predictions, without considering their direction, where all individual differences have equal weight. If the absolute value is not taken (the signs of the errors are not removed), the average error becomes the Mean Bias Error (MBE) and is usually intended to measure average model bias. Despite the various number of separate evaluation techniques which can be used for skeletal age estimation, it is most appropriate it make use of all evaluation techniques which will allow better literature comparisons to be made. Moreover, techniques such as RMSE will provide larger error for systems which produce larger errors within the respective age categories. This can be extremely useful when a model performs well on most age groups but provides inaccurate predictions for a particular age group which has a deviation further than other predictions made. This will result in a high RMSE, thus providing a more appropriate protocol for reducing the class errors as much as possible. The mean absolute error uses the same scale as the data being measured and therefore it is known as a scale dependent measure and cannot be used to make comparisons between series using different scales. RMSE is the standard deviation of the residuals, also known as prediction errors. Residuals are a measure of how far from the regression line data points are. In other words, the RMSE measures how spread out the residuals are or how concentrated the data is around the line of best fit. Root mean square error can be used for regression analysis to verify experimental results.

The RMSE is defined mathematically as:

$$RMSE = \sqrt{\frac{\sum_{i=1}^{n} |y_i - x_i|}{n}} \tag{5}$$

Both MAE and RMSE express average model prediction error in units of the variable of interest with the metrics ranging from 0 to $\infty$ and are indifferent to the direction of errors. The MAE and RMSE are negatively-oriented scores, which means lower values are better Taking the square root of the average squared errors has some interesting implications for RMSE. Since the errors are squared before they are averaged, the RMSE gives a relatively high weight to large errors. This means the RMSE should be more useful when large errors are particularly undesirable.

## 5   Results

Following the methodology shown in Fig. 1, results are split and discussed in 3 main areas. The first area is the performance of each of the deep learning models by itself, known as the plain performance. The second area is the performance of the deep learning models when average ensemble is applied to the classification results. Lastly, the performance of models when weighted ensemble is applied to the models where the better performing plain models have a higher weight contribution than lower performing models. The models were all pretrained on the ImageNet dataset. Thereafter, the weights of the models were altered by fine-tuning each model using the RSNA Bone Age dataset with only 5 epochs of training being allowed. Limiting the training epochs allows performance evaluations and improvements across methods to be done without allowing the plain models to be trained to exhaustion. This allows better evaluation of the ensemble techniques. All performance evaluations are represented in the 3 main metrics to allow comparison among current and future literature.

Table 2 represents the plain model performance. The worst performing models under the mentioned specifications was the $InceptionResNetV2$ and $InceptionV3$. The $InceptionResNetV2$ achieved a $MSE$ of 445.22 and $MAE$ of 16.75 months. Under the same specifications, the $DenseNet201$ performed the best and achieved a $MSE$ and $MAE$ of 160.83 and 9.96 months respectively. All 5 deep learning models achieved reasonable results in 5 epochs of tuning with $MAE$ ranging between 16.75 and 9.96 months. Figure 3 shows a visual comparison of $MAE$ and $RMSE$ of the models.

From the plain models, averaging ensemble was introduced. The results for this is represented in Table 3. When an ensemble of 2 of the best performing models are done ($VGG16\, and\, DenseNet201$) a $MSE$ and $MAE$ of 152.24 and 9.55 months respectively is achieved. This result already surpasses the best single plain model's result. Interestingly, when an average ensemble of the $VGG16 + DenseNet201 + InceptionResNetv2$ is done, a $MSE$ and $MAE$ of 170.54 and 10.20 months respectively is achieved. This implies that even though $InceptionResNetV2$ one of the lowest plain model results as shown in Table 2,

**Table 2.** Model performances of plain deep learning models trained on the ImageNet dataset and fine-tuned for only 5 epochs on the RSNA dataset.

| Model | Gender | Evaluation | | |
|---|---|---|---|---|
| | | MSE | MAE | RMSE |
| VGG16 | Male + Female | 250.53 | 12.32 | 15.82 |
| | Male | 462.92 | 16.32 | 21.51 |
| | Female | 240.14 | 13.26 | 15.49 |
| ResNet50 | Male + Female | 291.47 | 13.24 | 17.07 |
| | Male | 414.91 | 15.70 | 20.36 |
| | Female | 360.16 | 14.95 | 18.97 |
| InceptionV3 | Male + Female | 851.00 | 23.30 | 29.17 |
| | Male | 775.46 | 22.03 | 27.84 |
| | Female | 421.75 | 15.45 | 20.53 |
| InceptionResNetV2 | Male + Female | 445.22 | 16.75 | 21.10 |
| | Male | 598.31 | 18.90 | 24.46 |
| | Female | 367.56 | 15.13 | 19.17 |
| DenseNet201 | Male + Female | 160.83 | 9.96 | 12.68 |
| | Male | 183.53 | 10.71 | 13.54 |
| | Female | 145.81 | 9.26 | 12.07 |

**Table 3.** The following table represented the deep learning model performances when averaging ensemble is applied.

| Model | Gender | Evaluation | | |
|---|---|---|---|---|
| | | MSE | MAE | RMSE |
| VGG16 + DN201 | Male + Female | 152.24 | 9.55 | 12.33 |
| | Male | 270.93 | 12.57 | 16.46 |
| | Female | 149.12 | 10.03 | 12.21 |
| VGG16 + DN201 + IRNV2 | Male + Female | 170.54 | 10.20 | 13.05 |
| | Male | 306.40 | 13.06 | 17.50 |
| | Female | 163.63 | 10.43 | 12.79 |
| RN50 + DN201 | Male + Female | 851.00 | 23.30 | 29.17 |
| | Male | 775.46 | 22.03 | 27.84 |
| | Female | 421.75 | 15.45 | 20.53 |

when added with 2 better performing models it managed to achieve more acceptable results, closer to the best performing. This shows that there is a possibility that even though $InceptionResNetV2$ performs poorly as a plain model, it can correct some of the regression errors made by better performing models. This can be explored through weighted ensemble.

Table 4 represented the performance results of the application of weighted ensemble applied to the plain models, where the percentage contribution of each model is calculated based on each model's plain performance. The best result achieved a $MAE$ of 9.32 months. This was achieved by a weighted ensemble of $VGG16(0.2) + DenseNet201(0.7)$ and also tied with the weighted ensemble of $VGG16(0.25) + DenseNet201(0.7) + IRNV2(0.1)$. The tie breaker was decided on the $MSE$ and $RMSE$ evaluations where the model with the added weight

**Table 4.** The following table represented the deep learning model performances when weighted ensemble is applied.

| Model | Weight | Gender | Evaluation | | |
|---|---|---|---|---|---|
| | | | MSE | MAE | RMSE |
| VGG16 + DN201 | 0.25/0.75 | Male + Female | 143.18 | 9.32 | 11.96 |
| | | Male | 211.09 | 11.32 | 14.52 |
| | | Female | 133.2 | 9.13 | 11.54 |
| RN50 + DN201 | 0.1/0.9 | Male + Female | 158.63 | 9.89 | 12.59 |
| | | Male | 176.42 | 10.78 | 13.28 |
| | | Female | 150.54 | 9.42 | 12.26 |
| VGG16 + DN201 + IRNV2 | 0.2/0.7/0.1 | Male + Female | 142.78 | 9.32 | 11.94 |
| | | Male | 198.56 | 11.33 | 14.09 |
| | | Female | 141.65 | 9.38 | 11.90 |

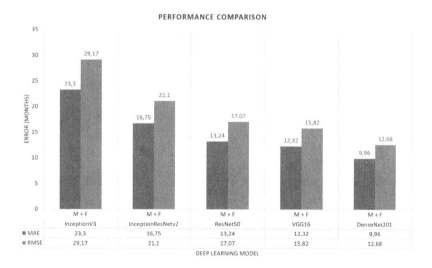

**Fig. 3.** Bar graph representing performance of plain models using MAE and RMSE evaluations. We can clearly see that both inception models perform poorly under 5 epochs of fine tuning, while the DenseNet201 and VGG16 perform much better under the same conditions

of the $IRNV2$ at 0.1 achieved a $MSE$ and $RMSE$ of 142.78 and 11.94 respectively, compared to the model without the $IRNV2$ which achieved a $MSE$ and $RMSE$ of 143.18 and 11.96 respectively. This shows that even though the $IRNV2$ model performed poorly compared to the other models, when added to a weighted ensemble of the better performing models it did in fact increase overall performance.

Overall performance improvements across the plain, average ensemble and the weighted ensemble is shown in Table 5. Figure 4 shows a scatter plot and line of best fit. Figure 4a shows the regression of the $InceptionResNetV2$ plain performance. We can observe outliers begin to appear and disappear as average and weighted ensemble is applied, as shown in Fig. 4c and Fig. 4d. With the introduction of the $InceptionResNetV2$, we see the improvement from Fig. 4c to Fig. 4d as outlies get reduced (Table 6).

**Table 5.** The following table represents the performance improvements across the explored approaches. The best plain approach has a significantly higher MSE and MAE while the best performing approach was the weighed ensemble which had a MSE, MAE and RMSE improvement of 18.05, 0.64 and 0.74 months respectively compared to the best plain performing model.

| Model | Regressor | Evaluation | | |
|---|---|---|---|---|
| | | MSE | MAE | RMSE |
| DenseNet201 | Plain | 160.83 | 9.96 | 12.68 |
| VGG16 + DN201 | Averaging | 152.24 | 9.55 | 12.33 |
| VGG16 + DN201 + IRNV2 | Weighted 0.2/0.7/0.1 | 142.78 | 9.32 | 11.94 |

**Table 6.** Comparison of results obtained from literature indicate that the performance of weakly fine-tuned model ensembling falls in range of other approaches which use more structural information extraction techniques from the radiographs.

| Method | Evaluation | | |
|---|---|---|---|
| | MAE | MSE | RMSE |
| [2] VGG16 | 16.88 | – | – |
| [2] VGG16 | 11.45 | – | – |
| **DenseNet201** | 9.96 | 160.83 | 12.68 |
| **VGG16 + DN201** | 9.55 | 152.24 | 12.33 |
| [3] DL + Carpal | 9.43 | – | – |
| **VGG16 + DN201 + IRNV2** | 9.32 | 142.78 | 11.94 |
| [3] DL + Metacarpals | 8.42 | – | – |
| [3] DL + Hand | 8.08 | – | – |
| [2] VGG16 | 6.80 | – | – |
| [9] Residual Learning | 6.44 | – | – |

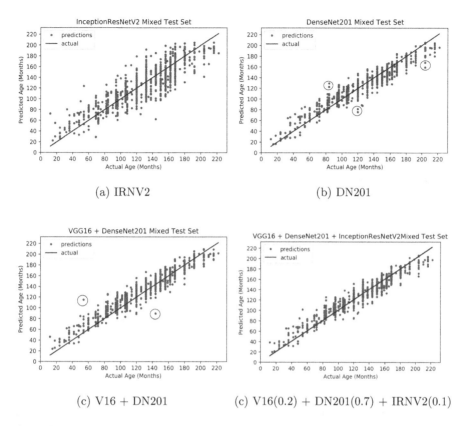

(a) IRNV2    (b) DN201

(c) V16 + DN201    (c) V16(0.2) + DN201(0.7) + IRNV2(0.1)

**Fig. 4.** Scatter plot representing the performance of various models in each of the tested categories. Figure 4a represents the scatter plot of the InceptionResNetV2, which is shown to perform poorly compared to other models. Figure 4b and c show the best performing plain and average models. Both of these regression graphs show correct outliers with the introduction of new but lower error outliers. Figure 4c shows the addition of the InceptionRenNetV2 into the weighted ensemble and its performance improvements can be seen by the reduction of outlies.

## 6    Conclusion

In this paper we explored the issue of skeletal age estimation from hand radiographs, with specific insight to performance improvements using weakly fine-tuned deep learning models originally trained on the ImageNet dataset. The weakly fine-tuned models on plain evaluations achieved MSE of 160.83 months. With the introduction of average ensembling the MSE had dropped to 152.24 months. Despite InceptionResNetV2 achieving a plain model MSE evaluation of 445.22 months, under weighted ensemble with the VGG16 and DenseNet201 models it managed to achieve the best result of a MSE of 142.78 months. These performance improvements indicate that weakly fine-tuned models can still performed increasingly better under ensemble environments even with poor performing models such as the InceptionResNetV2 which most likely will perform better if trained more. Furthermore, this indicates that even poor performing models can extract particular features that better performing models can't, and only under weighted ensemble can we see the performance improve. Further exploration can be done to evaluate the performance of these weakly trained models if used as feature extractors and not classifiers. Therefore, exploration of various types of regressor classifiers under the training data of features extracted from weakly fine-tuned deep learning models.

# References

1. Budka, M., Gabrys, B.: Density-preserving sampling: robust and efficient alternative to cross-validation for error estimation. IEEE Trans. Neural Netw. Learn. Sys. **24**(1), 22–34 (2013)
2. Castillo, J.C., Tong, Y., Zhao, J., Zhu, F.: RSNA Bone-age Detection using Transfer Learning and Attention Mapping, pp. 5
3. Iglovikov, V., Rakhlin, A., Kalinin, A., Shvets, A.: Pediatric Bone Age Assessment Using Deep Convolutional Neural Networks, vol. 11045, pp. 300–308 (2018). arXiv:1712.05053 [cs]
4. Kattukaran, M.S., Abraham, A.: Bone age assessment using deep. Learning **9**(2), 4 (2018)
5. Pietka, E., Gertych, A., Pospiech, S., Cao, F., Huang, H.K., Gilsanz, V.: Computer-assisted bone age assessment: image preprocessing and epiphyseal/metaphyseal ROI extraction. IEEE Trans. Med. Imaging **20**(8), 715–729 (2001)
6. Poznanski, Andrew K., Garn, Stanley M., Nagy, Jerrold M., Gall, John C.: Metacarpophalangeal pattern profiles in the evaluation of skeletal malformations. Radiology **104**(1), 1–11 (1972)
7. Rakhlin, A.: Diabetic Retinopathy detection through integration of Deep Learning classification framework. bioRxiv, June 2018
8. Rakhlin, A., Shvets, A., Iglovikov, V., Kalinin, A.: Deep Convolutional Neural Networks for Breast Cancer Histology Image Analysis. bioRxiv, April 2018
9. Souza, D., Oliveira, M.M.: End-to-end bone age assessment with residual learning. In: 2018 31st SIBGRAPI Conference on Graphics, Patterns and Images (SIBGRAPI), pp. 197–203, Parana, October 2018. IEEE
10. Tiulpin, A., Thevenot, J., Rahtu, E., Lehenkari, P., Saarakkala, S.: Simo: automatic knee osteoarthritis diagnosis from plain radiographs: a deep learning-based approach. Scientific Report **8**(1), 1–10 (2018)

# Fractal Geometry for Early Detection and Histopathological Analysis of Oral Cancer

Santisudha Panigrahi$^{(\boxtimes)}$, Juber Rahmen, Swagatika Panda, and Tripti Swarnkar

SOA Deemed to be University Bhubaneswar, Bhubaneswar 751030, Odisha, India
santisudha.nanda@gmail.com

**Abstract.** Oral squamous cell carcinoma (OSCC) has complex molecular structure stimulated by certain chromatin architectural changes which are not easy to be detected by the naked eye. Prediction of OSCC can be done through various clinical and histological factors. As the OSCC treatment is dependent on histological grading the recent focus is to discover the morphological changes studied by computer-assisted image analysis. One of such more specific diagnostic and prognostic factor is the analysis of the fractal geometry. Fractal Dimension (FD) is the analysis and quantification of the degree of complexity of the fractal objects. FD provides a way to precisely analyse the architecture of natural objects. The purpose of this research is to estimate Minkowski fractal dimension of histopathological images for early detection of oral cancer. The proposed model is developed for analysis medical images to estimate Minkowski fractal dimension using a box-counting algorithm that allows windowing of images for more accurate calculation in the suspected areas of oral cancerous growth.

**Keywords:** Histopathological analysis · Oral squamous cell carcinoma (OSCC) · Image processing · Oral cancer · Fractals · Minkowski dimension

## 1 Introduction

Oral squamous cell carcinoma (OSCC) is the most recurrent type of malignancy affecting oral cavity. Over the past several decades, the survival rate of oral cancer has not improved and still remains a severe public health issue [1]. Clinical and histological features can estimate the survival rate of OSCC patients and there is a need for more specific indicative and predictive factors. Recently, computer-aided image analysis has gained importance, several research has been done on biologic markers and morphological features of malignant cells studied through image analysis [28–30].

Oral cancer nuclear image analysis techniques are broadly categorized into two types: firstly the standard method based on of the nuclei size and secondly the contemporary and more precise technique including fractal analysis with mathematically proven and reliable outcomes [7].

The main objective of using medical images is to detect the potential abnormalities by identifying distinctive image patterns and the association between them. From the images the texture features are the key component, and important source of visual information for

© Springer Nature Switzerland AG 2020
B. R. Purushothama et al. (Eds.): MIKE 2019, LNAI 11987, pp. 177–185, 2020.
https://doi.org/10.1007/978-3-030-66187-8_17

image analysis. By using texture analysis methods to extract the significant information from medical images has given promising results [31]. Fractal geometry has become a prominent tool in the analysis of medical images, among various measures of texture analysis. The notion of fractal dimension has been applied to different fields of science and engineering such as shape analysis [2] and image segmentation [3]. Most applications of fractal concept has been seen in natural objects like mountains, clouds and trees [4–6]. Fractal measurement can depict and portray unpredictability of the images or their texture composition.

Fractal geometry is a mathematics concept introduced by Benoit Mandelbrot in 1982 [7]. The term fractal means irregular and rough shapes. The fractal objects' structures are extremely complex and also characterized by self-similarity. The investigation and evaluation of the level of unpredictability and abnormality of these objects provides estimations called "fractal dimensions" (FDs). There are many methods for estimation of FDs [8]. The most common method used to estimate the fractal dimension of natural objects is the box counting technique. The number of boxes of size needed to cover a fractal set $N = N_0 * R^{(-DF)}$, where DF $<=$ D (D is the dimension of the space, usually D $= 1,2,3$) which is repeated with different box sizes. DF is known as Minkowski-Bouligand dimension, N is the number of boxes with size R(The box sizes are powers of 2 i.e. R $= 1,2,4,.....2^p$ where p is the smallest integer such that MAX(SIZE(C)) $<=$ $2^p$,C is a D-dimensional array.

It has been observed that numerous structures of the human body, such as the retina vessels, air channels of the lungs and the vein tree of the kidneys, can be characterised as fractal objects [10–13]. In addition, fractal geometry is used in various areas of prescription. In cardiology for heartbeat valuation [14, 15], in neurology for the investigation of varying arrangements in electro encephalograms [16, 17], in radiology for radiographic examination and investigation of mammographic sores and tomographies [18–21].

Fractal analysis has also been applied for histopathology and cytology for the approximation of the fractal measurements of numerous neoplasms, for example, carcinomas of the gallbladder [23], lung [24], uterus [25], breast [26], larynx [27] and oral cavity [22].

The aim of our present study is to use image processing technique and nuclear fractal geometry to compare the morphometric complexity in the OSCC cases and different grades of OSCC such as well differentiated, moderately differentiated, and poorly differentiated will be verified.

## 2    Materials and Methods

Conventional histopathology detects the nuclear abnormalities for the calculation of the degree of variation. Nuclear complexity assessed by fractal study is a target and refined method for measurement of nuclear attribute. The morphological changes that the nucleus undergoes can also be used as an index for their transformation into neoplastic. It is observed that by using image processing techniques combined with fractal dimension, can help to automate the diagnosis process.

Minkowski-Bouligand dimension also known as box counting dimension is a method for defining the fractal dimension of a set S in a measurement space (X,d). To determine the fractal dimension for a fractal S, we have to imagine this fractal lying on a grid that is uniformly spaced, and check what number of boxes are required to cover the set. The box counting dimension is calculated by using a box counting algorithm to see how this number changes as we make the grid finer. Assume that N($\varepsilon$) is the number of boxes of side length $\varepsilon$ needed to cover the set, then the box-counting dimension is defined as in Eq. (1).

$$\dim_{box}(S) := \lim_{\varepsilon \to 0} logN(\varepsilon)/\log(1/\varepsilon) \tag{1}$$

Box counting method gathers information to analyze complicated patterns by splitting the image into smaller and smaller pieces, typically "box"- shaped and analysing the pieces at each smaller scale. This technique can be used for pattern extraction from the digital media.

### 2.1 Dataset Used

Histological H & E stained sections of normal mucosa and different grades OSCC are collected from the Institute of Dental Sciences (IDS, Siksha 'O' Anusandhan University). The data has been collected considering the patient concern and ethical committee clearance (Ref No./DMR/IMS.SH/SOA/1800040) of the IDS, SUM Hospital, Bhubaneswar, Odisha. A total of 114 samples of cases of OSCC were collected and included for this study. The slides were viewed under Lawrence and Mayo research microscope and images captured with 5 MP CMOS camera and stored digitally on the computer as high quality JPEG images. All images are 4032 × 3024 pixels in resolution and 24–bit with 16.7 million colors. To calculate the nFD we used 100X magnification of high power fields.

### 2.2 Proposed Model

The following steps go through our proposed model for the nFD values from the histopathological images. The block diagram of our proposed framework is illustrated in Fig. 1.

*a) Image Pre-Processing:* The data collected from the Institute of dental science is considered for pre-processing steps for our proposed model. The original image is filtered through Gaussian filter [34] which reduces the noise in the image. Then histogram equalization [35] is applied to enhance the contrast. It is accomplished by spreading the most frequent intensity values. The color image is converted to gray-scale which is required for proper fractal analysis.

*c) Segmentation:* Convolving mask is applied for sharpness and edge detection. For foreground (nucleus) and background (cytoplasm) separation, the image is subjected through a segmentation procedure known as Otsu methodology. This method is a means of finding an optimal threshold automatically based on the observed pixel value distribution (Otsu 1979) [32]. Then watershed algorithm [33] is applied to improve the effect of the image obtained by Otsu methodology.

*d) Feature Extraction:* In this phase the morphological feature, nuclear fractal dimension is extracted with the widely used box counting method of Minkowski-Bouligand dimension [22–27].

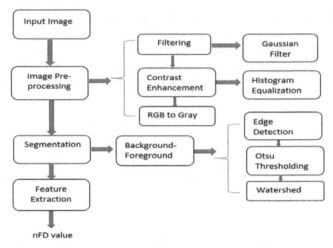

**Fig. 1.** Block diagram of the proposed model

# 3    Results and Discussion

Our proposed model is used to process the histopathological image of OSCC to extract a feature as nuclear fractal dimension. The different steps of image processing techniques can be made to enhance the raw image, and often the difference between the raw images and fully processed image is significant as seen from Table 1. It is observed that the value of nFD is significantly improved after image enhancement.

Our proposed method is assessed based on the following criteria.

i.   Extraction of morphological feature in terms of fractal dimension
ii.  Improvement in clinical interpretation using the fractal dimension

## 3.1    Extraction of Morphological Feature in Terms of Fractal Dimension

Figure 2 represents the overall steps of the proposed method for getting the nuclear fractal dimension as a morphological feature. Figure 2(a) represents the original histopathological image of oral mucosa. Gaussian filter is applied to reduce the noise in the image and histogram equalization is applied for contrast enhancement represented in Fig. 2(b). The color image is converted to greyscale, by which the complexity of the 3D pixel value is decreased in Fig. 2(c). Then the convolving mask is applied for sharpness and edge detection as shown in Fig. 2(d). Figure 2(e) represents the binary image obtained through a segmentation procedure known as otsu methodology. Fractal dimension algorithm is applied to extract the nFD using Fig. 2(f) obtained from watershed method.

Calculating fractal dimension with ImageJ software as in [21, 22] follows the selection of individual nuclei with Adobe Photoshop or the free hand selection tool. This selection of nuclei is a manual process followed by conversion to binary image suitable for fractal analysis. The box counting algorithm (FracLac plugin) is used to estimate the nuclear fractal dimension on each image. Then fractal dimension of the image is calculated by taking average of all the fractal dimensions of each nucleus.

2(a)                              2(b)                              2(c)

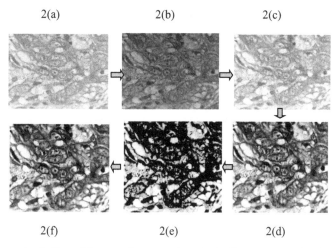

2(f)                              2(e)                              2(d)

**Fig. 2.** Shows the finding of the overall proposed method of image processing for oral mucosa

Our proposed method is more efficient compared to the above mentioned method, which requires human expertize to perform each and every step of extraction region of interest from the given input image. In our method there is no user interaction in between the input and recorded output. Only the input image will be given to the model, it automatically pre-processes, segments and extract the feature as nFD with widely used box-counting algorithm.

Calculating the nFD of each individual nucleus and then taking the average for a particular histopathological image will take more time, as the whole process is semi-manual [21, 22]. Selecting the nuclei with the free hand tool is totally user dependent. There will be a time variation from an expert to a general pathologist.

The below Table 1 shows the nuclear fractal dimension of 10 sample observation with respect to image enhancement and without image enhancement.

From the Table 1 it's clear that the nFD values are quietly improved compared to the direct image. The image processing methods are more suitable for display or further image analysis. For biomedical images these methods are very much required to remove unwanted noise, detect edges and enhance, making it easier to identify the key features.

### 3.2   Improvement in Clinical Interpretation Using the Fractal Dimension

The histological grading of oral squamous cell carcinoma is based mostly on the physical and functional nature of tumour epithelial cells. Grading based upon cellular and nuclear pleomorphism could play even a more important role. However, this grading system is subjected to subjective variation among pathologist which can be overcome by objective approach. Nuclear fractal dimension is attempted to utilize the objective evaluation potential of fractal dimension and co-relate with grading system as shown in Table 2.

Nuclear fractal dimension can be used as a classifier, since it is observed that there was a clear variance in the survival rate of the patients with fractal dimension values above and below the median value of 1.4 as seen in Fig. 3(a). These observations obtained

**Table 1.** Nuclear fractal dimension

| Sample image | nFD without enhancement | nFD with enhancement |
|---|---|---|
| 1 | 1.102160767 | 1.356722395 |
| 2 | 1.021704975 | 1.306379908 |
| 3 | 0.880899565 | 1.589653802 |
| 4 | 0.958915919 | 1.536753781 |
| 5 | 1.006295207 | 1.036371907 |
| 6 | 1.022639069 | 1.500007512 |
| 7 | 0.388706436 | 1.3843483 |
| 8 | 0.846874667 | 1.45136558 |
| 9 | 1.2451507 | 1.373278046 |
| 10 | 0.856874678 | 1.46236557 |

**Table 2.** OSCC grading based on nFD

| | | nFD of images | | Total |
|---|---|---|---|---|
| | | Low | High | |
| Grade | Moderate | 8 | 40 | 48 |
| | Poor | 0 | 1 | 1 |
| | Well | 11 | 54 | 65 |
| Total | | 19 | 95 | 114 |

from Table 2 and Fig. 3(a) supports the hypothesis that the nuclear fractal dimension may act as a self-determining predictive factor for the investigation of OSCC.

The above Fig. 3 shows the nuclear fractal dimension distribution of different images and its range. Figure 3(a) represents the box plot for the enhanced image that is after applying the image processing techniques. Figure 3(b) represents the nFD distribution of the raw image. It is observed that the value of nFD is significantly improved after image enhancement. Figure 3(a) represents the range of fractal dimension from 1.01 to 1.59 with lower quartile as 1.34, median 1.4 and upper quartile with 1.52. Table 2 represents the 114 cases of patients classified into three well defined categories of OSCC as (i) well differentiated (57.02% (n = 65)), (ii) moderately differentiated (42.10% (n = 48)), and (iii) poorly differentiated (0.88% (n = 1)) patients.

The study observes the statistically significant variation of FD between the poor quality and high evaluation tumor considering the P value as 0.001. Similarly a significant progressive and statistically increase of FD value from well differentiated to poorly differentiated cases is observed considering P = 0.003. From above study it can be

Boxplot grouped by Fractal-Dimension

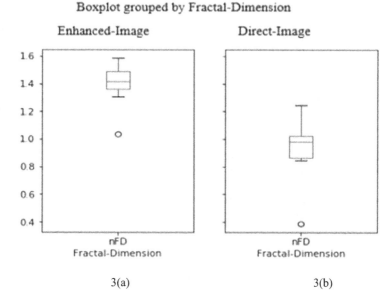

Fig. 3. Box plot of nuclear fractal dimension with the enhanced image and direct image

postulated that in the late period of OSCC tumorigenesis there is a significant increase in the complexity of the nuclear.

Therefore, it is necessary to identify, morphological ways to deal with recognize early changes that invigorate the intrusive development, for the most part on account of complex shapes where traditional morphometrical techniques may fail.

## 4   Conclusion

The study concludes that nuclear fractal dimension (nFD) acts as an important independent feature to predict the survival rate of oral malignant growth patients. However, extra studies are required with expanded number of patients to get the definite finding. Digital pathology based nFD scoring provide a more reliable and objective indicator of prognosis. The comprehensive approach towards the nuclear fractal dimension analysis using image processing methods and applying fractal dimension algorithms, is a promising approach towards the prognosis and diagnosis of OSCC.

## References

1. Silverman Jr., S.: Demographics and occurrence of oral and pharyngeal cancers. The outcomes, the trends, the challenge. J. Am. Dent. Assoc. 132(Suppl), 7S–11S (2001)
2. Orford, J., Whalley, W.: The use of the fractal dimension to quantify the morphology of irregular-shaped particles. Sedimentology 30, 655–668 (1983)
3. Keller, J., et al.: Texture description and segmentation through fractal geometry. Comput. Vis. Graph. Image Process. 45, 150–166 (1989)

4. Voss, R.F.: Random fractal forgeries. In: Earnshaw, R.A. (ed.) Fundamenfal Algorithms for Computer Graphics, pp. 805–836. Springer-Verlag, New York (1985). https://doi.org/10. 1007/978-3-642-84574-1_34
5. Fournier, A., Fussell, D., Carpenter, L.: Computer rendering of stochastic models. Commun. Ass. Comput. Mach. **25**(6), 371–384 (1982)
6. Barnsley, M.F., Ervin, V., Hardin, D., Lancaster, J.: Solution of an inverse problem for fractals and other sets. Proc. Not. Acad. Sci. **83**, 1975–1977 (1986)
7. Goutzamanis, L., Pavlopoulos, P.M., Papageorgakis, N.: Fractal analysis in the study of oral cancer. Aust Asian J Cancer **11**, 5–12 (2012)
8. Neha, U., Shubhangi, K., Alka, D., Kumar, M.R., Rohit, M.: A study of morphometrical differences between normal mucosa, dysplasia, squamous cell carcinoma and pseudoepitheliomatous hyperplasia of the oral mucosa. IOSR J. Pharm. Biol. Sci. **5**, 66–70 (2013)
9. Deepa, S., Tessamma, T.: Fractal features based on differential box counting method for the categorization of digital mammograms. Int. J. Comput. Inf. Syst. Ind. Manage. Appl. **2**, 011–019 (2010)
10. Family, F., Masters, B.R., Platt, D.E.: Fractal pattern formation in human retinal vessels. Physica **38**, 98–103 (1989)
11. Mainster, M.A.: The fractal properties of retinal vessels: embryological and clinical implications. Eye **4**(Pt1), 235–241 (1990)
12. Nelson, T.R., West, B.J., Goldberger, A.L.: The fractal lung: universal and species-related scaling patterns. Experientia **46**(3), 251–254 (1990). https://doi.org/10.1007/BF01951755
13. Cross, S.S., Start, R.D., Silcocks, P.B., Bull, A.D., Cotton, D.W., Underwood, J.C.: Quantitation of the renal arterial tree by fractal analysis. J. Pathol. **170**(4), 479–484 (1993)
14. Yeragani, V.K., Srinivasan, K., Vempati, S., Pohl, R., Blon, R.: Fractal dimension of heart rate time series: an effective measure of autonomic function. J. Appl. Physiol. **75**, 2429–2438 (1993)
15. Otsuka, K., Cornelissen, G., Halberg, F.: Circadian rhythmic fractal scaling of heart rate variability in health and coronary artery disease. Clin. Cardiol. **20**, 631–638 (1997)
16. Pradhan, N., Dutt, D.N.: Use of running fractal dimension for the analysis of changing patterns in electroencephalograms. Comput. Biol. Med. **23**, 381–388 (1993)
17. Preissl, H., Lutzenberger, W., Purvermuller, F., Birbaumer, N.: Fractal dimensions of short EEG time series in humans. Neurosci. Lett. **225**, 77–80 (1997)
18. Southard, T.E., Southard, K.A., Jakobsen, J.R., Hillis, S.L., Najim, C.A.: Fractal dimension in radiographic analysis of alveolar process bone. Oral Surg. Oral Med. Oral Pathol. Oral Radiol. Endod. **82**, 569–576 (1996)
19. Veenland, J.F., Grashius, J.L., Van der Meer, F., Beckers, A.L., Gelsema, E.S.: Estimation of fractal dimension in radiographs. Med. Phys. **23**, 585–594 (1996)
20. Velanovich, V.: Fractal analysis of mammographic lesions: a feasibility study quantifying the difference between benign and malignant masses. Am. J. Med. Sci. **311**, 211–214 (1996)
21. Dougherty, G., Henerby, G.M.: Fractal signature and lacunarity in the measurement of the texture of trabecular bone in clinical CT images. Med. Eng. Phys. **23**, 369–380 (2001)
22. Goutzanis, L., Papadogeorgakis, N., Pavlopoulos, P.M., et al.: Nuclear fractal dimension as a prognostic factor in oral squamous cell carcinoma. Oral Oncol. **44**, 345–353 (2008)
23. Waliszewski, P.: Distribution of grand-like structures in human gallbladder adenocarcinomas possesses fractal dimension. J Surg. Oncol. **71**, 189–195 (1999)
24. Oczeretko, E., Juczewska, M., Kasacka, I.: Fractal geometric analysis of lung cancer angiogenic patterns. Folia Histochem. Cytobiol. **39**(Suppl. 2), 75–76 (2001)
25. Dey, P., Rajesh, L.: Fractal dimension in endometrial carcinoma. Anal. Quant. Cytol. Histol. **26**(2), 113–116 (2004)

26. Yokoyama, T., Kawahara, A., Kage, M., Kojiro, M., Takayasu, H., Sato, T.: Image analysis of irregularity of cluster shape in cytological diagnosis of breast tumors: cluster analysis with 2D-fractal dimension. Diagn. Cytopathol. **33**(2), 71–77 (2005)
27. Delides, A., Panayoiotdes, I., Alegakis, A., Kyroudi, A., Banis, C., Pavlaki, A., et al.: Fractal dimension as a prognostic factor for laryngeal carcinoma. Anticancer Res. **25**, 2141–2144 (2005)
28. Zhao, Y.-Q., Gui, W.-H., Chen, Z.-C., Tang, J.-T., Li, L.-Y.: Medical images edge detection based on mathematical morphology. In: 2005 IEEE Engineering in Medicine and Biology 27th Annual Conference, pp. 6492–6495. IEEE (2006)
29. Chen, S., Zhao, M., Wu, G., Yao, C., Zhang, J.: Recent advances in morphological cell image analysis. Comput. Math. Methods Med. **2012**, 101536 (2012)
30. Pattanaik, P.A., Swarnkar, T., Sheet, D.: Object detection technique for malaria parasite in thin blood smear images. In: 2017 IEEE International Conference on Bioinformatics and Biomedicine (BIBM), pp. 2120–2123. IEEE (2017)
31. Pietikäinen, M.K.: Texture Analysis in Machine Vision. World Scientific, Singapore (2000)
32. Otsu, N.: A threshold selection method from gray-level histograms. IEEE Trans. Syst. Man Cybern. **9**(1), 62–66 (1979)
33. Beucher, S.: The watershed transformation applied to image segmentation. In: Scanning Microscopy-Supplement, p. 299 (1992)
34. Wang, M., Zheng, S., Li, X., Qin, X.: A new image denoising method based on Gaussian filter. In: 2014 International Conference on Information Science, Electronics and Electrical Engineering, vol. 1, pp. 163–167. IEEE (2014)
35. Zhihong, W., Xiaohong, X.: Study on histogram equalization. In: 2011 2nd International Symposium on Intelligence Information Processing and Trusted Computing, pp. 177–179. IEEE (2011)

# Under-Sample Binary Data Using CURE for Classification

T. Kathirvalavakumar[1]([✉]), S. Karthikeyan[2], and Rajendra Prasath[3]

[1] Department of Computer Science, VHNSN College, Virudhunagar, India
kathirvalavakumar@yahoo.com
[2] Department of Information Technology, VHNSN College, Virudhunagar, India
[3] Indian Institute of Information Technology, Sri City, Chittoor, AP, India
rajendra.prasath@iiits.in

**Abstract.** Classification is a major break-through in the field of research. The performance of a classifier is highly dependent on the preprocessing. Drawback with most of the classifiers is its performance. It always focuses on the class having a high number of samples and ignores the class having fewer numbers of samples. This problem is identified through state-of-the-art evaluation metrics. To overcome this problem, the data in imbalanced form are converted into balanced form before the classification process. In the proposed work, instead of balancing, samples are re-sampled with the help of cluster based technique CURE. It performs under-sampling by reducing the majority samples but not balancing with minority samples. The experimental results show that the data re-sampled through CURE performs better.

**Keywords:** K-means · Cure · Clustering · Under-sampling · Class imbalance

## 1 Introduction

Data is more precious in most real world problems. As the size of data increases tremendously the data distribution between classes can vary considerably which will create a high number of samples in one (majority) class and less number of samples in other (minority) classes. The skewness of the class distribution is represented using the Imbalance Ratio (IR) [1]. IR is defined by the proportion of samples in the majority class to that of the minority class.

In machine learning, classifiers are taking part in performing classification tasks. Classifiers effectively handle majority data, but for minority data its misclassification rate gets considerably increased [2]. Most of the existing classifiers are capable of handling data in balanced nature but it may not be able to handle imbalanced data in an efficient way. The performance of a classifier is justified using its accuracy. When the data are imbalanced, the percentage accuracy of minority class is not closer to majority class. Since the samples in the minority class are less in numbers, it might not influence much on accuracy prediction.

Problems with the imbalanced data set is often found in medical diagnosis, fraud detection and many other fields [3]. One way to increase the count of minority class

© Springer Nature Switzerland AG 2020
B. R. Purushothama et al. (Eds.): MIKE 2019, LNAI 11987, pp. 186–195, 2020.
https://doi.org/10.1007/978-3-030-66187-8_18

samples is by collecting needed numbers of samples from the real time environment. If the possibility of collecting samples from the environment is rare then data are re-sampled from the existing samples. Re-sampling techniques often used are over sampling, under sampling and hybrid sampling.

Oversampling is the process of increasing the number of minority samples to the number of majority samples. Random oversampling is a technique which helps to increase the count of minority samples. While using random sampling, instances get duplicated and that leads to over-fitting. This problem has been eradicated using certain methods. Synthetic Minority Oversampling TEchnique (SMOTE) [1] is used to generate synthetic samples by joining all the minority samples using a statistical line. Required number of synthetic samples is obtained along the line segment through computation. Data preprocessed using SMOTE is best suited for many classification algorithms. SMOTE generates data without considering the neighboring samples which causes overlapping of classes. Difficulties with SMOTE can be eliminated by its extensions as Adaptive SMOTE [4], Safe-level SMOTE [5] and Borderline SMOTE [5]. These algorithms avoid the overgeneralization of synthetic data.

In contrast to this strategy, under-sampling down sampled the majority samples to the count of minority samples. Edited Nearest Neighbor (ENN) [6] algorithm removes samples, which do not have the same opinion with the neighbors, from the dataset. Here the nearest neighbors rule is applied k-times in the data samples, which eliminates the samples which do not fit for the criteria. Tomek [7] has well formed the data by eliminating overlapping samples from the majority class until all minimally distanced nearest neighbor pairs are formed.

Clustering is an unsupervised learning method which groups the data based on the similarity measures. Clustering based under sampling approach [8] can replace the traditional methods of resampling. Clustering may be done through partitional or hierarchical. Both methods have the ability to produce a predetermined number of clusters. Many clustering methods are formulated during the past decades to infer useful information from various domains.

Partitional clustering has the ability to create exactly N clusters, it works by splitting a large group of majority data samples to the count of minority samples so as to balance the total number of samples in both classes. Every problem has its own IR, so the number of clusters to be created is depending on the problem. In turn, Hierarchical agglomerative clustering algorithms work by splitting the data to different clusters and merge them based on the similarity.

Altincay and Ergan [9] have followed a centroid based approach. They use the $k$-means algorithm to obtain training samples in the ratio 1:1. Major drawback with their work is that the under-sampled data works on balanced adaboost and not on adaboost. The classifier involved in this work uses a neural network. Yen and Lee [10] have used to under-sample the data in the ratio 1:1. In their work, they have distributed major and minor classes into a separate cluster and they have picked samples for the consecutive stage based on the euclidean distance between the samples. Their work was compared against the Near Miss algorithm and they have used neural networks with backpropagation to demonstrate the results. Rahman and Davis [11] have undersampled in the ratio 1:1 based on cluster. They have used C4.5 and Fuzzy unordered Induction algorithms to work with clinical data. Parinaz Sobhani et al. [12] have performed ensemble based clustering to down sample the majority class data. They have used NearMiss1, NearMiss2 and Nearest Neighbor algorithms to demonstrate the efficiency of their work. Srividya and Mallika [13] have performed under-sampling by dividing each cluster into concentric circles and picking samples from each cluster. They have used the Neural Network to classify the samples. Anuradha and Varma [14] have performed under-sampling with the help of adaptive k-means algorithm. They have used L1-norm instead of euclidean distance to select samples as L1-norm is less sensitive to outliers. Arafat et al. [15] have used the Random forest algorithm to under-sample the data. They compare their results against Adaboost, RUSBoost and SMOTEBoost to demo the accuracy.

Extensively used clustering based approach is k-means [16, 17], which is a popular Partitional Clustering algorithm for more than five decades. The popularity is due to its ability to handle data in an unsupervised manner. Its modified versions [18, 19] also shows a better accuracy in clustering data. The problem with the k-means algorithm is that it gets struck at Local minima. k-means is sensitive to outliers, so it may not handle outliers effectively. Lin et al. [16] have under sampled the majority class data using the k-means algorithm. In their work, the majority class samples are down sampled to generate k-samples where k indicates total number of instances in the minority class. As per their results, the overall accuracy of each dataset under-sampled under k-means does not provide good accuracy for some datasets.

Hybrid sampling on the other hand jointly uses both over and under sampling techniques [20]. Problems based on the Imbalanceness can be solved either through the adjustment in the algorithm level or through the data level [21].

The literature survey of the classification performance of the imbalanced dataset shows that the ratio of classification accuracy of majority and minority classes is not same and also not even closer. Many researches are going on to overcome this problem. The proposed work provides a data level solution for the imbalanced data based on the hierarchical agglomerative clustering. During under sampling the number of majority samples is made equivalent to double the size of minority samples. The method chosen to under sample the majority class is Clustering Using REpresentatives (CURE) [22]. The contents of this paper is organized as follows, Sect. 2 describes the proposed method. Section 3 demonstrates the experimental results and Sect. 4 shows the concluding remarks.

## 2   CURE

CURE method is used to under sample the majority data. CURE generates required 'N' samples from a large amount of available samples. Samples are clustered based on representatives. It handles data of higher dimensions with more time. But, as the generated samples consider the minority samples in classification accuracy, the time constraint becomes vanished. For small and medium scale datasets, it takes much less time for under-sampling than other cluster based methods.

CURE is capable of handling outliers. It does many consecutive merges and splits throughout the process of clustering. Initially, each sample in the dataset is considered as an individual cluster. Cluster means are calculated for each cluster by averaging the components of the representative of the cluster. Based on the means, clusters are arranged in ascending order. The cluster with minimum mean value and the second minimum mean value are merged to form a new cluster. After merging, the cluster representative for the new cluster is calculated by finding the mean of all samples in the cluster. The process of clustering continues until the number of clusters equivalent to the value of N. After the data are under-sampled, the classifier is used for classification. The pseudo code of CURE is shown in the Algorithm.

### 2.1  Algorithm

1. Let N be the user defined cluster count
2. Treat each pattern as a separate cluster (Totally N clusters)
3. Pattern in a cluster is representative of the cluster
4. Find a value for a cluster by adding all components of the representative of the cluster
5. Sort the values of the clusters in ascending order
6. Merge the two clusters in the first two positions
7. Find representative for the merged cluster by finding average of each components in the cluster
8. Find new value for this merged cluster
9. Keep the clusters in the ascending order based on its value
10. Repeat steps 6–9 until the number of clusters equal to user defined value

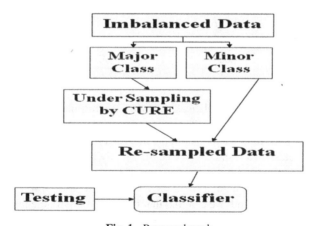

**Fig. 1.** Proposed work

The proposed work is shown in Fig. 1.

## 3   Experimental Results and Discussion

### 3.1  Datasets

The small and medium scale datasets are downloaded from [23] for the experiment. The Weka 3.8 tool is used for classification. Classifiers involved in this work include C4.5,

Multi layer perceptron (MLP) and Bagging. C4.5 is a decision tree classifier which is used to generate decision-tree based on certain criteria. Multi layer perceptron is a type of feedforward artificial neural network. Bagging is an ensemble based classifier; it uses a series of classifiers instead of classifying data using a single classifier. The final result is produced by aggregating the results of each classifier through voting or averaging. The information regarding the total number of majority data points, minority data points and its imbalance ratio of the downloaded data samples are specified in Table 1. The process of clustering starts by knowing the total number of minority data instances in a particular data set.

**Table 1.** Small and medium datasets and its imbalanced ratio

| Name | #Instances | # of instances in majority class | # of instances in minority class | IR |
|------|-----------|----------------------------------|----------------------------------|-----|
| Abalone9vs18 | 731 | 689 | 42 | 16.40 |
| Ecoli0vs1 | 220 | 143 | 77 | 1.86 |
| Glass0 | 214 | 144 | 70 | 2.06 |
| Haberman | 306 | 225 | 81 | 2.77 |
| Iris0 | 150 | 100 | 50 | 2.00 |
| New-thyroid1 | 215 | 180 | 35 | 5.14 |
| Pima | 768 | 500 | 268 | 1.86 |
| Vehicle0 | 846 | 647 | 199 | 3.25 |
| Vowel0 | 988 | 898 | 90 | 9.97 |
| Yeast1 | 1484 | 1,055 | 429 | 2.46 |

To analyze the effect of imbalanced datasets, the original dataset is used in the classifier without any preprocessing. The effect of each classifier is given in Table 2 and 3. Each table shows the information about the dataset, total number of instances in each dataset, correctly classified instances (CCI), incorrectly classified instances (ICI), total number of minority samples in ICI and its accuracy.

Each classifier produces a good accuracy under each dataset. But if we analyze the classifier performance in depth we can find that it doesn't classify the minority samples in a right way. This problem is explored when we have a closer look at the confusion matrix of a classifier. In particular, when we analyze the false predictions of a classifier, it is clear that the number of instances in minority class is high among the total number of instances in false predictions. It has been observed from Tables 2 and 3 that classifiers are not trained to reduce the misclassification rate of minority samples when the dataset is imbalanced in nature (Table 4).

To overcome this difficulty the dataset undergo under-sampling by CURE as to support classifier to achieve best result by considering samples in the minority class too. Re-sampling with the ratio 1:1 might not get enough samples to represent the characteristics of whole group, misclassification rate get decreased, but accuracy is becoming a

**Table 2.** Classifier performance and confusion matrix measures of C4.5

| Dataset | #instances | C4.5 | | | |
|---|---|---|---|---|---|
| | | CCI | ICI | ICI under minority class | Accuracy (%) |
| Abalone9vs18 | 731 | 708 | 23 | 22 | 96.8 |
| Ecoli0vs1 | 220 | 218 | 2 | 2 | 99.1 |
| Glass0 | 214 | 205 | 9 | 4 | 95.8 |
| Haberman | 306 | 236 | 70 | 45 | 75.6 |
| Iris0 | 150 | 150 | 0 | 0 | 100 |
| New-thyroid1 | 215 | 214 | 1 | 0 | 99.5 |
| Pima | 768 | 646 | 122 | 90 | 84.2 |
| Vehicle0 | 846 | 835 | 11 | 8 | 98.7 |
| Vowel0 | 988 | 985 | 3 | 2 | 99.7 |
| Yeast1 | 1484 | 1240 | 244 | 173 | 83.1 |

**Table 3.** Classifier performance and confusion matrix measures of multilayer perceptron and bagging

| Dataset | #instances | Multi layer perceptron | | | | Bagging | | | |
|---|---|---|---|---|---|---|---|---|---|
| | | CCI | ICI | ICI under minority class | Accuracy (%) | CCI | ICI | ICI under minority class | Accuracy (%) |
| Abalone9vs18 | 731 | 705 | 26 | 22 | 96.1 | 704 | 27 | 27 | 96.4 |
| Ecoli0vs1 | 220 | 218 | 2 | 2 | 99.1 | 217 | 3 | 2 | 98.6 |
| Glass0 | 214 | 188 | 26 | 16 | 88.2 | 198 | 16 | 5 | 92.5 |
| Haberman | 306 | 235 | 71 | 59 | 74.7 | 250 | 56 | 47 | 81.3 |
| Iris0 | 150 | 150 | 0 | 0 | 100 | 150 | 0 | 0 | 100 |
| New-thyroid1 | 215 | 214 | 1 | 1 | 99.5 | 212 | 3 | 3 | 98.6 |
| Pima | 768 | 627 | 141 | 100 | 81.5 | 667 | 101 | 73 | 86.9 |
| Vehicle0 | 846 | 845 | 1 | 0 | 99.9 | 827 | 19 | 4 | 97.8 |
| Vowel0 | 988 | 988 | 0 | 0 | 100 | 982 | 6 | 5 | 99.4 |
| Yeast1 | 1484 | 1179 | 305 | 196 | 78.6 | 1290 | 194 | 143 | 86.8 |

major issue. In-order to improve the classification performance while maintaining accuracy, instead of keeping data in balanced form, the majority class samples are generated

**Table 4.** Classification accuracy under C4.5, MLP and bagging with under-sampling ratio of 1:1

| Dataset | K-means | | CURE | | |
|---|---|---|---|---|---|
| | C4.5 (%) | Adaboost C4.5 (%) | C4.5 (%) | MLP (%) | Bagging (%) |
| Abalone9vs18 | 69.9 | 80.8 | 57.71363 | 56.43346 | 54.05251 |
| Ecoli0vs1 | 98.3 | 98.2 | **99.67532** | **99.67532** | **99.67532** |
| Glass0 | 77.2 | 89 | **95** | 87.7381 | 82.85714 |
| Haberman | 62 | 64.1 | 61.23059 | 58.24373 | **65.86022** |
| Iris0 | 99 | 99 | **100** | **100** | **100** |
| New-thyroid1 | 93.8 | 93.3 | 92.46753 | **100** | 90.19481 |
| Pima | 75.3 | 77 | 72.20997 | 73.6807 | **79.65085** |
| Vehicle0 | 94.2 | 97.4 | 80.46261 | 77.52143 | 77.52143 |
| Vowel0 | 94.1 | 95.5 | **100** | **100** | **100** |
| Yeast1 | 74.1 | 74 | **75.53738** | 72.85477 | **75.99146** |

double in number of minority class samples using CURE. Sometimes in the existing dataset, number of majority samples may be less than double the size of minority samples or closer to number of minority samples; in this case majority samples cannot be doubled to number of minority samples, so we keep the dataset in a balanced form after processing. The classifier is trained using generated data samples and available minority samples. The classification accuracy of the actual dataset is calculated from the trained classification system. The results of the classifiers are shown in the Table 5. The classification accuracy obtained after balancing the data by k-means are compared with the re-sampled data obtained by CURE. Data generated by the proposed method classifies better through C4.5, MLP and Bagging classifiers. In most cases, MLP provides best results. The classification accuracy of Vehicle0 is closer to the accuracy obtained by the k-means + classifier system.

**Table 5.** Accuracy under C4.5, MLP and bagging

| Dataset | K-Means | | CURE | | |
|---|---|---|---|---|---|
| | C4.5 (%) | Adaboost C4.5 (%) | C4.5 (%) | MLP (%) | Bagging (%) |
| Abalone9vs18 | 69.9 | 80.8 | 64.23679 | **84.31724** | 56.55577 |
| Ecoli0vs1 | 98.3 | 98.2 | **99.67532** | **99.67532** | **99.67532** |
| Glass0 | 77.2 | 89 | **95** | 87.7381 | 82.85714 |
| Haberman | 62 | 64.1 | **79.45042** | 65.21306 | **72.79304** |
| Iris0 | 99 | 99 | **100** | **100** | **100** |
| New-thyroid1 | 93.8 | 93.3 | **97.01299** | **100** | 90.19481 |
| Pima | 75.3 | 77 | 72.20997 | 73.6807 | **79.65085** |
| Vehicle0 | 94.2 | 97.4 | 86.89104 | 96.47059 | 87.56317 |
| Vowel0 | 94.1 | 95.5 | **100** | **100** | **100** |
| Yeast1 | 74.1 | 74 | **81.86616** | 79.22436 | **85.55013** |

Number of iterations needed by k-means is much lesser than CURE as CURE is hierarchical. Comparison results are shown in Table 6.

**Table 6.** Number of iterations to preprocess

| Number of iterations | | | |
|---|---|---|---|
| Name | k-means | CURE | |
| | | 1:1 | 2:1 |
| Abalone9vs18 | 42 | 647 | 605 |
| Ecoli0vs1 | 2 | 66 | 66 |
| Glass0 | 4 | 37 | 37 |
| Haberman | 5 | 144 | 63 |
| Iris0 | 12 | 50 | 50 |
| New-thyroid1 | 5 | 145 | 110 |
| Pima | 4 | 232 | 232 |
| Vehicle0 | 4 | 448 | 249 |
| Vowel0 | 10 | 808 | 718 |
| Yeast1 | 5 | 626 | 197 |

Even though CURE takes multiple iterations for under-sampling the data, execution time of the algorithm is lesser than k-means. The execution time for resample the data by k-means and CURE are shown in Table 7.

**Table 7.** Execution time to under-sample using k-means and CURE

| Execution time | | | |
|---|---|---|---|
| Name | K-means (ms) | CURE | |
| | | 1:1 (ms) | 2:1 (ms) |
| Abalone9vs18 | 1,933 | 286 | 308 |
| Ecoli0vs1 | 3,367 | 85 | 8 |
| Glass0 | 3,701 | 161 | 5 |
| Haberman | 3,103 | 97 | 11 |
| Iris0 | 1,983 | 71 | 2 |
| New-thyroid1 | 1,755 | 95 | 9 |
| Pima | 2,304 | 181 | 52 |
| Vehicle0 | 1,937 | 341 | 185 |
| Vowel0 | 1,610 | 511 | 347 |
| Yeast1 | 2,291 | 507 | 178 |

# 4 Conclusion

In this work, imbalanced data are re-sampled by CURE the hierarchical agglomerative clustering algorithm. When the number of majority samples is equivalent to double the number of minority samples, it gets good accuracy in classification and also it considers the minority samples for classification and classifies it correctly than the experimental data in the balanced form. The execution time of the proposed work is much lesser than the k-means method for re-sampling. Classification accuracy is also better than the data generated by k-means for the 9 dataset among 10. Also it has been observed that mostly classifiers C4.5 and MLP performs well in most of the dataset. In the proposed work, misclassification rate of minority samples is considerably reduced which is a major contribution of the proposed work.

# References

1. García, V., Sánchez, J.S., Mollineda, R.A.: On the effectiveness of preprocessing methods when dealing with different levels of class imbalance. Knowl.-Based Syst. **25**(1), 13–21 (2012)
2. Weiss, G.M., Provost, F.: Learning when training data are costly: the effect of class distribution on tree induction. J. Artif. Intell. Res. **19**, 315–354 (2003)
3. Fawcett, T.O.M.: Adaptive fraud detection **316**, 291–316 (1997)
4. Dorn, K.H., Jobst, T.: Innenreinigung von Rohrleitungssystemen aus Stahl. JOT J. fuer Oberflaechentechnik **42**(5), 56–57 (2002)
5. Han, H., Wang, W.-Y., Mao, B.-H.: Borderline-SMOTE: a new over-sampling method in imbalanced data sets learning. In: Huang, D.-S., Zhang, X.-P., Huang, G.-B. (eds.) ICIC 2005. LNCS, vol. 3644, pp. 878–887. Springer, Heidelberg (2005). https://doi.org/10.1007/11538059_91
6. Wilson, D.L.: Asymptotic properties of nearest neighbor rules using edited data. IEEE Trans. Syst. Man Cybern. **2**(3), 408–421 (1972)
7. Tomek, I.: Two modifications of CNN. IEEE Trans. Syst. Man Cybern. **SMC-6**(11), 769–772 (1976)
8. Yen, S.J., Lee, Y.S.: Under-sampling approaches for improving prediction of the minority class in an imbalanced dataset. In: Huang, D.S., Li, K., Irwin, G.W. (eds.) Intelligent Control and Automation. Lecture Notes in Control and Information Sciences, vol. 344, pp. 731–740. Springer, Heidelberg (2006). https://doi.org/10.1007/978-3-540-37256-1_89
9. Altınçay, H., Ergün, C.: Clustering based under-sampling for improving speaker verification decisions using AdaBoost. In: Fred, A., Caelli, T.M., Duin, R.P.W., Campilho, A.C., de Ridder, D. (eds.) SSPR/SPR 2004. LNCS, vol. 3138, pp. 698–706. Springer, Heidelberg (2004). https://doi.org/10.1007/978-3-540-27868-9_76
10. Yen, S.-J., Lee, Y.-S.: Cluster-based sampling approaches to imbalanced data distributions. In: Tjoa, A.M., Trujillo, J. (eds.) DaWaK 2006. LNCS, vol. 4081, pp. 427–436. Springer, Heidelberg (2006). https://doi.org/10.1007/11823728_41
11. Rahman, M.M., Davis, D.N.: Cluster based under-sampling for unbalanced cardiovascular data. In: Proceedings of World Congress on Engineering (2013), vol. III, pp. 1–6 (2013)
12. Sobhani, P., Viktor, H., Matwin, S.: Learning from imbalanced data using ensemble methods and cluster-based undersampling. In: Appice, A., Ceci, M., Loglisci, C., Manco, G., Masciari, E., Ras, Z.W. (eds.) NFMCP 2014. LNCS (LNAI), vol. 8983, pp. 69–83. Springer, Cham (2015). https://doi.org/10.1007/978-3-319-17876-9_5

13. Srividhya, S., Mallika, R.: Cluster concentric circle based undersampling to handle imbalanced data. **24**, 314–319 (2016). Spec. Issue Innov. Information, Embed. Commun. Syst.
14. Anuradha, N., Varma, G.P.S.: PBCCUT-priority based class clustered under sampling technique approaches for imbalanced data classification. Indian J. Sci. Technol. **10**(18), 1–9 (2017)
15. Arafat, M.Y., Hoque, S., Farid, D.M.: Cluster-based under-sampling with random forest for multi-class imbalanced classification. In: International Conference on Software, Knowledge, Information Management & Applications, SKIMA, December 2017, pp. 1–6 (2018)
16. Lin, W.C., Tsai, C.F., Hu, Y.H., Jhang, J.S.: Clustering-based undersampling in class-imbalanced data. Inf. Sci. (Ny) **409–410**, 17–26 (2017)
17. Jo, T., Japkowicz, N.: Class imbalances versus small disjuncts. ACM SIGKDD Explor. Newsl. **6**(1), 40 (2004)
18. Olukanmi, P.O., Twala, B.: k-means-sharp: modified centroid update for outlier-robust k-means clustering. In: 2017 Pattern Recognition Association of South Africa and Robotics and Mechatronics International Conference, PRASA-RobMech 2017, January 2018, November, pp. 14–19 (2018)
19. Bradley, P.S., Fayyad, U.M.: Refining initial points for k-means clustering. In: ICML, pp. 91–99 (1998)
20. Seiffert, C., Van Hulse, J., Raton, B.: Hybrid sampling for imbalanced data. In: IEEE International Conference on Information Reuse and Integration, pp. 202–207 (2008)
21. Monard, M.C.: A study of the behavior of several methods for balancing machine learning training data
22. Guha, S., Rastogi, R., Shim, K.: CURE: an efficient clustering algorithm for large databases. Inf. Syst. **26**(1), 35–58 (2001)
23. Small Scale Data Set. https://sci2s.ugr.es/keel/

# Extraction of White and Grey Lesion Features for the Inference of ADHD

K. Krishnaveni$^{(\boxtimes)}$ and E. Radhamani

Sri S. Ramasamy Naidu Memorial College, Sattur, Tamil Nadu, India
kkveni69@gmail.com, radhamaniphd2015@gmail.com

**Abstract.** ADHD is a neurological disorder caused by various factors. To perform the risk factor analysis for the existence of ADHD symptoms in children with brain abnormality, a novel technique to extract the features of white and grey matters of brain magnetic images is proposed in this paper. Initially a data set containing 40, T2 axial Human Brain MRI Images is created and non-cerebral tissues such as skull, Cerebro Spinal Fluid (CSF) and vein which are not needed in the diagnosis of the brain images are removed by morphological based double thresholded Skull stripping technique. Since the brain abnormality refers to the abnormal volume and structure of grey and white lesions of the brain, Fuzzy - C means (FCM) clustering Algorithm is applied to segregate these lesions from the MRI images and then the texture, intensity and shape based features are extracted and tabulated to carry out the research for finding the inference of ADHD. The evaluation of these extracted features will be further utilized to recognize the influence of brain abnormality for the incidence of ADHD.

**Keywords:** Attention Deficit Hyperactivity Disorder · Grey matter · White matter · Cerebro spinal fluid · Skull stripping · Fuzzy - C means

## 1 Introduction

Attention Deficit Hyperactivity Disorder (ADHD) is the most common developmental disorder, affecting 6–7% of school-aged children. It is characterized by the symptoms of inattention, impulsivity and hyperactivity and wide-ranging behavioral and cognitive mutilations including deficits in working memory, inhibitory control and altered motivational style. In children and teenagers, the severity of ADHD symptoms was related to decrease frontal and temporal grey matter, caudate and cerebella volumes and the reduced brain connectivity is not only in the frontal but also in the anterior cingulated and parietal regions. The ADHD associated with grey and white matter concentrations as well as shape differences will reduce the brain volume compared to controls (normal person). MRI is one of the most commonly used approaches to measure the brain structures. MRI T2-weighted imaging is used to evaluate the brain structure. Since brain abnormality is one of the causing factors of ADHD, in this paper, a methodology to

This work is supported by the University Grants Commission, Delhi under Grant (F. No. 43-277/2014(SR)), (Major Research Project).

B. R. Purushothama et al. (Eds.): MIKE 2019, LNAI 11987, pp. 196–209, 2020.
https://doi.org/10.1007/978-3-030-66187-8_19

segregate the grey and white lesions and to extract their features from MRI brain images is proposed. This paper is organized into IV sections. The proposed methodology is discussed in Sect. 2. The experimental results are represented and tabulated in Sect. 3. The conclusion and future direction of work are finally made in Sect. 4.

## 2   Methodology

The methodology to identify and extract the features of structural brain abnormality to detect the Inference of ADHD is proposed in this research work. The architecture of the proposed work is represented in Fig. 1.

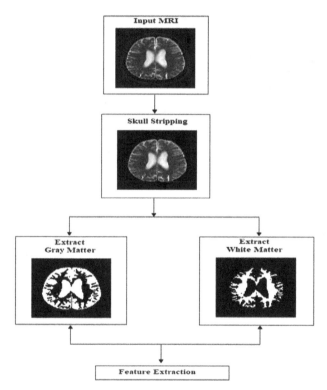

**Fig. 1.**  Architecture of the proposed method

### 2.1   MRI Image Acquisition

Children and adolescents ranging from 2 to 50 years were scanned at Stanly Medical College, Chennai, Tamil Nadu. T2-weighted (T2W) brain images in the axial plane were obtained with a Symens syngo Fast View tool for DICOM Images 1.5-T MRI scanner with the following parameters: 23 contiguous slices; TR = 5400 ms, TE = 97 ms, TI =

1000 ms, flip angle $= 7°$, mutation angle $= 90°$, slice thickness $= 3$ mm, inter-slice gap $= 0.3$ mm, voxel size $= 1.0 \times 1.0 \times 1.0$ mm, field of view $= 300$ mm. and matrix size $= 256 \times 256$.

## 2.2 Skull Stripping

Skull stripping is a technique refers to the removal of non-cerebral tissues such as skull, Cerebrospinal Fluid (CSF) and vein from the MRI brain images. While skull is a significant part in the human body, it is not required for any diagnosis. The anatomical structure of the cerebral and non-cerebral tissues of the sample MRI image is shown in Fig. 2.

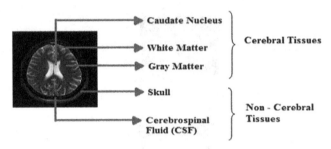

**Fig. 2.** Anatomical structure of cerebral and non-cerebral tissues

### 2.2.1 Double Thresholding

To remove the non-cerebral tissues from the image initially a double thresholding technique is proposed to convert the given image into binary form, i.e., gray scale brain image into binary image.

From the input MRI images, it has been identified that the average intensities of the non-cerebral tissues are within the range of 0 to 0.2 and 0.88 to 1.0. Whereas the upper intensity values above 0.88 is identified as skull since it appears brighter than other non-cerebral tissue. These intensities are listed in Table 1. The double thresholding is performed to remove the skull as below.

$$g(x, y) = \begin{cases} 0; 0.1 \le f(x, y) \le 0.88 \\ 1 \end{cases} \tag{1}$$

where, $g(x, y) =$ binary image & $f(x, y) =$ original image

### 2.2.2 Erosion

After thresholding, morphological erosion is applied to remove the unwanted pixels from the boundary of the brain image. Erosion of the image A using the structuring element

**Table 1.** Average intensities of cerebral and non-cerebral tissues

| Non-cerebral tissues | Average intensities |
|---|---|
| Skull | 0.88–1.00 |
| CSF | 0.00–0.20 |
| **Cerebral tissues** | 0.20–1.00 |

B is denoted as (2) which will display a set of all points Z such that B, translated by Z, is contained in A.

$$A \ominus B = \{Z | (B_Z) \subseteq A\} \tag{2}$$

### 2.3 Region Filling

After erosion, region filling technique is proposed to fill the holes in an image to have continuous boundary.

The resultant skull Stripped image is shown in Fig. 3.

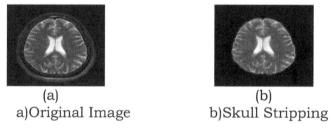

(a)                               (b)
a)Original Image        b)Skull Stripping

**Fig. 3.** a) Original image b) Skull stripping

### 2.4 Gray and White Lesions Extraction

After Skull stripping, the grey and white lesions of the brain image are isolated using Fuzzy C-Means Segmentation technique proposed in [4]. The grey and white lesions of the sample MRI brain image are shown in Fig. 4.

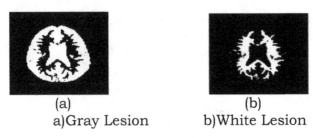

(a)                          (b)
a)Gray Lesion            b)White Lesion

**Fig. 4.** a) Gray lesion b) White lesion

## 2.5  Feature Extraction

Feature extraction methodologies are proposed to extract the most prominent features of the various classes of objects from the images. The purpose of feature extraction is to reduce the original data by features which will represent the characteristics of the input images. In this research work, the Textural, Intensity and Shape Based features of the Grey and White lesion images are calculated and extracted by the procedures given below.

### 2.5.1  Textural Based Features

Textural feature analysis is very much helpful in the assessment and diagnosis of abnormal brain tissues and its stages. Gray Level Co-occurrence Matrix (GLCM) is proposed to extract the Textural features of the lesions.

A GLCM is a matrix where the number of rows and columns is equivalent to the number of gray levels in the image (G). The matrix component P(i, j | d, θ) is the relative frequency with two pixels, separated by distance d, and in direction specified by the particular angle (θ), one with intensity i and the other with intensity j. The steps given below describe the GLCM algorithm.

1. Read the preprocessed image. Count all pairs of pixels in which the first pixel has an intensity value i, and its matching pair displaced from the first pixel by the distance d having the intensity value of j.
2. The image consists of varying shapes and sizes which are arranged in horizontal and vertical directions penetrate in the ith row and jth column of the matrix Pd[i, j].
3. The elements of Pd[i, j] can be normalized by dividing each entry by the total number of pixel pairs.
4. Normalized GLCM N[i, j] is defined by:

$$N[i, j] = \frac{P[i, j]}{\sum_i \sum_j P[i, j]} \tag{3}$$

From the Normalized GLCM, the following textural features are extracted [13].

(i)  Contrast

Contrast of an image is the measure of intensity values between a pixel and its neighboring pixel. The contrast of an image is calculated using (4).

$$\text{Contrast} = \sum_{i,j=0}^{N-1} P_{ij} \, (i-j)^2 \tag{4}$$

(ii)  Energy

Energy is given as the sum of square of all grey levels or the pixel values calculated using (5).

$$\text{Energy} = \sum_{i,j=0}^{N-1} \left( P_{ij} \right)^2 \tag{5}$$

(iii)  Homogeneity

Homogeneity gives a measure of value that measures the distribution of elements in the GLCM calculated using (6).

$$\text{Homogenity} = \sum_{i,j=0}^{N-1} \frac{P_{ij}}{1+(i-j)^2} \tag{6}$$

(iv)  Correlation

Correlation gives a value of how a pixel is correlated with its neighboring pixel throughout the whole image. It is calculated using (7).

$$\text{Correlation} = \sum_{i,j=0}^{N-1} P_{ij} \frac{(i-\mu)(j-\mu)}{\sigma^2} \tag{7}$$

where,

$$\mu = \sum_{i,j=0}^{N-1} iP_{ij}$$

$$\sigma^2 = \sum_{i,j=0}^{N-1} iP_{ij}(i - \mu)^2$$

Pij = The element at (i, j) in the GLCM Matrix.
N = Number of Gray levels in the image.
μ = GLCM Mean.

### 2.5.2 Intensity Based Features

The following intensity based features of are the grey and white lesions extracted.

(i) Mean

The mean value depends upon the brightness of the MRI image. Mean is distinct as the summation of all pixel values divided by the whole number of pixels and calculated using (8).

$$\text{Mean}(M) = \left(\frac{1}{mn}\right) \sum_{y=0}^{m-1} \sum_{y=0}^{n-1} f(x, y) \tag{8}$$

(ii) Variance

Variance gives a measure of how each pixel differs from the mean value of the image and is calculated by the differences between each number in the dataset and the mean. The variance of the image is calculated using (9).

$$\text{Variance} = \left(\frac{1}{mn}\right) \sum_{y=0}^{m-1} \sum_{y=0}^{n-1} (f(x, y) - M)^2 \tag{9}$$

(iii) Standard deviation

Standard deviation (SD) can be expressed as the square root of variance. SD is calculated using Eq. (10).

$$\text{SD}(\sigma) = \sqrt{\left(\frac{1}{mn}\right) \sum_{y=0}^{m-1} \sum_{y=0}^{n-1} (f(x, y) - M)^2} \tag{10}$$

where,

f(x, y) = Lesion Image    m × n = Size
M = Mean                SD = Standard Deviation

### 2.5.3  Shape Based Features

Area and volume are two shape based features calculated as below.

(i)  Area

The area of brain tissue is calculated using Eq. (11).

$$\text{Area} = ((P * 0.264)/100)\text{cm}^2 \tag{11}$$

where,

$$P = \text{Total Number of White Pixels}$$
$$= \sum_{W=0}^{255} \sum_{H=0}^{255} [f(x, y))] \text{ where } f(x, y) = 1.$$

(ii)  Volume

The volume of brain tissue is calculated using (12).

$$V = ((P * S * G * N)/1000)\text{cm}^3 \tag{12}$$

$$\text{where, } P = \text{Area,} \quad S = \text{Slice Thickness of MRI}$$
$$G = \text{Slice gap,} \quad N = \text{Number of slices}$$

## 3  Experimental Results

The research work has been done in MATLAB platform (Version R2017b, 64-bit) with a dataset of 40 T2 axial Human Brain MRI Images. The sample 10 input brain MRI images and the extracted Grey and White lesion images are shown in Table 2. The texture, intensity and shape features of the extracted white and grey matters which can be further used to identify the brain abnormality are listed in Tables 3, 4, 5, 6 and 7 and the corresponding charts are represented in Figs. 5, 6, 7, 8 and 9.

**Table 2.** Grey and white matter extraction

**Table 3.** Texture features

| S. no | Contrast | Energy | Homogeneity | Correlation |
|-------|----------|--------|-------------|-------------|
| Img 1 | 0.2438 | 0.2526 | 0.9170 | 0.9534 |
| Img 2 | 0.1322 | 0.3004 | 0.9490 | 0.9694 |
| Img 3 | 0.1953 | 0.3144 | 0.9391 | 0.9665 |
| Img 4 | 0.2156 | 0.2828 | 0.9224 | 0.9553 |
| Img 5 | 0.1443 | 0.3679 | 0.9475 | 0.9652 |
| Img 6 | 0.2938 | 0.2848 | 0.9184 | 0.9570 |
| Img 7 | 0.2197 | 0.3118 | 0.9272 | 0.9583 |
| Img 8 | 0.1600 | 0.2983 | 0.9409 | 0.9606 |
| Img 9 | 0.2977 | 0.3040 | 0.9189 | 0.9331 |
| Img 10 | 0.2047 | 0.2170 | 0.9307 | 0.9752 |

**Table 4.** Intensity features of gray matter

| S. no | Mean | S.D | Variance |
|-------|------|-----|----------|
| Img 1 | 0.2787 | 0.4483 | 0.2010 |
| Img 2 | 0.2343 | 0.4236 | 0.1794 |
| Img 3 | 0.2759 | 0.4469 | 0.1998 |
| Img 4 | 0.2641 | 0.4409 | 0.1944 |
| Img 5 | 0.2790 | 0.4485 | 0.2012 |
| Img 6 | 0.2832 | 0.4506 | 0.2030 |
| Img 7 | 0.2574 | 0.4372 | 0.1912 |
| Img 8 | 0.2750 | 0.4465 | 0.1994 |
| Img 9 | 0.2858 | 0.4518 | 0.2041 |
| Img 10 | 0.2790 | 0.4485 | 0.2012 |

**Table 5.** Intensity features of white matter

| S. no | Mean | S.D | Variance |
|-------|------|-----|----------|
| Img 1 | 0.1472 | 0.3543 | 0.1255 |
| Img 2 | 0.0836 | 0.2768 | 0.0766 |
| Img 3 | 0.1113 | 0.3145 | 0.0989 |
| Img 4 | 0.1544 | 0.3613 | 0.1306 |
| Img 5 | 0.0749 | 0.2632 | 0.0693 |
| Img 6 | 0.1512 | 0.3583 | 0.1284 |
| Img 7 | 0.1642 | 0.3704 | 0.1372 |
| Img 8 | 0.1177 | 0.3222 | 0.1038 |
| Img 9 | 0.0883 | 0.2838 | 0.0805 |
| Img 10 | 0.1652 | 0.3714 | 0.1379 |

**Table 6.** Shape features of gray matter

| S. no | Area | Volume |
|---|---|---|
| Img 1 | 35.6361 | 99.5741 |
| Img 2 | 32.7126 | 83.9065 |
| Img 3 | 35.3691 | 98.0877 |
| Img 4 | 30.1365 | 71.2118 |
| Img 5 | 35.5392 | 99.0331 |
| Img 6 | 35.9680 | 101.4376 |
| Img 7 | 29.5255 | 68.3537 |
| Img 8 | 35.2645 | 97.5084 |
| Img 9 | 36.0358 | 101.8202 |
| Img 10 | 29.1047 | 66.4192 |

**Table 7.** Shape features of white matter

| S. no | Area | Volume |
|---|---|---|
| Img 1 | 25.7085 | 51.8227 |
| Img 2 | 25.6270 | 51.4948 |
| Img 3 | 24.2765 | 46.2103 |
| Img 4 | 25.4414 | 50.7516 |
| Img 5 | 25.8154 | 52.2544 |
| Img 6 | 25.9057 | 52.6206 |
| Img 7 | 25.6719 | 51.6751 |
| Img 8 | 27.1111 | 57.6318 |
| Img 9 | 25.7112 | 51.8336 |
| Img 10 | 27.2240 | 58.1127 |

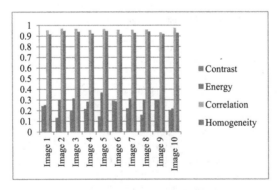

**Fig. 5.** Chart for texture features

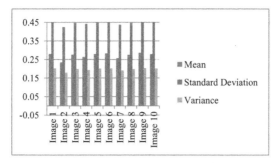

**Fig. 6.** Chart for intensity features of gray matter

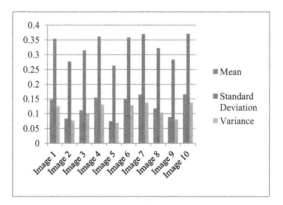

**Fig. 7.** Chart for intensity features of white matter

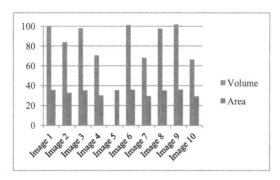

**Fig. 8.** Chart for shape features of gray matter

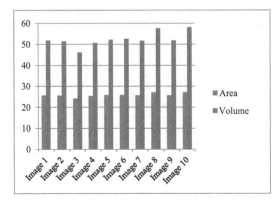

**Fig. 9.** Chart for shape features of white matter

# 4 Conclusion

In this paper, a brain image data set containing 40, T2 axial Human Brain MRI Images is created as input data set. A Skull stripping technique for the deduction of non-cerebral tissues such as skull, Cerebro Spinal Fluid (CSF) and vein which are not needed for diagnosing the MRI images is implemented. Then FCM Algorithm is applied to segregate the grey and white lesions from the MRI images. The brain abnormality is one of the major risk factors for the existence of the ADHD symptoms in children. Since the brain abnormality refers to the abnormal volume and structure of grey and white lesions of the brain, the texture, intensity and shape based features of these lesions are extracted and tabulated to carry out the research for finding the inference of ADHD. The extracted features are evaluated to recognize the influence of brain abnormality for the prevalence of ADHD in our future research.

**Acknowledgment.** I am very thankful to Dr. Sakthivelrajan M.B.B.S., MD (Radiology), Stanly hospital, Chennai for contributing MR images for this work.

# References

1. Radhamani, E., Krishnaveni, K.: Diagnosis and evaluation of ADHD using MLP and SVM classifiers. Ind. J. Sci. Technol. **9**(19) (2016). https://doi.org/10.17485/ijst/2016/v9i19/93853. ISSN 0974-5645
2. Radhamani, E., Krishnaveni, K.: Diagnosis and evaluation of ADHD using Naïve Bayes and J48 classifiers. In: 2016 International Conference on Computing for Sustainable Global Development (INDIA Com). IEEE (2016). 978-9-3805-4421-2/16/$31.00_c
3. Radhamani, E., Krishnaveni, K.: Prognosis of ADHD using R programming and MATLAB tools. Int. J. Emerg. Technol. Adv. Eng. **7**(7) (2017). ISSN 2250-2459, ISO 9001:2008 Certified Journal

4. Radhamani, E., Krishnaveni, K.: Diagnosis and inference of ADHD. Int. J. Eng. Res. Appl. (IJERA) **7**(6) (2017). ISSN 2248-9622
5. Radhamani, E., Krishnaveni, K.: Diagnosis of ADHD using statistical measures. Int.J. Eng. Res. Comput. Sci. Eng. (IJERCSE) **5**(3) (2018). ISSN 2394-2320
6. Radhamani, E., Krishnaveni, K.: Analysis of brain data attributes to detect the prevalence of ADHD using R programming. Int. J. Manage. Technol. Eng. **8**(XI) (2018). ISSN 2249-7455
7. Deepa, V., Benson, C.: Gray Matter and white matter segmentation from MRI Brain images using clustering methods. Int. Res. J. Eng. Technol. (IRJET) **02**(08) (2015). ISSN 2395-0056
8. Roy, S., Ganguly, D.: Computerized white matter and gray matter extraction from MRI of brain image. Biomed. Sci. Eng. (2015)
9. Kaushik, K.S., Rakesh Kumar, K.N., Suresha, D.: Segmentation of the white matter from the brain MRI images. Int. J. Adv. Res. Comput. Eng. Technol. (IJARCET) **2**(4) (2013)
10. Kabade, R.S.: Segmentation of brain tumour and its area calculation in brain MR images using K-mean clustering and fuzzy cmean algorithm. Int. J. Comput. Sci. Eng. Technol. (IJCSET) **4**(05) (2013). ISSN 2229-3345
11. Igual, L., Soliva, J.C., Escalera, S.: Supervised brain segmentation and classification in diagnostic of attention-deficit/hyperactivity disorder. In: Computerized Medical Imaging and Graphics, Elsevier Ltd. (2012)
12. Roslan, R., Jamil, N.: Skull stripping magnetic resonance images brain images: region growing versus mathematical morphology. Int. J. Comput. Inf. Syst. Ind. Manage. Appl. **3** (2011). ISSN 2150-7988
13. Joshi, J.: Feature extraction and texture classification in MRI. In: International Conference (ICCT 2010), Special Issue of IJCCT, vol. 2, no. 2 (2010)
14. Dubey, R.B., Hanmandlu, M., Gupta, S.K.: Region growing for MRI brain tumor volume analysis. Ind. J. Sci. Technol. **2**(9) (2009)
15. https://www.sciencedirect.com/science/article/pii/S2213158216300468
16. https://www.ncbi.nlm.nih.gov/pmc/articles/PMC5314130

# Skin Lesion Segmentation Techniques Based on Markov Random Field

Omran Salih$^{(\boxtimes)}$ and Serestina Viriri

School of Mathematics, Statistics and Computer Science,
University of KwaZulu-Natal, Durban 4000, South Africa
omran@aims.ac.za, viriris@ukzn.ac.za

**Abstract.** Several segmentation models based on Markov Random Field (MRF) theory have achieved great success in medical images. This paper presents a detailed and robust survey of the techniques based on MRF theory for performing skin lesion segmentation. Five types of models based on MRF theory namely Pixel-Based MRF model, Region-Based MRF model, Edge-Based MRF model, (Pixel, Region)-based MRF model and (Pixel, Region, Edge)-based MRF model, have been examined and utilized for segmentation of skin lesion images. The performance analysis of the five models have been conducted. Evaluation and comparison of these five models were also carried out. This work finds out and proposes possible improvements of these methods on the segmentation of skin lesions. It is also a systematic comparison of these models on the segmentation of skin lesion images. The paper discovers how MRF theory models can be explored using a supervised approach to get accurate results with less complexity possible. The models were evaluated on skin lesion dataset in PH2 dermoscopic images archives.

**Keywords:** Markov random field · Skin lesion · Segmentation

## 1 Introduction

Melanoma skin lesion has been reported as the deadliest skin cancer with high mortality [4]. Segmentation is an imprtant task in automating disease diagnosis. It aids in identification and recognition of disease pattern. Early detection of this disease can reduce the mortality rate [1]. In the past few years, with the advantages in technology, various computer aided techniques have evolved for the analysis and segmentation of medical images. Automatic medical image analysis methods have been successful in medical image analysis over the past two decades [16]. Automated analysis of skin lesion has assisted clinicians in making quick and accurate decisions in melanoma detection. Segmentation plays very important role in computer vision and it has various applications in various fields such as remote sensing, pattern recognition, medical diagnostic etc. [9,12,14,22,23].

In recent years image segmentation had different approaches based on MRF theory to improve the performance of the segmentation such as, iterative stochastic region merging method [21] that utilised merging strategy to solve an image

© Springer Nature Switzerland AG 2020
B. R. Purushothama et al. (Eds.): MIKE 2019, LNAI 11987, pp. 210–220, 2020.
https://doi.org/10.1007/978-3-030-66187-8_20

segmentation problem. Automatic segmentation of skin lesion using MRF that presents a new method to segregate the skin lesions through level set concept with regard to the level of homogeneity and MRF was done by [20]. A hybrid method [8] was developed by combining particle swarm optimization and MRF methods, in order to delineate the border of the lesion area in the images. A unified Markov random field (UMRF) model which is a probabilistic graphical method and provides statistical way to model the image information as the prior information was presented by [2]. Furthermore, the implementation of UMRF model has been used to detect skin lesion segmentation by the authors in [17]. This combines Pixel-Based and Region-Based MRF models. An enhanced unified Markov random field model [18] which combines various skin lesion features achieved a good skin lesion segmentation accuracy.

MRF theory has a significant potential role in image segmentation field. It uses (Pixel, Region, Edge)-based on MRF theory to detect objects, boundaries and other relevant information in an image. In this study we will discuss various model based on their feature extraction such as pixel features, region features and edge features. Also based on combining the benefits of region and edge feature instead of considering specific information. These techniques can be classified as Pixel-Based MRF model [6], the Region-Based MRF model [10], the Edge-Based MRF model [7], (Pixel, Region)-Based MRF model [2] and (Pixel, Region, Edge)-Based model [18]. The main purpose of this paper is to study and analyzing skin lesion segmentation performance of the previous techniques.

## 2    Techniques Based on MRF

In this section, various model based on MRF theory is discussed. These models can be classified according to their feature extraction such as pixel feature, region feature, edge feature etc. More details will be provided below.

### 2.1    MRF Model

Let $S = \{s_i | i = 1, 2, \cdots, N \times M\}$ be an input image where $N \times M$ denotes the size of the image and $s_i$ represents each pixel in the image. $X = \{X_s | s \in S\}$ represents the label random field defined on $S$. Each random variables $X_s$ in $X$ represents the class of pixel $s$, the class set is $\Lambda = \{1, 2, \cdots, n\}$ where $n$ is the number of classes. $Y = \{y_s | s \in S\}$ represents the observed image defined on $S$. Let $x = \{x_s | s \in S\}$ an instantiation of the region label field. In the MRF method, the main goal of segmentation is to find an optimal estimation of $x$ given the observed image $Y$, formulated as the following Maximum a Posteriori (MAP) estimation problem:

$$\hat{x} = \arg\max_x P(x|Y), \tag{1}$$

where $P(x|Y)$ is the posteriori. By using Bayes' theory, the posterior $P(x|Y)$ in Eq. (1) is equivalent to

$$\hat{x} = \arg\max_x P(Y|X)P(X). \tag{2}$$

The probability of the label random field $P(X)$ is used to model the label random field $X$. According to the theory of Harmercley-Clifford [13], $P(X)$ is a Gibss distribution, which is given by

$$P(X = x) = \frac{1}{Z} \exp\left(-U(x)\right), \quad Z = \sum_x U(x) \tag{3}$$

where $Z$ is the normalisation factor, $U(x)$ denotes the energy function, that is

$$U(x) = \sum_{s \in S} U(x_s, x_{N_s}), \text{ where } U(x_s, x_{N_s}) = \sum_{t \in N_s} V(x_s, x_t) \tag{4}$$

where $N_s$ is the set of pixels neighbouring pixel $s$ and each $V(x_s, x_t)$ is the potential function between pixel $s$ and pixel $t, t \in N_s$. The potential function $V(x_s, x_t)$ is defined by the multilevel logistic (MLL) model [7], which is

$$V(x_s, x_t) = \begin{cases} \beta & \text{if } x_s = x_t \\ -\beta & \text{if } x_s \neq x_t \end{cases}, \text{ where } \beta > 0 \text{ and } t \in N_s. \tag{5}$$

The conditional probability function $P(Y|X)$ needs to be determine in quation (2) in order to find the estimation to the problem defined on (2). But it is not easy task to determine $P(Y|X)$ due to complex challenges to skin lesion segmentation in a give image, such as noise and artifacts, multiple lesion regions, structural variations, illumination and color variations, and weak boundary separation between surrounding skin regions and unhealthy skin regions. Researches have been presented various models based on MRF theory to estimate the conditional probability function $P(Y|X)$ defined in Eq. (2). In the following subsection some of these models will be discussed in more details to determine The conditional probability function $P(Y|X)$ in order to solve the problem (2) which will lead to the desire skin lesion segmentation.

## 2.2   Pixel-Based MRF Model

Extract spectral value as the pixel feature to model the micro texture pattern and the detailed information using the likelihood function $P(Y_s^P|X)$. This technique used Gaussian distribution to determine the distribution of the likelihood function of $P(Y_s^P|X)$ which is obtained by

$$P(Y_s^P|X_s = h) = \frac{1}{(2\pi)^{D/2}\sqrt{\det(\Sigma_h^P)}} \exp\left(-\frac{(Y_s^P - \mu_h^P)^T \cdot (Y_s^P - \mu_h^P)}{2(\Sigma_h^P)}\right), \tag{6}$$

where $Y_s^P$ is the pixel feature for every pixel $s$, the Gaussian distribution parameters are $\mu_h^P, \Sigma_h^P$, and $D$ is the dimension of $Y_s^P$.

## 2.3  Region-Based MRF Model

This technique used algorithm provided by [2], to extract the regional feature of an input image. It highlighted that one of over segmented should be used to obtain the initial segmentation because it is very important in the final segmentation accuracy. Several methods of over-segmented are proposed in the literature to provide a better over segmentation result, i.e., watershed [3], mean shift (MS) [5], normalisation cut (Ncut) [19], and tuberpixel [11]. In this paper, MS is used to extract the over-segmented. Then the regional feature formula $Y_s^R$ is applied to extract the spectral value information from over-segmented image for each pixel $s$. The regional feature $Y_s^R$ is given as follows

$$Y_s^R = p_{R_s}\left[1 - \log(p_{R_s})\right] + \frac{1}{|N_{R_s}|} \sum_{T \in N_{R_s}} p_T\left[1 - \log(p_T)\right], \tag{7}$$

where $R_s$ represents the initial over-segmented region including $s$. $p_{R_s}$ denotes the area ratio of the region $R_s$ to the whole image, and $N_{R_s}$ is the set of neighbour regions of $R_s$. On solving for the likelihood function of regional feature $P(Y_s^R|X)$, the Gaussian distribution have been used to determine the distribution of the likelihood function of $P(Y_s^P|X)$, which is given by

$$P(Y_s^R|X_s = h) = \frac{\sqrt{\alpha} \times \exp\left(\frac{-1}{2}(Y_s^R - \mu_h^R)^T \cdot (\Sigma_h^R/\alpha)^{-1}(Y_s^R - \mu_h^R)\right)}{(2\pi)^{D'/2}\sqrt{\det(\Sigma_h^R)}} \tag{8}$$

Here $D'$ is the dimension of $Y_s^R$, $\mu_h^R$, and $\Sigma_h^R$ are the parameters of Gaussian distribution, $\det(\Sigma_h^R)$ is the determinant of $\Sigma_h^R$, $1 \leq h \leq n$, and $\alpha$ is proposed to show the interaction between the regional feature and the edge feature.

## 2.4  Edge-Based MRF Model

Edges of a color image by the max gradient method [7] is used, to extracts the edges of a color image without converting it to grayscale. This clearly shows that a significant amount of information is lost by the standard method, but it is recovered with the max gradient method [7]. The RGB color of each pixel is treated as a 3D vector, and the strength of the edge is the magnitude of the maximum gradient. This also works most especially when the image is in any other dimension (3-dimensional) color space. Direct formulas for the jacobian eigenvalues were used [7] to calculate the maximum eigenvalue (gradient magnitude), so this function is vectorized and yields good results without sacrificing performance.

Assume $f : R^2 \rightarrow rgb, (x,y) \in R^2$ is a continuous color image. The color components will be denote $r(x,y), g(x,y)$ and $b(x,y)$, so that the image as a whole can be denote $f = (r,g,b)$ or, more explicit, $f(x,y) = (r(x,y), g(x,y), b(x,y))$. Let $J$ is the Jacobian, its elements are the partial derivatives of $r,g,b$ with respect to $x,y$. The edge strength is the greatest eigenvalue of the product of Jacobian and its transpose.

$$J' * J = \begin{pmatrix} \frac{\partial r}{\partial x} & \frac{\partial g}{\partial x} & \frac{\partial b}{\partial x} \\ \frac{\partial r}{\partial y} & \frac{\partial g}{\partial y} & \frac{\partial b}{\partial y} \end{pmatrix} \begin{pmatrix} \frac{\partial r}{\partial x} & \frac{\partial r}{\partial y} \\ \frac{\partial g}{\partial x} & \frac{\partial g}{\partial y} \\ \frac{\partial b}{\partial x} & \frac{\partial b}{\partial y} \end{pmatrix} = \begin{pmatrix} J_x & J_{xy} \\ J_{xy} & J_y \end{pmatrix}. \tag{9}$$

The edge color image is obtained by finding the greatest eigenvalues of Eq. (9), which is given by the following formula:

$$Y^E = (J_x + J_y) + \sqrt{|(J_x^2 - 2J_xJ_y + J_y^2 + 4J_{xy}^2)|}. \tag{10}$$

where $Y^E$ is the edge color image for a whole image. The partial derivatives is obtained using Sobel filter. For solving the likelihood function of edge feature $P(Y_s^E|X)$, the Gaussian distribution have been used to determine the distribution of the likelihood function of $P(Y_s^E|X)$, which is

$$P(Y_s^E|X_s = h) = \frac{\exp\left((Y_s^E - \mu_h^E)^T \cdot (\Sigma_h^E)^{-1} \cdot (Y_s^E - \mu_h^E)\right)}{(2\pi)^{D/2}\sqrt{\det(\Sigma_h^E)}} \tag{11}$$

where $Y_s^E$ is the pixel feature for every pixel $s$, the Gaussian distribution parameters are $\mu_h^E, \Sigma_h^E$, and $D$ is the dimension of $Y_s^E$.

## 2.5  (Pixel, Region)-Based MRF Model

Chen et al. [2] stated that the observed image $Y$ can be divided into pixel feature $Y^P = \{Y_s^P | s \in S\}$, and the regional feature $Y^R = \{Y_s^R | s \in S\}$, in order to incorporate more priority for the segmentation result. Therefore, the conditional probability function have been divided into two parts as mentioned in [2]: the pixel likelihood function, and the regional likelihood function, which can be expressed into $(Y^P, Y^R)$. The pixel values, and the stochastic region-merging features are used to extract the pixel features and the region features, respectively. In order find a solution to the Maximum a Posteriori (MAP) estimation which leads to the desire skin lesion segmentation. This lead Eq. (2) to

$$\hat{x} = \arg\max_x P(X) \cdot P(Y^P|X) \cdot P(Y^R|X). \tag{12}$$

Solving Eq. (12) can be obtained using Pixel-Based MRF model and Region-Based MRF model equations.

## 2.6  (Pixel, Region, Edge)-Based MRF Model

This model is a probabilistic model based on MRF theory. It combines the benefits of several models based on MRF into its account. This technique put into account the advantages of three MRF models: (i) the Region-Based MRF model, (ii) the Pixel-Based MRF model, (iii) the Edge-Based MRF model. It combine the benifits of these models by computing the product of the pixel likelihood function, regional likelihood function and edge likelihood function. This lead Eq. (2) to

$$\hat{x} = \arg\max_{x} P(X) \cdot P(Y^P|X) \cdot P(Y^R|X) \cdot P(Y^E|X). \tag{13}$$

The solution of problem (13) can be obtained using Pixel-Based MRF model, Region-Based MRF model and Edge-Based MRF model equations.

### 2.7  Parameters Setting

The proposed method has eight parameters, $\mu_h^R, \Sigma_h^R, \mu_h^E, \Sigma_h^E, \beta$ and $\alpha$ are used in Eqs. (11) and (8) respectively. Furthermore, they are known as the mean value and the variance value for the Gaussian distribution, which can be calculated as follows.

$$\mu_h^P = \frac{1}{|X^h|} \sum_{s \in X^h} Y_s^P, \qquad \Sigma_h^P = \frac{1}{|X^h|} \sum_{s \in X^h} \left(Y_s^P - \mu_h^P\right)' \left(Y_s^P - \mu_h^P\right). \tag{14}$$

$$\mu_h^R = \frac{1}{|X^h|} \sum_{s \in X^h} Y_s^R, \qquad \Sigma_h^R = \frac{1}{|X^h|} \sum_{s \in X^h} \left(Y_s^R - \mu_h^R\right)' \left(Y_s^R - \mu_h^R\right). \tag{15}$$

$$\mu_h^E = \frac{1}{|X^h|} \sum_{s \in X^h} Y_s^E, \qquad \Sigma_h^E = \frac{1}{|X^h|} \sum_{s \in X^h} \left(Y_s^E - \mu_h^E\right)' \left(Y_s^E - \mu_h^E\right). \tag{16}$$

$\beta$ is the potential parameter in Eq. (5), which is used for finding $P(X)$, and $\alpha$ is used to reflect the interaction between $P(Y^P|X)$, $P(Y^R|X)$, $P(Y^E|X)$ and $P(X)$.

## 3  Performance Analysis

### 3.1  Data Sets

The evaluation of these models have been done using the PH2 dataset [15] which is a well-established publicly available datasets. PH2 contains 200 skin lesion image with highest resolution of $765 \times 574$ pixels. They were gotten at Dermatology Service of Hospital Pedro Hispano. The ground truth for segmentation is also included in the dataset as binary masks. The input dataset are skin lesion image in BMP format while the ground truth are mask image in BMP format as well.

### 3.2  Evaluation Metric Calculation

The most common skin lesion segmentation metrics were used for comparison including: The Jaccard index (JI) compares similarity for the pixels in the ground truth and automatic segmentation to see which pixels are shared and which are distinct. It's a measure of similarity for the two sets of data, with a range from 0% to 100%. The formula to find the index is:

$$\mathbf{JI} = \frac{|X \cap Y|}{|X \cup Y|} \tag{17}$$

where $X, Y$ are the number of pixels in the ground truth and automatic segmentation respectively.

Dice similarity coefficient (DICE) measure the similarity or overlap between the ground truth and automatic segmentation. It is defined as

$$\mathbf{DICE} = \frac{2TP}{FP \cup 2TP \cup FN} \tag{18}$$

Accuracy (ACC) measures the proportion of true results (both true positives and true negatives) among the total number of cases examined.

$$\mathbf{ACC} = \frac{TP \cup TN}{TP \cup TN \cup FP \cup FN} \tag{19}$$

Sensitivity (SEN) measure the proportion of those with positive values among those who are actually positive.

$$\mathbf{SEN} = \frac{TP}{TP \cup FN} \tag{20}$$

Specificity (SPE) is the proportion of those that are negative among those who actually tested negative.

$$\mathbf{SPE} = \frac{TN}{TN \cup FP} \tag{21}$$

where $FP$ is the number of false positive pixels, $FN$ is the number of false negative pixels, $TP$ is the number of true positive pixels and $TN$ is the number of true negative pixels.

### 3.3   Performance Evaluation Analysis

Various techniques based on MRF theory have been developed and applied for segmentation of skin lesions in time past. This section captures the application of some techniques and their performance on the segmentation of skin lesion image datasets of PH2. The performance evaluation results of these techniques is shown in Table 1 and Fig. 1. Pixel-Based MRF model [6] applied to extract the pixel feature for skin lesion segmentation. The results of the performance analysis of the technique was able to give the average score of 66%, 77%, 83%, 88% and 83% for Jaccard index, dice coefficient, accuracy, sensitivity and specificity, respectively which shows that a reasonably high percentage of similarity and low level of diversity between the samples set of data used for its experiment. This techniques does not perform well where there is high level of diversity in the sample set. The techniques is sensitive to outliers.

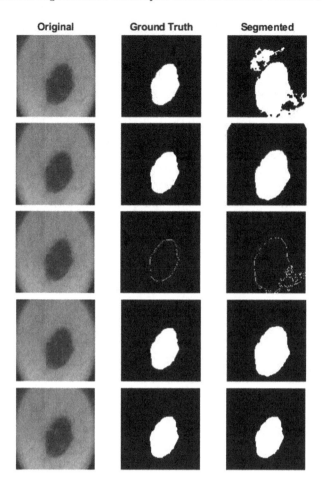

**Fig. 1.** Example of skin lesion segmentation techniques based on MRF: (1st row) Pixel-Based MRF model (2nd row) Region-Based MRF model (3rd row) Edge-Based MRF model (4th row) (Pixel, Region)-based MRF model and (5th row) (Pixel, Region, Edge)-Based MRF model

Region-Based MRF model [6] has been done to extend the MRF model from the pixel-based to the region-besed in order to reduce the time-consuming as well as modelling more macro and complex spatial patterns in a large neighbourhood. The technique tends to outperform the pixel-based MRF model for skin lesion images segmentation: The region-based MRF segmentation techniques with a high sensitivity and specificity average of 88% and 86% showing good rates of correct predictions. Edge-Based MRF model has been presented to extend the MRF model the pixel-based to the edge-based as well. The technique was based on discriminative edge feature and outperforms many techniques with sensitivity and specificity of 90% and 83% showing good rates of positive predictions.

(Pixel, Region)-Based MRF model [17] is presented to build one model of multi-features such as pixel feature and region feature and took advantages of both MRF models and solve pitfalls of each model. The performance analysis of this technique was able to give us the average score of 89% and 87% for sensitivity and specificity. This shows a high rate of performance when compared with Pixel-Based MRF model and Region-Based MRF model but the system requires more time in order to finish the task. (Pixel, Region, Edge)-Based MRF model [18] is applied to combine the benefits of several models based on MRF into its account. The technique put into account the advantages of three MRF models: (i) the Region-Based MRF model, (ii) the Pixel-Based MRF model, (ii) the Edge-Based MRF model. The performance analysis of this technique was able to give the average score of 93% and 87% for sensitivity and specificity. This shows a high rate of performance when compared with other MRF model.

**Table 1.** Lesion segmentation performances of various frameworks.

| Model | JI | DICE | ACC | SEN | SPE |
|---|---|---|---|---|---|
| Pixel-Based MRF model [6] | 0.66 | 0.77 | 0.83 | 0.88 | 0.83 |
| Region-Based MRF model [10] | 0.68 | 0.79 | 0.85 | 0.88 | 0.86 |
| Edge-Based MRF model [7] | 0.68 | 0.79 | 0.85 | 0.90 | 0.83 |
| (Pixel, Region)-Based MRF model [17] | 0.72 | 0.81 | 0.86 | 0.89 | 0.87 |
| (Pixel, Region, Edge)-Based MRF model [18] | 0.71 | 0.82 | 0.87 | 0.93 | 0.87 |

## 4   Conclusion

The study is a critical and analytical survey of the present MRF techniques for performing segmentation of skin lesion images. These techniques were studied for their performance on skin lesion images. The evaluation techniques were also studied. Merits of these techniques were also examined. A conclusion can be drawn from the analysis made, about the best performing techniques. It was observed that the application of complementary of more model in one technique such as (Pixel, Region, Edge)-based MRF model for performing analysis of images gives a better performance in image analysis most especially in the segmentation process of skin lesions images.

## References

1. Emre Celebi, M., et al.: A methodological approach to the classification of dermoscopy images. Comput. Med. Imaging Graph. **31**(6), 362–373 (2007)
2. Chen, X., Zheng, C., Yao, H., Wang, B.: Image segmentation using a unified markov random field model. IET Image Process. **11**(10), 860–869 (2017)
3. Chien, S.-Y., Huang, Y.-W., Chen, L.-G.: Predictive watershed: a fast watershed algorithm for video segmentation. IEEE Trans. Circuits Syst. Video Technol. **13**(5), 453–461 (2003)

4. Codella, N., et al.: Skin lesion analysis toward melanoma detection 2018: A challenge hosted by the international skin imaging collaboration (ISIC). arXiv preprint arXiv:1902.03368 (2019)
5. Comaniciu, D., Meer, P.: Mean shift: a robust approach toward feature space analysis. IEEE Trans. Pattern Anal. Mach. Intell. **24**(5), 603–619 (2002)
6. Deng, H., Clausi, D.A.: Unsupervised image segmentation using a simple MRF model with a new implementation scheme. Pattern Recognit. **37**(12), 2323–2335 (2004)
7. Di Zenzo, S.: A note on the gradient of a multi-image. Comput. Vis. Graph. Image Process. **33**(1), 116–125 (1986)
8. Eltayef, K., Li, Y., Liu, X.: Lesion segmentation in dermoscopy images using particle swarm optimization and markov random field. In: 2017 IEEE 30th International Symposium on Computer-Based Medical Systems (CBMS), pp. 739–744. IEEE (2017)
9. Grosgeorge, D., Petitjean, C., Ruan, S.: Multilabel statistical shape prior for image segmentation. IET Image Process. **10**(10), 710–716 (2016)
10. Jie, F., Shi, Y., Li, Y., Liu, Z.: Interactive region-based MRF image segmentation. In: 2011 4th International Congress on Image and Signal Processing (CISP), vol. 3, pp. 1263–1267. IEEE (2011)
11. Levinshtein, A., Stere, A., Kutulakos, K.N., Fleet, D.J., Dickinson, S.J., Siddiqi, K.: Turbopixels: fast superpixels using geometric flowsf. IEEE Trans. Pattern Anal. Mach. Intell. **31**(12), 2290–2297 (2009)
12. Li, C., Lin, L., Zuo, W., Wang, W., Tang, J.: An approach to streaming video segmentation with sub-optimal low-rank decomposition. IEEE Trans. Image Process. **25**(5), 1947–1960 (2016)
13. Li, S.Z.: Markov Random Field Modeling in Image Analysis. Springer, London (2009). https://doi.org/10.1007/978-1-84800-279-1
14. Liu, G., Zhao, Z., Zhang, Y.: Image fuzzy clustering based on the region-level Markov random field model. IEEE Geosci. Remote Sens. Lett **12**(8), 1770–1774 (2015)
15. Mendonça, T., Ferreira, P.M., Marques, J.S., Marcal, A.R.S., Rozeira, J.: PH$^2$-a dermoscopic image database for research and benchmarking. In 2013 35th Annual International Conference of the IEEE Engineering in Medicine and Biology Society (EMBC), pp. 5437–5440. IEEE (2013)
16. Nguyen, N.-Q., Lee, S.-W.: Robust boundary segmentation in medical images using a consecutive deep encoder-decoder network. IEEE Access **7**, 33795–33808 (2019)
17. Salih, O., Viriri, S.: Skin cancer segmentation using a unified Markov random field. In: Bebis, G., et al. (eds.) ISVC 2018. LNCS, vol. 11241, pp. 25–33. Springer, Cham (2018). https://doi.org/10.1007/978-3-030-03801-4_3
18. Salih, O., Viriri, S.: Skin lesion segmentation using enhanced unified Markov random field. In: Groza, A., Prasath, R. (eds.) MIKE 2018. LNCS (LNAI), vol. 11308, pp. 331–340. Springer, Cham (2018). https://doi.org/10.1007/978-3-030-05918-7_30
19. Shi, J., Malik, J.: Normalized cuts and image segmentation. IEEE Trans. Pattern Anal. Mach. Intell. **22**(8), 888–905 (2000)
20. Torkashvand, F., Fartash, M.: Automatic segmentation of skin lesion using Markov random field. Can. J. Basic Appl. Sci. **3**(3), 93–107 (2015)
21. Wong, A., Scharcanski, J., Fieguth, P.: Automatic skin lesion segmentation via iterative stochastic region merging. IEEE Trans. Inf. Technol. Biomedicine **15**(6), 929–936 (2011)

22. Zand, M., Doraisamy, S., Halin, A.A., Mustaffa, M.R.: Ontology-based semantic image segmentation using mixture models and multiple CRFs. IEEE Trans. Image Process. **25**(7), 3233–3248 (2016)
23. Zhou, D., Zhou, H.: Minimisation of local within-class variance for image segmentation. IET Image Process. **10**(8), 608–615 (2016)

# Performance of Coronary Plaque Feature Extraction and Identification of Plaque Severity for Intravascular Ultrasound B-Mode Images

C. Mahadevi[1(✉)] and S. Sivakumar[2]

[1] NMSSVellaisamy Nadar College, Nagamalai, Madurai 625019, Tamilnadu, India
kanstamil23@gmail.com
[2] Cardamom Planter's Association College, Bodinayakanur, Theni 625513,
Tamilnadu, India
sivaku2002@yahoo.com

**Abstract.** The process of extraction of blood vessel boundaries in the case of Intravascular Ultrasound (IVUS) images is extremely indispensable in the quantitative examination of cardiovascular functions. The affected region of plaque in the IVUS image has to be measured quantitatively to fix the stent challenges. In this paper, the lumen and coronary plaque feature extraction are done by the adjacent pattern method. To get appropriate features, sequential feature selection is carried out and directed with the assistance of the area under the precision and recall value. Subsets of appropriate image characteristics for lumen, plaque, and adjoining tissue characterization acquired are trained with the assistance of Support Vector Machine (SVM) based Convolution neural network (CNN). These features were able to accurately recognize plaque regions of the predicted class label based on the weighted matrix and display the plaque severity level. The proposed SVM based CNN classifier is compared with CNN-Basic and SVM classifier and the performance of feature extraction and classification methods are evaluated with quantifiable metrics like true positive (TP), true negative (TN), false positive (FP) and false negative (FN). The performance of plaque feature detection evaluated with quantitative values for accuracy, sensitivity, specificity, precision, recall, and F-score.

**Keywords:** IVUS image · Feature extraction · SVM · CNN Classifier

## 1 Introduction

Atherosclerosis an infection of the vessel wall is the foremost source of cardiovascular diseases for instance heart attack or stroke [3]. IVUS is an intra-operative imaging instrument assists in supervising and quantify the state of the vessel wall and lumen. It is used for quantification and categorization of coronary plaque

© Springer Nature Switzerland AG 2020
B. R. Purushothama et al. (Eds.): MIKE 2019, LNAI 11987, pp. 221–233, 2020.
https://doi.org/10.1007/978-3-030-66187-8_21

employed for effective diagnostic functions, facilitates the visualization of high resolution images of interior vascular structures. IVUS is a primary instrument for stent exploitation since it does compute the interference and the accurate position.

The segmentation process is essential to assess morphological characteristics of the vessel and plaque such as lumen diameter, minimum lumen cross-section area, and total atheroma volume. This information is mandatory to decide whether a stent is needed to restore blood flow in an artery. The plaque feature extraction also necessary to find out the plaque severity level such as mild, moderate, and severe. Plaque, lumen, and adventitia regions are determined through two textural characteristics and categorize them in an unsupervised manner [1]. Segmentation algorithms evaluated for the detection of plaque border and wall cross-sectional area in IVUS Images [9]. A scheme in accordance with a learning task applied to tissue features by defining the class calcification and vessel border and categorized the feature by a Fisher classifier [2]. Statistical texture-dependent schemes, Grey Level Co-occurrence Matrix (GLCM), and Grey Level Run Length Matrix (GLRLM) descriptors stay amongst the top options and the subset of GLCM and Run Length (RL) descriptors makes the most of the classification accuracy of the training dataset [13]. The efficiency of GLCM, Gabor filters, Local Binary Patterns (LBP), and RL scheme was exhibited for plaque evaluation [19]. The active shape scheme is employed for the purpose of recognizing object shapes. The existence of noise in addition to image artifacts for dented fractions. The deformations in the training set could take into account and has restrictions with respect to unpredicted shapes [11]. The local information of a pattern LBP schemes can be effectively implemented at the same time as the overall texture information can be explained with the assistance of the GLCM scheme [21].

Border discovery in IVUS images is completely dependent on supervised learning schemes. The lumen border identified with the assistance of supervised learning and the Ada-Boost (Adaptive Boosting) classifier. The prior details were integrated with a Support Vector Machine classifier model for the purpose of separating the lumen from the non-lumen features [10,14]. By using the hybrid feature extraction technique the plaque feature extracted and its accuracy evaluated with metric measurement [15]. The classification between lumen and non-lumen, performed well to determine the correct location of the lumen and plaque features [8]. The Artificial Neural Networks (ANN) classifier was used for the media-adventitia feature classification with a snake active contour model to trace the true boundary of each region [7,18]. The plaque features were classified with the Error Correcting Output Codes (ECOC) classifier performed well [12]. The combination of binary classifiers based on discrete Ada-boost using ECOC applied on the IVUS image to classify the features and measured its accuracy [6]. The GLCM method is used to extract suitable lumen and plaque features from IVUS image and extracted feature used by Fuzzy C-Means Clustering (FCM) [17].

Deep learning is a fraction of a broader family of machine learning schemes in accordance with learning data representation, as against the hard code machine schemes The Convolutional Neural Networks have a smaller amount of connection and hyper constraint that build CNN model easy to train and execute slightly worse than remaining models [5]. CNN's learn regarding thousands of objects from millions of images, as a result, this method has a huge learning capability. It creates tough and typically accurate suppositions regarding the nature of images. Consequently, when compared against the standard feed forward neural networks with similarly-sized layers, CNNs have an extremely smaller amount of constraints and connections, hence it is simpler to train, offer the most excellent performance [4, 16, 20].

In this paper by using the adjacent pattern feature extraction method, the lumen and plaque features are extracted from the IVUS image and it is classified further to achieve good features. CNN has smaller amount of connection and hyper parameter so they are simpler to train and provide the best performance. The CNN capability can be effectively managed through altering their breadth, deepness, and make sturdy that predominantly provide accurate assumptions regarding the nature of images. Hence the author proposed SVM based CNN classifier to train and test the plaque features and to characterize the plaque severity level automatically.

## 2   Materials and Methods

The proposed segmentation and classification scheme includes the following steps

- Removal of the speckle-noise, artifacts, smoothen and enhance the edge features
- Finding of the lumen, plaque, and adventitia sections on the fundamental of feature vector values
- Calculation of quantitative metrics for lumen, vessel, and wall cross-sectional shape parameters
- Extraction of texture characteristics of lumen and plaque
- Test and train the plaque features to display plaque severity level type as mild, moderate, and severe.

The frame works for the complete automatic feature extraction and display the plaque severity level is shown in Fig. 1.

### 2.1   IVUS Image Data Acquisition

The Data set for this work is acquitted from Volcano S5$^{TM}$ Imaging System the Eagle Eye Platinum RX Digital IVUS Catheter with 20 MHz transducer tip size of 3.2–3.5 F (1.2–1.5 mm) is used which will go over 5–6 F guiding catheter. The "DICOM" video format with 500 × 500 pixel size images are produced by this system. For each patient the video frame provides by the system is varied i.e. 250–500 frames. This video frame is converted into JPG format by using the MicroDicom viewer software tool and stored as a Joint Photographic Experts Group (JPEG) file format for processing. The spatial resolutions of the still images are kept at 500 × 500 pixels.

The data set is collected from four different patients with various ages, genders, and additional body aspects that possibly will affect vessel heart thickness and shape. Three different patients with dissimilar ages and genders of IVUS images are taken as a dataset for further development is shown in Fig. 2.

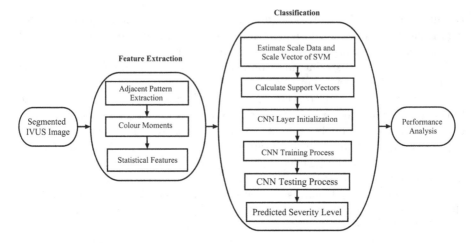

**Fig. 1.** Framework to extract the plaque features and find out the plaque severity level by classifier.

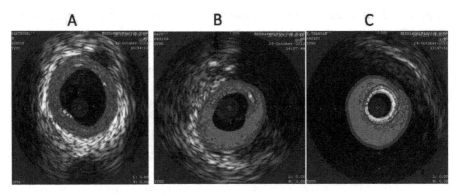

**Fig. 2.** IVUS images –(A) Data Image-1, (B) Data Image-2, (C) Data Image-3.

## 2.2  Adjacent Pattern – Feature Extraction

Take the segmented output region as input to the feature extraction. The entire segmentation result region is separated into $3 \times 3$ block. For each $3 \times 3$ pixel the centre pixel is find out and block region of neighbouring vectors estimated. Based on the center pixel value separate into odd and even pixel value and find the neighbouring vector using the Eq. (1). That result form the neighbouring vectors, based on that compute the binary pattern.

$$
N_d = \begin{cases} P_{1+ \ \mathrm{mod} \ (x+5,7)}, P_{1+ \ \mathrm{mod} \ (x+6,9)}, P_{x+1}, P_{\mathrm{mod} \ (x+2,8)} & if \ d == odd \\ P_{x-1}, P_{\mathrm{mod} \ (x+1,8)} & else \end{cases}
$$

$$(1)$$

Here $N$ indicates neighbour, d indicates dimension based on $3 \times 3$ outer pixel one binary pattern formed by using below equation of (2)

$$N_1(d) = \begin{cases} 1 \ if \ N_d \geq I_{seg(i,j)} \\ 0 \ else \end{cases} \tag{2}$$

Like manner $3 \times 3$ center pixel value formed another binary pattern by using below the equation of (3)

$$N_2(d) = \begin{cases} 1 \ if \ S_x \geq I_c \ \forall \ I_c \\ 0 \ else \end{cases} \tag{3}$$

Based on outer and center pixel result and logic again one binary pattern form by using below Eq. (4)

$$J_i(d) = \begin{cases} 0 \ if \ N_1(d) \ == \ 0 \ N_2(d) = 0 \\ 0 \ if \ N_1(d) \ == \ 1 \ N_2(d) = 1 \\ 1 \ else \end{cases} \tag{4}$$

When the current binary pattern greater than or equal to $N_d/2$, finally one binary pattern formed and process repeated until the final binary pattern got by using the Eq. (5).

$$Q(d) = \begin{cases} 1 \ if \ \dim(J_i \ == \ 1) \geq (\dim \ (N_d/2 \ )) \\ 0 \ else \end{cases} \tag{5}$$

Then performed local binary pattern(LBP) of either 0 or 1 pixel is multiplied by $2^{i-1}$ then performed summation that result is feature result. To get the test feature value perform the color moments of histogram and computed the statistical features by calculating mean, variance, median, co-variance, and correlation and combined all feature values. The plaque feature got in pixel values are converted into scale value by multiplied the area value with 0.0002645833 pixel value and performed square.

The plaque feature extraction algorithm is given below

---

**Adjacent Pattern Extraction**
**Input:** *Segmented Result $I_{seg}$*
**Output:** *Extracted features Fea*
**Procedure:**

    **Step 1:** *Perform the feature extraction for $I_{seg}$*
        *$[m \ n] = size(I_{seg})$*
        *For $i = 2 : m - 1$*
        *for $j = 2 : n - 1$*
        *$P = I_{seg}(i - 1 : i + 1, j - 1 : j + 1)$ // $3 * 3$ block taken*
    **Step 2:** *Estimate neighbouring vectors for the center pixel*
        *For $d = 1 : 8$*
        *Find Neighbouring dimension $N_d$*

---

**Step 3:** *Compute binary pattern*
**Step 4:** *Compute final neighbourhood pattern*
$$Fea = Q + (Q \times 2^{i-1})$$

## 2.3  SVM Based CNN Classifier

SVM is a kind of supervised machine learning scheme which predominantly utilized in classification complications. CNN is a multilayered neural network with a special structural design to detect complex features. To find out the features in IVUS image is a complex task so here we combine the supervised learning and deep learning algorithm and form a new algorithm of SVN based CNN algorithm, it characterizes the image pixels in the plaque/non-plaque categories separately.

By using training features CNN can able to operate but here before CNN operation the SVM matrix formed. Support vector matrix formed for every class and based on SVM matrix CNN will be trained and tested, to separate into classes and then apply CNN classifier in that class. Estimate the number of classes in the label as follows

$$U = unique(L)$$

where $L$ denotes the class labels for all images Form the features based on the grouping of unique classes form as the Eq. (6)

$$G = \lim_{o \to to\,size(U)} (U(o) == L) \tag{6}$$

$G$ - denotes the group contains binary values.

For every classes the support vector matrix i.e weight matrix formed by using Lagrange multipliers. Then the weight matrix is calculated using Lagrange multipliers and given in Eq. (7),

$$w(h, :) = \lim_{h \to 1\,to\,size(L)} \{\alpha \times G(h) \times Train_{fea}(h, :)\} \tag{7}$$

where, $w$ indicates the weight matrix and alpha represents the Lagrange Multiplier of the support vector, $\alpha \geq 0$.

The support vector or weight matrix separates the hyper plane and which values separate the hyper plane is decided by the weight matrix based on that the training and test features are calculated. Based on bias training and test matrix updated.

Estimate bias which separates the two parts by intercept of the hyper plane based on the Eq. (8),

$$Bi = \frac{1}{size(L)} \lim_{h \to 1\,to\,size(L)} G\,(h) - (Train_{fea}\,(h, :) \times W\,(h, :)) \tag{8}$$

Based on the calculated bias, the train features and the test features are updated based on the Eqs. (9) and (10).

$$Tr_i = (z_2(i) \times Train_{fea}(:,i)) + z_1(i) \tag{9}$$

$$Te_i = (z_2(i) \times Test_{fea}(:,i)) + z_1(i) \tag{10}$$

where, $i$ varies from 1 to number of feature dimension, $z_1$ is the mean of trained features, $z_2$ is scale factor given by,

$$z_2 = \frac{1}{std\,(Train_{fea})} \tag{11}$$

Then the updated the training and test features are passed into the CNN classifier by using the Eq. (11) and processed.

Predicted the class labels are based on the weight matrix of below Eq. (12).

$$C = L(Tr_i(Wt), Te_i) \tag{12}$$

The test and training features by SVM based CNN classification algorithm is given below

---

**Support Vector based CNN Classifier**
**Input:** *Train features $Train_{fea}$ , test features $Test_{fea}$ , Label L*
**Output:** *Predicted Class C*
**Procedure:**

**Step 1:** *Estimate number of class label for all images*
**Step 2:** *Form the features based on the grouping of unique classes*
**Step 3:** *The weight matrix is calculated using Lagrange multipliers*
**Step 4:** *Estimate bias which separates the two parts by the intercept of the hyper plane*
**Step 5:** *Based on the calculated bias, the train features, and the test features are updated*
**Step 6:** *Apply CNN for the updated train features,*
  – *Add 3×3 convolution layer with number filter*
  – *Apply ReLu activation function*
  – *3×3 max pooling layer*
  – *Add a fully connected layer*
  – *Use softmax function for calculation of the posterior probability*
  – *Estimated weight matrix $Wt$*
**Step 7:** *predicted the class label based on the weight matrix*
  $C = L((Wt), T_i)$

---

Finally, analyze the performance of the formulated scheme with state-of-the-art techniques. The supervised classifier of support vector based CNN classifier is estimating the support vectors for the trained and test features to execute the neural network operation. By formation of support vectors at the classification which separating the features for each class and finally the separated features from an image belongs to which plaque severity type whether Mild or Moderate or Severe type is displayed.

## 3   Results and Discussion

Intravascular ultrasound images are influenced by means of speckle noise and artifacts that hide the needed feature information. The segmented lumen, plaque regions, and their contours of output are taken as input for feature extraction. The lumen and plaque feature extraction from an IVUS image is shown in Fig. 2. The segmented result of border detection is shown in Fig. 3 1(A), 2(A), 3(A) this segmentation process discussed in our previous paper [9]. This segmented output is taken as input for the lumen and plaque feature extraction performed by adjacent pattern algorithm of neighbourhood pattern that produced the result of lumen and plaque feature is shown in Fig. 3 1(B), 2(B), 3(B) the inner yellow color is lumen feature and red color is plaque feature. For the segmented image, the color moments or histogram and the statistical features are found such as mean, median, variance, covariance, and correlation operations finally combined all to get the test features of plaque shown in Fig. 3 1(C), 2(C), 3(C) and plaque portion display in the RGB form that reflected the original image is shown in Fig. 3 1(D), 2(D), 3(D).

We aim to find out the blockage level of the artery, In the CathLab the physicians consider the heart blockage if the blockage is less than 40% is considered as mild, the moderate range is 50–70% and severe heart blockage is typically greater than 70% range. For 100% blockage, the physician tried stent procedure based on the plaque type otherwise they go for open-heart surgery. Only for the 70% and above blockage level only the stent going to be fixed. This blockage level percentage also follows in the data collected place of Meenakshi Mission Hospital & Research center, Madurai, Tamilnadu for this work. Also referred from the web site https://myheart.net/articles/heart-blockage-explained-with-pictures. In Table 1 the plaque area(WCSA-Wall cross-sectional area) and plaque in percentage calculation performed from Lumen cross-sectional area(LCSA) and Vessel cross-sectional area(VCSA) of shape parameters which is discussed in our previous paper [9]. In Table 1 the Data Image-1 has the plaque percentage 3.88 is less than 40% it belongs to mild plaque type, the Data Image -2 has the plaque percentage 53.12 is 50–70% it belongs to moderate plaque type, the Data Image -3 has the plaque percentage 82.93 is greater than 70% it belongs to severe plaque type.

To further enhance the feature extraction performance of the adjacent pattern method, the SVN based CNN algorithm is used for classification. The training progress and testing results of plaque are given in Fig. 4. As a result of the

Fig. 3 1(D) plaque type mild is shown in Fig. 4. a, the Fig. 3 2(D) plaque type moderate is shown in Fig. 4 b, the Fig. 3 3(D) plaque type severe is shown in Fig. 4 c.

## 3.1   Performance Measure for Classification

The performance of the feature extraction algorithm is examined and measured quantitatively with the metric measures. The proposed SVM based CNN classifier, compared with other two classifiers such as CNN-Basic and SVM method accurately predicts the positive class is true positive, model erroneously forecasts the positive class is false positive, model perfectly predicts negative class is true negative, and model imperfectly predicts negative class is a false negative. The TP, FP, TN, and FN are used as parameters to evaluate quantitatively for six metric measurements of accuracy, sensitivity, specificity, precision, recall, and F-score can be calculated by using the Eqs. 13–18 the values are tabulated in 2.

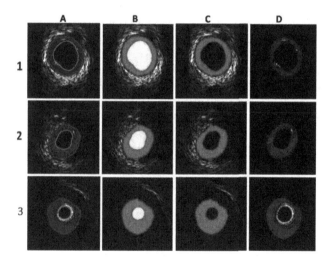

**Fig. 3.** Plaque feature extracted for the Fig. 2 images - column 1(A) 2(A) 3(A) lumen and plaque border detected (Green-lumen border, red-media-adventitia border), column 1(B) 2(B) 3(B) lumen and plaque feature extracted(yellow-lumen, red-plaque), column 1(C) 2(C) 3(C) plaque alone extracted, column 1(D) 2(D) 3(D) using color moments and statistical features the plaque area displayed. (Color figure online)

$$Accuracy = \frac{TP + TN}{TP + TN + FP + FN} \tag{13}$$

$$Sensitivity = \frac{TP}{TP + FN} \tag{14}$$

$$Specificity = \frac{TN}{TN + FP} \tag{15}$$

**Table 1.** Plaque area value displayed in percentage

| Original IVUS Image | Plaque Area (WCSA) | Plaque In Percentage (%) |
|---|---|---|
| Data Image -1 | 1.45 | 3.88 |
| Data Image -2 | 20.71 | 53.12 |
| Data Image -3 | 41.21 | 82.93 |

$$Precision = \frac{TP}{TP + FP} \tag{16}$$

$$Recall = \frac{TP}{TP + FN} \tag{17}$$

$$F - Score = 2 \times TP/(2 \times TP + FP + FN) \tag{18}$$

The plaque feature classification performed by three different classifiers SVM based CNN, CNN-Basic, and SVM are quantitatively measured and result values are shown in Table 2. It shows that the proposed method of SVM based CNN classifier provides high accuracy Value of 98.80 than the other two existing classifiers. The precision indicates the ratio of accurately predicted positive observations to the overall predicted positive observations. Precision can be seen as a measurement of exactness or quality. The call represents the ratio of perfectly predicted positive observations of the entire observations. The recall indicates a measure of completeness or quantity. F1-score represents a measure employed for evaluating binary classification with unbalanced classes.

**Table 2.** Comparison of different classification methods for different metrics of accuracy, sensitivity, specificity, precision, recall, and F-score for Fig. 3

| Original IVUS Images | Classifiers | Accuracy | Sensitivity | Specificity | Precision | Recall | F-Score |
|---|---|---|---|---|---|---|---|
| Data Image -1 | **SVM Based CNN** | 98.80 | 100 | 98.70 | 85.71 | 100 | 0.92 |
| | **CNN-Basic** | 98.80 | 100 | 98.70 | 85.71 | 100 | 0.92 |
| | **SVM** | 96.39 | 83.33 | 97.40 | 71.43 | 83.33 | 0.77 |
| Data Image -2 | **SVM Based CNN** | 98.80 | 100 | 98.70 | 85.71 | 100 | 0.92 |
| | **CNN-Basic** | 96.39 | 83.33 | 97.40 | 71.43 | 83.33 | 0.77 |
| | **SVM** | 96.39 | 83.33 | 97.40 | 71.43 | 83.33 | 0.77 |
| Data Image -3 | **SVM Based CNN** | 97.59 | 100 | 97.40 | 75 | 100 | 0.99 |
| | **CNN-Basic** | 96.39 | 83.33 | 97.41 | 71.43 | 83.33 | 0.77 |
| | **SVM** | 92.77 | 83.33 | 93.51 | 50 | 83.33 | 0.63 |

High precision indicates that an algorithm returned considerably more related results than immaterial ones from Table 2 the SVM based CNN classification algorithm provides high precision so this algorithm provides more relevant results. The high recall represents that a scheme returned most of the significant results from Table 2 the SVM based CNN classification algorithm provides high recall so this algorithm provides more relevant results.

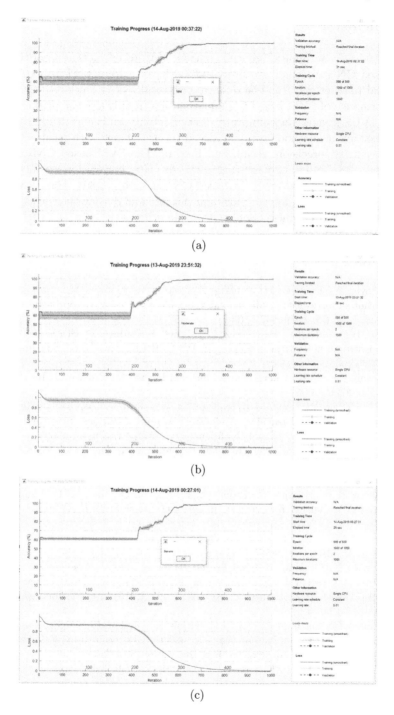

**Fig. 4.** Plaque severity level identified through SVM based CNN Classifier- (a) the Fig. 2 (A) Data Image -1 plaque severity level displayed as mild, (b) the Fig. 2 (B) Data Image -2 plaque severity level displayed as moderate, (c) the Fig. 2 (C) Data Image -3 plaque severity level display as severe.

# 4    Conclusion

In this study an automatic adjacent pattern feature extraction algorithm and SVM based CNN classifier are proposed in the new framework to extract the lumen and plaques feature. The quantitative results of this study demonstrate the performance of SVM based CNN method and it extracts the plaque feature from 2D IVUS images very efficiently. The reliability and reproducibility of the feature extraction methods were validated in accordance with accuracy, sensitivity, specificity, precision, recall, and F-score. The SVM based CNN method outperform than other two existing methods. The correlation coefficient i.e. accuracy value evaluated for SVM based CNN is high (98.80). The SVM based CNN method efficiently detects the plaque feature and display the corresponding plaque severity level in intravascular ultrasound images.

# References

1. Mojsilovic, A., Popovic, M., Amodaj, N., Babic, R., Ostojic, M.: Automatic segmentation of intravascular ultrasound images: a texture-based approach ease. Ann. Biomed. Eng. **25**, 1059–1071 (1997)
2. Gil, D., Hernandez, A., Rodriguez, O., Mauri, J., Radeva, P.: Statistical strategy for anisotropic adventitia modelling in IVUS. IEEE Trans. Med. Imaging **25**(6), 768–778 (2006)
3. Frostegard, J.: SLE, atherosclerosis and cardiovascular disease. J. Intern. Med. **257**, 13652796 (2005)
4. Lee, H., Grosse, R., Ranganath, R., Ng, A.: Convolutional deep belief networks for scalable unsupervised learning of hierarchical representations. In: Proceedings of the 26th Annual International Conference on Machine Learning, p. 609–616 (2009)
5. Shiddieqy, H.A., Hariadi, F.I., Adiono, T.: Implementation of deep-learning based image classification on single board computer. In: International Symposium on Electronics and Smart Devices (ISESD), pp. 133–137 (2017)
6. Caballero, K.L., Barajas, J., Pujol, O., Rodriguez, O., Radeva, P.: Using reconstructed IVUS images for coronary plaque classification. In: IEEE, pp. 2167–2170 (2007)
7. Kass, M., Witkin, A., Terzopoulos, D.: Snakes: active contour models. Int. J. Comput. Vis. **1**, 321–331 (1988)
8. Lo Vercio, L., Orlando, J.I., del Fresno, M., Larrabide, I.: Assessment of image features for vessel wall segmentation in intravascular ultrasound images. Int. J. Comput. Assist. Radiol. Surg. **11**(8), 1397–1407 (2016). https://doi.org/10.1007/s11548-015-1345-4
9. Mahadevi, C., Sivakumar, D.S.: Evaluation of segmentation algorithms for the detection of plaque border and wall cross-sectional area in b-mode intravascular ultrasound images. J. Int. Pharm. Res. **46**(4), 388–397 (2019)
10. Mendizabal-Ruiz, E.G., Rivera, M., Kakadiaris, I.A.: Robust segmentation of the luminal border in intravascular ultrasound using a probabilistic approach. Technical Report UH-CS-11-02, University of Houston, Houston, TX, USA (2011)
11. Mesejo, P., Ibanez, O., Cordon, O., Cagnoni, S.: A survey on image segmentation using meta heuristic-based deformable models: state of the art and critical analysis. Appl. Soft Comput. **44**, 129 (2016)

12. Taki, A., Roodaki, A., Setarehdan, S.K., Avansari, S., Unal, G., Navab, N.: An IVUs image-based approach for improvement of coronary plaque characterization. Comput. Biol. Med. **43**, 268–280 (2013)
13. Pazinato, D.V., et al.: Pixel-level tissue classification for ultrasound images. IEEE J. Biomed. Health Inform. **20**, 256–267 (2016)
14. Rotger, D., Radeva, P., Fernández-Nofrerías, E., Mauri, J.: Blood detection in IVUS images for 3D volume of lumen changes measurement due to different drugs administration. In: Kropatsch, W.G., Kampel, M., Hanbury, A. (eds.) CAIP 2007. LNCS, vol. 4673, pp. 285–292. Springer, Heidelberg (2007). https://doi.org/10.1007/978-3-540-74272-2_36
15. Sridevi, S., Sundaresan, M.: Hybrid feature extraction techniques for accuracy improvement in IVUS image classification. Int. J. Sci. Technol. Res. **9**(4), 720–724 (2020)
16. Turaga, S.C., et al.: Convolutional networks can learn to generate affinity graphs for image segmentation. Neural Comput. **22**(2), 511–538 (2010)
17. Dehnavi, S.M., Babu, M.P., Yazchi, M., Basij, M.: Automatic soft and hard plaque detection in IVUS images: a textural approach. In: IEEE Conference on Information and Communication Technologies (ICT 2013), pp. 214–219. IEEE (2013)
18. Su, S., Hu, Z., Lin, Q., Hau, W.K., Gao, Z., Zhang, H.: An artificial neural network method for lumen and media-adventitia border detection in IVUS. Comput. Med. Imaging Graph. **57**, 29–39 (2017)
19. Giannoglou, V.G., Theocharis, J.B.: Decision fusion of multiple classifiers for coronary plaque characterization from IVUS images. Int. J. Artif. Intell. Tools **23**, 1460005 (2014)
20. LeCun, Y., Huang, F.J., Bottou, L.: Learning methods for generic object recognition with invariance to pose and lighting. In: Proceedings of the 2004 IEEE Computer Society Conference on Computer Vision and Pattern Recognition, CVPR 2004, vol. 2, p. II97 (2004)
21. Zhang, L., Jing, J., Zhang, H.: Fabric defect classification based on LBP and GLCM. Appl. Soft Comput. **8**, 81–89 (2015)

# Identification of Palatal Fricative Fronting Using Shannon Entropy of Spectrogram

Pravin Bhaskar Ramteke[1(✉)], Sujata Supanekar[1], Venkataraja Aithal[2], and Shashidhar G. Koolagudi[1]

[1] National Institute of Technology Karnataka, Surathkal, India
ramteke0001@gmail.com, sujata.supanekar@gmail.com, koolagudi@nitk.edu.in
[2] Department of Speech and Hearing, SOAHS, Manipal, India
vrajaithal@manipal.edu

**Abstract.** In this paper, an attempt has been made to identify palatal fricative fronting in children speech, where postalveolar /sh/ is mispronounced as dental /s/. In children's speech, the concentration of energy (darkest part) of spectrogram for /s/ ranges 4000 Hz to 8000 Hz, whereas it ranges 3000 Hz 8000 Hz for /sh/. Gammatonegram follows the frequency subbands of the ear (wider for higher frequencies). Various spectral properties such as spectral centroid, spectral crest factor, spectral decrease, spectral flatness, spectral flux, spectral kurtosis, spectral spread, spectral skewness, spectral slope and Shannon entropy of the spectrogram (interval of 2000 Hz), extracted from the Gammatonegram are proposed for the characterization of /sh/ and /s/. The dataset recorded from 60 native Kannada speaking children of age between 3 1/2 to 6 1/2 years is considered for the analysis from NITK Kids' Speech Corpus. Support vector machine (SVMs) is considered for the classification. Various combinations of the proposed features are considered for the evaluation, along with the MFCCs(39) and LPCCs(39). Combination of MFCCs(39), LPCCs(39) and Entropy(4) is observed to achieve highest mispronunciation identification performance of 83.2983%.

**Keywords:** Shannon entropy · Gammatonegram · Support vector machine · Spectrogram

## 1 Introduction

Children are observed to face difficulty in pronouncing difficult sounds due to an underdeveloped vocal tract and lack of neuro-motor control [10]. Children replace difficult class of sounds with simpler ones. These mispronunciation patterns are known as phonological processes [10]. Based on the place of articulation of the substituted speech sound, the phonological processes can be classified into 3 categories: (i) syllable structure, (ii) assimilation or harmony, (iii) feature contrast or substitution [10]. Syllabic structure is simplification or modification of syllabic structure of the word. When the speech sound in a word becomes similar

© Springer Nature Switzerland AG 2020
B. R. Purushothama et al. (Eds.): MIKE 2019, LNAI 11987, pp. 234–243, 2020.
https://doi.org/10.1007/978-3-030-66187-8_22

to another sound in a word with the same place and manner of articulation is called assimilation or harmony. One class of sound is replaced with the another class of sound represents substitution. The phonological processes can be sub-categorized into different classes [5]. The phonological processes found in syllable structure are final consonant deletion, cluster reduction, etc. Assimilation can be sub-divided into velar assimilation, nasal assimilation, and so on. Substitution is further sub-classified into stopping, fronting, backing, etc [5]. The phonological processes get disappeared by the age of 8 years as the neuro-motor control, and vocal tract are completely developed. Disappearance of these processes in different age range provides a measure of language learning ability of children [12]. Speech-language pathologists (SLPs) analyze these phonological processes and their appearance in different age groups. Persistence of these processes after the age of 8 years, it represents the phonological disorder [12]. SLPs provide special practice sessions to overcome the pronunciation disability.

Unvoiced fricatives are produced by exciting the vocal tract with steady air-flow where it becomes turbulent in the region of a constriction. Some of the unvoiced fricatives are $/f/$, $/th/$, $/s/$, $/sh/$ etc. $/f/$ is produced by vocal constriction near the lips. Constriction near the teeth produces the fricative $/th/$. $/s/$ is a dental fricative pronounced by a constriction near the middle of the vocal tract whereas the $/sh/$ is postalveolar fricative with constriction near the back of the vocal tract. In general, children face difficulty in pronouncing the speech sound $/sh/$. In this paper, an attempt has been made to identify palatal fricative fronting in which $/sh/$ is replaced by $/s/$ in the Kannada language. $/sh/$ and $/s/$ are segmented using entropy extracted from spectrogram. Further, various spectral properties extracted from the Gammatonegram are proposed for the characterization of $/sh/$ and $/s/$. Support vector machine (SVMs) are used to evaluate the efficiency of the proposed features for the identification of mispronunciation of $/sh/$.

Rest of the paper is organized as follows. Section 2 gives the motivation behind this work. Analysis of the existing approaches in the field of mispronunciation detection is given in Sect. 3. Section 4 gives the details of the dataset used for the experimentation. The implementation detail of the proposed approach is given in Sect. 5. Results of the experimentation are analyzed and discussed in Sect. 6. Section 7 concludes the paper with some future directions.

## 2    Motivation

Phonological processes identification follows the manual analysis of children pronunciations by SLPs. Manual analysis of phonological processes has its limitations such as [7] (i) Time spent on the analysis (ii) continuous human expert attention (iii) errors in subjective evaluation by different experts (iv) appearance of phonological process varies from one language to another language of different nature. The substitution of $/sh/$ with $/s/$ is one of the phonological processes, where its presence after 8 years may result in phonological disorder. Hence, there is a need to develop an automatic system to identify substitution of $/sh/$ with $/s/$.

# 3    Literature Review

Various approaches have been proposed for identification mispronunciation. Efficiency of various features, classifiers, and parameters are explored for the task [2,3,6,9,23,31]. These approaches have focused on foreign language learning. Graphical analysis is one of the common and widely used approaches for mispronunciation analysis [17]. Waveform, spectrogram, pitch, intonation, and formants of the correct word and test word (pronounced by the learner) are displayed on the screen for comparison. Learner or experts visually compare the spectrogram and analyze the mispronunciation. Winpitch LTL, WinPitch LTL II, and KayPENTAX Auditory Feedback Tool (ADF) are some of the commercially available implementations of the graphical analysis systems [17]. These approaches involve continuous human intervention for mispronunciation analysis. Learners may not have sufficient expertise for analysis of acoustic features hence face difficulty in interpretation of the features.

'Goodness of pronunciation (GOP)' score based approaches have been proposed for automatic pronunciation error detection using Hidden Markov Model (HMMs) [2,3,6,9,23,31]. It is aimed at identification of phone level scores such as log-likelihood score, log posterior probability score, log-likelihood ratio (LLR) from the forced alignment phase of HMMs Viterbi decoding [3]. For performance analysis, phone level scores are correlated with the rating provided by human experts, where high correlation represents better performance. Log-likelihood ratio (LLR) is observed to perform better in comparison with the log-likelihood and log posterior probability scores. Pronunciation Space Model (PSMs) are efficient in modeling the deviations in the phone during pronunciation. Support vector machines (SVMs) are trained using PSMs for the identification of mispronunciation. GOPs are estimated from the automatic speech recognition system using Gaussian mixture model (GMMs) based HMM for parameter estimation. GMM is replaced by Deep neural network (DNN) to identify the mispronunciation errors [14,15,23]. The GOP scores obtained from the DNN-HMMs are claimed to be efficient in pronunciation error detection in comparison with the GOP scored obtained from the GMM-HMMs [23]. Native language may not have a certain set of phonemes that are present in the non-native language. These phonemes are substituted with the specific phonemes from the native language. Extended recognition network (ERNs) represents the encoded form of these commonly observed pronunciation error patterns in relation to phone level transcription of learner's speech [6]. This approach is efficient in the identification of very few and frequent mispronunciations patterns. Some approaches used Dynamic time warping (DTW) for the identification of mispronunciation. Native and corresponding non-native pronunciation of words are compared using Dynamic time warping (DTW) [13,18]. Various properties of the DTW comparison path and distance matrix are explored for the mispronunciation detection [13].

From the literature, it is observed that the features efficient in the identification of substitution of /sh/ with /s/ and vice versa are not explored. Also, the area of phonological process identification in children's speech is hardly explored. In this paper, an attempt has been made for the identification of the features efficient in characterization and identification of the phonological process where /sh/ is substituted with /s/ and vice versa.

## 4   Speech Dataset

The dataset used in this work is recorded from 60 children of age between $3\frac{1}{2}$ to $6\frac{1}{2}$ years having Kannada as a native language (NITK Kids Speech Corpus) [24]. The words to be recorded are chosen in such a way that it reflects child's typical use of speech sounds during everyday activities. This creates the recommended representative speech samples of size 112 words [26]. To add the contextual information, in our recordings of representative words, pictures representing the Kannada words are selected. Twenty words consisting of /s/ and /sh/ are considered for the analysis are: *icecream, autorickshaw, aushadhi, biskit, brash, ganesha, maragenasu, samaya, samudra, sangha, sayankala, shalage, shankha, shart, simha, snana, surya, vidhanasaudha*. From the analysis, it is observed that 200 pronunciations of these words are observed to have mispronunciation where /sh/ is substituted by /s/ and vice versa.

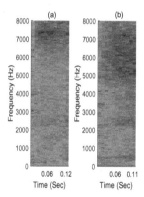

**Fig. 1.** (a) Spectrogram of speech segment /s/ ('*sangha*') (b) Spectrogram of speech segment /sh/ ('*shalage*').

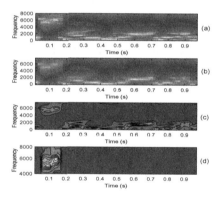

**Fig. 2.** Illustration of process of segmentation of /s/ from the speech (a) Spectrogram of speech of word '*sayankala*' (b) Spectrogram after Shannon entropy (c) Shannon entropy spectrogram after thresholding (d) Segmented fricative region of /s/

## 5   Methodology

Proposed approach is divided into three stages. First stage involves automatic segmentation of /s/ and /sh/ using entropy of the spectrogram. Further, spectral properties efficient in characterization of /s/ and /sh/ are extracted. Efficiency of the proposed features is calculated using SVMs.

## 5.1   Automatic Segmentation of /s/ and /sh/

Due to the absence of vocal tract vibration in voiceless fricatives, the resultant speech is of noise like nature and do not have specific formant structure, unlike voiced speech sounds. Spectrogram analysis of voiceless fricatives shown that the region of concentration of energy in frequency is different for each fricative. In children speech, the concentration of energy (darkest part) of spectrogram for /s/ ranges 4000 Hz to 8000 Hz (Fig. 1 (a)) whereas it ranges 3000 Hz 8000 Hz for /sh/ (Fig. 1 (b)). Entropy is a measure of randomness where higher the randomness larger is the entropy. Shannon entropy $(H(x))$ of a signal is given by,

$$H(x) = -\sum_{i=1}^{N} p(x) log_2 p(x) \tag{1}$$

where, $x$ is a random variable. $p(x)$ is the probability mass function $(pmf)$ associated with random variable $x$. Entropy of the voiced region is less compared to the fricative region due to less randomness. Hence, this property is explored for the segmentation of the /s/ and /sh/. For segmentation, $entropy$ of the spectrogram is calculated in the interval 2000 Hz e.g. 0 Hz–2000 Hz, 2000 Hz–4000 Hz, etc. A threshold of $\{thr = 0.04 \times max(entropy)\}$ is empirically set, where $\{entropy > thr\}$ represents fricative region. Figure 2 shows the process of segmentation of /s/ from the speech.

## 5.2   Feature Extraction

Analysis of spectrogram shown that the concentration of energy is different for /s/ and /sh/. Hence, spectral features are explored for the analysis.

**Mel-Frequency Cepstral Coefficients (MFCCs).** MFCCs are one of the most widely used features in the speech recognition [28]. It mimics the human perceptual and auditory system; hence it plays a significant role in various speech-related applications like speech recognition, speaker recognition, etc [19]. Total 39 features are extracted which consists of 13 MFCCs, 13 $\Delta$MFCCs and 13 $\Delta\Delta$MFCCs respectively.

**Linear Predictive Cepstral Coefficients (LPCCs).** LPCs are the coefficients of an auto-regressive model of a speech frame [16]. Vocal tract transfer function is obtained using all-pole representation. The detailed procedure to calculate LPCCs is given in [16]. LPCCs are well known for their performance in many speech-related tasks such as speech recognition, speaker recognition, etc. Total 39 features are extracted which consists of 13 LPCCs, 13 $\Delta$LPCCs and 13 $\Delta\Delta$LPCCs respectively.

**Gammatonegram.** Gammatone filters approximate the filtering process followed by the ear. It gives a simple wrapper function to generate the time-frequency surfaces based on a gammatone analysis. Gammatone function is a gamma distribution function modulated by tone given as [22]:

$$g(t) = t^{(N-1)}e^{-at}u(t)cos\omega_0 t \tag{2}$$

where $\omega_0$ represents the center frequency, $a$ is bandwidth parameter and $N$ represents the order of gammatone function. It is characterized by the closeness to experimentally obtained auditory response [30]. Gammatonegram follows the frequency sub-bands of the ear which get broad for higher frequencies; the traditional spectrogram use same bandwidth for all frequency channels. Hence, it can be used as an enhanced substitute for the conventional spectrogram. Different spectral properties extracted from the Gammatonegram for the characterization of /s/ and /sh/ are: Spectral Centroid (SC) [21], Spectral Crest Factor (SCF) [21], Spectral Decrease (SD) [21], Spectral Flatness (SFlat) [11], Spectral Flux (SF) [25], Spectral Kurtosis (SK) [21], Spectral Spread (SS) [21], Spectral Skewness (SSK) [21], Spectral Slope (SSP) [27]. These spectral variation are used in combination with the 39 MFCC and 39 LPCC features to characterize /s/ and /sh/ results in feature vector of size 91.

### 5.3   Classification Using Support Vector Machine (SVM)

Support Vector Machine is a well known classification algorithm which attempts to fit a large-margin hyperplane between two classes that act as a decision boundary [8]. SVMs in binary classification, given a training feature vector $X = \{x_1, x_2, ..., x_n\}$ in $d$ dimensional space, such that $X \subset R^d$ and their labels $y_1, y_2, ..., y_n$, where $y_i \in \{-1, 1\}$, it separate the training data by a hyperplane with maximal margin [1]. Support vectors are the data instances that lie closest to the hyperplane. The classifier can visualized in the form [29]:

$$f(x) = \sum_{i=1}^{n} \alpha_i K(x_i, x) \tag{3}$$

where, $K$ is Mercer kernel operator, which projects the training data on the higher dimensional feature space. Mercer kernel operator is defined as, $K(u, v) = \phi(u).\phi(v)$, where $\phi : X \longrightarrow F$ and "." represents an inner product. $F$ is a higher dimensional feature space to which $X$ is being projected. Further, Eq. 3 can be rewritten as:

$$f(x) = w.\phi(x), \quad where \quad w = \sum_{i=1}^{n} \alpha_i \phi(x_i) \tag{4}$$

SVM evaluates the $\alpha_i s$ corresponding to the hyperplane with maximal margin [20]. Polynomial and radial basis kernels are the most commonly used function kernels [29]. Polynomial kernel is given by $K(u, v) = (u.v + 1)^p$, where $p$ is the degree of polynomial boundaries. Radial basis kernel $(K(u, v) = exp^{\gamma(u-v).(u-v)})$ use weighted Gaussian to induce the boundary.

**Table 1.** Performance of mispronunciation identification using Support Vector Machine (SVMs)

| Featured considered | Average accuracy | Precision | Recall | F-Measure |
|---|---|---|---|---|
| MFCCs(39) | 78.8809% | 0.820 | 0.789 | 0.783 |
| MFCCs(39)+LPCCs(39) | 79.4699% | 0.820 | 0.795 | 0.790 |
| MFCCs(39)+LPCCs(39)+Entropy(4)+ SC(1)+SF(1)+SD(1)+SFlat(1)+SCF(1)+ SK(1)+SS(1)+SSK(1)+SSP(1) | 79.3437% | 0.816 | 0.793 | 0.789 |
| MFCCs(39)+LPCCs(39)+Entropy(4)+ SS(1)+SSK(1)+SF(1) | 79.7644% | 0.823 | 0.798 | 0.793 |
| MFCCs(39)+LPCCs(39)+Entropy(4) | **83.2983%** | 0.838 | 0.833 | 0.832 |

## 6   Results and Discussion

In this paper, an attempt has been made for the identification of phonological process where $/sh/$ is mispronounced as $/s/$ and vice versa. Dataset is recorded from the 60 children in the age range $3\frac{1}{2}$–$6\frac{1}{2}$ years (refer Sect. 4). Two hundred pronunciations are observed to have this phonological process. First, the automatic segmentation of unvoiced fricatives $/s/$ and $/sh/$ is performed using entropy of the spectrogram. The voiceless fricatives are random noise like in nature, hence have high entropy value in comparison with the voiced regions. The entropy of the spectrogram is calculated in the interval 2000 Hz over the range 0 Hz to 8000 Hz. A threshold is empirically set to $thr = 0.04 \times max(entropy)$, where the entropy value greater than $thr$ represents the region of fricatives $/s/$ and $/sh/$. The performance of the segmentation achieved is 92.58% within the tolerance range of ±100 ms. The segmented fricative regions are considered for the characterization and identification of mispronunciation. Spectrogram analysis shown that the energy values for $/s/$ are concentrated in the range 4000 Hz to 8000 Hz and for $/sh/$ it is concentrated in the range 3000 Hz to 8000 Hz. Here, the Gammatonegram is considered for the analysis. The spectral parameters extracted are: spectral centroid, spectral crest factor, spectral decrease, spectral flatness, spectral flux, spectral kurtosis, spectral spread, spectral skewness and spectral slope. MFCCs & LPCCs are found to be efficient in all speech tasks, hence it is considered in combination with the spectral feature for the characterization. This results in the feature vector of size 91. The performance of the various combination of features is tested using SVM (radial basis kernel (RBF)). We have used 80% of the instances for training the classifier and 20% for testing with 5-fold cross-validation. The commonly used metrics for the performance evaluation are accuracy, precision, recall, and F-measure [4].

The baseline system is implemented using 39 MFCC features on the correct pronunciation of $/s/$ and $/sh/$. The highest accuracy achieved using SVM (RBF kernel) is 85.221 %, with an average precision of 0.852, recall of 0.852 & F-measure of 0.848. The same model is used for the identification of mispronunciation with an average performance of 78.8809% on mispronounced data with an average precision, recall, and F-measure of 0.820, 0.789, 0.783 respectively (Table 1). Various combinations of 39 MFCCs and the proposed spectral features have been explored. Table 1 shows the performance metric of SVM classifier using various combinations of features. SVMs trained using 39 MFCCs and 39 LPCCs achieve an accuracy of 86.8824% on the correct pronunciation with an recall, precision, and F-measure of 0.868, 0.869, 0.866, respectively. The classification performance of 79.4699% is achieved on the mispronounced data with an average precision, recall and F-measure of 0.820, 0.795, 0.790 respectively. The combination of 39 MFCCs, LPCCs(39), Entropy(4), SC(1), SCF(1), SD(1), SFlat(1), SF(1), SK(1), SS(1), SSK(1) and SSP(1) is considered. The performance of 86.7018% is achieved on the correct pronunciation with the average precision of 0.866, recall of 0.867 and $F$-measure of 0.865. The classification performance of 79.3437% is achieved on the mispronounced data with an average precision, recall and F-measure of 0.816, 0.793, 0.789 respectively. /s/ and /sh/ are unvoiced sound where unvoiced speech is a result of random noise like excitation where vocal folds do not vibrate, it remain wide open. Hence, except the energy concentration over the frequency range, it do not exhibit any other variations in their spectral properties hence the spectral variations (SC, SCF, SD, SFlat, SF, SK, SS, SSK, SSP) considered for the classification do not show much improvement in the performance of the system. It is observed that the entropy of /s/ is high in the frequency range 3000 Hz to 8000 Hz, whereas for /sh/ entropy is high in the frequency range 2000 Hz to 8000 Hz. Hence, combination of MFCCs(39), LPCCs(39), SS(1), SSK(1), SF(1) and Entropy(4) observed to achieve an improvement in the performance of mispronunciation detection to 79.7644%. Considering the properties of entropy, combinations of MFCCs(39), LPCCs(39) and Entropy(4) are used for the analysis. The classification performance on correct pronunciation is observed to be dropped to 84.2314%, where it achieves a precision, recall and $F$-measure of 0.844, 0.842, 0.843 respectively. Using the same model, the performance of 83.2983% is achieved on the mispronunciation with an average precision of 0.838, recall of 0.833 and $F$-measure of 0.832. From the results, it is observed that the performance of the mispronunciation classification is improved by 4.4174% when compared to the baseline system. This shows that the entropy calculated at the interval 2000 Hz in combination with MFCCs(39) and LPCCs(39) are efficient in classification mispronounced /s/ and /sh/.

## 7   Summary and Conclusion

In this paper, an attempt has been made for the identification of mispronunciation where /sh/ is mispronounced as /s/ and vice versa. First, the automatic segmentation of /s/ and /sh/ is performed using the properties of Shannon entropy. Further, various spectral properties extracted from the Gammatonegram are proposed for the characterization of /sh/ and /s/. Various combinations of the proposed features are considered for the evaluation, along with the MFCCs(39) and LPCCs(39). For identification of mispronunciation, the system is first trained on correct pronunciations using SVM with 5 fold cross validation. The performance is evaluated on the mispronounced data. The highest classification performance of 83.2983% is achieved on the mispronunciation using a combination of MFCCs(39), LPCCs(39) and Entropy(4). Energy concentration is different for /s/ and /sh/, hence entropy improves the performance of the system. Other spectral variations do not show much improvement in the performance of the system as the random nature of the fricatives do not exhibit much variations in it. Further, various other spectral properties of the /s/ and /sh/ can be explored for the efficient identification of the mispronunciation.

**Acknowledgment.** The authors would like to thank the Cognitive Science Research Initiative (CSRI), Department of Science & Technology, Government of India, Grant no. SR/CSRI/ 49/2015, for its financial support on this work.

# References

1. Cortes, C., Vapnik, V.: Support-vector networks. Mach. Learn. **20**(3), 273–297 (1995). https://doi.org/10.1007/BF00994018
2. Cucchiarini, C., Strik, H., Boves, L.: Different aspects of expert pronunciation quality ratings and their relation to scores produced by speech recognition algorithms. Speech Commun. **30**(2–3), 109–119 (2000)
3. Franco, H., Neumeyer, L., Ramos, M., Bratt, H.: Automatic detection of phone-level mispronunciation for language learning. In: Sixth European Conference on Speech Communication and Technology, pp. 851–854 (1999)
4. García, V., Mollineda, R.A., Sánchez, J.S., Alejo, R., Sotoca, J.M.: When overlapping unexpectedly alters the class imbalance effects. In: Martí, J., Benedí, J.M., Mendonça, A.M., Serrat, J. (eds.) IbPRIA 2007. LNCS, vol. 4478, pp. 499–506. Springer, Heidelberg (2007). https://doi.org/10.1007/978-3-540-72849-8_63
5. Grunwell, P.: Clinical Phonology. Aspen Publishers, New York (1982)
6. Harrison, A.M., Lo, W.K., Qian, X.J., Meng, H.: Implementation of an extended recognition network for mispronunciation detection and diagnosis in computer-assisted pronunciation training. In: International Workshop on Speech and Language Technology in Education, pp. 45–48 (2009)
7. Hodson, B.W.: The Assessment of Phonological Processes. Interstate Printers and Publishers, Danville (1980)
8. Hsu, C.W., et al.: A practical guide to support vector classification, pp. 1–16 (2003)
9. Huang, X., Huang, X., Acero, A., Hon, H.W., Reddy, R.: Spoken Language Processing: A Guide to Theory, Algorithm, and System Development, 1st edn. Prentice Hall PTR, Upper Saddle River (2001)
10. Ingram, D.: Phonological rules in young children. J. Child Lang. **1**(1), 49–64 (1974)
11. Johnston, J.D.: Transform coding of audio signals using perceptual noise criteria. IEEE J. Sel. Areas Commun. **6**(2), 314–323 (1988)
12. Kent, R.D., Vorperian, H.K.: Speech impairment in down syndrome: a review. J. Speech Lang. Hear. Res. **56**(1), 178–210 (2013)
13. Lee, A., Glass, J.: A comparison-based approach to mispronunciation detection. In: 2012 IEEE Spoken Language Technology Workshop (SLT), pp. 382–387. IEEE (2012)

14. Li, K., Qian, X., Meng, H.: Mispronunciation detection and diagnosis in L2 English speech using multidistribution deep neural networks. IEEE/ACM Trans. Audio Speech Lang. Process. **25**(1), 193–207 (2017)
15. Li, W., Siniscalchi, S.M., Chen, N.F., Lee, C.H.: Improving non-native mispronunciation detection and enriching diagnostic feedback with DNN-based speech attribute modeling. In: International Conference on Acoustics, Speech and Signal Processing (ICASSP), pp. 6135–6139. IEEE (2016)
16. Makhoul, J.: Linear prediction: a tutorial review. Proc. IEEE **63**(4), 561–580 (1975)
17. Martin, P.: Winpitch LTL, un logiciel multimédia d'enseignement de la prosodie. Alsic. Apprentissage des Langues et Systèmes d'Information et de Communication **8**(2), 95–108 (2005)
18. Miodonska, Z., Bugdol, M.D., Krecichwost, M.: Dynamic time warping in phoneme modeling for fast pronunciation error detection. Comput. Biol. Med. **69**, 277–285 (2016)
19. Murty, K.S.R., Yegnanarayana, B.: Combining evidence from residual phase and MFCC features for speaker recognition. IEEE Signal Process. Lett. **13**(1), 52–55 (2006)
20. Pal, M.: Random forest classifier for remote sensing classification. Int. J. Remote Sens. **26**(1), 217–222 (2005)
21. Peeters, G.: A large set of audio features for sound description (similarity and classification). CUIDADO Project IRCAM Technical Report (2004)
22. Pour, A.F., Asgari, M., Hasanabadi, M.R.: Gammatonegram based speaker identification. In: 2014 4th International Conference on Computer and Knowledge Engineering (ICCKE), pp. 52–55. IEEE (2014)
23. Qian, X., Meng, H., Soong, F.K.: The use of DBN-HMMs for mispronunciation detection and diagnosis in L2 English to support computer-aided pronunciation training. In: Thirteenth Annual Conference of the International Speech Communication Association, pp. 775–778 (2012)
24. Ramteke, P.B., Supanekar, S., Hegde, P., Nelson, H., Aithal, V., Koolagudi, S.G.: NITK Kids' speech corpus. In: Proceedings of Interspeech 2019, pp. 331–335 (2019)
25. Scheirer, E., Slaney, M.: Construction and evaluation of a robust multifeature speech/music discriminator. In: International Conference on Acoustics, Speech, and Signal Processing, vol. 2, pp. 1331–1334. IEEE (1997)
26. Shriberg, L.D., Kwiatkowski, J.: Phonological disorders I: a diagnostic classification system. J. Speech Hear. Disord. **47**(3), 226–241 (1982)
27. Sturm, B.L.: An introduction to audio content analysis: applications in signal processing and music informatics by alexander lerch. Comput. Music J. **37**(4), 90–91 (2013)
28. Tiwari, V.: MFCC and its applications in speaker recognition. Int. J. Emerg. Technol. **1**(1), 19–22 (2010)
29. Tong, S., Koller, D.: Support vector machine active learning with applications to text classification. J. Mach. Learn. Res. **2**(Nov), 45–66 (2001)
30. Venkitaraman, A., Adiga, A., Seelamantula, C.S.: Auditory-motivated gammatone wavelet transform. Signal Process. **94**, 608–619 (2014)
31. Wei, S., Hu, G., Hu, Y., Wang, R.H.: A new method for mispronunciation detection using support vector machine based on pronunciation space models. Speech Commun. **51**(10), 896–905 (2009)

# Identification of Nasalization and Nasal Assimilation from Children's Speech

Pravin Bhaskar Ramteke[1]([✉]), Sujata Supanekar[1], Venkataraja Aithal[2], and Shashidhar G. Koolagudi[1]

[1] National Institute of Technology Karnataka, Surathkal, India
ramteke0001@gmail.com, sujata.supanekar@gmail.com, koolagudi@nitk.edu.in
[2] Department of Speech and Hearing, SOAHS, Manipal, India
vrajaithal@manipal.edu

**Abstract.** In children, nasalization is a commonly observed phonological process where the non-nasal sounds are substituted with nasal sounds. Here, an attempt has been made for the identification of nasalization and nasal assimilation. The properties of nasal sounds and nasalized voiced sounds are explored using MFCCs extracted from Hilbert envelope of the numerator of group delay (HNGD) Spectrum. HNGD Spectrum highlights the formants in the speech and extra nasal formant in the vicinity of first formant in nasalized voiced sounds. Features extracted from correctly pronounced and mispronounced words are compared using Dynamic Time Warping (DTW) algorithm. The nature of the deviation of DTW comparison path from its diagonal behavior is analyzed for the identification of mispronunciation. The combination of FFT based MFCCs and HNGD spectrum based MFCCs are observed to achieve highest accuracy of 82.22% within the tolerance range of ±50 ms.

**Keywords:** Group delay function · Nasalization · Nasal assimilation · Speech language pathologists (SLPs) · Zero Time Windowing (ZTW)

## 1 Introduction

Due to underdeveloped vocal tract, children face difficulty in pronunciation of speech sounds [9]. Hence, children try to substitute the difficult class of sounds with the simple class of sounds. These mispronunciation patterns are known as phonological processes [9]. Mispronunciation patterns in children speech can be categorized into three types: (i) syllable structure, (ii) assimilation or harmony, (iii) feature contrast or substitution. Change in the sound syllabic structure of the words is known as syllable structure. The class of sound when replaced with the other sounds from the same class is called as harmony or assimilation [9]. Substitution is a phonological process where one class of sound is replaced with the other simpler class of sound. Most commonly observed subclasses of these phonological processes in children are fronting, stopping, nasalization and nasal assimilation [5]. Substitution of velar sounds with the alveolar sounds is known

© Springer Nature Switzerland AG 2020
B. R. Purushothama et al. (Eds.): MIKE 2019, LNAI 11987, pp. 244–253, 2020.
https://doi.org/10.1007/978-3-030-66187-8_23

as fronting e.g. /k/ with /t/, /g/ with /d/, etc. When the fricatives are replaced with affricate stops, it is known as stopping, e.g. *"pan"* for *"fan"*. In nasalization, the non-nasal sounds are substituted with nasal sounds. Nasal assimilation is the assimilation of a non-nasal to a nasal consonant. Speech-language pathologists (SLPs) analyze these patterns in different age groups and evaluate the language learning ability of children. If these phonological processes persist after the age of 8 years, it may result in phonological disorder [10]. Special training can be provided to the children to overcome the disability.

Nasal phones have a periodic glottal source like vowels and amplitude is lower in comparison with vowels as the nasal membrane absorb the sound. Complete closure of the oral tract gives rise to anti-formants in the range 800 Hz to 1500 Hz. The average duration of nasal sounds /m/ is 86.40 ms, /n/ is 81.44 ms, and /nx/ is 74.15 ms in children below 6.5 years. In nasalization, it is observed that, the substitution of nasal sound leads to the nasalization of immediately following vowels. Nasalized voiced sounds are observed to have an extra nasal peak in near first formant. In this paper, an attempt has been made to identify the nasalization and nasal assimilation. The properties of nasal and nasalized voiced sounds are explored using MFCCs extracted from HNGD Spectrum. HNGD Spectrum highlights the formants in the speech and extra nasal formant in the vicinity of first formant in nasalized voiced sounds. It also provides a high spectral resolution with a smaller frame size of 5 ms to 10 ms. Features extracted from correctly pronounced and mispronounced words are compared using Dynamic Time Warping (DTW) algorithm. The nature of the deviation of DTW comparison path from its diagonal behavior is analyzed for the identification of mispronunciation.

Rest of the paper is organized as follows. Analysis of the existing approaches in the field of mispronunciation detection is given in Sect. 3. The implementation details of the proposed approach are given in Sect. 4. Results of the experimentation are analyzed and discussed in Sect. 5. Section 6 concludes the paper with some future directions.

## 2   Motivation

SLPs listen to the children pronunciations and manually analyze them [7]. Manual analysis of phonological processes needs continuous human expert attention, large amount of time is spent on the analysis and subjective evaluation varies among the experts. Chronological order of disappearance of the phonological processes in children varies in the languages of different nature. Nasalization and nasal assimilation are commonly observed phonological processes, where its presence after eight years may result in phonological disorder. Hence, automatic pronunciation error detection need to be developed for identification.

## 3   Literature Review

In the area of mispronunciation analysis, most of the research works have focused on identification mispronunciation in foreign language learning. Most common approach employed for mispronunciation analysis is graphical method, where waveform and spectrogram from the reference word and mispronounced word are displayed on the screen e.g. Winpitch LTL [15]. Learner or experts visually compare them and analyze the mispronunciation. Along with waveform other features such as spectrogram, pitch, intonation, and formants are used for the same. Main limitations of these approaches are (i) difficulty in interpretation of the features (learners may not have sufficient expertise for the analysis of acoustic features) (ii) Pronunciation of the same word by the same person varies, hence may result in the change of its acoustic features and duration. Automatic pronunciation error detection is proposed using variants of hidden Markov model (HMMs) [2,4,6,8,19,24]. Approaches aimed at identification of phone level pronunciation score from the forced alignment phase of HMMs Viterbi decoding [4]. Commonly used phone level scores are log-likelihood score, log posterior probability score, log likelihood ratio (LLR) and segment duration score [4]. LLR based score outperform posterior probability based approaches. Pronunciation Space Model (PSMs) are used to create parallel acoustic models for each phone [24]. These values are used as features to train support vector machine (SVMs). Deep neural network (DNN) is replaced with the GMM and used to detect the segment level mispronunciation errors in HMMs [13,14,19]. Posterior probabilities are extracted from basis function where DNN decompose input feature vectors into effective basis functions. The extracted posterior probabilities are better in pronunciation error detection [19]. Pronunciation errors in language learning may exhibit certain patterns. These patterns are encoded as extended recognition network (ERNs) in relation with phone level transcription of learner's speech [6]. Very few and particular mispronunciations can be identified using this approach. In some systems, native and corresponding non-native pronunciation of words are compared using Dynamic time warping (DTW) [12,16]. Various parameters from distance matrix and resultant DTW comparison path are explored for mispronunciation detection [12]. The method captures the phone and word level errors, but fails to detect the wrong lexical stress patterns as these patterns are dependent on pitch features. Analysis of the literature shows that mispronunciation analysis approaches have focused on foreign language learning. Problems related to the identification of phonological processes in children speech are hardly addressed.

## 4    Methodology

Proposed approach is divided into three stages: (i) Feature extraction from the speech signal (ii) Reference templates selection (iii) Comparison of reference templates with mispronounced words using DTW algorithm to estimate the region of mispronunciation.

### 4.1    Speech Dataset

The dataset used in this work is recorded from 75 children of age between $3\frac{1}{2}$ to $6\frac{1}{2}$ years having Kannada as a native language (NITK Kids Speech Corpus)

[21]. The words to be recorded are chosen in such a way that it reflects the child's typical use of speech sounds during everyday activities. This creates the recommended representative speech samples of size 112 words [22]. To add the contextual information in our recordings of representative words, pictures representing the Kannada words are selected and children are asked to describe the images. Figure 1 shows some of the pictures and corresponding words used for recording. 45 words are observed to have a nasalization and nasal assimilation.

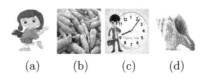

(a)       (b)       (c)       (d)

**Fig. 1.** Some of the representative speech samples for Kannada phonemes: (a) *"akka"* (sister) and *"shalage"* (school) (b) *"maragenasu"* (cassava roots) (c) *"samaya"* (time) (d) *"shankha"* (conch shell)

### 4.2  Preprocessing

Pronunciation of the same word varies from person to person due to his/her speaking style. Hence may result in different duration of word and small pauses in the pronunciations of same word. This property may affect DTW comparison path to warp due to longer duration of small pause and duration of word. Hence small pause removal and duration normalization is performed.

**Small Pause Removal.** Small pauses are removed using energy based threshold. For a given signal $x$, framewise energy of the speech signal is given by: $E_k = \frac{1}{2N} \sum_{i=1}^{N} x^2(i)$. Where, $E_k$ is the energy of speech signal in $k^{th}$ frame. $N$ is the length of the speech frame. Average energy $(Avg\_Ene)$ over entire speech signal having $L$ number of frames is calculated as in $Avg\_Ene = \frac{1}{L} \sum_{k=1}^{L} E_k$. From the analysis, an empirical threshold of $ene\_thr = 0.05 \times Avg\_Ene$ is set, where the energy values below $ene\_thr$ are considered as silence and removed.

**Duration Normalization.** Duration normalization is performed using a frequency modulation algorithm known as Time-Domain Pitch Synchronous Overlap and Add (TD-PSOLA) [17]. It can modify the duration of the speech signal to the target length without altering the segment identity.

### 4.3  Feature Extraction

MFCCs are extracted from the Fast Fourier transform (FFT) of the signal and HNGD spectrum obtained using Group delay function on Zero Time Windowing (ZTW) signal. The procedure of feature extraction is given in this section.

**Mel-Frequency Cepstral Coefficients (MFCCs).** MFCCs are one of the most widely used features in the speech recognition [23]. It mimics the human perceptual and auditory systems; hence it plays a significant role in various speech related applications like speech and speaker recognition, etc. Details of the MFCC feature extraction are given in [18]. Total 39 features are extracted which consists of 13 MFCCs, 13 $\Delta$MFCCs and 13 $\Delta\Delta$MFCCs respectively.

**MFCCs Extracted from HNGD Spectrum.** 13 MFCCs, 13 $\Delta$MFCCs and 13 $\Delta\Delta$MFCCs are extracted using HNGD spectrum. Here, a speech signal is multiplied with a Zero Time Window, where high weight is assigned to the few initial samples and low weights are given to the remaining samples of the signal. Figure 2 shows various phases of the HNGD spectrum extraction. ZTW function is given by equation [3],

$$w_1(n) = \begin{cases} 0 & n = 0 \\ \frac{1}{4sin^2(\pi n/2N)} & n = 1, 2, ..., N-1 \end{cases} \tag{1}$$

where $N$ is the window length. Spectrum for speech $(s)$ is extracted using ZTW as follows:

– Consider $s[n]$ of length $M$ samples, where $M$ varies from $n = 0$ to $M - 1$.
– Select DFT length $N$ such that $N >> M$ and equal the length of $s[n]$ to $N$ by padding $N - M$ zeros to it.
– Multiply $N$ length $s[n]$ with the window function $w_1[n]$.
– Truncation effect at the end of the window causes ripples in the spectrum. It is reduced by using a window function given in Eq. 2.

$$w_2[n] = 4cos^2(\pi n/2N) \qquad n = 0, 1, ..., M-1 \tag{2}$$

– Calculate N-point DFT of the double windowed signal: $x[n] = w_1[n]s[n]w_2[n]$.
– Calculate numerator of the group delay function $(g[k])$ from the N-point DFT $X[k]$ as given in Eq. 3 [1].

$$g[k] = X_R[k]Y_R[k] + X_I[k]Y_I[k] \qquad k = 0, 1, ..., N-1 \tag{3}$$

where, $X_R[k]$ and $X_I[k]$ are real and imaginary parts of the $N$-point DFT $X[k]$ of $x[n]$ and $Y_R[k]$ and $Y_I[k]$ are real and imaginary parts of the $N$-point DFT $Y[k]$ of $y[n] = nx[n]$ respectively.
– Highlight formants by differentiating the NGD 3 times in frequency domain.
– Compute Hilbert transform of the differenced NGD spectrum. It remove the effect of the spectral valleys in the spectrum and results in HNGD spectrum.

## 4.4   Feature Comparison and Decision Making

Dynamic time warping (DTW) is commonly used to similarity between two time-varying sequences [11]. Here, DTW based feature comparison is used for

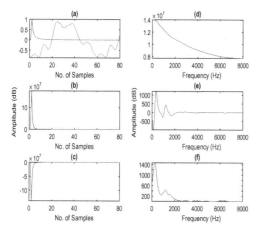

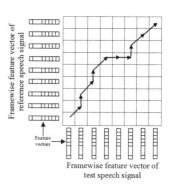

**Fig. 2.** Illustration of HNGD spectrum [3] (a) Speech segment (5 $ms$) of /n/ and ZTW function (b) Combined window function $w(n) = w^2(n) \times w2(n)$ (c) Windowed speech waveform $x(n) = s(n)w(n)$ (d) NGD spectrum of $x(n)$ (e) 3 times derivative of NGD spectrum (DNGD) (f) HNGD spectrum

**Fig. 3.** Illustration of working of DTW comparison algorithm [20]

reference template selection and location of the region of nasalization and nasal assimilation. It non-linearly warps one time sequence on the another. Consider two time series $X = \{x_1, x_2, ..., x_i, ..., x_n\}$ and $Y = \{y_1, y_2, ..., y_i, ..., y_m\}$ of length $n$ and $m$ respectively. The sequences $X$ and $Y$ are aligned to form a $n \times m$ matrix. Matrix element of location $(i^{th}, j^{th})$ stores Euclidean distance $d(x_i, y_j)$ of two data points $x_i$ and $y_j$ of the respective sequence. From this, the accumulated distance of comparison is calculated using equation: $D(i, j) = min[D(i-1, j-1), D(i-1, j), D(i, j-1)] + d(i, j)$. $D(m, n)$ stores the optimal distance between the two sequences. Value of $D(m, n)$ is small when the considered sequences are more similar to each other. The path shown in the Fig. 3 represents an optimal path which leads to the minimum distance between $X$ and $Y$. If the DTW comparison path deviates from its diagonal nature, it represents that the sequence around that region is dissimilar. This property can be used to identify the region of mispronunciation.

### 4.5 Reference Template Selection

Selected correct pronunciations of each word vary in their acoustic properties, hence selection of proper reference templates is crucial. 39 MFCCs are extracted. For each mispronounced word, selection procedure involves DTW comparison of reference words with each other. For each reference word, the distances are sorted in ascending order and the median value is set as a threshold. The count of words

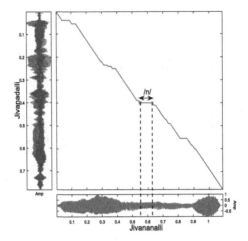

**Fig. 4.** Identification of nasalization using DTW algorithm: correct word *"jivanadalli"* compared with mispronounced word *"jivananalli"*

having DTW distance less than the set threshold is stored. Ten reference words having highest count are selected as final reference words.

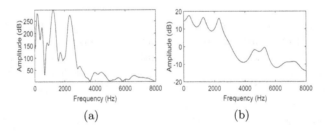

(a)                                 (b)

**Fig. 5.** Spectrum of nasalized vowel /aa/ from word 'billubANa' (a) HNGD (b) FFT

### 4.6   Identification of Nasalization

MFCCs extracted using HNGD spectrum are used for DTW comparison of the correct and mispronounced words. If the location of warped path appears at the substituted nasal sound and its duration is largest among the other deviations represents the region of nasalization or nasal assimilation. Figure 4 shows the DTW comparison path of the mispronounced word *"jivananalli"* and respective correct pronunciation *"jivanadalli"*. The longest DTW path warped at substituted nasal sound represents the region of mispronunciation.

# 5    Results and Discussion

In this approach, nasalization and nasal assimilation are considered for the analysis. Dataset is recorded from 75 children of age $3\frac{1}{2}$ years to $6\frac{1}{2}$ native Kannada language speakers. Total 125 pronunciations of 45 words are observed to have nasalization and nasal assimilation. For each word, ten correctly pronounced words are selected, as given in Sect. 4.5. As non-nasal sounds are replaced by nasal sounds, features efficient in characterizing nasal sound and nasalized voiced sounds, namely MFCCs using HNGD spectrum are extracted from the reference and mispronounced words. Features are extracted from 15 ms of frame with an overlap of 5 ms. DTW comparison path deviates from its diagonal nature in the region where signals under comparison are not similar. For the mispronunciation analysis, the longest horizontal or vertical path is considered. The longest horizontal or vertical DTW comparison path warped path at the substituted nasal sound represents the region of mispronunciation. To calculate the accuracy, majority voting of ten selected reference words is considered. Out of ten, if the identified region for more than two DTW comparison is overlapped with ground truth, the region is considered as correctly identified region. Tolerance range of the region identification is set to ±50 ms.

**Table 1.** Performance analysis of final consonant deletion using various combinations MFCCs and LPCCs

| Sl. No. | Featured considered | Average accuracy (%) |
|---|---|---|
| 1 | **MFCCs (FFT) (39)** | 56.67 |
| 2 | **MFCCs (HNGD) (39)** | 68.89 |
| 3 | **MFCCs (FFT) (39) + MFCCs (HNGD) (39)** | 82.22 |

First, the baseline system is implemented using 39 MFCCs after the small pause removal present within the words and duration normalization using TD-PSOLA. The system is observed to achieve the performance of 56.67%. The 39 MFCCs extracted from HNGD spectrum are considered for the analysis. The performance of the system is improved from 56.67% to 68.89% in comparison with the FFT based MFCCs. Further, the combination of FFT based MFCCs and HNGD spectrum based MFCCs are explored for the analysis. Highest accuracy achieved is 82.22% within the tolerance range of ±50 ms. This accuracy is high in comparison with the performance of 39 MFCCs and 39 LPCCs respectively. The performance of the various combinations of the features is given in Table 1. MFCCs are efficient in modeling the acoustic properties of speech units in the pronounced word. Due to substitution of nasal sounds, children tend to nasalize the immediately following vowel. HNGD spectrum highlights the nasal formants and nasal formant in the neighborhood of first formant of the nasalized vowels or voiced sounds. Figure 5 (a) shows the HNGD spectrum of nasalized vowel aa, where a nasalized spectral peak and spectral valley is highlighted in the neighborhood of first formant unlike FFT based formant spectrum (refer Fig. 5 (b)). Hence the combination of FFT based MFCCs and HNGD spectrum based MFCCs are observed to improve the accuracy of identification of nasalization. Though the performance of the system is 82.22%, the efficiency can be improved by exploring the spectral features efficient in highlighting the properties if nasal sounds.

## 6   Summary and Conclusion

In this paper, an attempt has been made to identify the nasalization and nasal assimilation from childrens' speech from age range 3.5–6.5 years. 45 mispronounced words having nasalization and nasal assimilation are considered for the analysis. Ten best reference samples are selected. The silence present within the words is removed using energy based threshold. Duration normalization is performed using TD-PSOLA. Various combinations of MFCCs extracted from the FFT spectrum and HNGD spectrum are considered for the identification of nasalization and nasal assimilation. DTW comparison is considered for the identification region of mispronunciation. From the results, it is observed that MFCCs extracted from FFT spectrum (39) and HNGD spectrum (39) are efficient in identification of nasalization and nasal assimilation with the highest accuracy of 82.22% within the tolerance range of $\pm 50$ ms. Further, the performance of the system can be improved by using the spectral features efficient in discriminating the nasal sounds from the other class of sounds.

**Acknowledgment.** The authors would like to thank the Cognitive Science Research Initiative (CSRI), Department of Science & Technology, Government of India, Grant no. SR/CSRI/ 49/2015, for its financial support on this work.

## References

1. Anand, J.M., Guruprasad, S., Yegnanarayana, B.: Extracting formants from short segments of speech using group delay functions. In: INTERSPEECH-2006, pp. 1009–1012. IEEE (2006)
2. Cucchiarini, C., Strik, H., Boves, L.: Different aspects of expert pronunciation quality ratings and their relation to scores produced by speech recognition algorithms. Speech Commun. **30**(2–3), 109–119 (2000)
3. Dubey, A.K., Prasanna, S.M., Dandapat, S.: Zero time windowing based severity analysis of hypernasal speech. In: 2016 IEEE Region 10 Conference (TENCON), pp. 970–974. IEEE (2016)
4. Franco, H., Neumeyer, L., Ramos, M., Bratt, H.: Automatic detection of phone-level mispronunciation for language learning. In: Sixth European Conference on Speech Communication and Technology, pp. 851–854 (1999)
5. Grunwell, P.: Clinical Phonology. Aspen Publishers, New York (1982)
6. Harrison, A.M., Lo, W.K., Qian, X.j., Meng, H.: Implementation of an extended recognition network for mispronunciation detection and diagnosis in computer-assisted pronunciation training. In: International Workshop on Speech and Language Technology in Education (SLaTE), pp. 45–48 (2009)

7. Hodson, B.W.: The Assessment of Phonological Processes. Interstate Printers and Publishers, Danville (1980)
8. Huang, X., Acero, A., Hon, H.W., Reddy, R.: Spoken Language Processing: A Guide to Theory, Algorithm, and System Development. Prentice Hall PTR, Upper Saddle River (2001)
9. Ingram, D.: Phonological rules in young children. J. Child Lang. 1(1), 49–64 (1974)
10. Kent, R.D., Vorperian, H.K.: Speech impairment in down syndrome: a review. J. Speech Lang. Hear. Res. 56(1), 178–210 (2013)
11. Keogh, E., Ratanamahatana, C.A.: Exact indexing of dynamic time warping. Knowl. Inf. Syst. 7(3), 358–386 (2004). https://doi.org/10.1007/s10115-004-0154-9
12. Lee, A., Glass, J.: A comparison-based approach to mispronunciation detection. In: 2012 IEEE Spoken Language Technology Workshop (SLT), pp. 382–387. IEEE (2012)
13. Li, K., Qian, X., Meng, H.: Mispronunciation detection and diagnosis in L2 English speech using multidistribution deep neural networks. IEEE/ACM Trans. Audio Speech Lang. Process. 25(1), 193–207 (2017)
14. Li, W., Siniscalchi, S.M., Chen, N.F., Lee, C.H.: Improving non-native mispronunciation detection and enriching diagnostic feedback with DNN-based speech attribute modeling. In: 2016 IEEE International Conference on Acoustics, Speech and Signal Processing (ICASSP), pp. 6135–6139. IEEE (2016)
15. Martin, P.: WinPitch LTL II, a multimodal pronunciation software. In: InSTIL/ICALL Symposium (2004)
16. Miodonska, Z., Bugdol, M.D., Krecichwost, M.: Dynamic time warping in phoneme modeling for fast pronunciation error detection. Comput. Biol. Med. 69, 277–285 (2016)
17. Moulines, E., Charpentier, F.: Pitch-synchronous waveform processing techniques for text-to-speech synthesis using diphones. Speech Commun. 9(5–6), 453–467 (1990)
18. Murty, K.S.R., Yegnanarayana, B.: Combining evidence from residual phase and MFCC features for speaker recognition. IEEE Signal Process. Lett. 13(1), 52–55 (2006)
19. Qian, X., Meng, H., Soong, F.K.: The use of DBN-HMMs for mispronunciation detection and diagnosis in L2 English to support computer-aided pronunciation training. In: INTERSPEECH, pp. 775–778 (2012)
20. Ramteke, P.B., Koolagudi, S.G., Afroz, F.: Repetition detection in stuttered speech. In: Nagar, A., Mohapatra, D.P., Chaki, N. (eds.) Proceedings of 3rd International Conference on Advanced Computing, Networking and Informatics. SIST, vol. 43, pp. 611–617. Springer, New Delhi (2016). https://doi.org/10.1007/978-81-322-2538-6_63
21. Ramteke, P.B., Supanekar, S., Hegde, P., Nelson, H., Aithal, V., Koolagudi, S.G.: NITK Kids' speech corpus. In: Proceedings of Interspeech 2019, pp. 331–335 (2019)
22. Shriberg, L.D., Kwiatkowski, J.: Phonological disorders I: a diagnostic classification system. J. Speech Hear. Disord. 47(3), 226–241 (1982)
23. Tiwari, V.: MFCC and its applications in speaker recognition. Int. J. Emerg. Technol. 1(1), 19–22 (2010)
24. Wei, S., Hu, G., Hu, Y., Wang, R.H.: A new method for mispronunciation detection using support vector machine based on pronunciation space models. Speech Commun. 51(10), 896–905 (2009)

# Kannada Dialect Classification Using CNN

Pradyoth Hegde[1(✉)], Nagaratna B. Chittaragi[1,2(✉)],
Siva Krishna P. Mothukuri[1(✉)], and Shashidhar G. Koolagudi[1(✉)]

[1] National Institute of Technology Karnataka, Surathkal, India
pradyothhegde@gmail.com, nbchittaragi@gmail.com, msivakrish@gmail.com,
koolagudi@nitk.edu.in
[2] Siddaganga Institute of Technology, Tumkur, India

**Abstract.** Kannada is one of the prominent languages spoken in southern India. Since the Kannada is a lingua franca and spoken by more than 70 million people, it is evident to have dialects. In this paper, we identified five major dialectal regions in Karnataka state. An attempt is made to classify these five dialects from sentence-level utterances. Sentences are segmented from continuous speech automatically by using spectral centroid and short term energy features. Mel frequency cepstral coefficient (MFCC) features are extracted from these sentence units. These features are used to train the convolutional neural networks (CNN). Along with MFCCs, shifted delta and double delta coefficients are also attempted to train the CNN model. The proposed CNN based dialect recognition system is also tested with internationally known standard Intonation Variation in English (IViE) dataset. The CNN model has resulted in better performance. It is observed that the use of one convolution layer and three fully connected layers balances computational complexity and results in better accuracy with both Kannada and English datasets.

**Keywords:** Kannada dialect classification · MFCC · Convolutional neural networks

## 1 Introduction

We know that different languages have a different styles of speaking. Within a language, there are different styles or patterns of speaking. These pronunciation variations of any language are called dialects. Dialects for any language are resulted due to long term effects of contact of foreign language, geographical regions, social, economic, cultural factors. Among dialects, even though language remains the same; however, there will be variations in the use of vocabulary, tones, words, sentence formation, and etc. Dialects can be classified into two categories: regional dialects and ethnic dialects.

Identification of a dialect will help in the understanding nativity of the person, his socio-economic, and cultural background. Kannada is a matured Dravidian language mostly spoken in the state of Karnataka in the southern part of

© Springer Nature Switzerland AG 2020
B. R. Purushothama et al. (Eds.): MIKE 2019, LNAI 11987, pp. 254–259, 2020.
https://doi.org/10.1007/978-3-030-66187-8_24

India. Several dialects are observed in the Kannada language due to its diverse geographical regions and the influence of neighboring state languages. There are more than 20 recognized dialects. In this paper, five prominent Kannada regional dialects are identified and considered. Instead of using whole utterances, sentence-level utterances are used for the development dialect classification system. Standard 13 MFCC features, delta, and double delta features are extracted from each sentence. The Convolutional Neural Network approach is used for modeling the explored features. The proposed dialect classification system uses a CNN which is a lightweight neural network. In this work, both Kannada dataset with 5 dialects and IViE dataset with 9 dialects are used for evaluation of the system performance.

The rest of the paper is organized as follows. Section 2 discusses the feature and approaches used in the literature for CNN based dialect classification. Section 3 explains the proposed methodology. Section 4 discusses the results obtained. Section 5 concludes the paper.

## 2   Literature Review

Dialect or accent classification is a popular and active research area in the speech processing domain due to its widespread applications [1]. Blackburn et al. have proposed a text-dependent accent classification system for dialects of the English language from continuous speech. Prosodic features such as pitch contours, spectral structures, and so on are explored to identify the English speakers of foreign accents [6]. Apart from HMMs, classification techniques such as GMMs, SVMs, DNNs, CNNs, RNNs, LSTMs are used for classification [2]. A combination of DNNs and RNNs trained with long-term and short-term features respectively are used for classification of dialects [8]. A CNN model is built with a fixed length of MFCC features as input extracted from 30 s of audio for identification of dialects [3]. In this work, they have used, Foreign Accented English v1.2 dataset consisting of the English language of Arabic, Italian, Japanese, and Korean accents. An automatic text-independent Kannada dialect identification system is proposed [4]. In their work, the audio file is split into smaller sentence level utterances, then MFCCs and its derived features are given to SVM and neural networks for classification. Test accuracy of 83.09% is achieved for sentence-level data.

The foreign accent classification in English is well explored. Few works can also be seen in the literature on Arabic, Spanish, and Chinese languages for classification of dialects [9]. In specific, Hemakumar and Punitha have proposed a text-dependent approach for speaker accent identification for Kannada language [7]. They considered the Baum-Welch algorithm and normal fit method and claimed 95.5% and 90.86% of word recognition rate (WRR) for Known Kannada accent speakers and unknown Kannada accent speakers respectively. A text-independent automatic accent identification system is proposed by Soorajkumar R. et al. [10]. Where they collected dialect data from three regions of Karnataka with significant variations in dialect. They achieved 79.5% accuracy with MFCC, pitch, and energy with GMMs. Based on our literature review, we

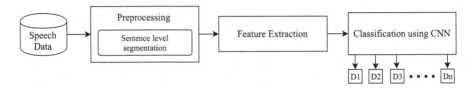

**Fig. 1.** Flow diagram of the proposed approach

set our objective to classify a text-independent dialect classification system, in which the input audio can be of variable length.

## 3    Proposed Methodology

The proposed approach consists of three steps namely, data collection & pre-processing, feature extraction, and classification using convolutional neural networks. A flow diagram of the proposed methodology is presented in Fig. 1.

### 3.1    Dataset Details

Kannada dialect dataset consists of five dialects spoken in five different regions of Karnataka. The recording is done in a relatively quite environment. Participants are native speakers of the particular dialect and recordings are done in a conversational manner. There are 32 speakers from each dialects. The recordings are done with 44.1 kHz sampling frequency and 16-bit depth. IViE dataset is a publicly available dataset with nine British English dialects. In this work we used semi-read dataset for conduction of experiments and for comparison of results.

From Kannada and English speech data, separate datasets of sentence-level utterance are derived. Initially, the audio was converted to mono. Later, audio file is split into sentences automatically by a segmentation algorithm through spectral centroid and short term energy features. Generally, a sentence utterance will be less than 5 s. Generated Sentences that are less than 1 s are neglected. The details of IViE semiread and Kannada datasets are given in Table 1. Complete details of both datasets can be found in [4] and [5].

**Table 1.** Kannda and IViE dialect dataset details

| Datasets | D1 | D2 | D3 | D4 | D5 | D6 | D7 | D8 | D9 |
|---|---|---|---|---|---|---|---|---|---|
| Kannada dataset | 200 | 213 | 201 | 233 | 202 | – | – | – | – |
| IViE dataset | 511 | 464 | 575 | 602 | 513 | 508 | 427 | 615 | 477 |

## 3.2    Feature Extraction

Mel Frequency Cepstral Coefficients (MFCCs) are the most widely used features for speech tasks. The Mel scale mimics the human auditory system. So, dialect-specific features are exploited for the dialect classification task. Delta and delta-delta features are also extracted along with MFCCs to capture dynamic variations across dialects. Totally 39 MFCCs (13 MFCC + 13 delta + 13 delta-delta) features are extracted from sentence level utterances with 20 ms frame size with 10 ms overlap.

## 3.3    Convolutional Neural Network

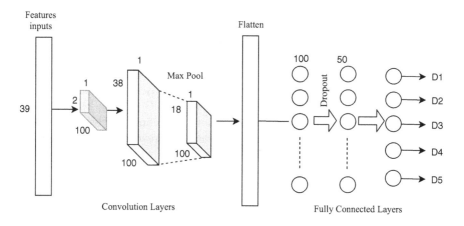

**Fig. 2.** Architecture of convolutional neural network

A convolutional neural network (CNN) model, as shown in Fig. 2 is built for classification of dialects. The input for the system is 39x1 MFCC + delta + delta delta feature vector. Input is convoluted with 100 filters of size 2X1. Max pooling is performed to reduce the dimension of the resultant feature vector by half. Now the feature size is 18x1x100. This is flattened and fed into the fully connected layers. The first layer is with 100 and second with 50 neurons. A dropout of 5% is added between the first and second layers. Output layer neurons equal to the number of classes; for Kannada, it is 5 and English; it is 9. Input and the hidden layer are set with the ReLu activation function and an output layer with softmax. The final layer predicts the dialect with probability.

# 4    Results and Discussion

This section describes the results achieved from the experiments. A CNN model is used for dialect classification. In general, CNN models have been used with layers of convolutions to extract complex features and create deep networks for classification of images. In this work, a lightweight CNN model is built with only one convolution layer and three layers of neurons for classification of dialects. Several experiments are carried out with different architectures of CNN model consisting of different numbers and sizes of convolutional and fully connected layers. In convolution layers, filters of (256, 100), (100, 100), (100) of size 2x1 is tried. In fully connected layers (200, 200, 100), (200, 100, 50), (200, 100), (100, 50), (50, 50) combinations of hidden layers have been tried. The output layer has either 5 neurons for Kannada or 9 neurons for the English dataset. The activation functions are set to ReLU in hidden layers, and softmax in output layer. "adam" algorithm is used for optimization and CNN model ran for 100 epochs. Input data has been split in 80:20 ratio for training and testing. In Kannada dataset, there are 1049 sentence-level utterances, where, 839 sentence units are use for training and 210 for testing. Similarly, English dataset has 4712 sentences split into 3769 for training and 943 for testing.

In a CNN model with two layers of convolution of (256, 100) and three fully connected layers (200, 200, 100), the test accuracy observed with Kannada and IViE dataset are 86.19 and 84.41 respectively. It is observed that, increase the number of convolution layers, the accuracy decreases. It is mainly because the convolution layers extract features from the MFCC feature, but when it is repeated, the feature complexity increases, and it becomes difficult to classify. Even in fully connected layers, when we increase the breadth of the architecture, there is no significant improvement in the accuracy, when depth is increased, there is noticeable degradation in accuracy.

**Table 2.** Performance analysis of CNN using MFCCs

|       | Kannada   |          | IViE      |          |
|-------|-----------|----------|-----------|----------|
|       | 13 MFCCs  | 39 MFCCs | 13 MFCCs  | 39 MFCCs |
| Train | 97.97     | 97.50    | 87.93     | 97.50    |
| Test  | **87.62** | **88.10**| **84.09** | **84.31**|

From Table 2, we can observe that for both Kannada and IViE, 39 MFCC features perform slightly better over MFCCs features. The margin is less than 1%, so considering the computation for this lightweight system, 13 MFCC features are enough to get good accuracy.

## 5    Conclusion

This paper presents a dialect classification method from the sentence level. The length of the utterance varies from one second to five seconds. Text independent Kannada dialect data is collected and used for this purpose. This system is also compared with an already published Intonation Variation in the English dataset.

MFCC features captures the shape of the vocal tract for dialect classification. This helps in differentiating the dialects based on the phonological features. Further, a lightweight CNN is designed to perform the classification task. The proposed CNN model has shown better performance with the balance between accuracy and model complexity. Hyper-parameter tuning can be done to achieve higher accuracy.

# References

1. Blackburn, C.S., Vonwiller, J.P., King, R.W.: Automatic accent classification using artificial neural networks. In: Third European Conference on Speech Communication and Technology (1993)
2. Chen, T., Huang, C., Chang, E., Wang, J.: Automatic accent identification using gaussian mixture models. In: IEEE Workshop on Automatic Speech Recognition and Understanding, 2001. ASRU'01, pp. 343–346. IEEE (2001)
3. Chionh, K., Song, M., Yin, Y.: Application of convolutional neural networks in accent identification
4. Chittaragi, N.B., Limaye, A., Chandana, N.T., Annappa, B., Koolagudi, S.G.: Automatic text-independent Kannada dialect identification system. In: Satapathy, S.C., Bhateja, V., Somanah, R., Yang, X.-S., Senkerik, R. (eds.) Information Systems Design and Intelligent Applications. AISC, vol. 863, pp. 79–87. Springer, Singapore (2019). https://doi.org/10.1007/978-981-13-3338-5_8
5. Grabe, E., Post, B.: Intonational variation in the British Isles. In: Speech Prosody, pp. 127–132 (2002)
6. Hansen, J.H., Arslan, L.M.: Foreign accent classification using source generator based prosodic features. In: 1995 International Conference on Acoustics, Speech, and Signal Processing, vol. 1, pp. 836–839. IEEE (1995)
7. Hemakumar, G., Punitha, P.: Speaker accent and isolated Kannada word recognition. Am. J. Comput. Sci. Inf. Technol. (AJCSIT) 2(2), 71–77 (2014)
8. Jiao, Y., Tu, M., Berisha, V., Liss, J.M.: Accent identification by combining deep neural networks and recurrent neural networks trained on long and short term features. In: Interspeech, pp. 2388–2392 (2016)
9. Lei, Y., Hansen, J.H.: Dialect classification via text-independent training and testing for Arabic, Spanish, and Chinese. IEEE Trans. Audio Speech Lang. Process. 19(1), 85–96 (2010)
10. Soorajkumar, R., Girish, G.N., Ramteke, P.B., Joshi, S.S., Koolagudi, S.G.: Text-independent automatic accent identification system for Kannada language. In: Satapathy, S.C., Bhateja, V., Joshi, A. (eds.) Proceedings of the International Conference on Data Engineering and Communication Technology. AISC, vol. 469, pp. 411–418. Springer, Singapore (2017). https://doi.org/10.1007/978-981-10-1678-3_40

# Robust Handwritten Digit Classification Using Tensors Decomposition

Dhouha Rahmani[1] and Haïfa Nakouri[1,2(✉)]

[1] Université de Tunis, Institut Supérieur de Gestion, LARODEC, Le Bardo, Tunisia
dhouharahmani1920@gmail.com
[2] Université de la Manouba, Ecole Supérieure de l'Economie Numérique,
La Manouba, Tunisia
nakouri.hayfa@gmail.com

**Abstract.** Various handwritten digits recognition methods have been developed and their good performances have been reported. Nonetheless, recognizing digits types and patterns remains a challenging task. Recognition performance is highly affected by image corruption, perspective and illumination variation. On the other hand, vectors and matrices are sometimes not suitable or enough to describe the intrinsic nature of data from various fields of data processing. In this paper, we propose a handwritten digit classification method based on robust higher-order tensors. The proposed approach handles invariance to occlusions, misalignment and illumination variation. Evaluation of the MNIST and USPS handwritten numeral databases is performed to assess the performance and effectiveness of the proposed method. Substantial results are achieved in terms of recognition accuracy, image alignment, numerical stability and computational speed.

**Keywords:** Robust digit classification · HOSVD · Low-rank approximation

## 1 Introduction

Handwritten digits classification is a classic topic in pattern recognition whose major challenge engages to correctly assign digits into one of the 10 digit classes. Most of the early works on digits classification are based on Principal Component Analysis (PCA) [7] for dimensionality reduction and classification.

However, PCA is computationally efficient and powerful for data that are mildly corrupted by trivial noises. On the other hand, handwritten images are often subject to all types of geometric distortion due to hand-writing variation and diversity, to illumination variation and to different types of corruptions namely noise and occlusions. PCA has shown its lack of robustness in many works when poorly recognizing partially occluded objects [2,3] and recovering information from noisy data. One other major shortcoming of PCA-based approaches is that they are based on an image vectorization approach while vectors are not

© Springer Nature Switzerland AG 2020
B. R. Purushothama et al. (Eds.): MIKE 2019, LNAI 11987, pp. 260–269, 2020.
https://doi.org/10.1007/978-3-030-66187-8_25

always the most suitable data structure to describe the intrinsic nature of data. It can only handle a 2-way matrix data. However, real world data are represented in a multi-dimensional way, also referred to as tensor. In this context, tensors [1] represent an alternative for the data structure that explicitly captures the $2D$ structure of images. This two-dimensional problem described so far can be hardly handled by matrix theory and a multidimensional data structure would be more suitable to consider both the digit identity and the image corruption. Higher order Singular Value Decomposition (HOSVD) [15] is an SVD-based tensor and it can be viewed as a higher order PCA for dimensionality reduction. Experiments show that recognition performance obtained by tensor PCA technique is higher than that obtained by classic PCA [11].

Besides, Yang et al. [16], Ye [17] and Nakouri et al. [12] noted that classic PCA often runs up against computational limits due to the high time and space complexity for dealing with large image matrices, especially for images and videos. Moreover, a family of powerful robust approaches has emerged in the last two decades, collectively referred to as robust low-rank modeling [5,10,14]. These approaches are based on the observation that, in several real-life cases, uncorrupted information is of low-rank whereas noise is sparse. This approach is known as Robust Alignment by Sparse and Low-rank Decomposition for Linearly Correlated Images (RASL). In this spirit, Zhang et al. [18] suggested a reflection and alignment tensor method for distorted images.

The objective of this paper is twofold: first, we study the problem of simultaneously aligning a batch of linearly correlated digit images, initially held in a tensor structure, despite corruption (e.g., occlusion, illumination). The proposed method, called Robust Tensor (RTensor), seeks an optimal set of image domain transformations such that the transformed images can be decomposed as the sum of a sparse component of errors and a low-rank component of recovered aligned images. Second, for the sake of digit recognition, a similarity measure needs to be determined. To correctly perform this task, the chosen distance measure should allow any test digit image, likely misaligned and distorted, to be fairly compared to the yet aligned and uncorrupted digit images from the training set. To evaluate the effectiveness of the proposed approach, experiments on the MNIST [4] and the USPS [6] benchmark data sets are performed in comparison with PCA, HOSVD and RASL based on three evaluation criteria, namely recognition accuracy, alignment performance and runtime.

The rest of this paper is organized as follows. Section 2 introduces the RASL and high order tensors. Section 3 outlines the proposed robust tensor. Finally, Sect. 4 presents experimental results showcasing the proposed method's performance on handwritten digits learning and classification.

## 2    RASL: Robust Alignment by Sparse and Low-Rank Decomposition for Linearly Correlated Images

Peng et al. [14] introduced the Robust Alignment by Sparse and Low-rank decomposition (RASL) algorithm to robustly align linearly correlated images.

Their work addresses the major issue of pixelwise image alignment since domain transformations make it difficult to measure image similarity for recognition or classification. The goal of RASL is to align multiple images of an object or objects of interest to a fixed canonical template. Given $n$ images of an object that are not well-aligned to each other and assuming that the degree of misalignment is not too large, the algorithm models the misalignment as a global domain transformation belonging to a finite-dimensional group. As a result, it computes these transformations and obtain the well-aligned images. Besides, considering $A$ to be a matrix whose columns represent well-aligned images of an object and that these images exhibit high linear correlation, the matrix $A$ is expected to have low-rank. However, in practice, there are various sources of error in images (self-shadowing, specularities, etc.) that violate this model. For that, RASL represents such large, sparse errors by a matrix $E$. Hence, $A + E$ will represent a matrix whose columns correspond to well-aligned images of an object. By this formulation, they represent $[I_1 \circ \tau_1, ..., I_n \circ \tau_n] = A + E$. Therefore, the main goal is to find a low-rank matrix $A$ and a sparse matrix $E$ such that this equation is satisfied. This is precisely formulated as the following optimization problem:

$$\min_{A,E,\tau} \; rank(A) + \lambda \|E\|_0 \;\; s.t \;\; D \circ \tau = A + E, \tag{1}$$

where $D$ is a matrix whose columns represent the misaligned input images, $\tau$ is the set of all transformations such that $D \circ \tau = [I_1 \circ \tau_1, ..., I_1 \circ \tau_n], \lambda$ is a positive weighting parameter and $\|E\|_0$ represents the number of non-zero entries in matrix $E$.

## 3   The Proposed Robust Tensor (RTensor)

The focus of this paper is handwritten digit classification based on robust high order tensors. In this section, we study low-rank recovery problem of 3-order tensors. We consider a low-rank 3-order data tensor $\mathcal{D} \in \mathbb{R}^{I_1 \times I_2 \times I_3}$ that we assume to be naturally corrupted by noise. We model the noise with an additional sparse error term $\mathcal{E}$, the low-rank term with $\mathcal{A}$ and the robust tensor data can accordingly be represented as

$$\mathcal{D} = \mathcal{A} + \mathcal{E} \tag{2}$$

where $\mathcal{A}$ and $\mathcal{E}$ should be accurately recovered from the corrected observations $\mathcal{D}$ Eq. (2) assumes that the original tensor data to be well aligned. However, for real visual data (i.e., for handwritten digits specifically), data are inevitably misaligned. Unluckily, even a small misalignment might disrupt the low-rank structure and compromise its fair recovery. To deal with possible misalignments, we extend the RASL approach to tensors and consider a set of geometric transformations $\mathcal{T} = \tau_1, ..., \tau_{I_3}$ to apply to the unfolded tensor data. Therefore, Eq. (2) can be altered to

$$\mathcal{D} \circ \mathcal{T} = \mathcal{A} + \mathcal{E}, \tag{3}$$

where $\mathcal{D} \circ \tau$ refers to the application of transformation $\tau_i$ to each matrix or data slice (i.e., unfolded tensor) $\mathcal{D}(:, :, i), i = 1, ..., I_{I_3}$.

Now that the low-rank, corruption and misalignment components are modeled, we can formulate the low-rank recovery for tensors with the following optimization problem.

$$\min_{\mathcal{T},\mathcal{A},\mathcal{E}} = rank(\mathcal{A}) + \lambda \parallel \mathcal{E} \parallel_0 \quad s.t. \quad \mathcal{D} \circ \mathcal{T} = \mathcal{A} + \mathcal{E}. \tag{4}$$

Similarly to RASL, the outlined optimization problem in Eq. (4) has two major shortcomings: it is not tractable due to the nonconvexity of the $l_0$ norm form one hand and to the nonlinearity of the constraint $\mathcal{D} \circ \mathcal{T} = \mathcal{A} + \mathcal{E}$ (caused by the transformation domain $\mathcal{T}$) on the another. To address the nonconvexity limitation, we consider the rank definition based on Tucker decomposition [8]. Accordingly, the rank of tensor $\mathcal{A}$ can be translated to computing a set of matrices' rank. Given that the nuclear norm is the convex envelope of the rank matrix [14], we replace $rank(\mathcal{A})$ with the nuclear norm or sum of the singular values: $\parallel A_{(i)} \parallel_* = \sum_{k=1}^{m} \sigma_k(A_{(i)})$, where $\sigma_k(A_{(i)})$ is the $k^{th}$ singular value of matrix $A_{(i)}$. Moreover, we use the $l_1$-norm relaxation as an efficient convex surrogate to the $l_0$ one. Applying this convex relaxation to Problem (4) yields to a new optimization problem:

$$\min_{\mathcal{T},\mathcal{A},\mathcal{E}} = \parallel A_{(i)} \parallel_* + \lambda \parallel \mathcal{E} \parallel_1 \quad s.t. \quad \mathcal{D} \circ \mathcal{T} = \mathcal{A} + \mathcal{E}. \tag{5}$$

Subsequently, constraint $\mathcal{D} \circ \mathcal{T} = \mathcal{A} + \mathcal{E}$ is nonlinear due to the accordance of $\mathcal{D} \circ \mathcal{T}$ with the $\mathcal{T}$ transformation set. When the change in $\tau$ is small or incremental, the constraint can be approximated by linearizing with respect to the transformation $\mathcal{T}$ parameters. This leads to a convex optimization problem in unknowns $\mathcal{A}, \mathcal{E}, \Delta\mathcal{T}$:

$$\min_{\mathcal{T},\mathcal{A},\mathcal{E}} = \parallel A_{(i)} \parallel_* + \lambda \parallel \mathcal{E} \parallel_1$$
$$s.t. \quad \mathcal{D} \circ \mathcal{T} + (\sum_{i=1}^{n} J_i \Delta\mathcal{T}_k \epsilon_i^T) = \mathcal{A} + \mathcal{E}, \tag{6}$$

where $J_i$ represents the Jacobian of $\mathcal{D}(:,:,i)$ $(D_{(i)})$ with respect to the transformation parameter $\tau_i$ and $\epsilon_i$ points out the basis for $\mathbb{R}^n$.

Now that the optimization Problem (6) is convex, to relax the equality constraints and solve the tensor recovery problem, we use the Augmented Lagrangian Multiplier (ALM) which is a version of the first-order alternating linearization methods [9]. The ALM method is a schema for converting an optimization problem with equality constraints into an unconstrained problem. In this section, we propose an ALM-based approach to obtain a smoothed version of Problem (6) and make it easier to solve. We build the partial Augmented Lagrangian function of Problem (6) as:

$$f_\mu(\mathcal{A}, \mathcal{E}, \Delta\mathcal{T}, Y, \mu) = \| A_{(i)} \|_* + \lambda \| \mathcal{E} \|_1$$

$$+ \langle Y_i, \mathcal{A} + \mathcal{E} - \mathcal{D} \circ \mathcal{T} - (\sum_{i=1}^{n} J_i \Delta\mathcal{T}_k \epsilon_i^T) \rangle$$

$$+ \mu/2 \langle \mathcal{A} + \mathcal{E} - \mathcal{D} \circ \mathcal{T} - (\sum_{i=1}^{n} J_i \Delta\mathcal{T}_k \epsilon_i^T) \rangle$$

$$= \| A_{(i)} \|_* + \lambda \| \mathcal{E} \|_1 \qquad (7)$$

$$+ \mu \| \mathcal{A} + \mathcal{E} - \mathcal{D} \circ \mathcal{T} - (\sum_{i=1}^{n} J_i \Delta\mathcal{T}_k \epsilon_i^T) + Y_i/\mu \|_F^2$$

$$\| Y_i/\mu \|_F^2 /(2\mu),$$

where $\langle . \rangle$ denotes the inner product between two matrices, $\mu$ is a positive penalty factor and $Y_i$ are Lagrangian multiplier matrices. The robust tensor (RTensor) algorithm that we propose aims to solve the optimal solution of Problem 7. It is a typical iterative minimization process based on ALM whose pseudo code is explicitly outlined in Algorithm 1. We use the alternative method in this algorithm, where we assume in each iteration that one variable, in turn, is unknown and fix the other variables as if they were known. Hence, the original multivariable optimization problem is transformed to a single-variable one. Afterward, solving the original problem becomes more workable along iterations.

---

**Algorithm 1.** Robust Tensor algorithm (RTensor)

**INPUT:**     Matrices $\mathcal{A}^0, \mathcal{E}^0, \Delta\mathcal{T}^0$
1. **WHILE** not converged **DO**
2.     $(U, \Sigma, V) \leftarrow svd(D_{(i)} \circ \mathcal{T} + \sum_{i=1}^{n} J_i \Delta\mathcal{T}_k \epsilon_i^T + \frac{1}{\mu_k} - \mathcal{E}_k)$
3.     $\mathcal{A}_{k+1} \leftarrow U \mathcal{S}_{\frac{1}{\mu_k}} \sigma V^T$
4.     $\mathcal{E}_{k+1} \leftarrow \mathcal{S}_{\frac{1}{\mu_k}}[D_{(i)} \circ \mathcal{T} + \sum_{i=1}^{n} J_i \Delta\mathcal{T}_k \epsilon_i \epsilon_i^T + \frac{1}{\mu_k} - \mathcal{A}_{k+1}]$
5.     $\Delta\mathcal{T}_{k+1} \leftarrow \sum_{i=1}^{n} J_i^\dagger (\mathcal{A}_{k+1} + \mathcal{E}_{k+1} - D_{(i)} \circ \mathcal{T} - \frac{1}{\mu_k} Y_k) \epsilon_i \epsilon_i^T$
6.     $Y_{k+1} \leftarrow Y_k + \mu_k h(\mathcal{A}_{k+1} + \mathcal{E}_{k+1} + \Delta\mathcal{T}_{k+1})$
7. **END WHILE**
**OUTPUT:**     Solution $\mathcal{A}^*, \mathcal{E}^*, \Delta\mathcal{T}^*$

---

Steps 3, 4 and 5 require solving a convex problem, which can be efficiently determined in a single step. Hence, a soft-thresholding or shrinkage operator for scalars is presented to define the solutions as follows:

$$S_\alpha[x] = sign(x). \max |x| - \alpha, 0, \alpha \geq 0 \qquad (8)$$

## 3.1   Similarity Measure for Digit Classification

Now that we trained our handwritten digit data, a convenient distance/similarity metric needs to be set to perform digits classification. Nakouri and Limam [13] proposed an incremental version to RASL where they suggest to estimate $\tau_{n+1}$, $A_{n+1}$ and $E_{n+1}$, for a freshly upcoming observation $I_{n+1}$ based on the batch RASL, previously computed for a $n$-sized training set. In that respect, we propose to use this algorithm to estimate the low-rank component $A_{n+1}$ of a new observation and compare the obtained low-rank term to the $\mathcal{A}$ terms recovered over Algorithm 1. The closest low-rank item in the $\mathcal{A}$ tensor structure would correspond to the class of the digit test image.

# 4   Experiments

For the sake of robust digits recognition, extracting a neutral, vertically aligned and corruption-free is a basic data preparation task. The presence of misalignment, occlusions and illumination variation on digit images makes this problem quite challenging. Luckily, the proposed method yields to low-rank approximation components of recovered aligned images representing the low-rank digits. The sparse components decently represent the corruption in images, noise and illumination variation. We compare the proposed method to three other algorithms: PCA, RASL and HOSVD.

## 4.1   Experimental Setting

For handwritten digits classification, we used two benchmark handwritten digits data sets: MNIST (Modified National Institute of Standards and Technology database) [4] and USPS (US Postal) [6]. These two large databases of handwritten digits are commonly used for training various image processing systems. The MNIST database originally contains $60,000$ training images and $10,000$ testing images. Each digit image represents one of the 10 digits (ranging from 0 to 9), is grayscale, centered and normalized to a $28 \times 28$ image size. As for the USPS data set, it offers 7291 training and 2007 test images. The digits are automatically scanned from envelopes by the US Postal Service, they are binary, of various sizes and orientations, resulting in $16 \times 16$ grayscale images. To evaluate the efficiency of the proposed method 100 training images and 100 test images are randomly selected in each experiment. Besides, we boosted the data corruption by adding artificial noise to 20% of the samples. We also set the stopping threshold to 0.03 and $\lambda$ to 2, so when the difference between two successive iterations in the value of the cost function is small, the algorithm ends. Figure 1 illustrates the performance of the proposed RTensor algorithm on both data sets. It shows that most of the misalignments were detected and accurately recovered. Besides, most of the noise has been captured by the sparse component to become left with a well-aligned low-rank structure $\mathcal{A}$. The recovered low-rank items in the $\mathcal{A}$ component illustrate how well and evenly aligned same-class digits are (e.g., digit 1). The alignment feature represents a key property to evaluate the recognition performance.

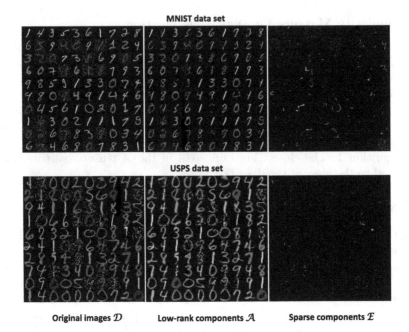

**Fig. 1.** Original digits $\mathcal{D}$ with various illumination, occlusions and noise. Low-rank tensor $\mathcal{A}$ and sparse errors tensor $\mathcal{E}$ are efficiently recovered for the MNIST data set.

## 4.2 Recognition Performance

**Table 1.** Recognition performance

| Method | MNIST | | USPS | |
|---|---|---|---|---|
| | Average rate | Best rate | Average rate | Best rate |
| PCA | 63% | 66% | 64% | 66% |
| HOSVD | 68% | 70% | 69% | 72% |
| RASL | 73% | 74% | 74% | 76% |
| RTensor | 80% | 81% | 88% | 89% |

Table 1 shows the recognition rate for PCA, HOSVD, RASL and the proposed RTensor on MNIST and USPS data sets. For each method, the best and average performance runs, across 10 trials, are given. Results show that the best recognition rate is given by the proposed RTensor algorithm. RASL gives less better classification performance, though and this leads us to conclude that aligning images on its own is not enough to reach a high recognition performance. The advantage of considering a high order tensor structure that fairly snatches the natural multidimensional data is showcased in the outperformance of RTensor over RASL. PCA and HOSVD low performance towards our data set can be justified by their poor processing of misalignments and corruptions no matter how much variation is captured. Classification results also show that accuracy is better on USPS because digits on this data set are naturally better aligned than those of MNIST (Fig. 1). Figure 2 shows the confusion matrix of the MNIST data set. This matrix for the analysis of classification of digits 0 to 9 has 10 columns, for the target classes (actual labels) and 10 rows, for the output classes (predicted labels). The sum of values along each column corresponds to the number of images tested for each digit. The sum of each row is less than the number of each digit's images due to imperfect classification. However, the classification algorithm has the largest values along the main diagonal, marking that the majority of test images were correctly classified. This is because the main diagonal indicates the number of times the predicted class corresponds to the target class.

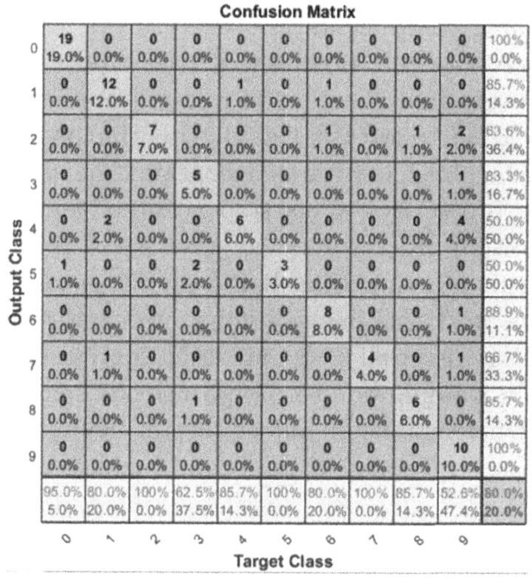

**Fig. 2.** The confusion matrix of the MNIST data set classification

## 4.3 Alignment Performance

Table 2 represents a quantitative measure (in pixel unit) of our RTensor method, the max error is represented as:

$$\frac{exactpositionvalue - approximatepositionvalue}{positionpositionvalue}.$$

The statistics of errors in handwritten digits was inspired from Peng et al. [14] and it is calculated as the distance from the estimated vertical position of the digit to the center line of the initial digit. After computing this quantitative measure for the MNIST data set, RTensor produces alignments within 0.13 pixels accuracy, with standard deviations of about quarter a pixel and a maximum error of slightly less than a pixel.

**Table 2.** Alignment performance

| Algorithm | Mean error | Standard deviation | Max error |
|-----------|------------|--------------------|-----------|
| RTensor   | 0.13       | 0.26               | 0.99      |

### 4.4  Runtime Performance

All the experiments were run on a 1.7 GHz Intel core $i3$ processor with a 4 GB RAM. Table 3 shows that our implementation requires 5.32 min to align, cover the low-rank and sparse components and classify the 100 test images of size $28 \times 28$ of the MNIST data set. However, RASL requires over 4.5 min to only align images without rotation, classification or tensor's structure. Our method requires a tad extra time to accomplish due to the projection of the tensor components into the Jacobian matrix that contains the spatial transformations parameters (affine or projective). This step is fundamental to get the images aligned for the recognition process. On the other hand, both PCA and HOSVD process in a considerably less time than RASL and RTensor for the trivial reason that neither of the two performs image alignment or low-rank approximation of data. Nevertheless, it is necessary to note that for larger training sets, both PCA and RASL fail in running due to computational boundaries caused by the $2D$-matrix calculus, whereas tensors allow a better flexibility in regards to data unfolding.

**Table 3.** Execution time (training + recognition)

| Methods               | PCA | HOSVD | RASL | RTensor |
|-----------------------|-----|-------|------|---------|
| Execution time (min)  | 3   | 4     | 4.5  | 5.32    |

## 5  Conclusion

In this paper, we have proposed a robust handwritten digit classification method based on higher-order tensors which can realize alignment and denoising of given images. Based on the RASL work and augmented Lagrangian multiplier to solve the optimization problem we have shown that the convergence of our method is guaranteed and the efficiency of its performance is validated by comparing with existing methods.

# References

1. Comon, P.: Tensors: a brief introduction. IEEE Signal Process. Mag. **31**(3), 44–53 (2014)
2. Cox, M., Sridharan, S., Lucey, S., Cohn, J.: Least squares congealing for unsupervised alignment of images. In: Proceedings of the 2008 IEEE Conference on Computer Vision and Pattern Recognition, pp. 1–8 (2008)
3. Croux, C., García-Escudero, L.A., Gordaliza, A., Ruwet, C., Martín, R.S.: Robust principal component analysis based on trimming around affine subspaces. Statistica Sinica **29**(6), 1437–1459 (2017)
4. Deng, L.: The MNIST database of handwritten digit images for machine learning research [best of the web]. IEEE Signal Process. Mag. **29**(6), 141–142 (2012)
5. Goldfarb, D., Qin, Z.: Robust low-rank tensor recovery: models and algorithms. SIAM J. Matrix Anal. Appl. **35**(1), 225–253 (2014)
6. Hull, J.J.: A database for handwritten text recognition research. IEEE Trans. Pattern Anal. Mach. Intell. **16**(5), 550–554 (1994)
7. Jolliffe, I.: Principal Component Analysis, 2nd edn. Springer, Heidelberg (2011). https://doi.org/10.1007/978-3-642-04898-2
8. Kim, Y.D., Choi, S.: Nonnegative tucker decomposition. In: Proceedings of the 2007 IEEE Conference on Computer Vision and Pattern Recognition, pp. 1–8. IEEE (2007)
9. Lin, Z., Chen, M., Ma, Y.: The augmented lagrange multiplier method for exact recovery of corrupted low-rank matrices. arXiv:1009.5055 (2010)
10. Lu, C., Feng, J., Chen, Y., Liu, W., Lin, Z., Yan, S.: Tensor robust principal component analysis: exact recovery of corrupted low-rank tensors via convex optimization. In Proceedings of the 2016 IEEE Conference on Computer Vision and Pattern Recognition, pp. 5249–5257 (2016)
11. Lu, H., Plataniotis, K.N., Venetsanopoulos, A.N.: MPCA: multilinear principal component analysis of tensor objects. IEEE Trans. Neural Netw. **19**(1), 18–39 (2008)
12. Nakouri, H., El-Aroui, M.A., Limam, M.: Robust low-rank approximation of images for background and foreground separation. In: Proceedings of the 2017 IEEE International Conference on Parallel and Distributed Computing Applications and Technologies, pp. 1637–1645 (2017)
13. Nakouri, H., Limam, M.: Incremental robust principal component analysis for face recognition using ridge regression. Int. J. Biom. **9**(3), 186–204 (2017)
14. Peng, Y., Ganesh, A., Wright, J., Xu, W., Ma, Y.: RASL: robust alignment by sparse and low-rank decomposition for linearly correlated images. IEEE Trans. Pattern Anal. Mach. Intell. **34**(11), 2233–2246 (2012)
15. Savas, B., Eldén, L.: Handwritten digit classification using higher order singular value decomposition. Pattern Recogn. **40**(3), 993–1003 (2007)
16. Yang, J., Zhang, D., Frangi, A.F., Yang, J.: Two-dimensional PCA: a new approach to appearance-based face representation and recognition. IEEE Trans. Pattern Anal. Mach. Intell. **26**(1), 131–137 (2004)
17. Ye, J.: Generalized low rank approximations of matrices. Mach. Learn. **61**(1–3), 167–191 (2005)
18. Zhang, X., Wang, D., Zhou, Z., Ma, Y.: Simultaneous rectification and alignment via robust recovery of low-rank tensors. Adv. Neural Inf. Process. Syst. **26**, 1637–1645 (2013)

# Clustering of Interval Valued Data Through Interval Valued Feature Selection: Filter Based Approaches

D. S. Guru and N. Vinay Kumar[(✉)]

Department of Studies in Computer Science, University of Mysore,
Manasagangotri, Mysuru 570006, India
dsg@compsci.uni-mysore.ac.in, vinaykumar.natraj@gmail.com

**Abstract.** In this paper, a problem of selectively choosing a few best interval valued features out of several available features is addressed in an Un-supervised environment. Various models belonging to two categories viz., models which transform interval data to crisp and models which accomplish feature selection through clustering of interval valued features are explored for clustering of interval valued data. Extensive experimentation is conducted on two standard benchmarking datasets using suitable symbolic clustering algorithms. The experimental results show that the approaches presented outperform the state-of-the-art models in terms of correct rand index score and number of features selected.

**Keywords:** Symbolic data · Interval valued data · Mutual similarity value · Feature ranking criteria · Symbolic clustering

## 1 Introduction

Nowadays, Data Science is a widely accepted domain among the community of many researchers across the globe. It covers various applications of Data Mining, Knowledge Discovery, Pattern Recognition, Information Retrieval, and Image Processing. In designing any Data Science application, dimensionality reduction techniques play an important role in improving the prediction rate of learning algorithms. Dimensionality reduction is a process of reducing the number of features based on richness of features in discriminating each data object from rest of the objects. It can be accomplished in two different ways viz., feature extraction (transformation) and feature selection (subsetting). The former technique applies a transformation function on original features in a higher dimensional space to map them onto features in a lower dimensional space, whereas, the latter technique selects a smaller subset of features from a given larger set of features. When the data size is too big, that too with a very high dimensional feature description, dimensionality reduction through feature transformation becomes unwieldy in addition to being inefficient. Therefore, in recent years, feature selection techniques have received greater attention.

Recently, it has been argued that real world objects can be better described by the use of symbolic features, which are extensions of classical data types. Symbolic data are

B. R. Purushothama et al. (Eds.): MIKE 2019, LNAI 11987, pp. 270–285, 2020.
https://doi.org/10.1007/978-3-030-66187-8_26

unified by means of relationships and they appear in the form of continuous ratio, discrete absolute interval and multi-valued. The concept of symbolic data has been extensively studied in the area of pattern classification. It has been shown experimentally that the symbolic approaches outperform the conventional clustering techniques and have a high consistency with human perception. However, there is a lot many challenging issues yet to be addressed related to proposal of effective feature selection techniques to reduce the number of features described by interval valued type data.

The use of symbolic data outperform the approaches based on conventional data in most of the classification tasks, such as shape retrieval [1], signature verification [2]. In this direction there are quite a good number of interesting works on classification [3–5] and clustering [6, 7, 20–22] of symbolic data in general, interval valued data in particular.

The aforementioned symbolic approaches have been demonstrated well for their superiorities over the respective conventional approaches for the corresponding classification tasks. However, the feature vectors being used are of high dimensional. Unfortunate that the problem of curse of dimensionality is still not being fully addressed especially on interval valued features. Only few attempts [3, 4, 8–10] could be traced on reduction of dimensionality of symbolic data. But, no works are found on dimensionality reduction of symbolic interval valued data for clustering which are evaluated in an un-supervised environment.

In this paper, we present simple yet effective dimensionality reduction techniques for symbolic data in general, and interval valued data in particular. The presented techniques belong to the class of sub-setting. The interval valued feature selection is realized through the proposal of various filter based approaches viz., models which transforms interval data to crisp [11, 12], and models which accomplishes feature selection through feature clustering of interval valued features. Extensive experimentation is conducted on benchmarking interval valued datasets. To demonstrate the efficacy of the techniques, the performance of the same is evaluated in an un-supervised environment using suitable symbolic learning algorithms. The experimental results obtained show that the proposed models outperform in terms of performance with only a subset of features compared to a full set of features in consideration.

The rest of the paper is organized as follows. Section 2 gives a background of interval valued data and its representation. Section 3 discusses on filter based feature selection approaches. The experimental results and analysis are presented in Sect. 4. Finally, comparative analysis and conclusion are given in Sect. 5 and Sect. 6 respectively.

## 2  Background

Let us consider an augmented supervised interval valued feature matrix say $AIFM \rightarrow [IFM : Y]$, with N number of rows and $d + 1$ number of columns. Each row corresponds to a sample, each column corresponds to a feature of type interval and the last column of the matrix corresponds to a set of class labels. A row in AIFM is denoted by $\left( S_i^j, y_i^j \right)$, where $S_i^j$ represents the $i^{th}$ sample of a class $C_j$ and $y_i^j$ represents its class label. Each sample $S_i^j$ in an interval valued feature matrix IFM is described by $d$ interval valued features and is given by:

$$S_i^j = \left( IF_1^i, IF_2^i, \ldots, IF_d^i \right) = \left( [if_1^-, if_1^+], [if_2^-, if_2^+], \ldots, [if_d^-, if_d^+] \right)$$

Here, $if_k^-$ and $if_k^+$ are the lower and upper limits of the $k^{th}$ interval feature respectively with $if_k^- \leq if_k^+$ and $if_k^-, if_k^+ \in \mathbb{R}$.

## 3   Interval Valued Feature Selection

In this section, we present two major approaches viz., transformation based and feature clustering based approaches along with their variants for selecting best interval valued features.

### 3.1   Transformation Based Approaches

In this sub-section, the details on three interval-crisp data transformation methods viz., Vertex transformation, Random Sampling and Min - Max transformation are presented. The first method transforms an interval into Hyper-rectangle vertices; the second one performs random sampling on an interval data and the last method transforms an interval to minimum and maximum crisp values.

Once the features are transformed into crisp type features, we recommend applying conventional feature filtering criteria for selecting the best subset of features.

**Vertex Transformation.** A vertex transformation technique [13] transforms the interval valued feature matrix into a matrix called Vertex-Coordinate matrix, where each row corresponds to a vertex and a column corresponds to a coordinate of a Hyper-rectangle. Thus, the interval valued samples are transformed to a set of Hyper-rectangle vertices, where each interval valued sample is associated with at most $2^d$ number of d-dimensional vertices. The general structure of a vertex transformed feature matrix is illustrated in Fig. 1.

Let us consider a sample $S$ described by $d$ interval features and let $IF_k$ be the $k^{th}$ interval feature described by $[if_k^-, if_k^+]$. Cazes et al. [13] categorized an interval into two forms viz., non-trivial and trivial intervals. The interval $IF_k$ is said to be a non-trivial interval if $if_{ik}^- < if_{ik}^+$ and otherwise it is said to be a trivial interval ($if_{ik}^- = if_{ik}^+$). The sample $S = (IF_1, \ldots, IF_d)$, with $d$ intervals can be re-described as a hyper-rectangle $H$ defined by $q$ number of $d$ dimensional vertices (where, $q = 2^d$, if all the $d$ intervals are non-trivial intervals otherwise $q < 2^d$).

Let us consider only 4 samples $S_1^1, S_2^1, S_1^2,$ and $S_2^2$ described by 3 interval features which form a matrix of dimension $4 \times 3$. Here, the sample $S_1^1$ is with 3 non-trivial intervals, the sample $S_2^1$ is with 2 non-trivial intervals, the sample $S_1^2$ is with 1 non-trivial interval and the sample $S_2^2$ is with only trivial intervals. The vertex transformation for these samples is illustrated in Table 1.

After vertex transformation, the dimension of the matrix $4 \times 3$ is transformed to the dimension of $15 \times 3$. In Table 1, we observe the variations in the number of vertices

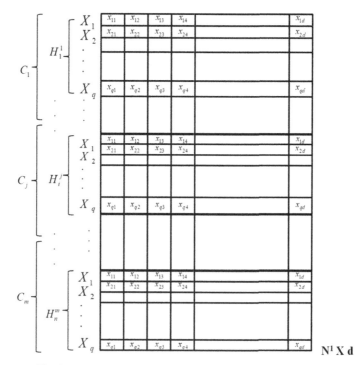

**Fig. 1.** General structure of a vertex transformed feature matrix.

of hyper-rectangles $H_1^1$, $H_2^1$, $H_1^2$, and $H_2^2$ corresponding to the samples $S_1^1$, $S_2^1$, $S_1^2$, and $S_2^2$ respectively. This is due to the presence of non-trivial and trivial intervals. Here, the hyper-rectangle $H_1^1$ has 8 vertices and can be visualized as a rectangle in 3-dimensional space, the hyper-rectangle $H_2^1$ has 4 vertices and can be visualized as a plane in 3-dimensional space, the hyper-rectangle $H_1^2$ has 2 vertices and can be visualized as a line in a 3-dimensional space and the hyper-rectangle $H_2^2$ has 1 vertex and can be visualized as a point in a 3-dimensional space. In general, a sample with $d$ intervals can be visualized as a Hyper-rectangle with at most $2^d$ vertices in $d$-dimensional space.

**Random Sampling.** If the value of $d$ increases, then the row dimension of the feature matrix (vertex transformed) also increases exponentially with time complexity $O(2^d)$. It is very tedious task to process such a huge feature matrix. Hence, we thought of notion of random sampling. The random sampling helps in generating a crisp values belonging to every interval features, thus resulting with $d$ single valued features for a sample. The random sampling is repeated for say '$r$' times. Hence for a given $N \times d$ interval feature matrix, one can get $r N \times d$ dimensional feature matrix of type crisp. This method is followed, only if the $d$ is relatively high.

**Min-Max Transformation.** In this sub-section, we present an alternative transformation method viz., Min-Max transformation, which takes relatively negligible amount of time for transformation of interval valued features into crisp features which is of order

**Table 1.** Illustration of vertex transformation.

| Sample | Corresponding hyper-rectangle after vertex transformation |
|---|---|
| $S_1^1 = ([1.2, 3.5], [25, 38], [100, 105])$ | $H_1^1 = \begin{pmatrix} 1.2 \ 25 \ 100 \\ 1.2 \ 25 \ 105 \\ 1.2 \ 38 \ 100 \\ 1.2 \ 38 \ 105 \\ 3.5 \ 25 \ 100 \\ 3.5 \ 25 \ 105 \\ 3.5 \ 38 \ 100 \\ 3.5 \ 38 \ 105 \end{pmatrix}$ |
| $S_2^1 = ([1.6, 3.8], [27, 41], [103, 103])$ | $H_2^1 = \begin{pmatrix} 1.6 \ 27 \ 103 \\ 1.6 \ 41 \ 103 \\ 3.8 \ 27 \ 103 \\ 3.8 \ 41 \ 103 \end{pmatrix}$ |
| $S_1^2 = ([0.5, 0.8], [16, 16], [75, 75])$ | $H_1^2 = \begin{pmatrix} 0.5 \ 16 \ 75 \\ 0.8 \ 16 \ 75 \end{pmatrix}$ |
| $S_2^2 = ([0.3, 0.3], [18, 18], [78, 78])$ | $H_2^2 = \begin{pmatrix} 0.3 \ 18 \ 78 \end{pmatrix}$ |

$O(2d)$. The Min-Max transformation transforms an interval valued data into two independent crisp single valued data which represents the minimum and maximum values of the interval respectively.

Let us consider a sample $S$ described by $d$ interval features and let $IF_k$ be the $k^{th}$ interval feature described by $[if_k^-, if_k^+]$ If the interval $IF_k$ is represented as a minimum $[if_k^-]$ and maximum $[if_k^+]$ feature values, then the sample $S = (IF_1, \ldots, IF_d)$ with $d$ intervals can be re-described as $S^- = (if_1^-, \ldots, if_d^-)$ and $S^+ = (if_1^+, \ldots, if_d^+)$ associated with minimum and maximum feature values of $S$ respectively. The Min - Max transformation thus results with a two crisp type single valued feature matrices termed as Min-Matrix and Max-Matrix. More details on this approach are found in [11, 12].

**Feature Ranking and Selection.** After transformation of interval valued data to crisp type data, it is recommended to use any of the existing conventional feature ranking criteria viz., Fisher score [14] and variants of Class Co-variance Score [11, 12] to rank the features. For ranking the features, each feature is considered at a time independent of every other features (i.e., uni-variate data analysis) to compute its degree of class separability, which defines the ability of the feature in keeping all m classes well separated. During ranking, a feature is assigned with a highest rank if it possesses a high degree of class separability and is assigned with a lowest rank if it possesses a low degree of class separability. Based on the computed degree of class seperability, the features are sorted and the top $d' \ll d$ are selected.

Here, in our work we adopt feature ranking criterion called Class Covariance Score criterion [11, 12]. As we know that the co-variance between two samples/objects results with the highest value if the two samples/objects are very similar and it results with the lowest value if they are different [16]. This made us think about the co-variance as the ranking criterion which is basically a similarity measure. Hence, the degree of class separability is realized through the degree of similarity. Here, the co-variance is computed between the samples of two classes, hence it is called as class co-variance score (CCS). The co-variance computation demands for equal number of samples to be present in each class. In this connection, it is made uniform using the Bagging strategy [19] and hence $n_1 = n_2 = n_3 = \ldots = n_m = n$.

A co-variance matrix is computed across the samples (vertices) of different classes with respect to $k^{th}$ feature and hence it is called as class co-variance matrix ($CCM^k$) and is given by:

$$CCM_{ab}^k = CC(V_a, V_b) \in \mathbb{R}, \ \forall a = 1, 2, \ldots, m; \ b = 1, 2, \ldots, m$$

Where, $CCM^k$ is a class covariance matrix corresponds to $k^{th}$ feature; $V_a = (x_{1k}^a, x_{2k}^a, \ldots, x_{nk}^a)'$ and $V_b = (x_{1k}^b, x_{2k}^b, \ldots, x_{nk}^b)'$ are respectively the features of the samples associated with $a^{th}$ and $b^{th}$ classes. $CC(.\ ,\ .)$ is a class co-variance (CC) computed between samples of two classes and is defined by:

$$CC(V_a, V_b) = \frac{1}{n} \sum_{i=1}^{n} \left( x_{ik}^a - \mu_a \right) \left( x_{ik}^b - \mu_b \right)$$

$$\mu_a = \frac{1}{n} \sum_{i=1}^{n} x_{ik}^a \text{ and } \mu_b = \frac{1}{n} \sum_{i=1}^{n} x_{ik}^b$$

A complete illustration of the computation of the class co-variance matrix associated with $k^{th}$ feature considered from the vertex transformed feature matrix is shown in Fig. 2.

Further, the average class covariance value (ACCV) for each class is computed to measure the degree of similarity from one class to the rest of the classes in terms of a single value and is given by,

$$ACCV_a = \frac{1}{m} \sum_{b=1}^{m} CCM_{ab}^k \ ; \ \forall a = 1, 2, \ldots, m$$

Now, we have obtained with $m$ average class covariance values. Thus class co-variance score $(CCS^k)$ corresponding to $k^{th}$ feature named as CCS-Min criterion is given by:

$$CCS^k = \min \left\{ (ACCV_1, ACCV_2, \ldots, ACCV_m)' \right\}$$

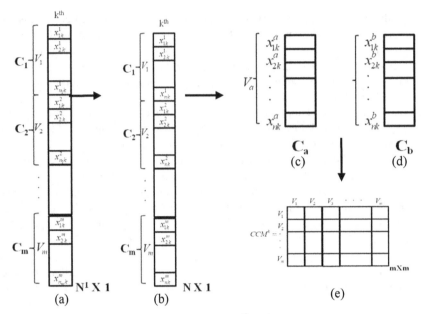

**Fig. 2.** Computation of class covariance matrix, (a) $k^{th}$ feature vector with un-equal number of samples (vertices) per class, (b) $k^{th}$ feature vector after bagging with equal number of samples (vertices) per class, (c)-(d) Samples of two arbitrary classes, (e) Class covariance matrix corresponds to $k^{th}$ feature.

The choice of minimum statistics for computing the relevancy score of a feature is recommended over others due to the fact that the co-variance is a measure of similarity. The minimum will be the co-variance score; higher is the degree of separability between the samples of respective classes.

Once class co-variance scores are computed for all $d$ features as their respective relevancies, the features are ranked based on their relevancy.

## 3.2   Feature Clustering Based Approaches

During feature selection, the top $d'$ ranked features are selected based on their relevancy scores. Let us assume that we have a set of top $d'$ ranked features say $RFS = \{IF_{R1}, IF_{R2}, \ldots IF_{Rd^1}\}$ obtained from any of the feature ranking criterion discussed in the previous section. The set usually consists of both most relevant and relatively least relevant features. If there exists two features say $IF_{Ri}$, $IF_{Rj} \in RFS$ which possess similar behaviour in separating (non-separating) samples among classes, then such features are treated to be redundant to each other. Such feature redundancies usually exist when features are selected through a feature ranking criterion [14]. Hence, in this section, we present a model for selecting the discriminating features by taking care of such feature redundancy during feature selection. This can be accomplished by feature clustering.

Clustering is the process of grouping data samples into a set of disjoint groups called clusters, so that the data samples of a same cluster will have a high degree of similarity to each other and the data samples of different clusters will have a low degree of similarity to each other. Here in this work, we recommend clustering of features considering them as samples so that most similar features in terms of their degree of similarity would go together into a same cluster and less similar features would go to different clusters. Once clustering is achieved, we propose to chose one representative from each cluster as the feature selected, thereby if K clusters are found then we end up selecting K features. Notice here that as we take one cluster representative from each cluster, automatically redundancy in feature selection is avoided. Though, multiple cluster representatives can be selected from each cluster; as an initial attempt we restricted the cluster representative selection to only one.

For clustering the interval valued data, a modified interval K-means clustering algorithm has been recommended. Further, the cluster representative of a cluster of features is selected based on the maximum affinity that a feature exhibits to all other features in the cluster.

The feature selection through clustering is realized in two ways viz., Class Independent Feature Selection (*CIFS*) and Class Dependent Feature Selection (*CIDFS*). The former one performs clustering of features by considering all the samples of all classes together, whereas the latter one performs clustering by considering only samples with respect to each class [15, 18].

**Pre-processing.** A transposed feature matrix of dimension $d \times N$, say *TIFM* of the interval valued feature matrix *IFM* of dimension $N \times d$ is obtained. Subsequently, the matrix *TIFM* is fed into the interval valued clustering algorithm for clustering the features. Later, the cluster representatives are selected using a cluster representative selection method.

During feature selection, the behaviour of the structure of the transposed feature matrix also changes accordingly. In case of *CIFS*, the transformed feature matrix *TIFM* of dimension $d \times N$ is directly fed into an interval K-Means clustering algorithm to obtain K clusters, where $d$ features are spread across K different clusters. Where as in case of *CIDFS*, the samples are separated based on their class correspondence and obtained with a sub-matrix $TIFM_j$ of dimension $d \times n_j$ ($n_j$ is the number of samples per class) corresponding to a class $C_j$ ($j = 1, 2, \ldots, m$; $m = no.\ of\ classes$) and is fed into interval K-Means clustering algorithm to obtain $K$ clusters for each sub-matrix $TIFM_j$. Thus, K and mK be the number of clusters obtained from the clustering algorithm associated with *CIFS* and *CIDFS* respectively.

**Interval K-Means Clustering: A modified K-Means Clustering.** The K-Means clustering, being a partitional clustering technique, initially fixes up with the number of clusters (K) and the centroid points. Then the algorithm uses a kernel to compute the proximity among the samples [16]. Later those samples which have greater affinity would go to a same cluster and samples with a little affinity would go to different clusters. Then, the new centroids will be computed for each K clusters. The same procedure is repeated until certain convergence criteria are satisfied. Usually, the said procedure is followed in K-Means clustering algorithm which works on conventional crisp numeric type data. But, in this work, as we are handling interval valued data, a kernel which adapts for the interval valued data during clustering is required. Hence, a slight modification has been brought out at the kernel level and recommended a kernel called as Symbolic Similarity Kernel (SSK), which is suitable for handling the interval valued data effectively. The SSK kernel computes the similarity $S_{ab}$ between two features $IF_a$ and $IF_b$ based on Mutual Similarity Value [17] as in Eq. 1. The rest of the interval K-Means clustering procedure follows the same procedure of the conventional K-Means clustering.

$$S_{ab} = \sqrt{\sum_{j=1}^{m} \sum_{i=1}^{n_j} \left( \frac{\left| IF_{ia}^j \cap IF_{ib}^j \right| \cdot \left( \left| IF_{ia}^j \right| + \left| IF_{ib}^j \right| \right)}{2 \cdot \left| IF_{ia}^j \right| \cdot \left| IF_{ib}^j \right|} \right)^2} \tag{1}$$

Where, $IF_{ip}^j$ is the $p^{th}$ feature of $i^{th}$ sample of $j^{th}$ class and I denotes the length of the interval.

**Selection of Cluster Representative.** Let us consider a cluster $Cl_w$, containing $z$ number of features ($\forall w = 1, 2, \ldots, K$). A feature is said to be a cluster representative ($ClR_w$), if it possesses a maximum similarity with all the remaining features in the cluster. In this regard, the similarity computation among the features within a cluster $Cl_w$ is recommended. Hence, it results with a similarity matrix $SM^w$, which is given by:

$$SM_{ab}^w = S_{ab} \in \mathbb{R}, \forall a = 1, 2, \ldots, z; b = 1, 2, \ldots, z$$

Further, the average similarity value with respect to each feature in the cluster $Cl_w$ is computed from one feature to the rest of the features in terms of a single value and is given by:

$$ASV_a = \frac{1}{z} \sum_{b=1}^{z} SM_{ab}^w$$

Now, we have obtained with $z$ average similarity values corresponding to cluster $Cl_w$. Now, the cluster representative $ClR_w$ is given by:

$$ClR_w = \arg \max_{IF_a} \{ASV_1, ASV_2, \ldots, ASV_z\}$$

The feature $IF_a$ which has a maximum $ASV_a$ value is considered as a cluster representative ($ClR_w$) of the cluster $Cl_w$. Thus, the above procedure is repeated for all the remaining clusters. Now, we have $K$ such cluster representatives ($ClR_1, ClR_2, \ldots, ClR_K$). The feature indices of these cluster representatives are further used to select features from original interval feature matrices.

**Class Independent Feature Selection (ClIFS).** The interval valued feature matrix TIFM is used to select features independent of classes. The matrix consisting of d interval valued features is directly fed into the interval K-means clustering algorithm which results with a K-clusters of interval valued features. Each cluster consists of say z number of features. Subsequently, each cluster is subjected to the cluster representative selection for the selection of K cluster representatives and are treated as a subset of K features selected from d interval valued features.

**Class Dependent Feature Selection (*CIDFS*).** The interval valued feature matrix TIFM is used to select the class dependent features. The matrix consists of d interval valued features along with the samples of the respective classes are separated resulting with m sub-matrices. These m sub-matrices are subjected to the interval K-means clustering algorithm separately to obtain K-clusters for each class. Therefore, m such K-clusters consisting of interval valued features are obtained. Subsequently, the clusters are subjected to the cluster representative selection for the selection of K cluster representatives associated with each class. Thus, mK cluster representatives are obtained.

# 4    Experimentation and Results

## 4.1    Datasets

In this work, two different supervised interval datasets are used viz., Water [9], and Flower [12] datasets. The more details on the datasets are found in Table 2.

**Table 2.** Details of the supervised interval valued datasets.

| Dataset | No. of samples | No. of features | No. of classes | No. of samples/class |
|---------|----------------|-----------------|----------------|----------------------|
| Water   | 316            | 48              | 2              | {93, 223}            |
| Flower  | 600            | 501             | 30             | 20                   |

## 4.2    Experimental Setup

In this section, the details of experimentation conducted on the two supervised interval valued datasets are presented for demonstrating the effectiveness of the models in selecting a best subset of features for clustering purpose.

During experimentation, feature relevancy score for individual interval feature is computed on each dataset. Later on, the features are sorted and top $d'$ features are selected based on their relevancy scores. With the support of symbolic clustering algorithms, the performance of the interval valued feature selection methods are evaluated in an un-supervised environment.

For the purpose of clustering, we have adopted three clustering algorithms with five different kernels. The kernels play a major role in computing the proximity between two samples. We recommend five different kernels for three different clustering algorithms viz., Clustering algorithm-1 [20], Clustering algorithm-2 [21], and Clustering algorithm-3 [22]. The first algorithm uses only one kernel viz., Euclidean distance. The second algorithm uses two kernel variants viz., squared Euclidean distance and adaptive squared Euclidean distance. Finally, the third clustering algorithm also makes use of two kernel variants viz., squared Euclidean distance along with a fuzzy Kohonen framework and adaptive squared Euclidean distance along with the same framework.

The Clustering algorithm-1 proposed by [20] is modified for clustering the interval valued data. The actual clustering algorithm proposed by Bezdek et al. [20] suits only for conventional crisp type of data. But, we have modified the original algorithm slightly to adapt for an interval valued data. The modification is brought out at kernel level. The modified Euclidean distance kernel is given by:

$$
ED(S_a, S_b) = \sqrt{ \sum_{k=1}^{d} \left[ \left(if_{ak}^- - if_{bk}^-\right)^2 + \left(if_{ak}^+ - if_{bk}^+\right)^2 \right] }
$$

$ED(.)$ is the Euclidean distance kernel which computes the distance between an interval sample and a cluster center with $d$ interval features.

The clustering algorithm proposed by Carvallho [21] for clustering the interval valued data. The algorithm is called as Interval Fuzzy C-Means Clustering algorithm and we have chosen this algorithm without any modification at any levels. The clustering algorithm comes with two different kernels viz., square Euclidean distance and adaptive square Euclidean distance. The technical details of the algorithm can be found in [21].

The clustering algorithm proposed by Almeida et al. [22] for clustering the interval valued data. The algorithm is called as Interval Fuzzy Kohonen clustering algorithm and hence we adopted this algorithm without any modification at any levels. The Kohonen network is an alternative name of self organizing map which is used for clustering. The Interval Fuzzy Kohonen clustering algorithm comes with two different kernels viz., square Euclidean distance and weighted square Euclidean distance. The technical details of the algorithm can be found in [22].

All the above three clustering algorithms being a partitional algorithms work on the same principle of K-means clustering, but differ only with respect to the metric (function) used to compute the proximity between two samples. The general steps involved in each of these are given in the following algorithm.

**Algorithm: Symbolic Clustering**
**Input:**
        IFM, Interval Feature Matrix
        $C_i$, Number of Cluster Centers
**Output:**
        $C_o$, Clusters obtained from the algorithm
**Method:**
        1.   Initialize the Fuzzy Membership matrix
        2.   Initialize the cluster centers
        3.   Repeat
                a) Compute the proximity between every sample and cluster centers.
                b) Update the Fuzzy Membership matrix
                c) Update the new cluster centers
      Until condition is satisfied
        4.   Return $C_o$
**Algorithm Ends**

## 4.3 Results

To evaluate the performance of the models presented in an un-supervised environment, the Correct Rand (CR) index is adopted to evaluate the performance of the proposed models. The definition of Correct Rand index is given below.

Let $S = (S_1, S_2,..., S_n)$ be a collection of n samples scattered across C classes. Let $V = \{v_1, v_2, ...,v_i, ..., v_C\}$ be the group of $C$ number of prior clusters (with class information) which is independent of clustering. If a partitional clustering algorithm is applied on the set V, then R number of cluster partitions are obtained and is represented by $U = \{u_1, u_2, ...,u_i, ..., u_R\}$. This set consists of same $n$ number of samples but with varied cluster membership. The external index for the clusters U and V is given by:

$$CR = \frac{\left[\sum_{i=1}^{R}\sum_{j=1}^{C}\binom{n_{ij}}{2}\right] - \left[\sum_{i=1}^{R}\binom{n_i}{2} * \sum_{j=1}^{C}\binom{n_j}{2}\right]/\binom{n}{2}}{\frac{1}{2}\left[\sum_{i=1}^{R}\binom{n_i}{2} - \sum_{j=1}^{C}\binom{n_j}{2}\right] - \left[\sum_{i=1}^{R}\binom{n_i}{2} * \sum_{j=1}^{C}\binom{n_j}{2}\right]/\binom{n}{2}}$$

Where, $\binom{n}{2} = n(n-1)/2$ and $n_{ij}$ represents the number of samples that are in clusters in $u_i$ and $v_j$. $n_i$ is the number of samples in cluster $u_i$ and $n_j$ is the number of samples in cluster $v_j$. n is the total number of samples in the dataset. The CR takes values between $-1$ and 1. If it takes the value equal to 1, then it is said to be perfect partition. If the value lies between 0 and $<1$, then the partition is said to be an approximate partition. If the value becomes negative, then the partition is said to be a random partition.

To select the top $d'$ features, the experimentation is conducted on the said datasets. The feature subset associated with maximum correct rand index is considered as the top $d'$ feature subset for clustering the interval valued samples and the same is tabulated. To show the effectiveness of the presented models, the correct rand indices obtained by considering all the features are also tabulated.

Table 3 and Table 4 show the correct rand index scores for both transformation based approaches using *CCS-Min* criterion for ranking of features on Water and Flower datasets respectively. While, Table 5 and Table 6 show the same for both the feature clustering based approaches on Water and Flower datasets respectively.

**Table 3.** Correct Rand (CR) Index scores obtained with **CCS-Min** Criterion on **Water** dataset for (a) **Random Sampling** approach (b) **Min-Max** Transformation.

(a)

| Existing Clustering Methods | | Clustering WFS | | Clustering WoFS | |
|---|---|---|---|---|---|
| | | # of Features | CR Index | # of Features | CR Index |
| Method [20] | | 6 | 0.108 | 48 | 0 |
| Method [21] | Euclidean | 6 | 0.108 | 48 | 0 |
| | Adaptive | 6 | 0.108 | 48 | 0.077 |
| Method [22] | Euclidean | 4 | 0.028 | 48 | 0.096 |
| | Adaptive | 1 | 0.096 | 48 | 0.096 |

(b)

| Existing Clustering Methods | | Clustering WFS | | Clustering WoFS | |
|---|---|---|---|---|---|
| | | # of Features | CR Index | # of Features | CR Index |
| Method [20] | | 5 | 0.107 | 48 | 0 |
| Method [21] | Euclidean | 5 | 0.107 | 48 | 0 |
| | Adaptive | 4 | 0.107 | 48 | 0.077 |
| Method [22] | Euclidean | 5 | 0.028 | 48 | 0.096 |
| | Adaptive | 2 | 0.134 | 48 | 0 |

**Table 4.** Correct Rand (CR) Index scores obtained with *CCS-Min* Criterion on **Flower** dataset for (a) **Random Sampling** approach (b) **Min-Max** Transformation.

(a)

| Existing Clustering Methods | | Clustering WFS | | Clustering WoFS | |
|---|---|---|---|---|---|
| | | # of Features | CR Index | # of Features | CR Index |
| Method [20] | | 40 | 0.235 | 501 | 0.109 |
| Method [21] | Euclidean | 20 | 0.228 | 501 | 0.113 |
| | Adaptive | 20 | 0.209 | 501 | 0.001 |
| Method [22] | Euclidean | 20 | 0 | 501 | 0 |
| | Adaptive | 40 | 0 | 501 | 0 |

(b)

| Existing Clustering Methods | | Clustering WFS | | Clustering WoFS | |
|---|---|---|---|---|---|
| | | # of Features | CR Index | # of Features | CR Index |
| Method [20] | | 20 | 0.235 | 501 | 0.109 |
| Method [21] | Euclidean | 20 | 0.228 | 501 | 0.125 |
| | Adaptive | 40 | 0.274 | 501 | 0.011 |
| Method [22] | Euclidean | 20 | 0 | 501 | 0 |
| | Adaptive | 20 | 0.007 | 501 | 0 |

**Table 5.** Correct Rand (CR) Index scores obtained with *CCS-Min* Criterion on **Water** dataset for feature clustering based approaches (a) *CIIFS* (b) *CIDFS*.

(a)

| Existing Clustering Methods | | Clustering WFS | | Clustering WoFS | |
|---|---|---|---|---|---|
| | | # of Features | CR Index | # of Features | CR Index |
| Method [20] | | 46 | 0.098 | 48 | 0.067 |
| Method [21] | Euclidean | 46 | 0.087 | 48 | 0.064 |
| | Adaptive | 45 | 0.074 | 48 | 0.071 |
| Method [22] | Euclidean | 5 | 0.048 | 48 | 0 |
| | Adaptive | 9 | 0.020 | 48 | 0 |

(b)

| Existing Clustering Methods | | Clustering WFS | | Clustering WoFS | |
|---|---|---|---|---|---|
| | | # of Features | CR Index | # of Features | CR Index |
| Method [20] | | 43 | 0.101 | 48 | 0.096 |
| Method [21] | Euclidean | 39 | 0.101 | 48 | 0.096 |
| | Adaptive | 45 | 0.074 | 48 | 0.077 |
| Method [22] | Euclidean | 2 | 0.039 | 48 | 0 |
| | Adaptive | 7 | 0.040 | 48 | 0 |

**Table 6.** Correct Rand (CR) Index scores obtained with *CCS-Min* Criterion on **Flower** dataset for feature clustering based approaches (a) *CIIFS* (b) *CIDFS*.

(a)

| Existing Clustering Methods | | Clustering WFS | | Clustering WoFS | |
|---|---|---|---|---|---|
| | | # of Features | CR Index | # of Features | CR Index |
| Method [20] | | 40 | 0.078 | 501 | 0.021 |
| Method [21] | Euclidean | 60 | 0.160 | 501 | 0.122 |
| | Adaptive | 60 | 0.121 | 501 | 0 |
| Method [22] | Euclidean | 40 | 0.320 | 501 | 0 |
| | Adaptive | 20 | 0.310 | 501 | 0 |

(b)

| Existing Clustering Methods | | Clustering WFS | | Clustering WoFS | |
|---|---|---|---|---|---|
| | | # of Features | CR Index | # of Features | CR Index |
| Method [20] | | 20 | 0.164 | 501 | 0.109 |
| Method [21] | Euclidean | 20 | 0.160 | 501 | 0.125 |
| | Adaptive | 40 | 0.161 | 501 | 0.011 |
| Method [22] | Euclidean | 20 | 0.453 | 501 | 0 |
| | Adaptive | 20 | 0.424 | 501 | 0 |

From Tables 3, 4, 5 and Table 6, it is understood that the clustering results obtained with feature selection (WFS) are better than the results obtained without feature selection (WoFS) for all variants of presented filter based feature selection approaches of interval valued data.

Further, it shall be noted that there shall be a considerable reduction in the number of features selected for the achieved better correct rand index scores.

## 5   Comparative Analysis

A comparative study on two datasets is illustrated with the aid of graphs. The X-axis of the graph represents the various clustering algorithms viz., Fuzzy C Means Clustering – Euclidean distance [20] (*Cl-1*), Interval Fuzzy C Means Clustering - Squared Euclidean Distance (*Cl-2*), Adaptive Squared Euclidean Distance (*Cl-3*) [21], Interval

Fuzzy Kohonen Clustering - Squared Euclidean Distance (*Cl-4*), Weighted Squared Euclidean Distance (*Cl-5*) [22] and the Y-axis represents the performance measured in terms of correct rand score. In addition to these, on top of each bin, a feature subset representing the top d' features associated with the clustering algorithm is represented. Initially, we compare the goodness of the presented feature selection approaches in terms of CR index. Later, the approach which performs well is used to compare against the state-of-the-art models.

The comparative analysis on the variants of transformation based approaches is given in Fig. 3 based on their best results obtained with respect to the *CCS-Min* feature ranking criterion. From Fig. 3, it is observed that the Min-Max approach with CCS-Min as a feature ranking criterion performs well on the datasets when compared to the Random Sampling approach in terms of number of features selected and correct rand index score. Hence, the results of Min-Max approach with CCS-Min criterion is used for further comparative study.

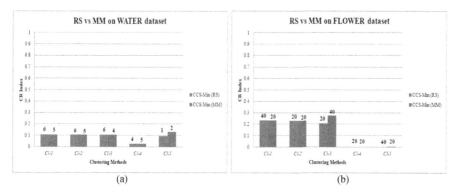

**Fig. 3.** Comparative analysis of the transformation based feature selection models Random Sampling, and Min-Max with *CCS-Min* feature ranking criterion on (a) Water dataset, and (b) Flower dataset.

A comparative study of both the variants of the feature clustering based approaches viz., Class Independent Feature Selection (*ClIFS*), and Class Dependent Feature Selection (*ClDFS*) is given in Fig. 4. From Fig. 4, it is observed that the method *ClDFS* has better results than that of *ClIFS*.

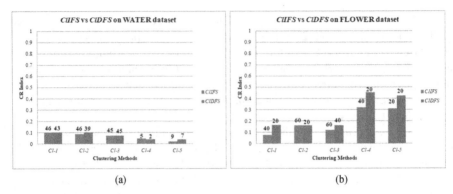

(a)                                                              (b)

**Fig. 4.** Comparative analysis of the two feature selection feature clustering based approaches *ClIFS* and *ClDFS* on (a) Water dataset, and (b) Flower dataset.

# 6 Conclusion

In this paper, filter based feature selection approaches along with necessary experimental results are presented for interval valued type feature evaluated in un-supervised environment. The approaches are based on different ways of representing an interval valued data and feature clustering based feature selection. Comparative analyses of the variants of filter based approaches are also presented. The experimental results and analysis show that the proposed approaches outperform in terms of correct rand index and number of features selected.

# References

1. Guru, D.S., Nagendraswamy, H.S.: Symbolic representation of two-dimensional shapes. Pattern Recogn. Lett. **28**(1), 144–155 (2007)
2. Guru, D.S., Prakash, H.N.: Online signature verification and recognition: an approach based on symbolic representation. PAMI **31**(6), 1059–1073 (2009)
3. Ichino, M.: Feature selection for symbolic data classification. In: Diday, E., Lechevallier, Y., Schader, M., Bertrand, P., Burtschy, B. (eds.) New Approaches in Classification and Data Analysis, Section 2, pp. 423–429. Springer, Heidelberg (1994). https://doi.org/10.1007/978-3-642-51175-2_48
4. Silva, F.C.D., de A.T. de Carvalho, F., de Souza, R.M.C.R., Silva, J.Q.: A modal symbolic classifier for interval data. In: King, I., Wang, J., Chan, L.-W., Wang, D. (eds.) ICONIP 2006. LNCS, vol. 4233, pp. 50–59. Springer, Heidelberg (2006). https://doi.org/10.1007/11893257_6
5. Souza, R.M.C.R.D., Cysneiros, F.J.A., Queiroz, D.C.F., Fagundes, R.A.D.A.: A symbolic pattern classifier for interval data based on binary probit analysis. LNAI **5243**, 340–347 (2008)
6. Guru, D.S., Kiranagi, B.B.: Multivalued type dissimilarity measure and concept of mutual dissimilarity value for clustering symbolic patterns. Pattern Recogn. **38**(1), 51–156 (2005)
7. Carvalho, F.A.T., Lechevallier, Y., Melo, F.M.: Relational partitioning fuzzy clustering algorithms based on multiple dissimilarity matrices. Fuzzy Sets Syst. **215**, 1–28 (2013)

8. Kiranagi, B.B., Guru, D.S., Ichino, M.: Exploitation of multivalued type proximity for symbolic feature selection. In: Proceedings of IEEE Conference, pp. 320–324 (2007)
9. Hedjazi, L., Martin, A.J., Lann, M.V.L.: Similarity margin based feature selection for symbolic interval data. PRL **32**, 578–585 (2011)
10. Izem, T.A., Harkat, M.F., Djeghaba, M., Kratz, F.: Sensor fault detection based on principal component analysis for interval-valued data. J. Qual. Eng. **30**(4), 635–647 (2018)
11. Guru, D.S., Kumar, N.V.: Novel feature ranking criteria for interval valued feature selection. In: IEEE ICACCI 2016, pp. 149–155 (2016)
12. Kumar, N.V., Guru, D.S.: A novel feature ranking criterion for interval valued feature selection for classification. In: 14th IAPR ICDAR, IEEE, pp. 71–76 (2017)
13. Cazes, P., Chouakria, A., Diday, E., Schektman, Y.: Extension de l'analyse en composantes principales a des donnees de type intervalle. Rev. Statistique Appliquee **45**(3), 5–24 (1997)
14. Ferreira, A.J., Figueiredo, M.A.T.: Efficient feature selection filters for high-dimensional data. Pattern Recogn. Lett. **33**, 1794–1804 (2012)
15. Guru, D.S., Kumar, N.V., Suhil, M.: Feature selection for interval valued data through interval k-means clustering. IJCVIP **7**(2), 64–80 (2017)
16. Duda, O.R., Hart, E.P., Stork, G.D.: Pattern Classification, 2nd edn. Wiley-Interscience (2000)
17. Guru, D.S., Kiranagi, B.B., Nagabhushan, P.: Multivalued type proximity measure and concept of mutual similarity value useful for clustering symbolic patterns. Pattern Recogn. Lett. **25**(10), 1203–1213 (2004)
18. Guru, D.S., Vinay Kumar, N.: Class specific feature selection for interval valued data through interval K-means clustering. In: Santosh, K.C., Hangarge, M., Bevilacqua, V., Negi, A. (eds.) RTIP2R 2016. CCIS, vol. 709, pp. 228–239. Springer, Singapore (2017). https://doi.org/10. 1007/978-981-10-4859-3_21
19. Breiman, L.: Bagging Predictors. Mach. Learn. **24**(2), 123–140 (1996). https://doi.org/10. 1007/BF00058655
20. Bezdek, J.C., Ehrlich, R., Full, W.: FCM: the fuzzy c-means clustering algorithm. Comput. Geosci. **10**(2–3), 191–203 (1984)
21. Carvalho, F.A.T.: Fuzzy c-means clustering methods for symbolic interval data. Pattern Recogn. Lett. **28**, 423–437 (2007)
22. Almeida, C.W.D., Souza, R.M.C.R., Candeias, A.L.B.: Fuzzy Kohonen clustering networks for interval data. Neurocomputing **99**, 65–75 (2013)

# Frequent Itemsets Based Partitioning Approach to Decision Tree Classifier

Shankru Guggari[1]([✉]), Vijayakumar Kadappa[2], and V. Umadevi[1]

[1] Department of Computer Science and Engineering, B.M.S. College of Engineering, Bengaluru, India
{shankru.16pej,umadevi.cse}@bmsce.ac.in
[2] Department of Computer Applications, B.M.S. College of Engineering, Bengaluru, India
vijaykumark.mca@bmsce.ac.in

**Abstract.** Decision tree is a classification technique which is widely used in many real world applications. It suffers from few challenges like structural instability, overfitting, curse of dimensionality etc. To address some of these issues, vertical partitioning paradigm is used in the literature. In vertical partitioning paradigm, the feature set is split into multiple subsets and these subsets are used for subsequent processing instead of original feature set. In this paper, we propose a novel partitioning approach using highest-size frequent itemsets. The efficiency of the method is evaluated using 5 standard datasets from UCI repository. The proposed method achieves significant improvement in classification accuracy and demonstrates better or competitive structural stability as compared to classical decision tree methods. The statistical significance of the results obtained by the proposed method is demonstrated using t-test, wilcoxon signed rank and pearson correlation tests.

**Keywords:** Vertical partitioning · Frequent itemsets · Decision tree

## 1 Introduction

Decision tree and frequent itemsets are popular and frequently used techniques in the domain of knowledge discovery from the databases [19]. Decision tree is a popular classification model in machine learning due to its efficiency, easier interpretation and understandability by human beings. It uses top-down induction paradigm and chooses splits heuristically. Some of its real world applications are: autism etiology and heterogeneity [13], road sign recognition [23], patient decision aids [8], education platform [5] etc. Decision trees are of varied types based on the splitting criteria, CART (Gini index) [3], C4.5 (Gain ratio) [18] and C5.0 (Gain ratio with boosting technique) [4] etc. Despite of its popularity, decision trees suffer from challenges like, structural instability, overfitting, lower classification accuracy for high dimensional data. Instability problem occurs when there is a slight change in number of data instances.

Frequent Itemset Mining (FIM) is a widely used technique in data mining to obtain frequently occurring items in transactional databases. An itemset is said to be frequent,

© Springer Nature Switzerland AG 2020
B. R. Purushothama et al. (Eds.): MIKE 2019, LNAI 11987, pp. 286–295, 2020.
https://doi.org/10.1007/978-3-030-66187-8_27

if its occurrence in the transaction database is more than the minimum support. Apriori [1], FP-growth [12], ECLAT [22] are some of the popularly used methods to generate frequent itemsets. FIM also discovers the correlations or relationships between the items. Discovery of frequent itemsets is an important task in many real world applications such as Stock portfolios [2], Long bilogical datasets [21], Social network analysis [7] etc. Frequent itemsets are helpful in classification, clustering and generating association rules.

Partitioning is a novel paradigm to address some of the challenges faced by decision trees. In partitioning, the dataset is divided into multiple subsets and these subsets are used for building models subsequently. The partitioning methods are categorised into horizontal and vertical types. Horizontal partitioning is based on splitting of the set of data instances, whereas vertical partitioning splits feature set of the data instances. The current study focuses on improving classification rate and structural stability of decision trees using vertical partitioning paradigm. In this paper, we exploit frequent itemsets to create item blocks and use them to build decision tree ensemble. To the best of our knowledge, frequent itemsets are not used for vertical partitioning in the literature.

The rest of the paper is organised as follows: Related works are discussed in Sect. 2. A detailed description about Frequent Itemsets based Partitioning technique is given in Sect. 3. Experimental analysis is described in Sect. 4 and Conclusions are presented in Sect. 5.

## 2  Related Works

In this section, we discuss some key papers [6, 9, 10, 15, 17, 20] related to vertical partitioning. Vertical partitioning helps to improve both classification accuracy and time complexity. An agent-based classification system is discussed to classify microRNA gene. This method is inspired by social choice theory and uses heterogeneous classifiers. Majority voting technique is used to combine the probabilities from multiple classifiers (KNN, Naive Bayes, C4.5, JRip and Support Vector Machines). The study uses microRNA dataset which has 34 features, which are divided into 5 groups like structural features (5 features), Thermodynamic (1 feature), Alignment features (2 features), Position-based features (20 features), seed features (6 features [17]. Similarly, theme based vertical partitioning method is introduced for teacher recruitment datasets. It identifies few themes such as research activity, work experience, publications etc. It shows improvement in classification accuracy as compared to classical methods, CART, C4.5 and C5.0 decision tree [14]. In another research work, the vertical partitioning is applied in a privacy preserving method. The method is evaluated using 6 standard datasets from UCI repository. It performs vertical partitioning of features randomly, holds private information about the features and does not share the information publicly. Gaussian perturbation is used to each local kernal and use proximal support vector machine for classification [15].

Vertical partitioning is based on the level of similarity and uses fuzzy technique to pre-process the features. Fuzzy technique helps to assign the features with the same similarity level to a partition. It combines features across equivalence classes generated by the partitions using Ordered weighted average [10]. Recently, non-sequential vertical partitioning techniques are proposed using Ferrer diagram and Bell triangle methods. It uses both low and medium dimensionality datasets to understand the performance of the method using metrics like classification accuracy, standard deviation and misclassification rate. It makes use of 10-fold cross validation technique to illustrate the significance of the method using classification accuracy and is compared with well known ensemble techniques such as Adaboost, Bagging etc. [9]. In another work, feature relevance method is introduced to improve the classification accuracy. It uses dominance rough set theory to obtain relevance features with the useful rules. It makes two partitions one with respect to punctuation marks and another partition with 17 words. It takes help of artificial neural network (ANN) classifier to measure the efficiency of the method [20].

Present study explores a vertical partitioning approach based on frequent itemsets. In upcoming section, we elaborate our proposed method in detail.

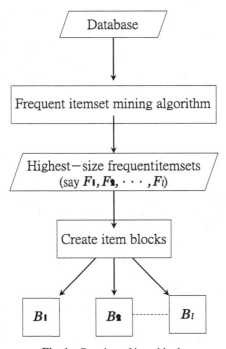

**Fig. 1.** Creation of item blocks

## 3  Frequent Itemsets Based Partitioning Decision Tree Technique (FIPDT)

In this section, we elucidate the Frequent Itemsets based Partitioning approach to Decision Tree (FIPDT). We use Apriori algorithm [1] to generate frequent *itemsets* with varied support based on the dataset. FIPDT uses frequent itemsets with highest size to choose features and create item blocks as shown in Fig. 1.

To illustrate the concept, we consider a transaction database $T = \{t_1: \{A, B, C\},$ $t_2: \{A, C\}, t_3: \{B, D\}, t_4: \{B, D, E\}\}$ with items $A, B, C, D$ and $E$. We assume 50% support for generating frequent itemsets. Using Apriori algorithm, we generate frequent itemsets as $\{\{A\}, \{B\}, \{C\}, \{D\}, \{A, C\}, \{B, D\}\}$. From these frequent itemsets, we consider frequent itemsets with highest size, that is, $\{\{A, C\}, \{B, D\}\}$.

We project the database on these frequent 2-itemsets to create the blocks, $B_1 = T$ $(\{A, C\}) = \{t_1: \{A, C\}, t_2: \{A, C\}\}$ and $B_2 = T (\{B, D\}) = \{t_1: \{B\}, t_3: \{B, D\}, t_4: \{B, D\}\}$ as demonstrated in step 3 of the algorithm and Fig. 1. Here $T (F_i)$ indicates the projection of database $T$, over the frequent itemset, $F_i$. In other words, each highest-size frequent itemset generates a block. The blocks thus generated may have common items.

## 3.1 Algorithm

A detailed explanation about the algorithm (Fig. 2) is given as follows: Consider the transaction database $T = \{t_1, t_2, \ldots, t_n\}$ with $n$ transactions and m-items $I = \{i_1, i_2, \ldots, i_m\}$. Each transaction $t_i$ is an itemset such that $t_i \subseteq I$.

Step 1:  *Generate highest-size frequent itemsets*: Use frequent item mining algorithms like Apriori, FP-growth to generate highest-size frequent itemsets (say $F_i$, $i = 1, 2, \cdots, l$)

Step 2:  *Create item blocks*: For each highest-size frequent itemset, $F_i$, $i = 1, 2, \cdots, l$: create a feature block $B_i$ as given by

$$B_i \leftarrow T(F_i) \tag{1}$$

Here $T (F_i)$ indicates the projection of database $T$, over the corresponding itemset, $F_i$. In other words, the database $T$ is projected on the items of $F_i$ to get a block (Mini database), $B_i$.

Step 3:  *Build a decision tree, $DT_i$ for each block, $B_i$*. In training phase, we build a model using CART, C4.5 or C5.0 decision tree for each block, $B_i$

$$DT_i \leftarrow BuildDecisionTree(B_i). \tag{2}$$

Step 4:  For each Test data instance, S:

a)  Create $l$ subsets, $S_1, S_2, \ldots, S_l$, based on the itemsets of $F_1, F_2, \cdots, F_l$.
b)  Classify each subset, $S_i$, $i = 1, 2 \ldots, l$ using the local decision tree, $DT_i$, as given by

$$(pr_i)_{c \times 1} = predict(S_i, DT_i); i = 1, 2, \ldots, l. \tag{3}$$

where $c$ is number of classes, $pr_i$ is the class membership probabilities.

c) Compute final class of $S$ by combining class memberships, $pr_i$; $i = 1, 2, ..$
., $l$, of its subsets (blocks). Here, we use majority voting rule as a combining
technique.

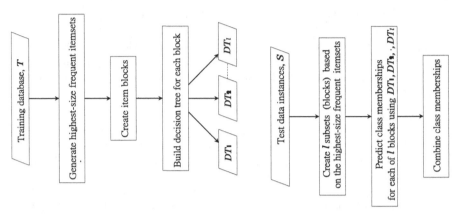

**Fig. 2.** The block diagram of the proposed method.

In the next section, we describe experimental set up and performance analysis of the
proposed method.

## 4   Experimental Analysis

In this section, we present the experimental results and compare classification accuracies
of the proposed method with Adaboost, Bagging, Stacking, Random forest and other
classical decision tree methods. The experiments are conducted using a computer system
with Windows 7 operating system, Intel i5 processor and 8 GB RAM. We use 5 popular
datasets from UCI repository as indicated in Table 1 to evaluate the performance of
the proposed method using 10 fold crossvalidation technique. We use R (version 3.6.1)
[16] and WEKA (version 3.8) [11] tools to obtain classification accuracies of various
methods as shown in Tables 2, 3 and 4.

Table 2 shows classification accuracies of FIPDT + CART method. In this approach,
CART is used to build a decision tree for each block. It indicates nearly 2% improvement
in classification accuracy for both Breast Cancer and Pima-Diabetics as compared to
CART. On an average, the proposed method exhibits better performance over stacking
and bagging and is competitive to CART. It is observed that Random forest and Adaboost
methods are better than the proposed method in terms of average classification accuracy.

Table 3 demonstrates classification accuracies that are obtained by FIPDT + C4.5.
In this approach, C4.5 is used to build a decision tree for each block. It shows classification improvement upto 4%, 8% and 15% for Breast cancer, Contactlenses and Weather
datasets respectively and shows competitive classification for both German credit and
Pima-diabetes datasets as compared to classical C4.5 decision tree. On an average, the
proposed method exhibits improved performance over all other benchmark methods.

**Table 1.** Characteristics of the datasets.

| Sl. no. | Data set | No. of features before discretization | No. of instances | No. of features after discretization | No. of classes |
|---------|----------|---------------------------------------|------------------|--------------------------------------|----------------|
| 1 | Breast Cancer | 10 | 286 | 51 | 2 |
| 2 | Contact lenses | 5 | 24 | 7 | 3 |
| 3 | Weather | 5 | 14 | 11 | 2 |
| 4 | German Credit | 21 | 1000 | 1077 | 2 |
| 5 | Pima-Diabetics | 9 | 768 | 1210 | 2 |

FIPDT + C5.0 uses C5.0 decision tree method to build a model for each block. It achieves approximately 6% higher classification accuracy for Breast cancer dataset as compared to C5.0 decision tree as indicated in Table 4. On an average, the proposed method shows 1.3%, 1.6%, 3.4%, 5.2%, and 0.4% better performance in terms of classification accuracies over C5.0, Adaboost, Bagging, Stacking and Random Forest methods respectively.

**Table 2.** Classification accuracies of FIPDT + CART method, CART, AdaBoost, Bagging, Stacking and Random Forest.

| Sl. no. | Datasets | Classification rate (%) | | | | | |
|---------|----------|-------|------|----------|---------|----------|---------------|
| | | FIPDT | CART | Adaboost | Bagging | Stacking | Random Forest |
| 1 | Breast Cancer | **72.36** | 70.6 | 71.62 | 68.41 | 70.3 | 69.75 |
| 2 | Contact-Lenses | 58.33 | 58.33 | 72.17 | 74.17 | 64.33 | **75.33** |
| 3 | Weather | **71.5** | **71.5** | 69 | 56 | 70 | 66 |
| 4 | German Credit | 77 | **80.08** | 71.27 | 74.19 | 70 | 76.33 |
| 5 | Pima-Diabetics | 71.59 | 69.89 | 74.92 | 75.86 | 65.11 | **76.1** |
| **Average** | | **70.15** | **70.08** | **71.79** | **69.72** | **67.94** | **72.70** |

In the next subsection, we describe structural instability analysis of the proposed method based on the standard deviation of the classification accuracies obtained using 10-fold cross validation.

### 4.1  Structural Instability

Standard deviation measure is used to evaluate the structural instability of a decision tree. The lower values of standard deviation indicate higher structural stability of a decision tree. The standard deviation values of 10 classification accuracies obtained by the proposed method are shown in Fig. 3. FIPDT + C4.5 shows better performance for

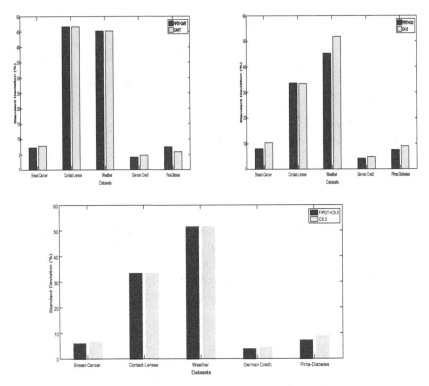

**Fig. 3.** Structural stability using standard deviation

**Table 3.** Classification accuracies of FIPDT + C4.5 method, C4.5, AdaBoost, Bagging, Stacking and Random Forest.

| Sl. no. | Datasets | Classification rate (%) | | | | | |
|---------|----------|-------|------|----------|---------|----------|---------------|
| | | FIPDT | C4.5 | Adaboost | Bagging | Stacking | Random Forest |
| 1 | Breast Cancer | **75.15** | 70.95 | 71.62 | 68.41 | 70.3 | 69.75 |
| 2 | Contact-Lenses | **81.67** | 73.33 | 72.17 | 74.17 | 64.33 | 75.33 |
| 3 | Weather | **71.5** | 55 | 69 | 56 | 70 | 66 |
| 4 | German Credit | **77** | 76.78 | 71.27 | 74.19 | 70 | 76.33 |
| 5 | Pima-Diabetics | 71.59 | 70.3 | 74.92 | 75.86 | 65.11 | **76.1** |
| **Average** | | **75.38** | **69.27** | **71.79** | **69.72** | **67.94** | **72.70** |

all the datasets except contact-lenses dataset. Both FIPDT + CART and FIPDT + C5.0 methods show relatively lower standard deviation for 3 datasets as compared to classical decision trees. In brief, the proposed method is structurally stable as compared to other methods.

**Table 4.** Classification accuracies of FIPDT + C5.0 method, C5.0, AdaBoost, Bagging, Stacking and Random Forest.

| Sl. no. | Datasets | Classiftcation rate (%) | | | | | |
|---------|----------|-------|------|----------|---------|----------|---------------|
| | | FIPDT | C5.0 | Adaboost | Bagging | Stacking | Random Forest |
| 1 | Breast Cancer | **75.48** | 69.21 | 71.62 | 68.41 | 70.3 | 69.75 |
| 2 | Contact-Lenses | **81.67** | 81.67 | 72.17 | 74.17 | 64.33 | 75.33 |
| 3 | Weather | 60 | 60 | 69 | 56 | **70** | 66 |
| 4 | German Credit | 77 | **77.11** | 71.27 | 74.19 | 70 | 76.33 |
| 5 | Pima-Diabetics | 71.59 | 71.3 | 74.92 | 75.86 | 65.11 | **76.1** |
| **Average** | | **73.14** | **71.85** | **71.79** | **69.72** | **67.94** | **72.70** |

## 4.2 Statistical Tests

We use $p-value$ as a metric to quantify the significance of the statistical tests, namely, t-Test, Wilcoxon Sign Test and Pearson correlation Test. We use 0.05 (that is, $\alpha = 0.05$) as the level of significance in our tests. If $p-value \leq \alpha$, the null hypothesis is rejected. Table 5 presents $p-values$ computed based on the classification accuracies of the proposed and other methods. For most of the cases, it is observed that $p < 0.05$ which confirms the statistical significance of the classification accuracies obtained by the proposed FIPDT method. Table 6 indicates $p-values$ obtained from standard deviation values of FIPDT. FIPDT method shows statistically significant values of standard deviation (that is, higher structural stability) as $p-value$ is less than $\alpha$ for all the cases.

**Table 5.** Various Statistical tests for FIPDT using classification accuracy.

| p-value | | | | |
|---------|------|------|------|------|
| Sl. no. | Tests | CART | C4.5 | C5.0 |
| 1 | t-Test | 1.45e−10 | 1.212e−10 | 2.897e−10 |
| 2 | Wilcoxon Sign Test | 0.0058 | 0.0019 | 0.0058 |
| 3 | Pearson correlation test | 0.0062 | 0.2583 | 0.0164 |

**Table 6.** Various statistical tests for FIPDT using standard deviation.

| *p-value* | | | | |
|---|---|---|---|---|
| Sl. no. | Tests | CART | C4.5 | C5.0 |
| 1 | t-Test | 0.0078 | 0.0056 | 0.0083 |
| 2 | Wilcoxon Sign Test | 0.0058 | 0.0019 | 0.0058 |
| 3 | Pearson correlation test | 2.973e−05 | 0.0006 | 5.661e−06 |

## 5   Conclusions

In this work, we proposed a vertical partitioning based decision tree ensemble method using frequent pattern concept. The proposed method shows improved classification rate and structural stability over other approaches. Highest-size frequent itemsets are used to create the item blocks. The significance of the results obtained by the proposed method is demonstrated using statistical tests. In future, we would like to explore evolutionary and statistical methods to bring in novel partitioning approaches.

## References

1. Agrawal, R., Srikant, R.: Fast algorithms for mining association rules in large databases. In: Proceedings of the 20th International Conference on Very Large Data Bases, VLDB 1994, pp. 487–499 (1994)
2. Baralis, E., Cagliero, L., Garza, P.: Planning stock portfolios by means of weighted frequent itemsets. Expert Syst. Appl. **86**, 1–17 (2017)
3. Breiman L: Classification and Regression Trees. Wadsworth Int. Group (1984)
4. C5.0: See5: An informal tutorial (1993). http://www.rulequest/see5-win.html
5. Chao, W., Junzheng, W.: Cloud-service decision tree classification for education platform. Cogn. Syst. Res. **52**, 234–239 (2018)
6. Domadiya, N., Rao, U.P.: Privacy preserving distributed association rule mining approach on vertically partitioned healthcare data. Procedia Comput. Sci. **148**, 303–312 (2019). The second international conference on intelligent computing in data sciences, ICDS2018
7. Farzanyar, Z., Cercone, N.: Efficient mining of frequent itemsets in social network data based on mapreduce framework. In: 2013 IEEE/ACM International Conference on Advances in Social Networks Analysis and Mining (ASONAM 2013), pp. 1183–1188 (2013)
8. Gheondea-Eladi, A.: Patient decision aids: a content analysis based on a decision tree structure. BMC Med. Inform. Decis. Mak. **19**(1), 137 (2019)
9. Guggari, S., Kadappa, V., Umadevi, V.: Non-sequential partitioning approaches to decision tree classifier. Future Comput. Inform. J. **3**(2), 275–285 (2018)
10. Gupta, M., Mohanty, B.K.: Attribute partitioning in multiple attribute decision making problems for a decision with a purpose a fuzzy approach. J. Multi-Criteria Decis. Anal. **23**(3–4), 160–170 (2016)
11. Hall, M., Frank, E., Holmes, G., Pfahringer, B., Reutemann, P., Witten, I.H.: The weka data mining software: an update. ACM SIGKDD Explor. Newsl. **11**(1), 10–18 (2009)
12. Han, J., Pei, J., Yin, Y., Mao, R.: Mining frequent patterns without candidate generation: a frequent-pattern tree approach. Data Min. Knowl. Disc. **8**(1), 53–87 (2004)

13. Hassan, M.M., Mokhtar, H.M.: Investigating autism etiology and heterogeneity by decision tree algorithm. Inform. Med. Unlocked **16**, 100215 (2019)
14. Kadappa, V., Guggari, S., Negi, A.: Decision tree classifier using theme based partitioning. In: 2015 International Conference on Computing and Network Communications (CoCoNet), pp. 540–546 (2015)
15. Sun, L., Mu, W.-S., Qi, B., Zhou, Z.-J.: A new privacy-preserving proximal support vector machine for classification of vertically partitioned data. Int. J. Mach. Learn. Cybernet. **6**(1), 109–118 (2014). https://doi.org/10.1007/s13042-014-0245-1
16. R: The R project for statistical computing (1993). http://www.r-project.org/
17. Recamonde-Mendoza, M., Bazzan, A.L.: Social choice in distributed classification tasks: dealing with vertically partitioned data. Inf. Sci. **332**, 56–71 (2016)
18. Salzberg, S.L.: C4.5: Programs for Machine Learning by J. Ross Quinlan. Morgan Kaufmann Publishers, Inc., 1993. Mach. Learn. **16**(3), 235–240 (1994)
19. Säuberlich, F., Gaul, W.: Decision tree construction by association rules. In: Decker, R., Gaul, W. (eds.) Classification and Information Processing at the Turn of the Millennium, pp. 245–253 (2000)
20. Stanczyk, U.: Decision rule length as a basis for evaluation of attribute relevance. J. Intell. Fuzzy Syst. Appl. Eng. Technol. **24**(3), 429–445 (2013)
21. Vanahalli, M.K., Patil, N.: Distributed mining of significant frequent colossal closed itemsets from long biological dataset. In: Intelligent Systems Design and Applications, pp. 891–902 (2020)
22. Zaki, M.J., Parthasarathy, S., Ogihara, M., Li, W.: New algorithms for fast discovery of association rules. In: Proceedings of the Third International Conference on Knowledge Discovery and Data Mining, KDD 1997, pp. 283–286 (1997)
23. Zheng, J., Yang, S., Wang, X., Xia, X., Xiao, Y., Li, T.: A decision tree based road recognition approach using roadside fixed 3D LiDAR sensors. IEEE Access **7**, 53878–53890 (2019)

# Investigating Fingerprint Quality
# Features for Liveness Detection

Ram Prakash Sharma$^{(\boxtimes)}$, Ashutosh Anshul, Ashwini Jha, and Somnath Dey

Indian Institute of Technology Indore, Indore, India
{phd1501201003,cse170001011,cse170001012,somnathd}@iiti.ac.in

**Abstract.** Fingerprint-based recognition systems are vulnerable to presentation attacks. To identify these attacks one of the solution is fingerprint liveness detection which ensures the presence of a live or fake fingerprint. In this paper, we have investigated the use of quality features for the detection of liveness of given fingerprint image. We have proposed a novel set of features which can be used for liveness detection in fingerprint images. Along with these features, efficacy of other existing quality features is also evaluated for the liveness detection. Based on these quality features fingerprint images are classified into fake and live fingerprints using various classifiers. The robustness of the proposed approach is evaluated on publicly available LivDet 2015 competition database. The advantage of the proposed method is that it utilizes the quality features for liveness detection which are also utilized for the quality analysis of fingerprint images. Therefore, it is possible to combine two different modules, namely, quality analysis and liveness detection of the Automatic Fingerprint Identification System (AFIS) using our proposed approach.

**Keywords:** Biometrics · Presentation attack · Quality features · Fingerprint liveness detection · Extra tree classifier

## 1 Introduction

The vulnerability of fingerprint recognition system against presentation attacks has gained attention due to its wide applicability in access control and security applications. The fingerprint sensors can be deceived by the fake fingerprints fabricated with different materials such as silicone, gelatin, playdoh, etc. To avoid these attacks strong counter-measures must be developed. Liveness detection is one of the solution to avoid presentation attacks. The liveness detection can be achieved using two types of techniques, software-based and hardware-based. The hardware-based methods [13] utilizes electrical conductivity of the skin, temperature of the fingertip using an external hardware. This extra hardware unit leads to increase the overall cost of the liveness detection system. The software-based methods [7,15,16] makes use of the image of fingerprint to detect the liveness. In this paper, we have emphasized on the software-based liveness detection systems due to their low-cost and faster implementation.

© Springer Nature Switzerland AG 2020
B. R. Purushothama et al. (Eds.): MIKE 2019, LNAI 11987, pp. 296–307, 2020.
https://doi.org/10.1007/978-3-030-66187-8_28

Perspiration and pores are some of the prominent features in addition to quality based features that are used in various software-based liveness detection methods [4,5,8,9,17,18]. However, the non-uniform pressure on the fingerprint sensors can lead to loss perspiration based features and pore based features will not be helpful if the fingerprint image is of low resolution($< 1000$ dpi). Also, the performance of existing quality based features is not good enough if the images are captured with different sensors or if different materials are used to generate the fake fingerprints. Therefore, in this work, we propose a novel set of sensors and material independent quality features that can help in performance improvement. These features have been identified by a careful observation of various live and fake fingerprints. The benefit of using quality features for fingerprint liveness is that the two important modules of AFIS system namely, quality analysis and liveness detection can be combined as they both relies on the quality information of fingerprint images.

In this paper, we propose a novel set of quality features for fingerprint liveness detection. For this, we have proposed four features namely, white circular patches (WCP), ridge bifurcation (RB), ridge ending (RE), and center intensity difference (CID) by carefully analyzing the differences between live and fake fingerprint images. These features are proposed based on the differences in the ridge-valley structure of the live and fake fingerprint made of different materials (gelatin, playdoh, silicon, etc.) and captured with different sensors. Apart from these features, we have also evaluated the effectiveness of some existing fingerprint quality features namely, orientation certainty analysis (OCL), mean intensity (MI), frequency domain analysis (FDA), and ridge valley uniformity (RVU). Extracted features undergo through a feature scaling and feature selection unit. These extracted features are then fed to various classifiers (multi-layer perceptron (MLP), logistic regression, support vector machine (SVM), decision tree, k- nearest neighbours(k-NN), random forest, and extra tree classifier) to identify live and fake fingerprint images. Experimental evaluations on LivDet 2015 show that extra tree classifier performs the best for liveness detection. Individual feature performance test is also performed to identify the best performing quality features. The major contributions of the proposed work are as follows:

– Novel quality features (WCP, RB, RE, and CID) are proposed to detect live or fake fingerprint.
– The effectiveness of the proposed as well as existing quality features is evaluated on well known publically available LivDet 2015 database.
– Effectiveness of individual quality features to differentiate live and fake fingerprint images is analyzed.
– The proposed method makes it possible to combined the livenesss detection and quality analysis modules of fingerprint recognition as both of these tasks can be accomplished with the same feature set.

The rest of the paper is organized as follows. In Sect. 2, related works of the fingerprint liveness detection are given. Section 3 presents the proposed method. The experimental evaluations are presented in Sect. 4. Finally, conclusions with future research direction are provided in Sect. 5.

## 2    Related Works

Some of the famous and well-known quality based fingerprint liveness detection methods from literature are discussed in this section. Abhayankar et al. [1] utilizes a wavelet-based approach to detect liveness which is integrated with the fingerprint matcher. They have also utilized changing pattern of pressure and moisture for liveness detection. Espinoza et al. [2] proposed an approach which utilizes the number of sweat pores as a distinguishing feature between live and fake fingerprints. Marasco et al. [9] proposed robust morphological and perspiration-based measures for the liveness detection in fingerprint images. They have tested their approach on LivDet 2009 data-set. Ghiani et al. [6] proposed the use of binarized statistical image features (BSIF), which is a local image descriptor. This descriptor is constructed by converting the responses of linear filters into binary data. Tan et al. [17] suggested that real-time perspiration pattern can be used for liveness detection. They have utilized an intensity based approach for analyzing static and dynamic perspiration features. In another approach, Tan et al. [18] detects the liveness by analyzing the difference of noise distribution along the valleys in fingerprint images. Galbally et al. [3] proposed use of some quality features, namely, ridge clarity, ridge continuity, and ridge strength for liveness detection over LivDet 2009 database. Experimental evaluations on LivDet 2009 and ATVS databases with an improved study is presented in [5]. Galbally et al. [4] presented a novel software-based presentation attack detection method that involves quality assessment of the image obtained and can be used in real time applications. To distinguish between real and fake samples of fingerprint, iris and face, they have used 25 quality features. Sharma et al. [14] proposed a quality feature based fingerprint liveness detection approach. Their approach is able to perform very well on the ivDet 2009, 2011, 2013, and 2015 database. Marcialis et al. [10] have utilized pores as a distinguishing feature for liveness detection. They have presented a detailed study of pores distribution including their location and frequencies to differentiate live and fake fingerprints. Manivanan et al. [8] proposed a technique in which active sweat pores are located and extracted for liveness detection in fingerprint sensors. Their technique utilizes high-pass filtering which is followed by correlation filtering.

## 3    Proposed Method

The proposed method extracts a set of novel quality features and combines these features with some of the existing quality features to form a complete feature vector for fingerprint liveness detection. The obtained feature vector is fed to feature scaling unit in order to scale the features uniformly. The scaled features are passed through feature selection unit and their results are tested using various classifiers. Figure 1 illustrates the flow mechanism of the proposed approach.

### 3.1    Quality Feature Extraction

The following section includes a brief description of the eight features extracted from the fingerprint image.

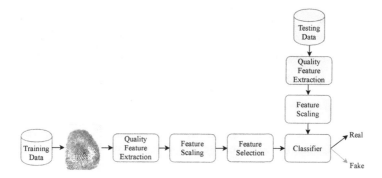

**Fig. 1.** Block diagram of the proposed liveness detection method

(a)                                    (b)

**Fig. 2.** Difference in area of white circular patches in a live and fake fingerprint, (a) Live, and (b) Fake

– **White Circular Patches:** The fake fingerprint fabrication process might cause loss of details (ridge-valley structure). This leads to sensor not detecting ridges in some regions, thus resulting in WCP in the fake fingerprint. Thus, the difference in the area of such circular regions can be used to differentiate live and fake fingerprints. The white circular patches are located by detecting all the elliptical contours and the smallest circles enclosing them. Based on a threshold (threshold = 0.3) on the ratio of elliptical contour area to the enclosing circle area, these regions are considered in WCP. The area of WCP is calculated at each pixel as given in Eq. 1.

$$WCP_{area} = \sum_{i=1}^{n_{contours}} \left\{ \frac{Contour_{area}(i)}{\pi \times r_i^2} > 0.3 \right\} \tag{1}$$

Here $r$ is the radius of the circle and $n_{contours}$ is the number of contours found in a fingerprint image.

– **Ridge Bifurcation and Ending:** The number of minutiae points (ridge bifurcation and ending) also plays an important role to discriminate live and fake fingerprints. The fingerprint fabrication process causes loss in some minute details of a fingerprint image due to the elastic property of various materials. Due to this, fake fingerprints have a lesser number of bifurcation and ending points as compared with live fingerprint. These features are extracted based on the thinning morphological operation. Figure 3 shows

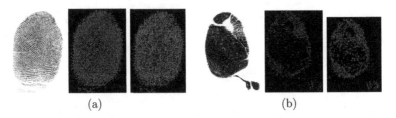

**Fig. 3.** Difference in number of ridge bifurcation and ridge ending in a live and fake fingerprint, (a) Live and (b) Fake

**Fig. 4.** Difference in average intensity of different regions in a live and fake fingerprint, (a) Live and (b) Fake

the distribution of ridge endings and bifurcation points in a fake and live fingerprint sample.

- **Center Intensity Difference:** The pressure applied while the acquisition of live fingerprint is more in the center part, therefore, the acquired images have darker center region as compared with other surrounding regions. However, in case of a fake fingerprint acquisition, this phenomenon is not found. Therefore, the intensity difference of the center block from its surrounding blocks of the segmented fingerprint image can be a distinguishing feature. The computation of this feature is done by dividing the foreground area of a fingerprint image in 9 blocks. The intensity difference in these 9 different regions can be seen from Fig. 4. Computation of CID from the average intensity of 9 blocks ($I_{avg}$) is done as given in Eq. 2.

$$CID = \sum_{i=1}^{i=3} \sum_{j=1}^{j=3} \left\{ I_{Avg}(i,j)[(i,j) \neq (2,2)] - I_{Avg}(2,2) \right\} \tag{2}$$

- **Orientation Certainty Level:** OCL considers a local block of the fingerprint image and measures its intensity gradient . It estimates the energy concentration in the direction of the dominant ridge. The computation of OCL is done as given in [12].
- **Mean Intensity:** This feature computes the mean intensity of the segmented fingerprint image region. The computation of this feature is done as given in [12].

- **Frequency Domain Analysis:** FDA is obtained by computing the DFT of the 1D signature of ridge-valley structure. The computation of the FDA is done as given in [12].
- **Ridge Valley Uniformity:** Ridge Valley Uniformity is computed as a ratio of ridge width to the valley width. The computation of this feature is also done as given in [12].

**Feature Vector from the Local Quality Features.** Some of the features $(FDA, OCL, RVU)$ are calculated on local level from the fingerprint images. The final set of features obtained is the combination of standard deviation and mean of these local quality features and WCP, RB, RE, CID, and M features. Therefore, the final features vector contains 11 features which are represented as given in Eq. 3.

$$Q = \Big\{ WCP, RB, RE, CID, MI, OCL^\mu, OCL^\sigma,$$
$$FDA^\mu, FDA^\sigma, RVU^\mu, RVU^\sigma \Big\} \tag{3}$$

### 3.2 Feature Scaling

The features extracted in the proposed approach have high variance in the magnitude and range. Due to this, it is possible that two equally important features may not have equal effect on the prediction model. To remove these variations, the extracted features are scaled by using robust scalar technique. Robust scalar removes the median and uses the quantile range given as input to scale the data.

### 3.3 Feature Selection

The features contained in feature vector might have high positive or negative correlation among themselves which might hamper the results. So in order to obtain best feature set, a simple feature selection procedure has been followed in this work. Let set $S$ denotes the selected features set. For each feature $f$ not in $S$, accuracy was checked for $S \cup f$. If addition of any feature $f$, results in maximum accuracy than that feature $f$ will be selected in feature set $S$. The same procedure is repeated for all the remaining features. In case for an iteration if no feature results in improvement of accuracy obtained with feature set $S$, the iteration stops and the resultant set $S$ contains the final selected features for the liveness detection.

## 4   Experimental Results

Experiments are carried out on three data-sets of the LivDet 2015 [11] competition database to evaluate the performance of quality features for liveness detection. Description of training and testing set in these data-sets is given in Table 1.

**Table 1.** Composition of the LivDet 2015 data-sets used for the tests

| Sensor | Resolution (dpi) | Live images Train/Test | Fake images Train/Test | Spoof materials |
|---|---|---|---|---|
| Crossmatch | 500 | 1000/1000 | 1473/1448 | BodyDouble, Ecoflex, PlayDoh, OOMOO, Gelatin |
| Digital Persona | 500 | 1000/1000 | 1000/1500 | Liquid Ecoflex, RTV, Gelatin, Latex, Ecoflex, WoodGlue |
| Hi-Scan | 1000 | 1000/1000 | 1000/1500 | Liquid Ecoflex, RTV, Gelatin, Latex, Ecoflex, WoodGlue |

## 4.1 Evaluation Results by Various Classifiers

We have tested the liveness detection performance with various classifiers. For each classifier, feature selection is performed to find the best feature set which results in highest accuracy. Different classifiers used in our experiments to predict the fingerprint liveness are as follows:

- **Multi-layer Perceptron (MLP):** A Multi-layer perceptron is a neural network that consists of three or more layers of nodes. These layers include an input and an output layer. The rest of the layers are hidden. The output of each node in each layer except the input layer is a nonlinear function of the input or set of inputs, which is termed as activation function. MLP uses back-propagation for training. In our experiments, the size of the hidden layers is selected as (200,200,200) and the solver used is Limited Memory Broyden Fletcher Goldfarb Shanno (LBFGS) which is an optimization algorithm.
- **Logistic Regression:** Logistic regression is a classification model that maps predicted values with probabilities and assigns its observation to set of classes. In case of binary logistic regression the predicted value is mapped to probability using sigmoid function. The obtained probability is used to predict the class of the object.
- **Support Vector Machines (SVM):** SVM is a supervised machine learning model, mostly used for classification. It generates suitable hyper-plane that differentiates between set of objects that belong to different classes. The dimension of the space is equal to the number of features used. The generation of hyper-plane considers many factors including the distance from objects of different class, the regularization parameter, and the kernel used. In our experiments, we have used redial basis function (RBF) kernel with $\gamma = 0.000001$ and the penalty parameter $C$ of the error term is selected as 10.

**Table 2.** Experimental results obtained with different classifiers

| Classifier | Result | Features selected |
|---|---|---|
| MLP | 74.52 | $FDA^\mu, RB$ |
| Logistic regression | 76.70 | $FDA^\mu, RB, CID, OCL^\sigma, FDA^\sigma, MI, RVU^\mu, WCP$ |
| SVM | 80.22 | $FDA^\mu, RB, CID, RVU^\mu, MI, OCL^\sigma, FDA^\sigma, OCL^\mu, RE, WCP$ |
| Decision tree | 83.22 | $FDA^\mu, RB, RVU^\mu, FDA^\sigma, CID, MI, OCL^\mu, WCP$ |
| KNN | 86.14 | $FDA^\sigma, RB, MI, OCL^\sigma, OCL^\mu, CID, RE, RVU^\mu$ |
| Random forest | 86.69 | $FDA^\sigma, WCP, RVU^\mu, RB, OCL^\mu, OCL^\sigma, CID, MI, RE$ |
| Extra tree classifier | 87.36 | $FDA^\sigma, RB, MI, CID, OCL^\sigma, RE, RVU^\mu, WCP$ |

- **Decision Tree:** A decision tree is also is a supervised machine learning model. It follows a tree-like structure. The internal nodes of the tree represents test on features, the leaf nodes represents class label or the output and the branches represents the outcome of the test. In our experiments, the max depth of 1000 is selected which provides the optimal results.
- **k- Nearest Neighbours (k-NN):** k-NN is a type of lazy learning where the output of a test case depends on neighbouring training examples. The neighbours are decided on the basis of their similarity with the test case. The decision depends on $k$, the number of neighbours to be considered. The contribution of the neighbours is weighted so that the neighbours that are nearer have more contribution than the distant ones. We have selected the number of neighbors as 15 for the optimal results.
- **Random Forest:** Random Forest is an ensemble technique where multiple decision trees work together to produce output. It generates multiple subsets of the training data-set and builds different decision tree models over them. Each tree produce their own class prediction from which the class with maximum votes is chosen to be the output. In the experimental evaluations, the number of trees and maximum depth is selected as 500 and 1000, respectively.
- **Extra Tree Classifier:** Extra Tree, like random forest builds multiple tree over subsets of data-set and treat them as an ensemble. The key difference between Extra tree and Random Forest are is that random forest generates samples from data-set with replacement but extra tree picks samples without replacement. Moreover, while random forest computes an optimal value for split, extra tree chooses a random value. These differences leads to a less variance in case of extra tree. The splitting criterion used for the classifier is "gini". The optimal parameters resulting in highest accuracy by Extra Tree classifier are number of trees $n_{estimators} = 500$, maximum depth of the tree $n_{depth} = 1000$, and random state parameter as 0.

The description of the maximum accuracy obtained with different classifiers and their corresponding selected feature set is given in Table 2. As seen from the results, the best accuracy is obtained by the Extra Tree Classifier (87.36%). Results also indicates the difference in the selected feature set, which shows that importance of the features varies based on the classifier. Moreover, it can be seen from the results that ensemble classifiers (random forest, and extra tree classifiers) are better than other classifiers in terms of performance.

## 4.2  Quality Features Performance

The performance of each individual quality feature is evaluated using the best performing extra tree classifier. The performance of the quality features for liveness detection on different data-sets and combined data-sets is given in Table 3. The results indicates that each feature perform differently for different data-sets. As an instance of this property we can see that RB features provides an accuracy of 80.58%, 52.61%, 54.32%, and 57.95% on Crossmatch, Digital Persona, Hi-Scan, and combined data-sets of these three, respectively. The best performing feature for the liveness detection as per the combined data-sets are as follows: $FDA^\sigma, RB, MI, CID, OCL^\sigma, RE, RVU^\mu, WCP$.

**Table 3.** Performance of individual quality features for extra tree classifier

| Features | Crossmatch | Digital person | Hi-Scan | Combined |
|---|---|---|---|---|
| WCP | 64.88 | 60.14 | 52.48 | 56.13 |
| RB | 80.58 | 52.61 | 54.32 | 57.95 |
| RE | 67.22 | 49.31 | 56.44 | 54.15 |
| CID | 57.29 | 53.62 | 57.84 | 57.87 |
| $OCL^\sigma$ | 50.56 | 60.14 | 58.64 | 55.94 |
| $FDA^\sigma$ | 64.30 | 66.04 | 57.44 | 59.01 |
| $RVU^\mu$ | 62.20 | 65.16 | 49.72 | 55.48 |
| Mean intensity | 65.05 | 51.15 | 56.52 | 52.97 |

**Table 4.** Liveness detection performance with additive increase in quality features

| Feature set | Crossmatch | Digital person | Hi-Scan | Combined |
|---|---|---|---|---|
| $FDA^\sigma$ | 64.16 | 66.04 | 57.44 | 59.01 |
| $FDA^\sigma$+RB | 82.35 | 70.72 | 65.56 | 68.54 |
| $FDA^\sigma$+RB+MI | 86.88 | 72.77 | 76.84 | 77.58 |
| $FDA^\sigma$+RB+MI+CID | 91.50 | 73.48 | 77.76 | 81.29 |
| $FDA^\sigma$+RB+MI+CID+$OCL^\sigma$ | 92.66 | 75.03 | 83.16 | 83.98 |
| $FDA^\sigma$+RB+MI+CID+$OCL^\sigma$+RE | 92.59 | 76.29 | 85.76 | 85.47 |
| $FDA^\sigma$+RB+MI+CID+$OCL^\sigma$+RE+$RVU^\mu$ | 92.49 | 76.29 | 86.68 | 86.64 |
| $FDA^\sigma$+RB+MI+CID+$OCL^\sigma$+RE+$RVU^\mu$+WCP | 92.62 | 76.79 | 86.88 | 87.36 |

## 4.3  Performance Improvement with Quality Features

The results in Table 4 indicates the progression in the performance using extra tree classifier for liveness detection. In the start of this evaluation we have only the best performing FDA feature for liveness detection. Now adding other features one by one in the existing feature vector continuously improves the performance. The liveness detection performance improves from 64.16 to 92.62 for Crossmatch, 66.04 to 76.79 for Digital Persona, 57.44 to 86.88 for Hi-Scan, and 59.01 to 87.36 for combined data-sets. The growth in performance while adding the quality features one by one is also shown in the Fig. 5.

## 4.4   Comparative Analysis

A comparative study of the results is performed with some of the existing fingerprint liveness detection methods present in LivDet 2015 competition [11].

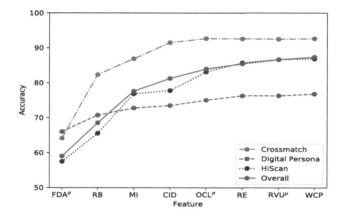

**Fig. 5.** Improvement in the liveness detection performance with additive increase in quality features. Each point represents the accuracy using feature set that contain the corresponding feature and previous features

**Table 5.** Comparative results of quality based fingerprint liveness detection

| Methods | Crossmatch | Digital Persona | Hi-Scan | Combined |
|---|---|---|---|---|
| Proposed method | **92.62** | 76.79 | 86.88 | **87.36** |
| Hectorn (Universidade Federal de Pernambuco) | 86.94 | **84.20** | **88.20** | 86.44 |
| CSI MM (Institute for Infocomm Research (I2R)) | 89.99 | 75.56 | 87.84 | 84.46 |
| CSI (Institute for Infocomm Research (I2R)) | 88.33 | 76.20 | 83.20 | 82.57 |
| COPILHA (Instituto de Biociencias, Letras e Ciencias Exatas) | 69.00 | 79.96 | 75.64 | 74.86 |
| UFPE II (Universidade Federal Rural de Pernambuco) | 61.16 | 75.44 | 71.24 | 69.28 |
| UFPE I (Universidade Federal Rural de Pernambuco) | 59.97 | 78.36 | 64.32 | 67.55 |

The comparative results are reported in Table 5. The results show that the proposed method performs best for the Crossmatch sensor while the hectron method submitted in LivDet 2015 competition performs better for Digital Persona and Hi-Scan data-sets. In terms of combined data-sets performance it can be seen that the proposed method outperforms other methods.

## 5    Conclusion

In this paper, we have proposed a novel set of quality features (i.e. $WCP$, $RB$, $RE$, $CID$) for fingerprint liveness detection. Additionally, we have evaluated the performance of some other existing quality features. The experimental evaluation show that the each of the quality feature is effective for liveness detection task. The accuracy obtained with each feature varies with the type of sensor used. Further, the experimental evaluation while adding the quality features one by one shows a continuous improvement in the performance. The study presented in this work is makes it evident that it is possible to combine the quality analysis and liveness detection module of AFIS system as both of these task can be performed with same feature set. In the future studies of this work, we look forward to explore the efficacy of other quality features for fingerprint liveness detection.

**Acknowledgment.** This research work has been carried out with the financial support provided from Science and Engineering Research Board (SERB), DST (ECR/2017/000027), Govt. of India.

## References

1. Abhyankar, A., Schuckers, S.: Integrating a wavelet based perspiration liveness check with fingerprint recognition. Pattern Recogn. **42**(3), 452–464 (2009)
2. Espinoza, M., Champod, C.: Using the number of pores on fingerprint images to detect spoofing attacks. In: International Conference on Hand-Based Biometrics, pp. 1–5 (2011)
3. Galbally, J., Alonso-Fernandez, F., Fierrez, J., Ortega-Garcia, J.: Fingerprint liveness detection based on quality measures. In: First IEEE International Conference on Biometrics, Identity and Security (BIdS), pp. 1–8 (2009)
4. Galbally, J., Marcel, S., Fierrez, J.: Image quality assessment for fake biometric detection: application to iris, fingerprint, and face recognition. IEEE Trans. Image Process. **23**(2), 710–724 (2014)
5. Galbally, J., Alonso-Fernandez, F., Fierrez, J., Ortega-Garcia, J.: A high performance fingerprint liveness detection method based on quality related features. Future Gener. Comput. Syst. **28**(1), 311–321 (2012)
6. Ghiani, L., Hadid, A., Marcialis, G.L., Roli, F.: Fingerprint liveness detection using binarized statistical image features. In: IEEE Sixth International Conference on Biometrics: Theory, Applications and Systems (BTAS), pp. 1–6 (2013)
7. Ghiani, L., Yambay, D.A., Mura, V., Marcialis, G.L., Roli, F., Schuckers, S.A.: Review of the fingerprint liveness detection (LivDet) competition series: 2009 to 2015. Image Vis. Comput. **58**, 110–128 (2017)

8. Manivanan, N., Memon, S., Balachandran, W.: Automatic detection of active sweat pores of fingerprint using highpass and correlation filtering. Electron. Lett. **46**(18), 1268–1269 (2010)
9. Marasco, E., Sansone, C.: Combining perspiration and morphology based static features for fingerprint liveness detection. Pattern Recogn. Lett. **33**(9), 1148–1156 (2012)
10. Marcialis, G.L., Roli, F., Tidu, A.: Analysis of fingerprint pores for vitality detection. In: 20th International Conference on Pattern Recognition, pp. 1289–1292 (2010)
11. Mura, V., Ghiani, L., Marcialis, G.L., Roli, F., Yambay, D.A., Schuckers, S.A.: LivDet 2015 fingerprint liveness detection competition 2015. In: IEEE 7th International Conference on Biometrics Theory, Applications and Systems (BTAS), pp. 1–6 (2015)
12. Olsen, M.A., Šmida, V., Busch, C.: Finger image quality assessment features: definitions and evaluation. IET Biometrics **5**(2), 47–64 (2016)
13. Shahzad, M., Nadarajah, M., Noor, A., Balachadran, W., Boulgouris, N.V.: Fingerprint sensors: liveness detection and hardware solutions. Sens. Biosens. MEMS Technol. Appl. **136**(1), 35–49 (2012)
14. Sharma, R.P., Dey, S.: Fingerprint liveness detection using local quality features. Vis. Comput. **35**, 1393–1410 (2018). https://doi.org/10.1007/s00371-018-01618-x
15. Sharma, R.P., Dey, S.: Local contrast phase descriptor for quality assessment of fingerprint images. In: Deka, B., Maji, P., Mitra, S., Bhattacharyya, D.K., Bora, P.K., Pal, S.K. (eds.) PReMI 2019. LNCS, vol. 11941, pp. 507–514. Springer, Cham (2019). https://doi.org/10.1007/978-3-030-34869-4_55
16. Sharma, R.P., Dey, S.: Quality analysis of fingerprint images using local phase quantization. In: Vento, M., Percannella, G. (eds.) CAIP 2019. LNCS, vol. 11678, pp. 648–658. Springer, Cham (2019). https://doi.org/10.1007/978-3-030-29888-3_53
17. Tan, B., Schuckers, S.: Comparison of ridge- and intensity-based perspiration liveness detection methods in fingerprint scanners. In: Proceedings of SPIE: Biometric Technology for Human Identification III, vol. 6202, pp. 1–10 (2006)
18. Tan, B., Schuckers, S.: New approach for liveness detection in fingerprint scanners based on valley noise analysis. J. Electron. Imaging **1**(17), 011009 (2008)

# Full Informed Digital Transformation Simpler, Maybe Better

Almeida Dias[1] , António Capita[2] , Mariana Neves[3] , Goreti Marreiros[4] ,
Jorge Ribeiro[5] , Henrique Vicente[6,7] , and José Neves[1,7(✉)]

[1] Instituto Politécnico de Saúde do Norte, CESPU, Gandra, Portugal
a.almeida.dias@gmail.com
[2] Instituto Superior Técnico Militar, Luanda, Angola
antoniojorgecapita@gmail.com
[3] Deloitte, London, UK
maneves@deloitte.co.uk
[4] Departamento de Engenharia Informática, Instituto Superior de Engenharia
do Porto, Porto, Portugal
goreti@dei.isep.ipp.pt
[5] Escola Superior de Tecnologia e Gestão, ARC4DigiT – Applied Research Center for Digital
Transformation, Instituto Politécnico de Viana do Castelo, Viana do Castelo, Portugal
jribeiro@estg.ipvc.pt
[6] Departamento de Química, Escola de Ciências e Tecnologia, Centro de Química de Évora,
Universidade de Évora, Evora, Portugal
hvicente@uevora.pt
[7] Centro Algoritmi, Universidade do Minho, Braga, Portugal
jneves@di.uminho.pt

**Abstract.** The digital age is upon us and challenges many of today's businesses. To succeed with digitalization, it is needed a well-integrated enterprise and *Information Technology* organization that works seamlessly and thrives towards common goals. This is easy to say, but harder to achieve. *Digital Transformation* is the integration of digital technology into all areas of a business, fundamentally changing how one operates and delivers value to customers. It is also a cultural change that requires organizations to continually challenge the status quo, experimenting and coming to terms with doing something rather than making it perfect. This will be the focus of this work, which will be delivered as a computational agency integrating the phases of data gathering, the anticipation of a logic representation of uncertainty and vagueness, as well as the phases of data processing and analysis of results.

**Keywords:** Digital Transformation (DT) · Information Management · DT or DX economy · Entropy · Logic programming · Knowledge Representation and Reasoning · Artificial Neural Networks

## 1 Introduction

*Digital Transformation* (*DT*) stands for the interference of digital technology in all areas of an organization. It essentially changes the way one works and deliver value

© Springer Nature Switzerland AG 2020
B. R. Purushothama et al. (Eds.): MIKE 2019, LNAI 11987, pp. 308–319, 2020.
https://doi.org/10.1007/978-3-030-66187-8_29

to customers. It is also a cultural revolution in which companies constantly need to question the status quo, experiment and come to terms with disappointment [1–3]. *DT* looks different for every business, and finding a definition that works for everyone can be difficult. *DT* is not about raiding a storm and hoping it will go away. It is about accepting and accelerating change. But the real hurry is when the acceleration of innovation and transformation becomes exponential. And that is exactly what many analysts mean when talking about the *DT* or *DX* economy. Not only speeding up interrupts and changes, but also speeding up the actual *DTs* and innovations, making the gap to the Junker's even bigger. However, change management is obviously primarily about the human dimension, i.e., internal customers, stakeholders, and the wider ecosystem in which organizations are located. No organization can realize a deep *DT* without putting people first and having people on board. If things change too fast for people, or if one does not consider the persons and their concerns, this can be a recipe for failure and, in the broader sense, even resistance [4]. It is this dimension that is the object of this work, i.e., even if information is at the heart of *DT*, the link between *Information Management* (*IM*) and *DT* is not often enough. What does it all mean and how will it develop, is the question.

The article is organized into 4 (four) sections. The former one is dedicated to the topic's *DT* and *DX Economy*. Section 2 discusses some theoretical matters, namely the issues of qualitative thinking, uncertainty and vagueness [5]. In Sect. 3, a computational make-up of a case study is presented and how it develops into an agency as a logic program that is used to derive the data sets that can be used to train *Artificial Neural Networks* (*ANNs*) [6, 7] to address the issues of *DT* evaluation and its rating or degree of sustainability. Section 4 contains the presentation and discussion of the results as well as prospects for further research.

## 2  Fundamentals

*Knowledge Representation and Reasoning* (*KRR*) practices may be understood as a process of energy devaluation [8]. A data item is to be understood as being in a given moment at a particular entropic state as untainted energy which ranges in the interval 0...1 and, according to the *First Law of Thermodynamics,* is a quantity well-preserved that cannot be consumed in the sense of destruction, but may be consumed in the sense of devaluation. It may be introduced as, viz.

- *exergy*, sometimes called available energy or more precisely available work, is the part of the energy which can be arbitrarily used or, in other words, the entropy correlated it. In Fig. 1 it is given by the dark colored areas;
- *vagueness*, i.e., the corresponding *energy values* that *may or may not have been consumed*. In Fig. 1 are given by the gray colored areas; and
- *anergy*, that stands for an *energetic potential* that was not yet consumed, being therefore available, i.e., *all of energy that is not exergy*. In Fig. 1 it is given by the white colored areas.

**Table 1.** *IMTQ – 6* employee answer.

| Questions | Scale | | | | | | | vagueness |
|---|---|---|---|---|---|---|---|---|
| | (4) | (3) | (2) | (1) | (2) | (3) | (4) | |
| Q1 | | | | | × | | × | |
| Q2 | × | × | | | | | | |
| Q3 | | | | | × | × | | |
| Q4 | | | | | | × | | |
| Q5 | | | | | | | | × |
| Q6 | | | | | | × | | |

Leading to ⟶ **Fig. 1 and 2** ⟵ **Leading to**

These terms denote all possible energy's operations as pure energy's consume practices. Taking as example a group of 6 (six) questions that make the *Information Management Team Questionnaire-Six-Item (IMTQ – 6)*, viz.

*Q1* – Our IT organization is very familiar with our business strategy and our digital goals;

*Q2* – Our digital strategy is in line with our business strategy;

*Q3* – Our IT organization has a scaling strategy that can handle the additional data and traffic load or peaks at a reasonable cost;

*Q4* – Our IT organization has a strategy for efficient interaction and data exchange with business partners or the public;

*Q5* – Our IT organization has a problem-solving strategy or methodology that ensures the security of our IT systems and data; and

*Q6* – Our IT organization has an integration strategy that may give external parties access to our internal system

to assess whether the digital strategy and the digital goals are well defined and shared with the organization's employees, on the assumption that business and *IT* have a very good match, i.e., that high scores are to be found in the answers to the questionnaire, leading to positive results and benefits at the organizational level. In terms of the scale one may have, viz.

*strongly agree* (4), *agree* (3), *disagree* (2), *strongly disagree* (1), *disagree* (2), *agree* (3), *strongly agree* (4)

Moreover, it is included a neutral term, *neither agree nor disagree*, which stands for *uncertain* or *vague*. The reason for the individual's answers is in relation to the query:

As a member of your organization, how much would you agree with each one of IMTQ – 6 referred to above (Table 1)?

On the other hand, the process is graphically displayed for better understanding (Fig. 1 and Fig. 2).

Where the input for *Q1* means that he/she *strongly agrees* but does not rule out that he/she will *agree* in certain situations. The inputs are be read from left to right, from *strongly agree* to *strongly disagree* (with increasing entropy), or from *strongly disagree* to *strongly agree* (with decreasing entropy), i.e., the markers on the axis correspond to any of the possible scale options, which may be used from *bottom → top* (from *strongly agree* to *strongly disagree*), indicating that the performance of the system decreases as entropy increases, or is used from *top → bottom* (from *strongly disagree* to *strongly agree*), indicating that the performance of the system increases as entropy decreases). The contribution of each individual to the system entropic state as untainted energy is evaluated as shown in Table 2.

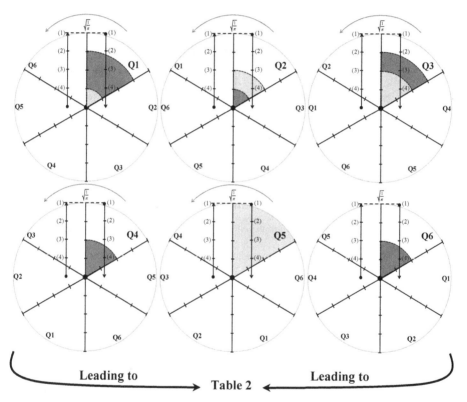

**Fig. 1.** A graphical representation of employee's answers to the *IMTQ – 6* questionnaire for the *Best-case scenario*.

However, once the performance of a system depends on its entropic state, the data collected above can be structured in terms of the extent of predicate *imtq – 6*, viz.

*imtq –* 6: *EXergy, VAgueness, System's Performance,*

*Quality-of-Information → {True, False}*

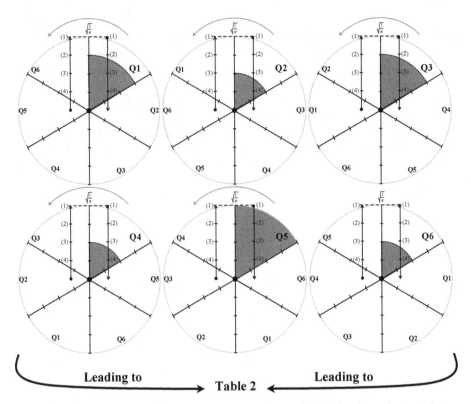

**Fig. 2.** A graphical representation of employee's answers to the *IMTQ – 6* questionnaire for the *Worst-case scenario*.

whose graphical depiction was given in Fig. 1 and Fig. 2, above. The corresponding logical program for the best-case scenario is given in Program 1. The values of *SP* and *QoI* presented in Table 3 for *IMTQ – 6* where evaluated as follow, viz.

- *SP* is figured out using $SP = \sqrt{1 - ES^2}$, where *ES* stands for an *exergy's* value in the *Best-case scenario* (i.e., $ES = exergy + vagueness$), a value that ranges in the interval $0\ldots1$ (Fig. 3).

$$SP = \sqrt{1 - (0.14 + 0.25)^2} = 0.92$$

- *QoI* is evaluated in the form, viz.

$$QoI = 1 - (exergy + vagueness) = 1 - (0.14 + 0.25) = 0.61$$

**Table 2.** *Best* and *Worst-Case's scenarios* assessment.

| Questions | Best Case Scenario | Worst Case Scenario |
|---|---|---|
| Q1 | $exergy_{Q_1} = \frac{1}{6}\pi r^2 \Big]_0^{\frac{1}{4}\sqrt{\frac{1}{\pi}}} =$ $= \frac{1}{6}\pi \left(\frac{1}{4}\sqrt{\frac{1}{\pi}}\right)^2 - 0 = 0.01$ | $exergy_{Q_1} = \frac{1}{6}\pi r^2 \Big]_0^{\frac{3}{4}\sqrt{\frac{1}{\pi}}} = 0.09$ |
| | $vagueness_{Q_1} = \frac{1}{6}\pi r^2 \Big]_0^{\frac{1}{4}\sqrt{\frac{1}{\pi}}} = 0.01$ | $vagueness_{Q_1} = \frac{1}{6}\pi r^2 \Big]_{\frac{1}{4}\sqrt{\frac{1}{\pi}}}^{\frac{1}{4}\sqrt{\frac{1}{\pi}}} = 0$ |
| | $anergy_{Q_1} = \frac{1}{6}\pi r^2 \Big]_{\frac{1}{4}\sqrt{\frac{1}{\pi}}}^{\sqrt{\frac{1}{\pi}}} = 0.16$ | $anergy_{Q_1} = \frac{1}{6}\pi r^2 \Big]_{\frac{3}{4}\sqrt{\frac{1}{\pi}}}^{\sqrt{\frac{1}{\pi}}} = 0.08$ |
| Q2 | $exergy_{Q2} = \frac{1}{6}\pi r^2 \Big]_0^{\frac{1}{4}\sqrt{\frac{1}{\pi}}} = 0.01$ | $exergy_{Q2} = \frac{1}{6}\pi r^2 \Big]_0^{\frac{2}{4}\sqrt{\frac{1}{\pi}}} = 0.04$ |
| | $vagueness_{Q2} = \frac{1}{6}\pi r^2 \Big]_{\frac{1}{4}\sqrt{\frac{1}{\pi}}}^{\frac{2}{4}\sqrt{\frac{1}{\pi}}}$ $= 0.03$ | $vagueness_{Q2} = \frac{1}{6}\pi r^2 \Big]_{\frac{2}{4}\sqrt{\frac{1}{\pi}}}^{\frac{2}{4}\sqrt{\frac{1}{\pi}}} = 0$ |
| | $anergy_{Q2} = \frac{1}{6}\pi r^2 \Big]_{\frac{1}{4}\sqrt{\frac{1}{\pi}}}^{\sqrt{\frac{1}{\pi}}} = 0.16$ | $anergy_{Q2} = \frac{1}{6}\pi r^2 \Big]_{\frac{2}{4}\sqrt{\frac{1}{\pi}}}^{\sqrt{\frac{1}{\pi}}} = 0.13$ |
| | The evaluation of Q3 is similar to Q1. | |
| Q4 | $exergy_{Q4} = \frac{1}{6}\pi r^2 \Big]_0^{\frac{2}{4}\sqrt{\frac{1}{\pi}}} = 0.04$ | $exergy_{Q4} = \frac{1}{6}\pi r^2 \Big]_0^{\frac{2}{4}\sqrt{\frac{1}{\pi}}} = 0.04$ |
| | $vagueness_{Q4} = \frac{1}{6}\pi r^2 \Big]_{\frac{2}{4}\sqrt{\frac{1}{\pi}}}^{\frac{2}{4}\sqrt{\frac{1}{\pi}}} = 0$ | $vagueness_{Q4} = \frac{1}{6}\pi r^2 \Big]_{\frac{2}{4}\sqrt{\frac{1}{\pi}}}^{\frac{2}{4}\sqrt{\frac{1}{\pi}}} = 0$ |
| | $anergy_{Q4} = \frac{1}{6}\pi r^2 \Big]_{\frac{2}{4}\sqrt{\frac{1}{\pi}}}^{\sqrt{\frac{1}{\pi}}} = 0.13$ | $anergy_{Q4} = \frac{1}{6}\pi r^2 \Big]_{\frac{2}{4}\sqrt{\frac{1}{\pi}}}^{\sqrt{\frac{1}{\pi}}} = 0.13$ |
| Q5 | $exergy_{Q5} = \frac{1}{6}\pi r^2 \Big]_0^0 = 0$ | $exergy_{Q5} = \frac{1}{6}\pi r^2 \Big]_0^{\sqrt{\frac{1}{\pi}}} = 0.17$ |
| | $vagueness_{Q5} = \frac{1}{6}\pi r^2 \Big]_0^{\sqrt{\frac{1}{\pi}}} = 0.17$ | $vagueness_{Q5} = \frac{1}{6}\pi r^2 \Big]_{\sqrt{\frac{1}{\pi}}}^{\sqrt{\frac{1}{\pi}}} = 0$ |
| | $anergy_{Q5} = \frac{1}{6}\pi r^2 \Big]_0^{\sqrt{\frac{1}{\pi}}} = 0.17$ | $anergy_{Q5} = \frac{1}{6}\pi r^2 \Big]_{\sqrt{\frac{1}{\pi}}}^{\sqrt{\frac{1}{\pi}}} = 0$ |
| | The evaluation of Q6 is similar to Q4. | |

Leading to → **Table 3** ← Leading to

**Table 3.** The scope of the *imtq-6* predicate from an employee's answer to the *IMTQ-6* questionnaire.

| Exergy BCS | Vague BCS | Anergy BCS | SP BCS | QoI BCS | Exergy WCS | Vague WCS | Anergy WCS | SP WCS | QoI WCS |
|---|---|---|---|---|---|---|---|---|---|
| 0.14 | 0.25 | 0.86 | 0.92 | 0.61 | 0.47 | 0 | 0.53 | 0.88 | 0.53 |

**Leading to** ⟶   **Table 5** ⟵   **Leading to**

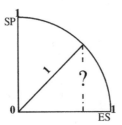

**Fig. 3.** *SP* evaluation.

# 3   Case Study

## 3.1   Digital Maturity Assessment

A string of tête-à-têtes can be carried out with service users, frontline employees, and executives in terms of skills, abilities, and governance. Along these lines one may visualize how mature each part of a company is and how ready it is for change. In fact, the first step in achieving *DT* starts with understanding the company's strengths and areas of improvement, i.e., departing with an assessment of where one's organization is will assist in the identification of the snags among different services and put in the picture further discussions. To help in doing just that one may need to answer to questions such as, viz.

*Q1 –  My organization understands the urgent need for digital transformation and the critical opportunities that digital technologies can offer snags;*

*Q2 –  My organization plans to implement an enterprise-wide strategy for digital transformation, such as the automation of core business activities or the conversion of the most important processes from analog to digital;*

*Q3 –  My organization has leaders, employees and suppliers to successfully implement a digital transformation strategy; and*

*Q4 –  There is a digital transformation strategy in my organization that is made available to employees, customers and partners and reviewed based on their feedback*

whose results are given in Table 4 and Table 5.

**Table 4.** Single answer to *DMAQ – 4* and *ENISAQ – 6* questionnaires.

| Questionnaire | Questions | (4) | (3) | (2) | (1) | (2) | (3) | (4) | *Vagueness* |
|---|---|---|---|---|---|---|---|---|---|
| | | | | | | *Scale* | | | |
| DMAQ – 4 | Q1 | | | | × | | × | | |
| | Q2 | × | | | | | | | |
| | Q3 | | | | | | | | × |
| | Q4 | | | | | | × | | |
| ENISAQ – 6 | Q1 | | | | | | × | × | |
| | Q2 | | | | | × | | | |
| | Q3 | | | × | × | | | | |
| | Q4 | | | | | | × | | |
| | Q5 | | | | | | | | × |
| | Q6 | | | × | × | | | | |

Leading to ⟶ **Table 5** ⟵ Leading to

**Table 5.** The *imtq – 6, dmaq – 4 and enisa – 6* results from an answer to the *IMTQ – 6, DMAQ – 4* and *ENISAQ – 6* questionnaires for the *Best* and *Worst-case* scenarios.

| Questionnaire | Exergy BCS | Vague BCS | Anergy BCS | SP BCS | QoI BCS | Exergy WCS | Vague WCS | Anergy BCS | SP WCS | QoI WCS |
|---|---|---|---|---|---|---|---|---|---|---|
| **IMTQ – 6** | 0.14 | 0.25 | 0.86 | 0.92 | 0.61 | 0.47 | 0 | 0.53 | 0.88 | 0.53 |
| **DMAQ – 4** | 0.28 | 0.42 | 0.72 | 0.71 | 0.30 | 0.75 | 0 | 0.25 | 0.66 | 0.25 |
| **ENISAQ – 6** | 0.34 | 0.12 | 0.66 | 0.93 | 0.54 | 0.78 | 0 | 0.22 | 0.62 | 0.22 |

Leading to ⟶ **Program 1** ⟵ Leading to

## 3.2 The Possible Role of an EU Body in the Future EU Cybersecurity Landscape

Given that it is always very difficult to predict how people, businesses and industries will explain the full potential of a new technology, how does one explain the tremendous political importance of this topic? Indeed, what we are seeing now is a possible reconfiguration of global commerce, the disputing for the technological and geopolitical leadership of the information age, where security reasons are paramount, and this is the issue that is now called in. Therefore, the following is a questionnaire to assess and review the role of the *European Union Network and Information Security Agency (ENISA)*, highlighting some gaps and needs in this digital revolution, i.e., providing insights on which guidelines must be account for, and in particular on the development or repositioning of standards in the context of the *European Union (EU) Network and Information Security Directive (NIS Directive)*, viz.

*Q1 – Developing and maintaining a high level of cybersecurity expertise;*

*Q2 – Supporting the development of EU policies;*

*Q3 – Supporting the implementation of EU policies;*

*Q4 – Supporting the EU institutions, agencies and bodies in strengthening their capacity and willingness to prevent, detect and respond to network and information security problems and incidents;*

*Q5 – Assisting Member States in strengthening their ability and willingness to prevent, detect and respond to network and information security problems and incidents; and*

*Q6 – Supporting cybersecurity community cooperation (e.g., through public-private cooperation, information exchange, community building, coordination of Cyber Europe exercise)*

whose results are given in Table 4 and Table 5.

Or, in other words, how does one see the future role of ENISA in addressing these gaps and needs?

### 3.3  Computational Make-Up

One's work that went step-by-step to understand the problem and come up with a solution was possible due to the power of *Computational Logic*, or *Computational Thinking*, i.e., a term that describes the decision-making progress used in programming and to turn up with algorithms. Here it is used deduction, i.e., starting from a conjecture and, according to a fixed set of relations (axioms and inference rules), try to construct a proof of the conjecture. It is a creative process. *Computational Logic* works with a proof search for a defined strategy. If one knows what this strategy is, one may implement certain algorithms in logic and do the algorithms with proof-finding [9].

**Program 1.** The extent of *imtq – 6*, *dmaq – 4* and *enisaq – 6* predicates for the *Best-case scenario.*

{

/* *The sentence below states that the extent of predicate imtq – 6 is made on the clauses that are explicitly stated plus the ones that cannot be discarded* */

$\neg\, imtq - 6\,(EX, VA, AN, SP, QoI) \leftarrow not\, imtq - 6\,(EX, VA, AN, SP, QoI),$

$$not\, abducible_{imtq-6}\,(EX, VA, AN, SP, QoI)$$

/* *the sentence below denotes an imtq–6's axiom* */

$imtq - 6\,(0.14, 0.25, 0.86,\ 0.92,\ 0.61).$

$\neg\, dmaq - 4\,(EX, VA, AN, SP, QoI) \leftarrow not\, dmaq - 4\,(EX, VA, AN, SP, QoI),$

$$not\, abducible_{dmaq-4}\,(EX, VA, AN, SP, QoI)$$

$dmaq - 4\,(0.28, 0.42, 0.72,\ 0.71,\ 0.30).$

$\neg\, enisaq - 6\,(EX, VA, AN, SP, QoI) \leftarrow not\, enisaq - 6\,(EX, VA, AN, SP, QoI),$

$$not\, abducible_{enisaq-6}\,(EX, VA, AN, SP, QoI)$$

$enisaq - 6\,(0.34, 0.12, 0.66,\ 0.93,\ 0.54).$

}

where $\neg$ denotes *strong negation* and *not* stands for *negation-by-failure*. It is now possible to generate the data sets that will allow one to train an *ANN* (Fig. 4), where the extent of predicates *imtq – 6*, *dmaq – 4*, and *enisaq – 6* are used to build the input to the *ANN*, that presents as output an evaluation of the *Organization Digital Transformation Stage* plus a measure of its *Sustainability* (*QoI*). With a group of 20 (twenty) workers, the *ANN* training sets may be obtained by making the sentence depicted below obvious (i.e., object of formal proof), viz.

$$\forall(EX_1, VA_1, AN_1, SP_1, QoI_1, \cdots, EX_3, VA_3, AN_3, SP_3, QoI_3),$$
$$\left(imtq - 6(EX_1, VA_1, AN_1, SP_1, QoI_1),\, dmaq - 4(EX_2, VA_2, AN_2, SP_2, QoI_2),\right.$$
$$\left. enisaq - 6(EX_3, VA_3, AN_3, SP_3, QoI_3)\right)$$

in every possible way, therefore generating all the different possible sequences that combine the extent of predicates $imtq - 6$, $dmq - 4$, and $enisaq - 6$, leading to a number of 1140 sets that are presented in the form, viz.

$$\{\{imtq - 6(EX_1, VA_1, AN_1, SP_1, QoI_1), dmaq - 4(EX_2, VA_2, AN_2, SP_2, QoI_2),$$
$$enisaq - 6(EX_3, VA_3, AN_3, SP_3, QoI_3)\}, \cdots\}$$
$$\approx \{\{(imtq - 6(0.14, 0.25, 0.80, 0.92, 0.61), dmaq - 4(0.28, 0.42, 0.68, 0.71, 0.30),$$
$$enisaq - 6(0.34, 0.12, 0.73, 0.93, 0.54)\}, \cdots\}$$

where $\{\}$ is the expression for sets and $\approx$ stands for itself. With respect to the output of the *ANN*, output values include both the *Digital Transformation Stage* (*DTS*) of the organization and its *Sustainability* (*QoI*), which are evaluated in the form, viz.

$$\{\{(SP_{imtq-6} + SP_{dmaq-4} + SP_{enisa-6})/3\}, \cdots\}$$
$$\approx \{\{(0.92 + 0.71 + 0.93)/3 = 0.85\}, \cdots\}$$

and, viz.

$$\{\{(QoI_{imtq-6} + QoI_{dmaq-4} + QoI_{enisaq-6})/3\}, \cdots\}$$
$$\approx \{\{(0.61 + 0.30 + 0.54)/3 = 0.48\}, \cdots\}$$

With this tool or agency one can study the basics, i.e., focus on changing the way people think and amending organizational culture and processes before deciding which digital tools to buy and how to use them. What members think about the future of the organization will drive technology, not the other way around.

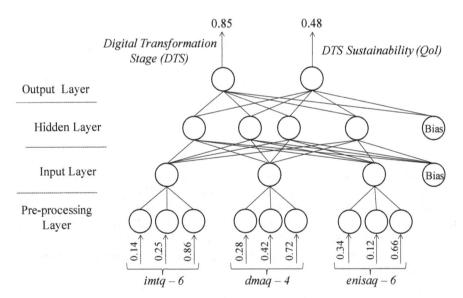

**Fig. 4.** A creative (abstract) view of the *ANN* topology for *DTS* assessment.

# 4  Conclusions

Worldwide, *DT* is accelerating. The private and public sectors continue to invest in disruptive technologies to stand out from the irrelevance, adapting their business models to rising customer expectations and public satisfaction. The pace of change continues to blur the boundaries of the physical and digital worlds, redefining the traditional industries and the public services and the way one lives and works. New technologies, growing amounts of data, and smarter ways to gain insights are changing the way people, businesses, and governments interact. One has to change the way of living, accept new challenges, adapt to new experiences, develop new behavioral, cognitive, and emotional responses. In fact, a human's adaptive performance becomes a key factor in maintaining persistence throughout the *DT* path, which must be mathematically evaluated and formally substantiated in real time. This was the main objective of this work, delivered as a computational agency that integrates the phases of data gathering, anticipating a logic representation of uncertainty and vagueness, plus the stages of data processing and results' analysis. In the future work, a vision of multivalued logic is to be pursued, a topic that has just been addressed here.

**Acknowledgements.** This work has been supported by national funds through FCT – Fundação para a Ciência e Tecnologia within the Project Scope UID/CEC/00319/2019 and UID/QUI/0619/2019.

# References

1. Fitzgerald, M., Kruschwitz, N., Bonnet, D., Welch, M.: Embracing Digital Technology: A New Strategic Imperative. MIT Sloan Management Review, Research Report, 12 p. (2013)
2. Ross, J., et al.: Designing Digital Organizations. CISR Working Paper N° 406, 19 p. (2016)
3. Matt, C., Hess, T., Benlian, A.: Digital transformation strategies. Bus. Inf. Syst. Eng. **57**(5), 339–343 (2015)
4. Zinder, E., Yunatova, I.: Synergy for digital transformation: person's multiple roles and subject domains integration. In: Chugunov, A.V., Bolgov, R., Kabanov, Y., Kampis, G., Wimmer, M. (eds.) DTGS 2016. CCIS, vol. 674, pp. 155–168. Springer, Cham (2016). https://doi.org/10.1007/978-3-319-49700-6_16
5. Neves, J., et al.: Entropy and organizational performance. In: Pérez García, H., Sánchez González, L., Castejón Limas, M., Quintián Pardo, H., Corchado Rodríguez, E. (eds.) HAIS 2019. LNCS (LNAI), vol. 11734, pp. 206–217. Springer, Cham (2019). https://doi.org/10.1007/978-3-030-29859-3_18
6. Cortez, P., Rocha, M., Neves, J.: Evolving time series forecasting ARMA models. J. Heuristics **10**, 415–429 (2004)
7. Fernández-Delgado, M., Cernadas, E., Barro, S., Ribeiro, J., Neves, J.: Direct Kernel Perceptron (DKP): ultra-fast kernel ELM-based classification with non-iterative closed-form weight calculation. J. Neural Netw. **50**, 60–71 (2014)
8. Wenterodt, T., Herwig, H.: The entropic potential concept: a new way to look at energy transfer operations. Entropy **16**, 2071–2084 (2014)
9. Neves, J.: A logic interpreter to handle time and negation in logic databases. In: Muller, R., Pottmyer, J. (eds.) Proceedings of the 1984 Annual Conference of the ACM on the 5th Generation Challenge, pp. 50–54. Association for Computing Machinery, New York (1984)

# CNN Pre-initialization by Minimalistic Part-Learning for Handwritten Numeral Recognition

Seba Susan$^{(\boxtimes)}$ (iD) and Jatin Malhotra

Department of Information Technology, Delhi Technological University,
Bawana Road, Delhi 110042, India
seba_406@yahoo.in

**Abstract.** The performance of all types of neural networks is affected by initialization of weights since most of these networks follow some form of the derivative gradient descent algorithm for weight optimization that tends to get trapped in local minima. A new scheme is presented in our work for initializing the weights of Convolutional Neural Networks (CNNs) by part-learning using only 5% of the training data, in a minimalistic approach. The problem at hand is the classification of handwritten numeral images. The parts that are learned, by two-way CNNs, comprise of the top-half and bottom-half of the numeral image respectively, with the second half of the image kept masked. The two set of weights initialized in this manner are respectively fine-tuned on the remaining 95% training images. The probabilistic softmax scores of the two CNNs are fused in the last stage to decide the test label. Our work validates the theory inspired from human cognition that learning in stages with increasing size and complexity of the training data improves the performance over time, rather than training on the complete dataset at one go. Experiments on the benchmark MNIST handwritten English numeral dataset yield high accuracies as compared to the state of the art.

**Keywords:** Convolutional Neural Network · Part-learning · Handwritten numeral recognition

## 1 Introduction

The advent of Convolutional Neural Networks (CNNs) brought about a revolution in the field of pattern recognition. Deep CNNs constitute the state of the art these days in all applications involving image and video processing such as face and object recognition [1], tracking activities over time [2] and multimedia content analysis [3]. CNNs employ filters at initial levels to extract low-level features such as textures and in higher layers for extracting the higher-level features such as specific shapes associated with the objects in the scene. The weights of CNNs are still being trained by the conventional gradient descent algorithm which is a derivative approach and the one used to train the conventional artificial neural network (ANN) [4]. These weights are randomly initialized at the beginning of the iterative training process. The initialization of network weights

© Springer Nature Switzerland AG 2020
B. R. Purushothama et al. (Eds.): MIKE 2019, LNAI 11987, pp. 320–329, 2020.
https://doi.org/10.1007/978-3-030-66187-8_30

affects the network performance, as proved in the case of the perceptron network in [5]. Alternatives have been suggested such as weight optimization by Particle Swarm Optimization [5], Genetic Algorithm [6] and newer metaheuristics like Whale Optimization algorithm [7] etc. that claim convergence to global minima at the cost of an increased computational complexity. However, the majority of the neural networks today still rely on the derivative backpropagation algorithm for weight optimization, that is sensitive to initialization. Optimal initialization of CNN weights has not been researched well enough in literature, since the focus has ever been on designing CNN architectures that gave high performance. In this paper, we address the problem of pre-initialization of CNN weights via the process of part-learning in which a part of the image is exposed to the part-specific CNN, using only 5% of the training data, in a minimalistic approach. The soft outputs of multiple CNNs are fused to decide on the class label. The organization of this paper is as follows: the CNN architecture, pre-initialization and part-learning concepts are reviewed in Sect. 2, the proposed part-learning is described in Sect. 3 along with the methodology. Section 4 presents the experimentation and the results and Sect. 5 draws the conclusions.

## 2 Convolutional Neural Network, Pre-initialization and Part-Learning-The Motivation for Our Work

### 2.1 Convolutional Neural Network (CNN) and Pre-initialization

Convolutional neural network (CNN) is the current state of the art for processing images and video. It accepts a 2D image input and filters out information through stages of convolutional layers, Rectified Linear Unit (ReLU) activation function and Pooling layer, terminated by a stage of one or more fully connected layers and an output softmax layer that predicts the class label [8]. Figure 1 shows a general CNN architecture.

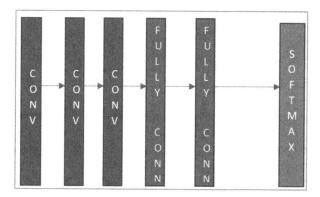

**Fig. 1.** A general CNN architecture

ReLU induces non-linearity in the filtered output and speeds up training. The Pooling layer downsamples the filtered (and rectified) signal using a Max or Average (Avg) function applied on a small sub-region of the filtered output. The aim is to increase the computational speed and to reduce over-fitting. The fully connected layer receives the flattened features as input and learns on similar lines as the Multi-Layer Perceptron ANN while training. The output layer is a softmax classifier that interprets the output label in the form of probability values, where the sum of all class probabilities is one. An intelligent combination of all these layers with careful selection of hyperparameters constitute the high-performance deep networks trending today.

## 2.2   Pre-initialization of CNNs

The weights of a CNN are the unknown parameters to be determined in any experiment. Conventionally, a derivative-based optimization algorithm like gradient decent is used for optimizing the weights. Such algorithms require the weights to be randomly initialized prior to the iterative procedure. In [9], it was stated that random weight initialization of CNNs is advisable rather than assigning zero initial weights. CNNs following this paradigm are known to be 'trained from scratch' [10]. Alternatively, pre-trained Deep CNNs can be used, that facilitate transfer learning from one domain (ImageNet object database) to other domains and applications such as the classification of medical images [11]. The weights of pre-trained Deep CNNs are pre-initialized while training on the ImageNet database. Hence the user fine-tunes the already trained weights to suit a particular application, yielding high performance for many computer vision problems [12, 13]. Pre-initialization of neural network weights, without crossing domains, is suggested in [14] as an optional hierarchical learning strategy for increasing the performance. This involves successive hierarchical training in stages, initially for smaller data subsets at lower data complexity levels, and later on, for larger training data subsets at increased data complexity. This is the learning approach followed in our current research on handwritten numeral recognition, that is described in greater detail in subsequent sections.

## 2.3   Learning from Image Parts

An improved learning performance has been observed, in several prior works, when subsets or parts of the image are learnt rather than the whole image itself. The most prevalent of these are patch-learning techniques, where image windows or image patches are cropped, processed and learned by a suitable classifier [15–17]. This approach is affine-invariant and immune to background clutter, to some extent. As the number of patches increase, the computational complexity also increases, and in most cases, an exhaustive annotation process for the patches is required. The application of patch-learning to handwritten numeral recognition is not investigated enough with some rare examples being the so-called 'box-partitioning' methods in [18, 19], possibly because image windows in handwritten numeral images are not semantically defined as in the cases of object detection and classification. Image patches are usually represented by patch-level feature vectors that are learned by suitable classifiers. In object detection experiments, class-specific image parts represented by HOG feature vectors are learnt with the help of a discriminative support vector machine in [20], followed by discriminative clustering that segregates the foreground from the background. A two-stream CNN was used in

[21] to compare image patches in a brute-force manner. Parallel processing of patches was done using two CNNs with a common fully connected layer at the output.

A previous work by the authors implements handwritten numeral recognition by fusing the hidden state activations emanating from five multi-layer perceptron neural networks that are trained separately on five image quadrants [27]. The final concatenated feature vector is used for training the Support Vector Machine classifier. This approach was adapted recently by the authors for recognizing symbols from the ancient Indic script Devanagari [28], where a separate 2D convolutional neural network was trained on each of the five image quadrants. As an extension to our investigations in [27, 28] that involved feature-level fusion, in the current work, we propose half-part learning of numeral images for weight pre-initialization of two separate CNNs with decision fusion of the probabilistic scores; the proposed scheme is explained in greater detail in Sect. 3.

## 3 Proposed CNN Pre-initialization by Minimalistic Part-Learning for Handwritten Numeral Recognition

### 3.1 Our CNN Architecture

The proposed CNN architecture for our experiments is given in Fig. 2. The details of the convolutional layers with the dropout and max-pooling layers interspersed in between, are outlined in Table 1. A 3 × 3 filter is used for all the convolutional layers. The three dropout layers have a dropout ratio of 0.25, 0.25 and 0.50 respectively.

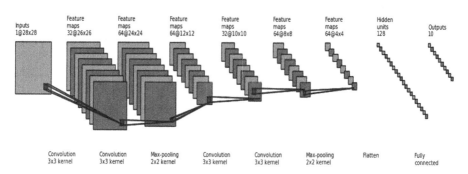

**Fig. 2.** CNN architecture for our experiments

### 3.2 Proposed Methodology for Minimalistic Part-Learning of Numeral Images

Inspired by the paradigm of hierarchical learning in small quantities starting from lower complexities of data, similar to the way humans learn, we devise a two-stage learning process in which parts of the image are first learnt by different CNNs and they, later on, fine-tune their knowledge by training on the remaining images after the weights are pre-initialized. The outputs of the separately trained CNNs are probabilistically combined in the decision phase. The proposed learning model is shown in Fig. 3.

**Table 1.** Chronological order of layers and the associated parameters of the CNN in Fig. 2

| Layer (type) | Output Shape | Param # |
|---|---|---|
| conv2d_1 (Conv2D) | (None, 26, 26, 32) | 320 |
| conv2d_2 (Conv2D) | (None, 24, 24, 64) | 18496 |
| max_pooling2d_1 (MaxPooling2 | (None, 12, 12, 64) | 0 |
| dropout_1 (Dropout) | (None, 12, 12, 64) | 0 |
| conv2d_3 (Conv2D) | (None, 10, 10, 32) | 18464 |
| conv2d_4 (Conv2D) | (None, 8, 8, 64) | 18496 |
| max_pooling2d_2 (MaxPooling2 | (None, 4, 4, 64) | 0 |
| dropout_2 (Dropout) | (None, 4, 4, 64) | 0 |
| flatten_1 (Flatten) | (None, 1024) | 0 |
| dense_1 (Dense) | (None, 128) | 131200 |
| dropout_3 (Dropout) | (None, 128) | 0 |
| dense_2 (Dense) | (None, 10) | 1290 |

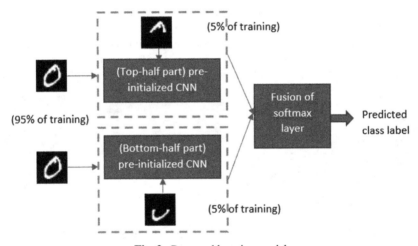

**Fig. 3.** Proposed learning model

The steps of the proposed methodology, pertaining to the model in Fig. 3, are summarized below.

1. Pre-initialize two duplicate CNNs 1 and 2, each having the architecture shown in Fig. 2 and Table 1, with 5% of the training data.
a. Train CNN1 with the top-half image parts.
b. Train CNN2 with the bottom-half image parts.

2. Fine-tune the weights of the two CNNs separately using the remaining 95% of the training data. This marks the completion of the training stage.
3. For a test sample, fuse the outputs of CNN1 and CNN2 by averaging the respective probabilistic softmax scores for each class, and alternatively, by taking the maximum of the two softmax scores for each class.
4. The maximum (fused) probabilistic score among the ten numeral classes indicates the class of the test label.

## 4   Experimental Results

### 4.1   Experimental Setup

The experiments are performed on handwritten numeral images from the MNIST dataset [22] for handwritten English numerals. Handwritten numeral images, for most languages, are divided into ten numeral classes representing the digits 0 to 9. There are 80K images in MNIST dataset, out of which 60K are segregated for training and 10K for testing, at the source itself. The images input to the CNN are of size 28 × 28. The masked images (top-half and bottom-half) used for CNN initialization are shown in Fig. 4 for each numeral category. We repeat the experiment with both 5% and 10% of the training data, for pre-initialization. The remaining 95% and 90% of the training set, respectively, are used for fine-tuning the pre-trained weights.

**Fig. 4.** MNIST numeral images: (i) Original image (ii) Image containing the top-half (to CNN1) (ii) Image containing the bottom-half (to CNN2)

### 4.2   Results Analysis

We implement the proposed model with both 5% and 10% of the training data, for pre-initialization. The software implementation of our model is provided online at [29]. Our results on the MNIST dataset are shown in Table 2. The percentage of correct classification (test accuracy in %) is the evaluation criterion. The best results are observed to be for the fusion of probability scores emanating from the two CNNs, from Table 2.

The results of some existing learning models on MNIST data are summarized in Table 3, for comparison purpose. These constitute some of the state-of-the art methods on deep learning prevalent in the field of computer vision and image processing.

**Table 2.** Implementation results (in percentage (%) accuracy) for the proposed model in Fig. 3 with 5% and 10% of the training data on the 10K test images of the MNIST dataset (Highlighted value in bold indicates the best performance)

| Method | Test accuracy (5% training for pre-initialization; 95% for fine-tuning) | Test accuracy (10% training for pre-initialization; 90% for fine-tuning) | Test accuracy (without pre-initialization and random initialization of weights) |
|---|---|---|---|
| Proposed CNN model (*Top-half part*) | 99.5% | 99.48% | 99.44% |
| Proposed CNN model (*Bottom-half part*) | 99.48% | 99.51% | 99.44% |
| Proposed CNN model (*after fusion of scores from both parts-AVERAGE*) | 99.53% | 99.55% | 99.44% |
| Proposed CNN model (*after fusion of scores from both parts-MAXIMUM*) | **99.56%** | 99.53% | 99.44% |

**Table 3.** Comparison to the state of the art for 10K test images of the MNIST dataset

| Method | Test accuracy |
|---|---|
| Interpretable deep CNN [23] | 92.8% |
| Deep representation learning with target coding [24] | 85.5% |
| Deep neural net + Hadamard code [24] | 84.85% |
| ReNet deep recurrent network [25] | 99.55% |
| Very deep CNN model [26] | 99.55% |

As observed, the proposed method gives high accuracies that supersede the performance of the complex (and deep) state of the art presented in Table 3, with the highest accuracies of 99.56% obtained by our method in Table 2. Fusion of the softmax scores emanating from the CNNs pre-trained on individual parts by taking the maximum of the two softmax scores, is observed to be more accurate than averaging the softmax scores. The 5% pre-training is overall found superior in performance to the 10% pre-training, as evident from the accuracies in Table 2. Hence, based on a minimalistic training approach (of 5% pre-training only), the CNN weights are pre-initialized to optimal values that gave higher performance. Learning by parts thus enhances the model performance. The performance of individual CNNs are lower than the fused result of two CNNs, as noted from the first two rows of Table 2. Our work thus validates the theory that learning hierarchically in stages, with increasing size and complexity of the training data, improves the performance, rather than training a single network on the complete dataset at one go. The methodology presented in this paper can be applied to CNNs of any complexity, as well as complex datasets, and for exploring optimal complexity of CNNs for various applications other than handwritten numeral recognition. This forms the future scope of the current work.

## 5  Conclusions

A novel learning paradigm for handwritten numeral images is proposed in this work that initializes CNNs by learning image parts in a pre-initialization phase using only 5% of the training data. Two image parts: the top-half and bottom-half are selected for initializing the weights of the two-way CNNs used in our model. The CNNs so trained are fine-tuned on the remaining 95% training images. The scores of the two CNNs are fused using the average/maximum function to predict the class label of the test sample. The use of maximum function is found more suited to our application. High accuracies that supersede the state of the art confirm the efficacy of our approach. Our work validates the theory inspired from human cognition, that learning in stages, with increasing size and complexity of the training data, improves the performance over time rather than training on the complete dataset at one go. Future scope involves adapting our learning paradigm to more fields and application areas of computer vision.

## References

1. Bansal, A., Ranjan, R., Castillo, C.D., Chellappa, R.: Deep features for recognizing disguised faces in the wild. In: Proceedings of the IEEE Conference on Computer Vision and Pattern Recognition Workshops, pp. 10–16 (2018)
2. Wang, J., Chen, Y., Hao, S., Peng, X., Lisha, H.: Deep learning for sensor-based activity recognition: a survey. Pattern Recogn. Lett. **119**, 3–11 (2019)
3. Shamsolmoali, P., Kumar Jain, D., Zareapoor, M., Yang, J., Afshar Alam, M.: High-dimensional multimedia classification using deep CNN and extended residual units. Multimedia Tools Appl. **78**(17), 23867–23882 (2018). https://doi.org/10.1007/s11042-018-6146-7
4. Susan, S., Dwivedi, M.: Dynamic growth of hidden-layer neurons using the non-extensive entropy. In: 2014 Fourth International Conference on Communication Systems and Network Technologies, pp. 491–495. IEEE (2014)
5. Susan, S., Ranjan, R., Taluja, U., Rai, S., Agarwal, P.: Neural net optimization by weight-entropy monitoring. In: Verma, N., Ghosh, A. (eds.) Computational Intelligence: Theories, Applications and Future Directions -, vol. II, pp. 201–213. Springer, Singapore (2019). https://doi.org/10.1007/978-981-13-1135-2_16
6. Montana, D.J., Davis, L.: Training feedforward neural networks using genetic algorithms. IJCAI **89**, 762–767 (1989)
7. Aljarah, I., Faris, H., Mirjalili, S.: Optimizing connection weights in neural networks using the whale optimization algorithm. Soft. Comput. **22**(1), 1–15 (2016). https://doi.org/10.1007/s00500-016-2442-1

8. Krizhevsky, A., Sutskever, I., Hinton, G.E.: Imagenet classification with deep convolutional neural networks. In: Advances in Neural Information Processing Systems, pp. 1097–1105 (2012)
9. Dewa, C.K.: Suitable CNN weight initialization and activation function for javanese vowels classification. Procedia Comput. Sci. **144**, 124–132 (2018)
10. Saini, M., Susan, S.: Comparison of deep learning, data augmentation and bag of-visual-words for classification of imbalanced image datasets. In: Santosh, K.C., Hegadi, Ravindra S. (eds.) RTIP2R 2018. CCIS, vol. 1035, pp. 561–571. Springer, Singapore (2019). https://doi.org/10.1007/978-981-13-9181-1_49
11. Saini, M., Susan, S.: Deep transfer with minority data augmentation for imbalanced breast cancer dataset. Appl. Soft Comput. **97**, 106759 (2020)
12. Carneiro, G., Nascimento, J., Bradley, Andrew P.: Unregistered multiview mammogram analysis with pre-trained deep learning models. In: Navab, N., Hornegger, J., Wells, William M., Frangi, Alejandro F. (eds.) MICCAI 2015. LNCS, vol. 9351, pp. 652–660. Springer, Cham (2015). https://doi.org/10.1007/978-3-319-24574-4_78
13. Bulat, A., Tzimiropoulos, G., Kossaifi, J., Pantic, M.: Improved training of binary networks for human pose estimation and image recognition. arXiv preprint arXiv:1904.05868 (2019)
14. Bishop, C.M.: Neural Networks for Pattern Recognition. Oxford University Press, Oxford (1995)
15. Tang, P., Wang, X., Huang, Z., Bai, X., Liu, W.: Deep patch learning for weakly supervised object classification and discovery. Pattern Recogn. **71**, 446–459 (2017)
16. Lin, W., Zhang, Y., Jiwen, L., Zhou, B., Wang, J., Zhou, Yu.: Summarizing surveillance videos with local-patch-learning-based abnormality detection, blob sequence optimization, and type-based synopsis. Neurocomputing **155**, 84–98 (2015)
17. Susan, S., Sethi, D., Arora, K.: CW-CAE: pulmonary nodule detection from imbalanced dataset using class-weighted convolutional autoencoder. In: Gupta, D., Khanna, A., Bhattacharyya, S., Hassanien, A.E., Anand, S., Jaiswal, A. (eds.) International Conference on Innovative Computing and Communications. AISC, vol. 1166, pp. 825–833. Springer, Singapore (2021). https://doi.org/10.1007/978-981-15-5148-2_71
18. Susan, S., Singh, V.: On the discriminative power of different feature subsets for handwritten numeral recognition using the box-partitioning method. In: 2011 Annual IEEE India Conference, pp. 1–5. IEEE (2011)
19. Huang, F.-A., Su, C.-Y., Chu, T.-T.: Kinect-based mid-air handwritten digit recognition using multiple segments and scaled coding. In: 2013 International Symposium on Intelligent Signal Processing and Communication Systems, pp. 694–697. IEEE (2013)
20. Sun, J., Ponce, J.: Learning discriminative part detectors for image classification and cosegmentation. In: Proceedings of the IEEE International Conference on Computer Vision, pp. 3400–3407 (2013)
21. Zagoruyko, S., Komodakis, N.: Learning to compare image patches via convolutional neural networks. In: Proceedings of the IEEE Conference on Computer Vision and Pattern Recognition, pp. 4353–4361 (2015)
22. LeCun, Y., Bottou, L., Bengio, Y., Haffner, P.: Gradient-based learning applied to document recognition. Proc. IEEE **86**(11), 2278–2324 (1998)
23. Liu, X., Wang, X., Matwin, S.: Interpretable deep convolutional neural networks via meta-learning. In: 2018 International Joint Conference on Neural Networks (IJCNN), pp. 1–9. IEEE (2018)
24. Yang, S., Luo, P., Loy, C.C., Shum, K.W., Tang, X.: Deep representation learning with target coding. In: Twenty-Ninth AAAI Conference on Artificial Intelligence (2015)
25. Visin, F., Kastner, K., Cho, K., Matteucci, M., Courville, A., Bengio, Y.: ReNet: a recurrent neural network based alternative to convolutional networks. arXiv preprint arXiv:1505.00393 (2015)

26. Srivastava, R.K., Greff, K., Schmidhuber, J.: Training very deep networks. In: Advances in Neural Information Processing Systems, pp. 2377–2385 (2015)
27. Susan, S., Malhotra, J.: Learning interpretable hidden state structures for handwritten numeral recognition. In: 2020 4th International Conference on Computational Intelligence and Networks (CINE), pp. 1–6. IEEE (2020)
28. Susan, S., Malhotra, J.: Recognising devanagari script by deep structure learning of image quadrants. DESIDOC J. Libr. Inf. Technol. **40**(5), 268–271 (2020)
29. https://github.com/JMalhotra7/CNN-Pre-Initialization-by-Minimalistic-Part-Learning-for-Handwritten-Numeral-Recognition. Accessed 20 Dec 2019

# GlosysIC Framework: Transformer for Image Captioning with Sequential Attention

Srinivasan Thanukrishnan$^{(\boxtimes)}$, R. Sai Venkatesh, and Prasad Rao Vijay Vignesh

Glosys Artificial Intelligence Research, Glosys Technology Solutions Private Limited,
Chennai, India
tsrini1969@gmail.com, venkysai.96@gmail.com,
vijayvigneshp02@gmail.com

**Abstract.** Over the past decade, the field of Image captioning has witnessed a lot of intensive research interests. This paper proposes "GlosysIC Framework: Transformer for Image Captioning with Sequential Attention" to build a novel framework that harnesses the combination of Convolutional Neural Network (CNN) to encode image and transformer to generate sentences. Compared to the existing image captioning approaches, GlosysIC framework serializes the Multi head attention modules with the image representations. Furthermore, we present GlosysIC architectural framework encompassing multiple CNN architectures and attention based transformer for generating effective descriptions of images. The proposed system was exhaustively trained on the benchmark MSCOCO image captioning dataset using RTX 2060 GPU and V 100 GPU from Google Cloud Platform in terms of PyTorch Deep Learning library. Experimental results illustrate that GlosysIC significantly outperforms the previous state-of-the-art models.

**Keywords:** Convolutional neural network · Transformer · Embedder · Positional encoder · Sequential attention

## 1 Introduction

Image Captioning is the process of automatically describing an image with an appropriate sentence. It incorporates two seemingly discrete concepts - Computer Vision and Natural Language Processing and hence, is a complex task. But recent advances in each of these domains have efficiently improved the performance of image captioning algorithms.

The most commonly used image captioning algorithm involves using an encoder-decoder framework, shown in Fig. 1, which came into usage with the emergence of many successful models [1, 5, 6, 8, 9, 11, 12, 17, 18, 19, 24]. These architectures employ Convolutional Neural Network (CNN) as the encoder and Recurrent Neural Network (RNN) as the decoder. CNN, essentially, is used to obtain the feature matrix from an image. The effectiveness of CNN is established by how well the feature matrix is able

---

S. Thanukrishnan—CEO & Director.
R. S. Venkatesh and P. Vijay Vignesh—Research Intern.

B. R. Purushothama et al. (Eds.): MIKE 2019, LNAI 11987, pp. 330–340, 2020.
https://doi.org/10.1007/978-3-030-66187-8_31

to capture the information from the given image. The efficiency of CNN decreases as the loss of information increases. Traditional RNN's are incapable of retaining long term dependencies. Although Long Short Term Memory (LSTM) [7] has addressed this disadvantage it is slow because of its increased complexity in computation. Moreover, it also neglects word-to-word self-attention. To overcome both these disadvantages, we use a modified version of the transformer. Our model not only reduces the complexity and incorporates self-attention, but also serializes the attention from more than one encoder, which proves to be effective in generating captions.

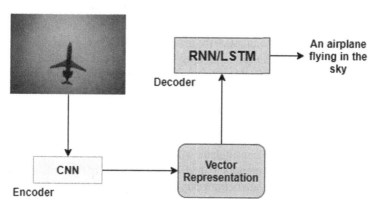

**Fig. 1. The Encoder-Decoder model.** Here, CNN is used as the encoder. The vector representation from the encoder is fed to the decoder, which comes up with an appropriate sentence based on the image feature matrix.

To summarize, the contribution of this study is two-fold:

- Our first proposal is to incorporate multiple CNN architectures. We observe that using more than one encoder significantly improves performance. We have utilized a combination of three CNN architectures, though, our model can be generalized to use *n* encoders.
- Our model also utilizes a sequential attention-based transformer. In this version, attended features from one sub-layer is sequentially passed on to the next.

The rest of the paper is organized as follows. Section 2 highlights the related work. Section 3 describes our proposed methodology. Section 4 delineates the performance comparison along with the experimental results to contrast the proposed strategy with other models. Finally, concluding remarks and future work is given in Sect. 5.

## 2   Related Work

In this section, we look into the various existing architectures and their efficacy in generating befitting captions. [11] uses a combination of VGGnet as the encoder and LSTM as the decoder. The image is converted into a one-dimensional array using the encoder and sent to the LSTM, which then builds the sentence. [12], effectively, replaces the one-dimensional vector with a two-dimensional vector and incorporates 'hard' and 'soft' attention to generate the appropriate descriptions. [17] applies three modules, i.e., Attention, Inference, and Generation modules in order to form captions from the images.

[18] computes a set of attributes from the images. These attributes are generated based on commonly used words in image captions, thereby, reducing the vocabulary size. The problem is, now, treated as a multi-label classification problem and a fixed-length vector is generated. This vector is then injected into the LSTM to construct captions. [20] uses Resnet101 to extract visual features. These features are then, parallelly, sent across two attention modules, i.e., conventional top-down attention, and stimulus-based attention. These two modules of attention are merged and, finally, incorporated into the language generation module to annotate the image. The recent breakthrough in Language Generation and, eventually, image captioning came with the invention of Transformer [4]. [21] encompasses a basic CNN as the encoder and Transformer with stacked Multi-Head Attention as the decoder. Our work is adjacent to [16] which applies more than one R-CNNs, parallelly, and uses a transformer which is an attention-based decoder, to formulate captions.

Our model contrasts in using CNNs as the encoder. This was done in order to reduce complexity. Our architecture consolidates attention of various image matrices along with the embeddings of the sentences, one after the other, using the transformer model. Since multiple image features are being generated for the same image, the entire model becomes relatively robust. The learning from one attention module is transferred and passed on to the next, which enables us to retain only the best features.

## 3  Methodology

In this section, we describe our model which encompasses multiple image encoders for extracting image features and transformers for generating captions based on them.

### 3.1  Encoder

All the training and test images are, initially, resized to a standard size. The encoder is used to extract essential features from the image. GlosysIC proposes to use more than one encoder, all of which are pre-trained on ImageNet dataset. Loss of information is a major factor to be considered during encoding. Traditional 1-D vectors tend to lose a lot of information. Hence, we use a multidimensional array. Each encoder outputs $d_c$ channels of $d_k \times d_k$ matrix and then it is reshaped to $d_k * d_k$. The dimension of each feature matrix finally becomes $X \in \mathbb{R}^{d_k * d_k \times d_c}$. These encoder outputs are, then, sent to the transformer in order to generate the required caption.

### 3.2  Decoder

This module incorporates attention on the feature matrices given by the encoders. The reference captions are first tokenized and trimmed to a maximum length of $l$ words. Each word is embedded as a word vector of dimension $y_i \in \mathbb{R}^{512}$ using the 512-D GloVe embeddings pre-trained on a large-scale corpus [10]. Sentences which contain less than $l$ words are padded using <pad> . The final representation is $Y = [y_1, y_2 \ldots y_n] \in \mathbb{R}^{n \times y_i}$

A positional encoder, then, injects the relative position to the embedded words using sine and cosine functions [4].

$$PE_{(pos,2i)} = \sin\left(pos/1000^{2i/d_{model}}\right) \tag{1}$$

$$PE_{(pos,2i+1)} = \cos\left(pos/1000^{2i/d_{model}}\right) \tag{2}$$

where $pos$ is the position and $i$ is the dimension and $d_{model}$ is the same as the dimension of the embedder, i.e., $y_i$.

The output from the positional encoder is then fed to the six layers of the transformer which are stacked one above the other. Each layer, in turn, is made up of $m$ sequential sublayers. The first $m$-$1$ sub-layers are the Multi Head Attention (MHA) modules, while the final sub-layer is a Feed-Forward Network (FFN). Each MHA module consisting of a query, key, and value are projected into n different sub-spaces or heads. The first MHA layer is used to perform self-attention on the ground truth captions, where the key, query, and value are the captions themselves. The output of this layer is passed on to the next MHA sub-layer as the query. The key and value is the image matrix corresponding to that sub-layer. All the $m$-$1$ image feature matrices are similarly attended one after another after which output is served to the FFN. The FFN sends this output to the next layer of the transformer. A similar pipeline is followed for all the six layers of the transformer after which a softmax layer is used to predict the sentence (Fig. 2).

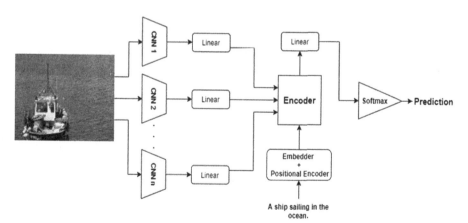

**Fig. 2. Flowchart of GlosysIC** showing the overall flow of data from the image to final caption generation. The image is sent through various encoders and provided to the decoder module, sequentially. The other input to the decoder module comes from the Positional Encoder. Softmax layer is used to finally predict the sentence.

### 3.3 Transformer

The principal component of our architecture is the Transformer, which leverages the power of scaled dot product attention. In order to attend to diverse parts of information, we use Multi-Head Attention, rather than a single attention. The input to the attention modules consists of a query, key and value, where $q, k, v \in \mathbb{R}^d$. Set of all keys $K = [k_1, k_2, .., k_n]$ and set of all values $V = [v_1, v_2, .., v_n]$ are represented as matrices. The attention for the queries $Q = [q_1, q_2, .., q_n] \in \mathbb{R}^{n \times d}$ is given as follows:

$$F = A(q, k, v) = softmax\left(\frac{QK^T}{\sqrt{d}}\right)V \qquad (3)$$

where $F \in \mathbb{R}^{n \times d}$.

The multi head attention function is represented as:

$$F = MHA(Q, K, V) = Concat(h_1, h_{2,..,} h_h)W^o \qquad (4)$$

$$h_i = A\left(QW_i^Q, KW_i^K, VW_i^V\right) \qquad (5)$$

where $W_i^Q, W_i^K, W_i^V \in \mathbb{R}^{h \times h_i}$ and $W^o \in \mathbb{R}^{h*d_h \times d}$.

Each head outputs a feature of dimension $d_h$. The first MHA sub-layer is used for self-attention on the training caption. The subsequent MHA sub-layers, till the last one, help in attending each of the encoders sequentially.

The Feed Forward Network contains two linear layers which is represented as

$$FFN(x) = FC(Dropout(ReLU(FC(x)))) \qquad (6)$$

Various image representations in our model act as teachers for the decoder, which will learn to focus on a specific area. The focused features get transferred, thereby, making our model more robust (Fig. 3).

### 3.4 GlosysIC

We follow a similar approach to [16], but our model is different from it in the way that we use sequential MHA sub-layers with the image representations. We feel that the feature learnings of the one attended sub-layer would be beneficial for the next. So, instead of parallel attention, we propose to use sequential attention. Essentially, when the attended features pass from one sub-layer to the next, only the most relevant features are captured.

Let $X_1, X_2,..., X_n$ be the feature matrices. Decoder caption is provided as the query, key and value and self-attention is performed.

$$F_1 = MHA(d_o, d_o, d_o) \qquad (7)$$

where $d_o$ is the decoder caption.

In the next step, we feed this normalized output as the query to the next sub-layer. The key and value are the outputs from the first encoder.

$$F_2 = MHA(F_1, X_1, X_1) \qquad (8)$$

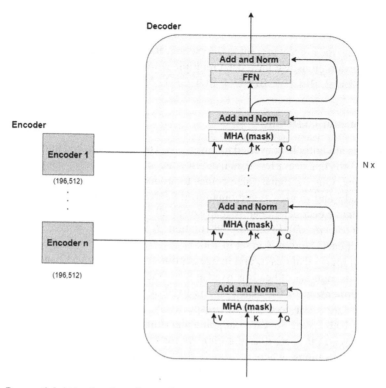

**Fig. 3. Sequential Attention based transformer of GlosysIC.** The first MHA sub-layer gets its input from the Positional Encoder. The value and key of each of the next sub-layers are the respective image feature matrices. The output from the final MHA sub-layer is sent to the Feed Forward Network and, eventually, to the subsequent Transformer layer. The output from the transformer is sent to the Softmax layer.

This output, in turn, is given as the query to the subsequent sub-layer whose key and value are the second encoder's feature matrices.

$$F_3 = MHA(F_2, X_2, X_2) \tag{9}$$

This process continues till the penultimate sub-layer.

$$F_{n+1} = MHA(F_n, X_n, X_n) \tag{10}$$

Finally, output of this sub-layer is normalized and given to the feed forward sub-layer.

## 4  Experiments

### 4.1  Datasets

The primary dataset that we have used for training and testing purposes is the MSCOCO dataset [14], which contains 118k images for training and 5k images for validation. Each image has five captions. All our CNN models have been pre-trained on the ImageNet dataset. ImageNet dataset contains more than 14 million images which have been annotated to indicate the objects present in the picture. It has more than 20,000 categories of objects. For evaluations, we have used multiple automatic evaluation metrics, namely, BLEU-1, BLEU-2, BLEU-3, BLEU-4, ROUGE-L, METEOR, and CIDEr [2, 3].

### 4.2  Implementation Details

The sentences are initially converted to lowercase. They are tokenized into words, based on spaces. Words that occur less than five times are labeled as <unk> and are neglected during training. Our vocabulary size comes to around 9345 words, including <start>, <end> , <pad> and <unk>. A combination of ResNet-101, ResNeXt-101, and VGGnet are used as image encoders. Feature matrices of all our encoders are brought to a fixed dimension of $(d_k * d_k, d_c)$. In our implementation, $d_k = 14$ and $d_c = 512$. The maximum word limit for each caption, $l$, is set to 100.

The input image features $d_x$ and image caption features $d_y$ are 512 and 512, respectively. Since the number of heads is fixed at 8 and the latent dimensionality is 512, each head has a dimension of 64. Batch size is fixed at 80. The encoder and the decoder learning rates are set at 1e-4 and 4e-4 respectively, which are, eventually, reduced by half after the 10th epoch. An early-stopping algorithm is incorporated which breaks the training process if the score does not improve for 4 epochs. We use the teacher forcing algorithm while training, where we supply the ground truth for generating every word. Additionally, we incorporate the masked MHA module to make sure the exact context is passed to predict the subsequent word and only the previous words contribute to the score.

Adam optimizer [15], which is an extension of the Stochastic Gradient Descent algorithm is chosen for training. To avoid overfitting, dropout layers with a probability of 0.5 are used. In addition, we have also used Cross-Entropy Loss for backpropagation. The model was trained without fine-tuning the CNN encoders. A total of 13 epochs were trained using the log loss. Each epoch took 8 h to train in RTX 2060 GPU and 1.5 h on V100 GPU from Google Cloud Platform.

### 4.3  Results

The scores produced by our model outperformed most of the existing architectures. Table 1 compares our architecture with other state-of-the-art architectures. Table 2 compares the two flavors of GlosysIC. The first one employs Resnet101 and VGGnet as encoders. The second flavor utilizes Resnet-101, VGGnet, and ResNeXt-101 as encoders. We found a slight improvement in the performance as the number of encoders increased. This shows that the use of multiple CNN architectures, sequentially, would be more effective. We have depicted the results of our comparisons in the table. Our models are evaluated on various metric scores like BLEU-1, BLEU-2, BLEU-3, BLEU-4, CIDEr, ROUGE-L and METEOR (Fig. 4).

**Table 1.** The table compares our metric scores with various other existing architectures. The results were obtained using the COCO Karpathy splits.

| Model | BLEU-1 | BLEU-2 | BLEU-3 | BLEU-4 | CIDEr | ROUGE-L | METEOR |
|---|---|---|---|---|---|---|---|
| Google NIC [11] | – | – | – | 27.7 | 85.5 | 23.7 | – |
| Soft-attention [12] | 70.7 | 49.2 | 34.4 | 24.3 | – | – | 24.0 |
| Hard-attention [12] | 71.8 | 50.4 | 35.7 | 25.0 | – | – | 23.0 |
| VAE [22] | 72.0 | 52.0 | 37.0 | 28.0 | 90.0 | – | 24.0 |
| ERD [23] | – | – | – | **29.8** | 89.5 | – | 24.0 |
| LRCN [25] | 62.79 | 44.19 | 30.41 | 21.0 | – | – | – |
| S&C ATT [26] | 70.8 | 53.6 | **39.1** | 28.4 | 89.8 | 52.1 | 24.8 |
| Phi-LSTM [27] | 69.5 | 52.3 | 38.5 | 28.2 | 90.5 | 51.7 | 24.3 |
| 3G [28] | 71.9 | 52.9 | 38.7 | 28.4 | – | – | 24.3 |
| CIC [29] | 70.6 | 53.2 | 38.9 | 28.4 | 89.9 | 51.9 | 24.4 |
| **GlosysIC (ours)** | **72.5** | **53.4** | 38.7 | 28.15 | **94.0** | **54.5** | **25.8** |

**Table 2.** The table compares the two flavors of GlosysIC. GlosysIC exercises a combination of Resnet-101, VGGnet, and ResNeXt-101 as encoders, though, it could be extended to include $n$ encoders. In backbone, R, V, Rx denote Resnet-101, VGGnet, ResNeXt-101, respectively.

| Model | Backbone | BLEU-1 | BLEU-2 | BLEU-3 | BLEU-4 | CIDEr | ROUGE-L | METEOR |
|---|---|---|---|---|---|---|---|---|
| GlosysIC (ours) | R, V | 72.3 | 53.4 | 38.2 | 28.07 | **94.1** | 54.4 | 25.4 |
| **GlosysIC (ours)** | R, V, Rx | **72.5** | **53.4** | **38.7** | **28.15** | 94.0 | **54.5** | **25.8** |

1. Large mustard yellow commercial airplane parked in the airport.
2. A brown jetliner sitting on top of an airport runway.
3. A brown LOT airliner sitting on the tarmac.
4. A gold colored, Polish airplane sitting on the runway.
5. A large golden airplane is on the runway.

A large jetliner sitting on top of an airport tarmac.

1. A man on a blue raft attempting to catch a ride on a large wave.
2. The boy is looking back at a wave in the ocean.
3. A young man is body surfing and paddling in the water.
4. A man in a black shirt plays on an ocean wave.
5. A boy riding a boogie board in the ocean waves.

A man in a wet suit riding a surfboard on a wave.

1. A little girl holds up a big blue umbrella.
2. A young girl stands with her arms wrapped around a large blue umbrella.
3. A girl in a pink shirt holding a blue umbrella.
4. A little girl who is holding an umbrella.
5. A little girl with a big, blue umbrella.

A little girl holding an umbrella while standing on a sidewalk.

1. A yellow dog runs to grab a yellow frisbee in the grass.
2. A dog is on the grass playing frisbee.
3. A dog in the grass catching a frisbee.
4. A tan dog leaping to catch a Frisbee.
5. A dog is opening his mouth to catch a Frisbee.

A dog jumps up to catch a frisbee in the grass.

**Fig. 4.** The figure compares the ground truth captions with the generated captions from GlosysIC Framework. Here, red color represents ground truth captions and green color represents captions from our model. (Color figure online)

## 5    Conclusion and Future Work

In this paper, we presented a novel approach to Image Captioning, which utilizes sequential attention on multiple CNN models using transformer in order to generate appropriate captions. On top of self-attention, GlosysIC, effectively transfers the learning from one sub-layer to the next, making it more effective. Our model has been, extensively, trained on the benchmark MSCOCO dataset. We have displayed example captions of our model on various validation images and have incorporated the ground truth captions to test its efficiency. It has been observed that GlosysIC Framework is quite effective in capturing minute details and, hence, generating apposite captions. Our future work involves using Graph Convolutional Network (GCN) to incorporate the relationships between different objects in the image [13]. We feel object relationships and their attributes could play a vital role in generating relevant captions to the image. Traditional Encoders are incapable of finding relationships between objects.

## References

1. Anderson, P., et al.: Bottom-up and top-down attention for image captioning and visual question answering. In: IEEE Conference on Computer Vision and Pattern Recognition (CVPR), June 2018

2. Papineni, K., Roukos, S., Ward, T., Zhu, W.-J.: BLEU: a method for automatic evaluation of machine translation. In: Association for Computational Linguistics (ACL), pp. 311–318. Association for Computational Linguistics (2002)

3. Vedantam, R., Zitnick, C.L., Parikh, D.: CIDEr: consensus based image description evaluation. In: IEEE Conference on Computer Vision and Pattern Recognition (CVPR), pp. 4566–4575 (20152015)

4. Vaswani, A., et al.: Attention is all you need. In: Advances in Neural Information Processing Systems (NIPS), pp. 6000–6010 (2017)

5. Yao, T., Pan, Y., Li, Y., Qiu, Z., Mei, T.: Boosting image captioning with attributes. In: IEEE International Conference on Computer Vision (ICCV), pp. 4894–4902 (201)

6. Yao, T., Pan, Y., Li, Y., Mei, T.: Exploring visual relationship for image captioning. In: European Conference on Computer Vision (ECCV), pp. 684–699 (2018)

7. Hochreiter, S., Schmidhuber, J.: Long short-term memory. Neural Comput. $9(8)$, 1735–1780 (1997)

8. Karpathy, A., Fei-Fei, L.: Deep visual-semantic alignments for generating image descriptions. In: IEEE Conference on Computer Vision and Pattern Recognition (CVPR), pp. 3128–3137 (2015)

9. Jiang, W., Ma, L., Jiang, Y.-G., Liu, W., Zhang, T.: Recurrent fusion network for image captioning. In: Ferrari, V., Hebert, M., Sminchisescu, C., Weiss, Y. (eds.) ECCV 2018. LNCS, vol. 11206, pp. 510–526. Springer, Cham (2018). https://doi.org/10.1007/978-3-030-01216-8_31

10. Pennington, J., Socher, R., Manning, C.: GloVe: global vectors for word representation. In: Conference on Empirical Methods in Natural Language Processing (EMNLP), pp. 1532–1543 (2014)

11. Vinyals, O., Toshev, A., Bengio, S., Erhan, D.: Show and tell: a neural image caption generator. In: IEEE Conference on Computer Vision and Pattern Recognition (CVPR) (2015)

12. Xu, K., et al.: Show, attend and tell: neural image caption generation with visual attention. In: International Conference on Machine Learning, vol. 3, pp. 2048–2057 (2015)

13. Kipf, T.N., Welling, M.: Semi-supervised classification with graph convolutional networks. In: Proceedings of ICLR (2017)

14. Lin, T.-Y., et al.: Microsoft COCO: common objects in context. In: Fleet, D., Pajdla, T., Schiele, B., Tuytelaars, T. (eds.) ECCV 2014. LNCS, vol. 8693, pp. 740–755. Springer, Cham (2014). https://doi.org/10.1007/978-3-319-10602-1_48

15. Kingma, D., Ba, J.: Adam: a method for stochastic optimization (2015)

16. Yu, J., Li, J., Yu, Z., Huang, Q.: Multimodal transformer with multi-view visual representation for image captioning. arXiv:1905.07841v1 (2019)

17. Sutskever, I., Vinyals, O., Le, Q.V.: Sequence to sequence learning with neural networks. In: Advances in Neural Information Processing Systems (NIPS), pp. 3104–3112 (2014)

18. Chen, H., Ding, G., Lin, Z., Zhao, S., Han, J.: Show, observe and tell: attribute-driven attention model for image captioning. In: Proceedings of the Twenty-Seventh International Joint Conference on Artificial Intelligence, pp. 606–612 (2018)

19. Wu, Q., Shen, C., Wang, P., Dick, A., van den Hengel, A.: Image captioning and visual question answering based on attributes and external knowledge. IEEE Trans. Pattern Anal. Mach. Intell. $40$, 1367–1381 (2018)

20. Chen, S., Zhao, Q.: Boosted Attention: Leveraging Human Attention for Image Captioning. In: Ferrari, V., Hebert, M., Sminchisescu, C., Weiss, Y. (eds.) ECCV 2018. LNCS, vol. 11215, pp. 72–88. Springer, Cham (2018). https://doi.org/10.1007/978-3-030-01252-6_5

21. Zhu, X., Liu, J., Peng, H., Niu, X.: Captioning transformer with stacked attention modules. Appl. Sci. $8$, 739 (2018)

22. Pu, Y., et al.: Variational autoencoder for deep learning of images, labels and captions. In: Proceedings of the 30th International Conference on Neural Information Processing Systems, pp. 2352–2360 (2016)
23. Yang, Z., Yuan, Y., Wu, Y., Salakhutdinov, R., Cohen, W.W.: Encode, review, and decode: reviewer module for caption generation. In: NIPS (2016)
24. Lu, J., Xiong, C., Parikh, D., Socher, R.: Knowing when to look: adaptive attention via a visual sentinel for image captioning. In: CVPR (2017)
25. Donahue, J., et al.: Long-term recurrent convolutional networks for visual recognition and description. In: CVPR (2015)
26. Cornia, M., Baraldi, L., Serra, G., Cucchiara, R.: Paying more attention to saliency: image captioning with saliency and context attention. ACM Trans. Multimed. Comput. Commun. Appl. (TOMM) **14**, 1–21 (2018)
27. Tan, Y.H., Chan, C.S.: Phrase-based image caption generator with hierarchical LSTM network. Neurocomputing **333**, 86–100 (2019)
28. Yuan, A., Li, X., Lu, X.: 3G structure for image caption generation. Neurocomputing **330**, 17–28 (2019)
29. Aneja, J., Deshpande, A., Schwing, A.: Convolutional image captioning. In: Proceedings of the IEEE Conference on Computer Vision and Pattern Recognition, Salt Lake City, UT, USA, pp. 5561–5570 (2018)

# Author Index

Printed in the United States
By Bookmasters